OBSERVING THE OU'   MW01482515

Describing Newfoundland Culture, 1950–1980

The years after Newfoundland's confederation with Canada were ones of rapid social and economic change, as provincial resettlement and industrialization initiatives attempted to reshape the lives of rural Newfoundlanders. At Memorial University in St John's, a new generation of faculty saw the province's transformation as a critical moment. Some hoped to solve the challenges of modernization through their rural research. Others hoped to document the island's "traditional" culture before it disappeared. Between them they created the field of "Newfoundland studies."

In *Observing the Outports*, Jeff A. Webb illustrates how interdisciplinary collaborations among scholars of lexicography, history, folklore, anthropology, sociology, and geography laid the foundation of our understanding of Newfoundland society in an era of modernization. His extensive archival research and oral history interviews illuminate how scholars at Memorial University created an intellectual movement that paralleled the province's cultural revival.

JEFF A. WEBB is an associate professor in the Department of History at Memorial University.

Observing the Outports

Describing Newfoundland Culture, 1950–1980

JEFF A. WEBB

UNIVERSITY OF TORONTO PRESS
Toronto Buffalo London

© University of Toronto Press 2016
Toronto Buffalo London
www.utppublishing.com
Printed in the U.S.A.

ISBN 978-1-4426-3741-2 (cloth)
ISBN 978-1-4426-2894-6 (paper)

♾ Printed on acid-free, 100% post-consumer recycled paper
with vegetable-based inks

Library and Archives Canada Cataloguing in Publication

Webb, Jeff A. (Jeffrey Allison), 1962–, author
Observing the outports : describing Newfoundland culture, 1950–1980 /
Jeff A. Webb.

Includes bibliographical references and index.
ISBN 978-1-4426-3741-2 (bound) – ISBN 978-1-4426-2894-6 (pbk.)

1. Newfoundland and Labrador – Civilization – Study and teaching –
History. 2. Newfoundland and Labrador – Social life and customs – Study
and teaching – History. 3. Newfoundland and Labrador – Study and
teaching – History. I. Title.

FC2169.W43 2015   306.09718   C2015-905458-3

This book has been published with the help of a grant from the Federation
for the Humanities and Social Sciences, through the Awards to Scholarly
Publications Program, using funds provided by the Social Sciences and
Humanities Research Council of Canada.

University of Toronto Press acknowledges the financial assistance to its
publishing program by the Canada Council for the Arts and the Ontario
Arts Council, an agency of the Government of Ontario.

Canada Council   Conseil des Arts
for the Arts   du Canada

ONTARIO ARTS COUNCIL
CONSEIL DES ARTS DE L'ONTARIO
an Ontario government agency
un organisme du gouvernement de l'Ontario

Funded by the   Financé par le
Government   gouvernement
of Canada   du Canada

Canadä

Contents

Acknowledgments

Writing this book has been a great pleasure, thanks in large part to the people that have helped me with it. I am a historian – not a lexicographer, folklorist, geographer, sociologist, or anthropologist – and I have been made welcome meandering in other people's fields. Many scholars were generous with their time and taught me something about their training and method and their individual disciplines, as well as shared their memories of working on Newfoundland society and culture. I appreciate their generosity and, in a few cases, their forbearance when they read drafts of what I had written about them or allowed themselves to be interviewed. Being the subject of inquiry may have sometimes provoked a little discomfort, even for people who spent their careers writing about other people. Their efforts to help and set down a record of this period in their lives are gratefully acknowledged. Misunderstandings and mistakes are mine, but many of the insights in this book I owe to others.

As I started this project, Professor William Kirwin tutored me in lexicography and linguistic research during many conversations over a two-year period, and he gave me free rein to use the files in the English Language Research Centre. Jenny Higgins and Suzanne Power of the centre helped provide access. Professor Kirwin also read and made corrections to my chapter on the writing of the *Dictionary of Newfoundland English*. He was in many respects the consummate student of Newfoundland culture; he quietly devoted himself to constantly and rigorously documenting the language of his adopted home. He was scrupulous in not telling me what to think, and his only instruction to me was to take a critical stance towards those about whom I was writing, including himself. That proved to be difficult, for I liked them, and

I hope that my efforts to contextualize and historicize my predecessors in Newfoundland studies pays them the respect of taking their work seriously even when I disagree.

Kirwin's surviving collaborator on the dictionary, John Widdowson, also shared with me his memories of working on the *DNE* and his folklore fieldwork with Herbert Halpert, and he read and made suggestions on chapters 1 and 3. The anthropologist James C. Faris allowed me to use his field notes of the year he lived in Lumsden North, to which Linda White of the Archives and Special Collections division of the QEII Library provided access. Faris discussed his Newfoundland fieldwork in both telephone conversations and email correspondence. Linda has been a great friend and supported this project in many ways, not the least by helping me select the accompanying photographs.

Several other scholars who conducted foundational fieldwork in Newfoundland in the 1960s also took time to be interviewed. Melvin Firestone, John Szwed, Gerald Mars, Ralph Matthews, and C. Grant Head all discussed their careers, and my account of the era would lack some nuance if it were not for their aid. The folklorists Peter Narváez, Neil Rosenberg, Michael Taft, and Philip Hiscock all reflected on their memories of Herbert Halpert, the field of folklore, and their own careers. Pat Byrne gave me permission to quote from his and Al Pittman's song "The Ode to Parzival Copes." Thomas Nemec made helpful suggestions regarding the history of anthropology and the development of ISER, both of which he has first-hand experience with, and he read the chapter on fieldwork. The geographers Alan MacPherson and Gordon Handcock also discussed their careers and the history of their field with me. My former professors, and later colleagues, in the Department of History, Shannon Ryan and James Hiller helped for the development of history. Rosemary Ommer discussed her own views of both the Departments of Geography and History. Heather Wareham of the Maritime History Archive discussed Keith Matthews's career, as did Kathleen (Kay) Matthews and Keith Matthews Jr. Gillian Cell recounted her early life and her work on Newfoundland.

Melvin Baker of the President's Office of Memorial provided access to university records and, equally importantly, expert guidance on the history of the university. Joan Ritcey of the Centre for Newfoundland Studies at the QEII Library aided my research. Colleagues at Memorial and other universities read and commented on portions of this book. Steve High of Concordia University read an early draft, and his insightful comments and his encouragement helped refine the book's argument. Tina Loo at the University of British Columbia did the same for chapter 4. Karen Stanbridge made helpful comments on the introduction. Neil McLaughlin at McMaster University introduced me to the literature on the sociology of knowledge, which helped sharpen my thinking. The anonymous peer reviewers solicited by the press provided comments that resulted in improvements to the book. Len Husband, editor at the press, was invaluable in marshalling this through the process of publication.

My fellow historians at Memorial, past and present, have made the Department of History an intellectually stimulating place to work. I especially thank my friends Terry Bishop-Stirling, Dominque Brégent-Heald, Skip Fischer, Neil Kennedy, Kurt Korneski, and Peter Pope.

Jeff Webb
St John's

OBSERVING THE OUTPORTS

Describing Newfoundland Culture, 1950–1980

Introduction

We were at the beginnings of that time in our contemporary history when university education was being heralded as the panacea to cure all our social and economic ills ... and when the pernicious doctrine of relevance began to settle like a deadly fungus upon the groves of academe. These fascinating developments coincided in time with the determined and much advertised efforts of the Newfoundland government to drag the province, kicking and screaming if necessary, into the 20th century. This meant the transformation of a backward society, trapped in a 17th century time warp, into a progressive, expansive model of 20th century industrialization ... Memorial's role was obvious. It was to be both the catalyst and the crucible through which the alchemical magic of transmutation from leaden disprized past to golden future would be accomplished. And, to strain the metaphor just a little, the fire to heat the crucible would derive from the scholarly fervour of scientists including social scientists and humanists.[1]

Newfoundland was the first part of northern North America to be known to Europeans, although, to many people, it is now unknown. In the nineteenth century the residents of the then British colony developed a self-awareness of a distinct language and history, but until the second half of the twentieth century their society and culture remained largely un-described and unstudied. (The province took the name Newfoundland and Labrador in 2001.) Following near bankruptcy during the Great Depression and an economic boom during the Second World War, a hard-fought campaign resulted in the decision to join the Canadian federation in 1949.

Meanwhile improved communications in rural Newfoundland, as in the Appalachian region of the United States, eroded the isolation of rural communities and threatened the destruction of local cultures by mainstream American popular culture. It is not surprising, therefore, that the study of both folklore and history underwent significant expansions after the Second World War. Soon after the existential crisis of the Confederation debate, key administrators and faculty members at the newly degree-granting Memorial University of Newfoundland launched a broad agenda of research into the history and culture of the province. They invented Newfoundland studies. This book is a history of that research program and follows the social and economic research initiatives of the 1950s and 1960s as they came to fruition in the 1970s and 1980s.

Those who grew up in the self-governing colony felt something had been lost, even as they welcomed the benefits of Confederation, and many newcomers to the island embraced the study of the place as well. It was as if, having relinquished the path towards being a nation state, Newfoundland-born intellectuals now wanted to preserve something of the national ethnos. For others, the island provided a virtual laboratory to study a traditional culture as it modernized – a subject which then attracted international attention in their respective fields. Some of the Canadian-, British-, and American-born scholars who made the province home identified with Newfoundland; they felt it was a distinctive part of North America and had a culture they wanted to help preserve even as they worked towards modernization of the society.

Modernization was one of the most influential concepts within the academy and government during the twentieth century. Scholars and policymakers alike assumed that in socially and economically disadvantaged societies, "tradition" dictated people's behaviour and that, over time, people moved towards having the "modern" attributes of rational decision making, individualistic economic relations, and secularization. Intellectuals in the middle of the century sometimes exaggerated the dichotomy between pre-modern and modern, and many worked to remove the impediments to modernization. Furthermore, for most people in North America and Europe after the Second World War, *modern* was synonymous with improved.[2] Newfoundland thus provided social scientists with an opportunity both to observe and to participate in a modernizing society.

During the three decades after the Second World War everyone in Newfoundland had an idea of what *modern* was, that the country was too slowly becoming modern, was modernizing unevenly, and needed help to develop. But neither government policymakers nor university-based intellectuals felt they had to define *modernization* in their writings since it seemed so obvious and profound. It meant capital-intensive rather than labour-intensive production, production for market rather than use within the family, exchange of commodities among people that had no social relationship, urban rather than rural life, taking values from popular culture rather than tradition, leadership through secular rather than religious institutions, bureaucratic systems of governance, knowledge gained from science rather than experience, consumption of goods produced outside the community, and valuing the new over the old. The study of modernization in outports was thus, to the scholars who undertook it, a local study with universal relevance.

The sea surrounding the island circumscribed Newfoundland – there was no question of how to define the boundaries, even though there were few aspects of Newfoundland culture that were not shared with their European ancestors and North American neighbours. This book will show how scholars brought different methods, theories, and concepts to bear on that community, even as those who worked in different disciplines shared much. Although their object was explicitly Newfoundland culture, their concept of *culture* varied depending on their discipline and ideology, and unfortunately they rarely defined the concepts most central to their studies. We can infer that a few scholars used the word *culture* in the sense of having acquired knowledge or taste, and elite culture was the best of what has been thought or created. Many more researchers used culture to mean performance or spiritual beliefs – folktales or the belief in witchcraft, for example. But most of the social scientists discussed in this book would have defined culture as something along the lines of the socially transmitted environmental adaptations and ways of interacting with others within their community. This "traditional culture" was a way of life passed from generation to generation, and they thought little changed from the remote past. It was the object of study either because of its intrinsic interest or because it was a counterpoint to the modern, individualistic urban way of life in which the scholars themselves had grown up.

The period after the Second World War, and especially after Newfoundland joined Canada, was one of dramatic economic and cultural change in rural areas of the province. In addition to the capital city, St John's, there were several oases of urbanity – the iron ore mine on Bell Island, the international airport at Gander, and the paper mill towns

of Grand Falls and Corner Brook, but a large portion of the population continued to live in communities of dozens of families or fewer.
In 1950 most of the workforce was employed seasonally in primary
resource extraction, particularly the fishery. During the second half of
the century, the portion of the workforce in the fishery declined rapidly
as that industry became more capital intensive and as other employment opportunities became available. Urbanization, and the further
development of industrial production, thus altered the lives of hundreds of families each year. For those who lived in the remotest of the
outports, as the coastal communities were known, their lives seemed
little changed from that of their parents and grandparents – but even
moving to a larger outport disrupted their ties of kinship and land use.

The 1950s was also a time of political reorganization as the new
province adjusted to being part of Canada after more than a century
of being a self-governing colony of the British Empire. National identities change in response to new circumstances, never more so than after
a dramatic change, such as becoming incorporated into a larger pol-
ity. The arrival of fisheries officers and the Royal Canadian Mounted
Police made a substantive change to families whose contact with the
outside world was often mediated by the local clergy, merchant, and
schoolteacher.

In April 1949 the government of Canada started to transfer money
directly to families in the form of family allowances and pensions, and
a few years later changes to the unemployment insurance program
made seasonal fishermen eligible for income support. Ottawa also provided money to the provincial government to help it raise the level of
government services to something closer to the average of the Maritime
provinces.

Joseph Smallwood, who had led the pro-Confederation forces
through the constitutional debates of the 1940s, was sworn in as premier, and his government rushed to build roads, schools, technical
colleges, and hospitals. He tried to push an industrial revolution. If
an individual was not personally affected by the changes, and few
were not, he or she could hardly have avoided the propaganda of
modernity. At every opportunity Smallwood cited each mile of road
paved, each school built, and each new industry developed. To him
they were concrete testaments to the benefits of Confederation and the
Liberal governments in St John's and Ottawa. The provincial government supported manufacturing, increased mining and paper production, and building fish plants and larger vessels to make an industrial

fishery that produced frozen fish rather than the beach-dried salted cod that had been the mainstay of the economy for centuries. The birthrate remained high in the 1950s and 1960s, and when small-scale manufacturing proved insufficient to absorb the workforce, Smallwood turned to mega projects such as an oil refinery and hydroelectric generation to provide the growth poles that would support industrialization. In the Confederation campaign Smallwood had emphasized the gap between Newfoundland and mainland standards of living, and he now capitalized on the voters' desire for greater opportunities for their children.

The days of bartering salted cod for provisions and fishing families being indebted to local merchants were now memories, but in the 1950s many families remained cash poor and continued to produce many of the necessities of life from the land. Becoming a province meant that Canadian social programs raised families' purchasing power and allowed greater purchases of mass-produced imported goods. Confederation also made the long-standing practice of travelling to the continent for work easier, which drained the province of some of its underused labour.

There were substantial regional variations in the province, and thus differences in the degree to which change affected people's lives. On the northeast coast of the island, many fishers prosecuted a small boat fishery, hauling cod traps and handlining, and each day splitting their fish, salting it, and drying it on beaches or flakes as their ancestors had done. Others produced frozen fish for the American market in a more capital-intensive fresh/frozen fishery. Many men continued in their annual rhythm of cutting wood and mending nets in the winter, harvesting seals in the spring, fishing in the summer, and shipping fish to the market in the fall. Women tended crops and livestock, made and mended clothing, and did the bulk of the labour in drying the fish.

On the Burin Peninsula, on the other hand, men went to the offshore fishing banks in schooners, leaving their families for extended periods, but they too worked long hours for varied and low income. Many Newfoundlanders engaged in occupational plurality – fishing for part of the year, picking up some wage-paying work in mines or on the roads, and cutting wood for the paper companies in the winter. But not everything was getting bigger and better, despite Smallwood's rhetoric. One of the greatest tensions in the first decade after Confederation resulted from paper producers paying low wages and providing poor working conditions to loggers, a dispute in which urban workers sided with the employers while rural workers suffered the coercion of the state siding with capital. Not everyone shared equally in progress.

Thousands of miles of roads were paved to connect rural communities, and a trans-island highway was finished in 1965. Radio had been bringing information of the outside world to even the most isolated of Newfoundlanders since the 1920s, and in 1955 the first television broadcasting station started transmitting. The gap in consumer goods available to Newfoundland and American families had never been more evident. Year by year, telephone service was extended into more remote areas. Rural electrification was as symbolic of modern life as it was essential to it, and rapid progress was made in that area too. These technologies diminished the feelings of isolation and eased the movement of goods, people, and ideas, but they did little for those who lived on small islands, and those who did not live near the trans-island railway continued to come and go by sea when not icebound.

Urbanization happened throughout the world during the twentieth century. The Newfoundland government also applied an accelerant to the process of the abandonment of the most isolated communities: Its centralization program subsidized the relocation costs of families moving to places that government services could be provided more cheaply. While many outports were disappearing on their own, the availability of subsidies and, in some instances, pressure from governments, business, or churches facilitated the trend. Unfortunately the lives of people in their new homes did not always meet their expectations, and feelings of resentment towards the Smallwood government became widespread. The rapid disappearance of a "rural way of life" in the half century after 1949 sometimes provoked nostalgia among urban dwellers, and a desire among some of them to maintain the sense of community that had been so evident in the lives of their parents and grandparents. Memorial University played a role in ushering in modernity and in promoting the idea that a traditional culture was being lost.

Twentieth-century universities were modernist institutions. When the new provincial government, in one of its first pieces of legislation, made the Memorial University College a degree-granting institution, it set the university the task of transforming the province. Training thousands of teachers to go out into the outports to prepare children for life in the new Newfoundland, for example, was a centrepiece of the cultural revolution Smallwood hoped to bring about.

From its modest beginnings in 1925 as little more than a teachers' college, Memorial began offering arts and science degrees in 1949 and later expanded into graduate degrees and to housing professional schools. The first premier hoped it would train the professional workforce his modernization agenda required, but he simultaneously believed that it would be a centre for the development and rejuvenation of Newfoundland culture. Many of the university's administrators, such as Raymond Gushue, Moses Morgan, and Leslie Harris, also wanted to balance Memorial's role in modernization with the study of Newfoundland's "traditional" culture.

As president of the university, Gushue approved of the proposal to study Newfoundland English and hired the university's first linguists and folklorists with the specific goal of studying oral culture. As dean of arts and sciences, vice president, and later president, Morgan supported those projects and was central in the creation of a Department of History and the Institute of Social and Economic Research. Harris followed the same career path as Morgan, and as dean, vice president, and president, he too gave financial and moral support to each of the initiatives outlined in this book.

Given the friendships, collaborations, and daily contacts between faculty members and the Newfoundland-born administrators, it is impossible to tell who originated which ideas and who supported whom. Morgan, a political scientist, and Harris, a historian, hired those with the expertise they believed would be needed to develop Memorial as a centre for the study of rural traditional culture. In this they often relied on the judgment of like-minded scholars such as Ronald Seary and George Story of the Department of English Language and Literature. Although Story never took up an administrative role, those who did, such as Morgan, valued his lifelong friendship, his advice, and his aid. Story shaped hiring priorities and the university's research agenda to a degree that would seem improbable in a more hierarchical management structure. Leadership was not solely a function of academic rank or role.

This book is about a particular place during a particular period, Newfoundland from the 1950s to 1980s, but it draws on the study of the history of the social sciences and humanities in other places and in other times. In the United States and Great Britain there are many biographies of important intellectuals, institutional histories of universities, and studies of the evolution of academic fields written by practitioners of those disciplines. Fewer such studies exist in Canada.[3]

Most biographies take an influential thinker, or a group of thinkers, most often at a prestigious institution, and work backwards from the master works to trace the origins of ideas or theories. Biographers use the context of intellectuals' lives, such as Darwin's studies at the University of Edinburgh and his trip on the *Beagle*, to illuminate the factors that influence the creation of knowledge. Studies of one discipline, such as history or anthropology, are sometimes prescriptive, but the guides to fieldwork or archival research only incidentally offer reflection on how knowledge is created.[4] There are few studies that examine the careers and scholarship of a set of intellectuals who work in a common field.[5] It is even rarer to have a study that examines different disciplines being brought to bear to create a common field of study for the period after the Second World War.[6] This is a study of a small group of scholars working in different academic departments and drawing on different scholarly practices who examined a common object – rural Newfoundland culture. It highlights aspects of the production of knowledge.

"Fields, of course, are made," Edward Said pointed out, and "they acquire coherence and integrity in time because scholars devote themselves in different ways to what seems to be a commonly agreed-upon subject matter."[7] Despite his widely influential study of "Orientalism," the shortage of broad studies of the intellectuals who create regional studies is not surprising; two of the characteristics of modern scholarship are specialization and professionalization. In fact, scholars writing about the roots of their respective fields, whether it is in the human or natural sciences, are often in the business of disciplinary boundary maintenance and canon building. That makes it difficult to write a coherent history of intellectuals who wrote on a common area of study but worked within different disciplines. Even the expression *renaissance man*, to refer to a scholar who works in many fields, suggests that he or she belongs to an earlier era. By focusing on different disciplines as they engage in the study of one region – in this case the island of Newfoundland – differences and similarities among disciplines can be seen.

In the twentieth century, however, no scholar worked exclusively within the intellectual milieu of his or her own discipline, although one might get that impression from biographies that present people as little more than the embodiment of their training. We divide historians into schools, speak of a Chomskian revolution in linguistics, introduce students to a succession of theories in anthropology, and refer to a *cultural turn* that reoriented the work in many disciplines. We also, sometimes, make a fetish of technologies, such as computers for quantitative research. Talk of *disciplines* can also be anachronistic: Sociology and anthropology, for example, overlapped and defined themselves in tension with each other. In fact, during much of the twentieth century British social anthropologists sometimes called themselves sociologists and used the terms *anthropology* and *sociology* interchangeably. They were particularly likely to call their work sociology when studying urban rather than rural populations, with little regard for any differences in method when speaking of the distinction.[8]

Accounts of the production of knowledge often emphasize the influential scholar or big breakthrough and add to the myth of the solitary mind as the motor of innovation. Most of the important work in Newfoundland studies, however, resulted from collaborations that arose among friends. Collaborations and institutional supports are as often the sources of creativity as the genius working alone in the garret, and individuals usually work among a community of scholars. The sociologist Michael Farrell has theorized the ways that friendship can blossom into productive creative partnerships. A "collaborative circle," to use his term, happens when "the members escalate their commitment to one another and deepen their interdependence until the circle becomes the centre of their creative lives."[9] This book examines several such collaborations.

Similarly, scholars of the history of ideas emphasize social cohesion and esprit de corps as essential ingredients in forging an intellectual field. The literature on the sociology of knowledge, on the other hand, "suggests that [disciplinary] cohesiveness and loyalty is often a socially constructed origin myth created after the fact to legitimate a school of thought."[10] When intellectuals saw themselves as working within a discipline, they often conducted boundary work to distinguish themselves from others, but they did not always see themselves in the ways that their successors identified them. What might now look like interdisciplinary work might have been perceived by past practitioners as staking a claim to a field for their discipline.

So, too, accounts of the founding father intellectuals can provide origin myths that embody the practices that make disciplines what they are.[11] The expositions of theory in textbooks may give students the impression of one paradigm giving way to its successor because the former was found unsatisfactory as new evidence was collected. Such accounts often use the names of scientists only as labels on decontextualized ideas. The theories are only slightly connected to the lives of individual scholars or the social context within which they lived and worked. Metaphors such as tipping points or revolutions or turns are handy, but they obscure the ways that interpretations, methods, and even facts remain contested. There is also, often, greater continuity in scholarship than implied by such analogies.

This book builds on the international literature in the history of social science, and the sociological literature on intellectual movements, in examining the scholars who developed the study of the culture of Newfoundland. There is symmetry in this. The social scientists I examine simultaneously engaged with the international theoretical and methodological bases of their disciplines (with an eye to contributing to international intellectual debates) while conducting deep study into local culture. Each chapter examines the international and local context of the work of a particular group of collaborators. Each discussion also balances between the assumption that the success of ideas as based on their rightness or usefulness and attention to the social factors that account for some interpretations being widely accepted and others neglected.[12]

Three sociologists of knowledge, Charles Camic, Neil Gross, and Michèle Lamont, call for studies of *practices*, by which they mean "the day to day actions and processes through which the producers of social knowledge actually go about the on-the-ground work of making, evaluating, and disseminating" social knowledge.[13] Historians of science, for example, have shown how the practice of science in both the lab and the field affect the work as much as does the theory underpinning our understanding of nature.[14] Each chapter examines just such practices. As a whole it contributes to the "contextual history" of twentieth-century social science; it is based on the premise that the production of knowledge is best understood through the biographies of intellectuals and an examination of their practices.[15] Just as historians may examine the folk culture of fishermen or study the *mentalité* of peasants, we can inquire into the combination of social factors, and the internal history of scientific inquiry, that determined what scholars believed. This is a history of disciplines, not a disciplinary history, although I hope that students in many departments will learn something from a study of their predecessors in their own branches of knowledge.[16] Objective description remains illusive; scholars create knowledge through the institutions in which they work. Theory, method, peer review, citations, departmental structures, mentor relationships, and many other practices all created and verified evidence. Inside and outside the academy, readers created an audience for the work that then gave it social significance.

This book examines the careers and publications of a *crowd*, to use the Newfoundland word that evokes both those who work on a common productive task and those who belong to a community.[17] This crowd of lexicographers, historians, folklorists, anthropologists, sociologists, and historical geographers worked to describe and understand the society and culture around them. I attempt to make a narrative out of these practitioners' encounters with Newfoundland. While the chapters overlap chronologically, they present vistas of the culture and history from several academic disciplines. Each chapter shows how the interplay of theory and method engaged in a dialogue with the culture of the place. These cases show how we know what we know of Newfoundland.

Chapter 1 examines the linguistic work at Memorial, which culminated in the *Dictionary of Newfoundland English* (*DNE*) and shows the scholars' recognition that the unique language could be the basis of a research university. The authors of the dictionary worked within the methods and theory of American and British lexicography and linguistics as they responded to local linguistic change. The writing, and professionalization, of history is the subject of chapter 2, which reveals the administration's desire to create research infrastructures. Newfoundland history grew out of the British and imperial historiography, as well as the broader quest for a scientific history, and the need to understand the past of the province. The study of folklore and Christmas mumming is examined in chapter 3. This was central to much of the interdisciplinary scholarship on the island, and it shows how enlisting students as collectors developed and how an intangible cultural artefact can be reinterpreted. The fourth chapter surveys the anthropological fieldwork of the first six Institute of Social and Economic Research fellows. Those community studies illustrate how the university worked with the state to study modernization. They reflect British and American sociology and anthropology, the methods of fieldwork, and the nature of the outports. Their colleagues in geography developed their own approach, as shown in chapter 5, as they worked to understand the distribution of people and resources on the island. Historical geography was grounded in the context of that discipline in Canada and shows the rise and fall of a Newfoundland school of approach. Chapter 6 examines the sociological counterpart of the work in the preceding chapters, as scholars were drawn into helping the state evaluate the Resettlement Program. It demonstrates how doing applied research led scholars who worked towards modernization of the economy to become critics of the state. Their work with government encouraged them to become sceptical of the policies they were employed to evaluate. This last chapter, on the resettlement of rural communities, engages with the American sociological theories of modernization that dominated academic discourse in the post-war world while adding to our knowledge of government policy.

All chapters are informed by archival research, reading key texts, and oral interviews, and each varies in the balance of sources and its approach. Readers will notice that nearly all of the scholars discussed in this book were men. Memorial hired few women before the 1970s, and for many years female faculty members were required to resign upon getting married. It was not exclusively men who studied Newfoundland, however. Female graduate students and research assistants collected and collated data, even if the professional and gender norms of the day meant that they often did so in ways that were anonymous. Some faculty wives worked in the library, and many more contributed to their husband's careers. The wives of anthropologists often worked in the field, collecting data from other women, and helped their husbands fit into the community. Other women participated in the research programs of their husbands as archivists, editors, and secretaries. If those collaborations had been recognized as co-authorship it would be easier to reconstruct how much women contributed to scholarship, but that did not happen. There was another sort of gender bias in the scholarly community. We can be confident that men's concerns were seen as community concerns – and thus the problems most likely to be the subject of inquiry of the male social scientists.

The earliest collaborations examined in this book started around 1952, and this phase of the study of Newfoundland lasted into the 1980s. It's helpful to think of this as a Newfoundland Studies Movement, since it was qualitatively different from anything that it preceded or followed. It had many of the characteristics of "scientific/intellectual movement" (SIM) described by Scott Frickel and Neil Gross.[18] "The history of almost every field of study," they argue, "is a history of a new scientific or intellectual movement that rose up to challenge established patterns of inquiry, became the subject of controversy, won or failed to win a large number of adherents, and either became institutionalized for a time, until the next movement came along, or faded into oblivion."[19]

The movements have as their central goal the production of knowledge and the circulation of those ideas within the intellectual community, rather than directly trying to change the world like the women's movement or socialism. The intellectual practices adopted by members of intellectual movements also exist in opposition to the dominant methods in their respective disciplines. Since these practices are contentious among scholars, and the participants in a SIM want greater influence in their fields, the movements are inherently political. They are *movements*, not individual actions, so they are usually collaborative enterprises that aim to change something and that take shape in tension with high-status intellectual networks that maintain the status quo. SIMs are also episodic in Frickel and Gross's estimation; the movements emerge, exist for a decade or two, and either dissipate or become institutionalized as an accepted set of practices. Lastly, characteristically, such movements either examine a previously undiscussed topic or argue for a new method to examine an established topic.[20]

The Newfoundland studies movement at the university had its leaders and its own internal dynamic, but it was also part of a broader cultural reaction to a loss of nationhood and modernization that included a folk music revival, efforts to preserve built heritage, the growth of an indigenous collective theatre, and the emergence of a visual arts scene. In 1976 the journalist Sandra Gwyn brought Canadian attention to a cultural "renaissance" then taking place in St John's. She pointed to the birth of politically engaged, collectively written theatre, such as Codco and the Mummers Troupe, the fusion of traditional music with popular music, such as the band Figgy Duff, and the burgeoning number of painters and artists, such as Christopher Pratt and Gerald Squires.[21] Intellectuals at the university, just as much as the city's artists, looked to rural Newfoundland, and the past, for inspiration and for material out of which to make their work.

Many of these artists and academics reacted against their parents' generation's embrace of American popular culture, or British drama, and believed they could make a new popular culture out of the Newfoundland folk culture. For the young people, it shared many elements with the American counterculture – including a desire to get "back to the land," a suspicion of authority figures, and a rejection of mass-produced culture. The magazine article did not recognize the continuity with earlier generations of Newfoundland artists, but Gwyn had put her finger on something exciting that was happening in the province, especially in the capital city. Urban Newfoundlanders, and people who moved to Newfoundland from the United States or Britain, may have been more likely to be nostalgic about rural life than those who had grown up in homespun clothing. The broad community interest in Newfoundland heritage made it easier for the university to gain the financial resources that made the social science and humanities research possible.

There are two possible avenues of explanation of why the movement occurred – the social and the psychological. Historians of intellectual movements sometimes focus on the elite institutions and highly successful scholars they assume are the source of significant innovations. They attribute the influence of such places to the resources and prestige that are necessary to break new ground and promote their achievements. This book provides a counter example – that of a new university and relatively young faculty who established their reputation by innovating from the margin of North American and European academic life.

Memorial University was not a magnet place attracting talent by virtue of its endowments of cash or prestige, but the excitement for the research made it an appealing place to work. The sociologist Charles Camic also suggests that "understanding any intellectual creation demands an analysis of both the historical setting in which it was originally constituted and the social position its producer occupied in that setting."[22] Situating the texts that make up what we know of Newfoundland in the biography of the authors, their collaborations, and the history of the university and province within which they worked, this book can help us understand the scholarship. I argue that the scholars in St John's were shaped by the dialectic between the local realities and the elite universities that defined standard theories and methodologies within their respective fields. Their interactions within the academic ecosystem of their peers also affected their research. Psychological factors (such as a desire to break with one's mentor), rivalries and friendships, and ego and affection all played roles in determining academic interactions.

When writing about the history of a university, we must not idealize disciplines or project anachronistic departmental boundaries. "No aspect of academic life is as taken for granted," Peter Novick observed, "as the division of inquiry into separate disciplines."[23] I might have organized this book by academic discipline or institutional departments – scholars often do so – but disciplinary boundaries are contested, and departmental divisions of labour are both arbitrary and are themselves the result of historical contingencies.[24] While universities are now divided into departments, such boundaries were created by men and women working within universities. Disciplines are, at one level, products of the way that universities segmented themselves into departments for particular reasons, but more fundamentally fields are the boundaries that scholars built.

Scholars broke up the study of life into fields as they developed techniques to study parts of the whole. They are also products of career aspirations and local conditions, more so than anything that was natural or predestined. Camic suggests that *localism*, "the pattern of relations obtaining among different disciplines at this or that particular university," should be incorporated into the history of the social sciences.[25] Memorial University followed a similar pattern of splitting into different departments and increasing specialization to that which had occurred in other universities. But while it replicated the departments common to other North American universities during the period I'm examining, it also founded a couple of departments that were uncommon. The Department of Folklore, for example, reflected the unique institutional commitment to documenting Newfoundland oral culture.

This study shows how individuals applied the tools of their different disciplines to the study of one object – Newfoundland culture. These intellectuals wrote descriptions of the culture that were based on their distinct methodologies, but they spoke to each other about their common goal of understanding the community about which they cared. In doing so they consciously, or in a few cases unintentionally, created a field of study. The common object gave scholars something to have a conversation about and made interdisciplinary collaborations possible. Professors spend most of their energy and time in teaching, administration, and community and social lives, but this book focuses on research as if it was sealed off from other duties – which it was not. The creation of courses in Newfoundland literature, history, folklore, geography, and anthropology established syllabi for the field and reproduced subsequent generations of Newfoundland specialists, and it played a role in defining the field of Newfoundland studies, as did the research and publication. Although there was no clear boundary between teaching and research, this book sets aside much of the work that made up their lives to focus on their research. The exception is the very great extent to which enlisting students in research became a teaching technique in apprenticing the young into disciplines.

I have elected to look at key texts and key individuals – the influence of which transcended their disciplines, made a mark on the province, and established the new university as a research institution. The people discussed in this book shared a common impetus and developed a particular Newfoundland social science approach. These individuals were celebrated by their peers as important in their fields, these texts were foundational in the study of Newfoundland culture, and in many cases the books remain in print. The accidents of archival preservation and my ability to interview surviving scholars from the era also shaped my selection. My access to the field notes of the anthropologist James Faris and my ability to speak to him, for example, allowed me to reflect on his work in ways that could not be matched for all of his contemporaries. Such close attention to the texture of the fieldwork experience can teach us as much about the creation of knowledge as the intention of the author or the exposition of theory.[26]

Every act of inclusion is an act of exclusion, and I am aware of my own, unintentional, role in establishing a canon. As my argument proceeds it will also become apparent that the scholars selected here, whether anthropologists or lexicographers, shared particular methods and assumptions, were in dialogue across departmental boundaries, and shared a commonly agreed-upon object to study. I chose the work of this particular set of men and women whose work laid the foundation of the study of Newfoundland society and culture. This treatment shows how individuals' lives, theory, and methodology within the academy; the institution for which they worked; their collaborations; and the place they studied and in which they lived shaped their practice and their perception of the world. I do not examine the career of every scholar or discuss every publication. As George Story, the central figure in this book, reminded his collaborators on the *DNE*: "Many a good piece of work has been spoilt by the vain passion for completeness."[27]

Universities engage with the city in which they are based. Some, such as the University of Chicago, built their international reputations and their influence on social observation of the cities in which they were housed. As one commentator put it, for Chicago-based social scientists "*modern society* was interpreted to mean urban society," particularly their own city.[28] The scholars at Memorial recognized that the study of the rural culture in Newfoundland could contribute to the broader understanding of societies that had not yet made the transition to modernity and that they could advance their careers while doing so. They cared about the community in which they lived. Individuals who taught in different departments regularly had coffee together in the Arts Building common room, or Arts Café, as it was also known, and they were all influenced by the leading intellectuals at the university. Many faculty members at Memorial were young and often still engaged in their graduate work when they were first hired. Their research and teaching were shaped by their continued relationship with universities elsewhere, but arguably more so by their daily interactions with colleagues at Memorial. A community of scholars existed, which has to be understood as such. As departmental and disciplinary divisions proliferated in the 1960s and 1970s and fields underwent increasing specialization, the nature of engagement changed. This book describes such changes in academic culture. Like those at other Canadian universities, faculty members at Memorial in the 1950s and 1960s were largely recruited from outside the local society because of the shortage of qualified people at a time when the institution was expanding. The mix of American and British intellectual approaches in a particular place created an amalgam.

Many late twentieth-century scholars discounted the importance of the author's intent and emphasized the multiple possible readings of texts. As fruitful as these approaches were, they downplayed the process by which authors created the texts, just as biographies of individual intellectuals risked missing the degree to which scholarship is often a community effort. An examination of the process of creating a particular book, or body of work, can add to our understanding. A few texts become iconic within a community of scholars or a nation. Classic works are often read without much thought given to how descriptions of the culture or society are themselves the creation of individuals.

I have organized each chapter around key texts and individuals, since that better reflects the projects in which people engaged than would the history of university departments. What follows is a series of overlapping studies. None of these projects existed in isolation of the others; friendships and collaborations transcended disciplines, and individuals played many roles in different research projects. No one study could describe the whole range of study and research within a twentieth-century university; I focus on the research into Newfoundland studies largely, but not exclusively, at Memorial University of Newfoundland. Several pioneering scholars who worked at other universities are included in my discussion, since their work was a foundational part of the corpus of social science and humanities research and was in dialogue with the work at Memorial.

The social sciences and humanities research into Newfoundland culture was a coherent body of intellectual activity and an important way that the university responded to the needs of the province. Faculty members in the Department of English Language and Literature, for example, also wrote critical essays on the fiction of many British authors, but it was their work on Newfoundland language that played an important part in the history of the university, and indeed the history of the province. Similarly, archaeologists, economists, and others all did valuable work that I do not examine here because such work was not central to the movement I am examining. The natural scientists at the university also contributed a great deal, and my decision to not examine their work is based on practicality rather than having judged their work to be less important than the humanities in the university's efforts to understand and serve the province.

A book similar to this one might be written about social factors in the history of the development of geology, physics, or marine biology. During the 1960s geologists at Memorial, for example, explored the province at the same time that they contributed important evidence to support the field's acceptance of the theory of plate tectonics. The debate over that theory had been stimulating, and the work of Memorial's geologists such as the Newfoundland-born Harold (Hank) Williams helped to make Memorial an exciting place to work. The enthusiasm for geological research in rural Newfoundland and the potential to contribute to science while based in Newfoundland spread to other disciplines. Biology, and the other sciences that emphasized fieldwork, encouraged an attitude among administrators, faculty, and students that knowledge was out there to be discovered. Getting out of the classroom, the laboratory, and city was a way to map unknown territories and challenge theories. Social scientists and humanists at Memorial, as this book will show, developed the same approach – fieldwork on the culture, society, and history was rewarded with promotion and the respect of peers. The scholars I examine in this book were the first within Memorial University to make oral culture a subject of scholarship, and they exemplified trends within North American and European universities.

Retrospective analyses of scholarship usually focus on a single academic discipline; each of us is trained within a particular methodology and has absorbed a particular body of theory. The ways that observers from the 1950s to the 1980s described the culture and society merits attention both for the foundation that scholarship laid for the research of our generation and for the history of engagement in culture that bore fruit. The overlapping studies in lexicography, history, folklore, anthropology, and historical geography came from a common impetus – the desire to document a way of life that was disappearing.

All fields were shaped by the leadership of the key intellectuals, and all developed methodologies that overlapped. The complexity and the development of each of these disciplines merit their own extended treatment – but they developed in relation to each other and are thus best understood in reference to each other. My interest in this is primarily historical; Memorial's Newfoundland studies movement of the 1950s to 1980s affected the province's development, and it occurred in tandem with the cultural revival of the 1970s. I hope future students of Newfoundland culture will find this reflection on the foundational works in Newfoundland studies useful to their own research. People working in many fields consult the *DNE*, for example, without thought as to the sources, methodologies, or the judgments made by that book's authors. An understanding of such projects may change the ways in which future scholars conduct their own studies.

Through its examination of a set of individuals engaged in overlapping research, this book illuminates themes in the intellectual history of the second half of the twentieth century. A dialogue between theory and evidence during a succession of worldwide academic fashions determined the questions people asked and the methodologies they used. Functionalism, structuralism, and Marxism, for example, all shaped the way people understood the world. Even as they worked together, there was a creative tension between the academic disciplines as increasing specialization encouraged faculty members to hive themselves off in their own field, while at the same time common problems and social factors encouraged their continued conversations with those who were nominally now in a different academic department. The creative synthesis that emerged made Memorial a leader in many fields.

The intellectual biography of several men and women shows how their training and personal lives affected the field and their daily practice as scholars. It demonstrates how both internal factors (the nature of Newfoundland and the institutional history) and external factors (the evolution of academic theory and methodology) shaped their work. While this study could be replicated for other Canadian universities, Newfoundland's case has its own character. Memorial University's administrative leaders directed much of the growth in scholarship by recruiting people to study Newfoundland culture and then promoting their research. That included the development of academic departments of linguistics and folklore, for example, which leaders at Memorial saw as methods of documenting the oral culture. Memorial's leaders valued that task both for its intrinsic qualities and as a way of leveraging that oral culture to develop a research profile for the young university.

The first generation of scholars who studied Newfoundland believed they were observing a society that was undergoing an unprecedented period of rapid modernization, and they had a sense of urgency about documenting the "traditional" before it was gone. Especially during the tenure of Premier Smallwood, between 1949 and 1971, the provincial government aggressively promoted urbanization, industrialization, and modernization. This was exemplified in Smallwood's, perhaps apocryphal but widely repeated, injunction to rural fishermen to "burn your boats" and take up employment in one of the new industries he hoped to attract. It can also be seen in Smallwood's patronage of the university. With the support of his government, Memorial expanded its role in ushering in social changes, offered free tuition for a while, and in 1961 opened a new campus. The architecture of the Elizabeth Avenue Campus showed Smallwood's love of the modern – not for its aesthetic qualities, but because it showed Newfoundland to be making progress in catching up to the rest of North America.[29]

As Newfoundland underwent social change, which many people at the time perceived as breaking the influence of the past and embracing the modern, social scientists and scholars within the humanities focused their attention on the rural culture. It seems that nearly everyone in this era believed that the cultural changes were causing the local culture to converge with the dominant North American one – giving them an opportunity, if not a duty, to examine the world that would be lost.

The university was the principal institution describing and promoting Newfoundland culture, and it was a catalyst for change even as it took on a preservationist agenda. This raises the question of whether the phenomenon at the centre of this book was a bourgeois effort to shape the culture. Historians are sensitive to the process by which what are commonly accepted as ancient traditions were recently invented for political purposes and the role that literature and newspapers played in people imagining themselves to be part of a community.[30]

As we will see, some people who were not affiliated with the university criticized the *DNE* for allegedly encouraging people to speak incorrectly, thought folklore was old foolishness, and criticized the anthropologists for reporting embarrassing beliefs such as witchcraft. But thousands of rural Newfoundlanders volunteered to fill in linguistic questionnaires, shared their food and stories with folklorists, and taught the anthropologists how to light the stove. Ascribing class identity to the scholars is also problematic. The Newfoundland-born scholars were from both urban and rural communities, and not all came from privileged backgrounds. The British- and American-born, more often than not, grew up in working-class families. The foreign-born often worked on Newfoundland culture not just out of convenience, or because they had some sense that like missionaries they were bringing civilization to the ignorant, but because their friendships with neighbours and colleagues made them feel part of the community.

While this book examines Newfoundland studies at Memorial, there was more continuity between pre-war and post-war examinations of the place than the foregoing implies. The *DNE*, for example, the first edition of which was published in 1982, was a high point of Newfoundland studies, but it was not the first time scholars had studied Newfoundland history, language, and oral culture. Journalists such as P.K. Devine, judges such as D.W. Prowse, and geologists such as J.P. Howley had done so in the late nineteenth and early twentieth centuries.

Similarly, both locals and outsiders had studied the island's musical traditions. Patrick O'Flaherty found that there was an awareness that there was a "Newfoundland culture" in the sense of "something created by an artistic and cultural community" by at least 1937.[31] That is strikingly late, and long post-dates the awareness of an oral culture and distinctive language. Among those who were suggesting efforts be made to create a national culture was the journalist and future premier of the province, Smallwood, who focused his own efforts on the writing of history. He even suggested that the government establish a "National Board of Newfoundland History and Culture" to foster the creative sector.[32] But before 1949, Newfoundland intellectuals had been mostly clergymen, lawyers, and journalists and were autodidacts or had been trained in other countries. Newfoundlanders' efforts to improve their standard of living encouraged them to ape the strategies of more advanced economies, and emulating the consumer culture and attitudes of those countries went hand in hand with such things as railway building. Modernizing was copying other countries. The first generation of faculty at Memorial University College, founded as a memorial to soldiers who had lost their lives during the First World War, had devoted themselves to training teachers who would go out into outports as missionaries of modernity. Some of these teachers had done more to change oral culture than continue it. But given that most of them had come from outports and received only the briefest of teacher training before being sent to other outports to teach students who were only slightly younger than themselves, they remained of the culture.

One could argue that when Newfoundlanders voted to join Canada in the referendum of 1948 they voted for participation in a North

American consumer culture and that the nearly half of the population who voted against union with Canada wanted to be a nation state. Newfoundland nationalist intellectuals on both sides of that debate reconciled their aspirations with being citizens of a new country. Some of the impetus behind the movement to study, preserve, and celebrate Newfoundland culture examined in this book was a reaction to a sense of loss that accompanied the political and economic changes. Business-man F.M. O'Leary, for example, maintained his sponsorship of cultural activities such as a prize for poetry, and the provincial government introduced an "Arts and Letters Competition" that it hoped would encourage artistic expression. Meanwhile the desire to modernize the society was also palpable during the 1950s, and those who advocated the preservation of the old could be castigated for not embracing the "New Newfoundland" (to borrow the title of one of Smallwood's books). The modernist novelist Harold Horwood, on the other hand, responding to the provincial government's Arts and Letters Competi-tion, claimed that there was no Newfoundland culture.

Among Newfoundland's favourite myths is the belief that we have in this province a very distinctive and flavourful culture which should be pre-served at all costs. Even the Government subscribes to this belief, offering annual prizes for the encouragement of arts and letters. We have no quar-rel with the prizes, provided it is realized that we are trying to interest people in laying the foundations for a cultural tradition rather than build-ing upon a foundation which already exists. The truth is that Newfound-land has no literature, no music, no art, little philosophy and less science. The only culture which we have is the culture of the fish flake, though even that isn't our own, having come with our peasant ancestors from England and the Channel Islands.[33]

It would be an error to assume that people fit neatly into one camp or another, that they either valued the "traditional" culture or saw it as an impediment to modernization. Many apostles of progress embodied a high regard for heritage – if only as a yardstick to measure how far the county had come or as an ideological response to the less desirable effects of the changes that were occurring. The university itself embod-ied the tension.

The Newfoundland studies movement was a phenomenon of the second half of the twentieth century. Many of the second generation of academics pursuing Newfoundland studies at Memorial in the years after Confederation were part of the broader cultural movement described by Gwyn. Artists and musicians often took inspiration and practical aid from faculty members at Memorial who had documented the oral culture of Newfoundland, and younger members of the faculty and graduate students became part of the broader cultural movement. That cultural movement was a success – actors, for example, no longer needed to adopt fake English accents or set their plays in ersatz English country villages – and artists were able to work within a Newfoundland context. They were then able to work within global forms. As Jerry Pocius suggested, when cultures feel threatened they turn inward, and when they feel confident they turn outward.[34] As for the members of the Newfoundland studies movement, their work documenting the culture and history laid a foundation that has subsequently been built upon. By the 1980s the sense of ongoing cultural loss had eased, and many artists' work had become less overtly nationalist and self-referential, so the impetus for documenting Newfoundland life waned. Their movement ended, in large part, because researchers had achieved their goals in documenting the culture and creating the research tools that would make scholarship possible and because the old ways had passed. While scholars continue to study aspects of Newfoundland culture and society, as I write this, they do so in a more individualistic way, and whole academic departments do not focus their efforts on Newfoundland scholarship. The sense of urgency is gone, and there are fewer of us now engaged in the study of the province. The Newfoundland studies movement was a product of its time.

Viewing the Universe through Newfoundland Eyes: The *Dictionary of Newfoundland English*

The Dictionary which is now presented to the public is part of a plan conceived at Memorial University more than two decades ago by members of the Department of English in which the languages (especially the English language), the place and family names, and the folklore of Newfoundland were to be subjected to a scrutiny worthy of their importance for Newfoundlanders and their interest to others in the English-speaking world.[1]

More than any other single intellectual, George Story was a key figure of the Newfoundland studies movement of the 1950s to 1980s. The *Dictionary of Newfoundland English* (*DNE*), of which Story was the principal author, was the most prominent effort at the university to preserve oral culture, and it was part of a broader cultural resurgence in the second half of the twentieth century. Story led the way among faculty members at Memorial, both native-born and non-Newfoundlanders, who advanced their careers through the virgin territory of the study of Newfoundland culture, making their mark in their respective fields. Scholars carried on a conversation with Newfoundlanders about themselves, as well as a dialogue with the methodological practices of various academic fields. The local context of a modernizing society informed the scholarship at Memorial even as the faculty participated in the conceptual and theoretical discussions of the day.

The preface of the *DNE* acknowledged the key people in the linguistic enterprise at the university: E.R. Seary, who helped initiate the whole study of language and took the lead role in studying both place names and family names; Herbert Halpert, who created the Folklore and Language Archive; and Agnes O'Dea, who built the reference collection of Newfoundland-related published material at the library (which became the Centre for Newfoundland Studies) and compiled the *Bibliography of Newfoundland and Labrador*. To these brief acknowledgments could have been added the names of dozens of others who contributed their local knowledge and professional expertise to the *DNE*. The dictionary itself, the focus of this chapter, was the culmination of the work of three scholars from different backgrounds, George M. Story, William J. Kirwin, and John D.A. Widdowson.

That introduction to the *DNE* also did something perhaps too rare among works of scholarship – it articulated the criteria by which the authors selected the words that became the corpus of Newfoundland English. Introductions are the least-read part of dictionaries, but they provide the key to understanding how the knowledge contained within their pages was created and how it might be used. The chapters of this book delve into how scholars learned of the culture around them and produced the texts that provide the foundation of what we know. The first of these explorations shows how the *DNE* was produced.

Several nineteenth- and early twentieth-century observers had identified the existence of a Newfoundland speech different from that of Canada, the United States, or Britain, and dabbling in the study of language in Newfoundland predates the creation of a Newfoundland institution of post-secondary education and research. The Reverend George Patterson published the first attempt at a scholarly description of a Newfoundland dialect in an essay in the *Journal of American Folklore* in 1895, but he was far from the first author from outside to have noted the particular lexicon.[2]

Newfoundlanders were aware of their linguistic identity as well. Their interest in the study of language on the island, and other aspects of their history and culture, are local examples of the nationalist agenda common throughout the world in the nineteenth century. Scholars in many countries worked to establish the essential national ethnos of their homelands and based it on history and the oral culture of peasants. A self-consciousness of vernacular languages and the proliferation of print capitalism are often linked with the emergence of modern nationalism.[3]

Two early twentieth-century Newfoundlanders stand out as precursors of the work examined in this chapter – Michael Francis Howley and P.K. Devine. A Newfoundland-born Roman Catholic bishop, Howley was an important nationalist intellectual during the last years of the nineteenth and early years of the twentieth century. He argued, for example, that John Cabot's landfall was indeed Newfoundland, in response to Nova Scotian claims for Cape Breton, and wrote an ecclesiastical history of Newfoundland (by which he meant the history of the country's Roman Catholic Church).[4] Of particular interest to us here, Howley was also the author of a series of essays on Newfoundland place names published in the *Newfoundland Quarterly* at the turn of the century, a topic to which E.R. Seary was to turn in the 1950s in one of the pioneering initiatives at the university.

Devine, the other notable figure, was a King's Cove, Bonavista Bay, native who was part of a cohort of nationalist organic intellectuals during the 1930s. That group included the lawyer Frederick Emerson, businessman Gerald S. Doyle, and journalist Joseph R. Smallwood. Emerson was an accomplished musician who taught music appreciation at Memorial College and had written on Newfoundland folk music.[5] Doyle had both collected and published folk music, while Smallwood collected and popularized oral culture in his *Barrelman* radio program and wrote history and biography of Newfoundlanders.

In 1937 Devine, who had studied at St Francis Xavier College in Nova Scotia, published his *Devine's Folk Lore of Newfoundland in old words, phrases and expressions, their origin and meaning*. While Howley was a representative of the venerable tradition of the gentleman-scholar of the cloth, Devine had been a journalist. He earned little money for his glossary, which was published with the aid of his nephew – businessman and fellow folk-culture enthusiast Doyle.[6] In 1936 the botanist Agnes Marion (Miller) Ayre had also published a study of Newfoundland names based on a broad reading of published texts.[7] These men and women contributed much to establish Newfoundland's oral culture as a subject of inquiry and a basis for nationalist sentiment. But, unlike larger countries, until a relatively late date Newfoundland lacked a post-secondary educational institution that could support research and publication.

That changed in 1925, when Memorial University College was founded as a living memorial to those Newfoundlanders who had died during the Great War. Under the leadership of a former English public school headmaster and classicist, J.C. Paton, the college functioned primarily to give students a grounding in the arts and science that would enable them to become teachers or to go on to a university in another country to train in one of the professions. A few faculty members at the college conducted research, some of which was relevant to Newfoundland's particular situation, but the support and opportunities for doing so were limited.

During the 1930s, perhaps prompted by Devine's pamphlet, a faculty member at Memorial, probably the modern-language teacher A.C. Hunter, had formed a "glossary club" in which his students collected Newfoundland vocabulary and created a file of about a thousand cards.[8] In doing so he was ahead of his time both in the sense of having anticipated the work on the *DNE* but also in having pressed his students into service as collectors of oral culture.

The process of collecting a glossary of Newfoundland words and usage was picked up again in the 1950s by George Story, a man at the centre of many of the scholarly initiatives to study Newfoundland from the 1950s to the 1980s. Story had been born in St John's in 1927, the son of an accountant with Imperial Tobacco and the grandson of a Methodist clergyman. The Storys were not a wealthy family, but they had relative economic security in a city that was the commercial and political capital of Britain's self-styled oldest colony, and they shared in a strong sense of neighbourhood living on the south side of the St John's harbour. In keeping with his lifelong interests in history and oral culture, George Story later reflected that his was "a happy family background, and one [with] great consciousness of ancestors and relationships, you know genealogy, not in an antiquarian sort of stuffy way but just talk, a lot of talk."[9]

While he was a Methodist (this self-identification among Newfoundland Methodists persisted well after they elected to join the United Church of Canada in 1925) who lived in the west end of the city, he attended Bishop Feild College, a Church of England boys' school in the east end of the city. As a teenager during wartime, he witnessed thousands of Canadian and American servicemen in the city, with their vibrant popular culture and ready cash. He may have also seen the disparaging attitudes towards local people's speech and manners that a few servicemen and mainland (as Newfoundlanders referred to the continent of North America) journalists shared. Story was a proud St John's man, and his first sustained contact with Newfoundland outside of "town," as the city was sometimes called, was summer employment as a land surveyor's assistant for the Commission of Government's agricultural settlements between 1942 and 1946. It gave the teenager experience working in the woods with other men, and although his tastes then included the popular music on the radio, he experienced first-hand the oral culture that he was to one day defend against condescension.

Story enrolled as an undergraduate at Memorial University College between 1946 and 1948, at a time when servicemen returned from the war swelled the small classrooms and added seriousness to the class work. During these years his countrymen were also embroiled in the debate over whether to join Canada or return to their status as a self-governing colony within the British Empire. That raised nationalist consciousness among many students, even as most faculty members were British expatriates.

Story took a range of courses at the college on Parade Street in St John's, and he did well in history (despite, he later commented, the lack of passion in the teaching style on the part of the college's sole lecturer in history, Alan Fraser). He wavered between pursuing history or English literature as a specialization, not only for the rest of his time as a student but throughout the rest of his life.[10] After completing the two years towards a BA in English that were then available at Memorial, he went to McGill University in Montreal in 1948, coincidentally just after Newfoundlanders voted to throw in their lot with Canada. He stayed there until 1950, by which time Newfoundland was the newest province in the Confederation. Although he had no dislike of Canada and always felt at home there in a way that he did not in the United States, his two years in Montreal gave him "no particular sentimental attachment to Canada."[11] His time at McGill had also established his professional path. A course on Shakespeare whetted his interest in textual criticism and encouraged his decision to edit a text for a dissertation topic when he took up graduate work.[12]

The experience of living in Montreal also sharpened his self-awareness as a Newfoundlander and his sense that Newfoundland English was something different from British, American, or Canadian English. "My first realization of the fact that I did not speak Canadian English came in Montreal," he once told a class, "when I sent fellow students into apparent convulsions by referring to a cut finger as very *nish* and calling a small dog a *crackie*."[13] In 1949 Story had also acquired a copy of Devine's glossary, which "first aroused my own interest in the Newfoundland lexicon."[14] Over the next few years, as a pastime and perhaps because he missed home, he added to the collection of words he made during his time in Montreal. It was not systematic collecting, and he rarely noted provenance or examples of the words in use, but it was a start on a glossary of his own.

Upon finishing his BA in 1951, Story returned to St John's, in time to see the momentous changes that had occurred while he was away. Following a divisive constitutional debate, the people of Newfoundland had voted by a slender margin to join Canada, so Story came home to what was now a different country than that of his boyhood. The people of the Avalon Peninsula, and the people of St John's in particular, had overwhelmingly voted to return to responsible government rather than become a Canadian province, and in some quarters a nationalist resentment towards the outcome quietly simmered.

On a more positive note, in 1949 the new provincial government made the college a full degree-granting institution and renamed it Memorial University of Newfoundland.[15] Although it was to embark on a period of growth and diversification, it then consisted of, in the words of a historian of Memorial, "a staff of thirty [who] offered fifteen predictable subjects."[16] The new premier, Joseph Smallwood, had been the leader of those who had advocated Confederation, and he was determined to modernize the province as quickly as possible. Smallwood intended the new university to an agent of modernization, but also, in keeping with his role as a nationalist intellectual, to promote Newfoundland culture. Smallwood had hand-picked at least one of the four members of the Department of English; in 1949 the premier had told the university to hire David G. Pitt (the first appointment after it became degree granting). Pitt had been born in Musgravetown, educated at Memorial College and Mount Allison University, and took a PhD in English literature at the University of Toronto. There he met the expatiate Newfoundlander E.J. Pratt, then Canada's foremost modernist poet, and, as Pitt put it, Pratt was "the only Newfoundlander of any note who'd made a name in the literary world ... He wasn't known that much in Newfoundland but his poems were in one or two of the school books."[17] The two men had much in common (they were both sons of Methodist clergymen who had ministered in outports), and Pitt devoted much of his career to the promotion of Pratt's poetry among Newfoundland undergraduates and the writing of a two-volume biography.

After teaching English as a lecturer at Memorial and briefly working for the *Evening Telegram* newspaper, a Rhodes Scholarship enabled Story to attend Oriel College, Oxford, between 1951 and 1954, where he trained in textual criticism of the Elizabethan era. A graduate degree at Oxford at that time consisted almost wholly of writing a dissertation, but he took three preparatory courses that would have been as good a training for a career as a historian of early modern Europe as they turned out to be for a professor of English language and literature.

The first was on Bibliography – broadly conceived to cover the whole subject of books, from papyrus roll to vellum codex and printed typographic book – their material, making, distribution, collection into libraries, cataloguing in the diverse ways of monastic institutions, royal and princely owners, the slowly emerging national libraries. The second course was Paleography – the hand writing of documents from the Carolingian renaissance of the tenth century and Anglo-Saxon England through the bewildering variety of medieval scripts – literary, court hand, specialized Chancery style, legal manner, informal cursive, and so on ... [The third course] was called "An Introduction to the Public Records" and it was given by Vivian Galbraith, the Regius Professor of Modern History ... It was his passionate mission to instruct us in the *use* of those records. And that *use*, he held, depended *not* on their present arrangement ... but on knowledge of the administrative structures of more than a thousand years of history which produced the records.[18]

His exercises during his time at Oriel College also included sorting the varied editions of early modern texts, based on an analysis of printers' errors and corrections, to determine the order in which they had been published. This was a prelude to establishing a definitive text with annotations to indicate the variants. During Story's first two years at Oxford he studied Elizabethan Catholic affairs under the supervision of the historian Hugh Trevor-Roper, who among many other things had written on the Elizabethan gentry. Story shared with Trevor-Roper, for example, a lifelong enthusiasm for Edward Gibbon's *Decline and Fall of the Roman Empire*, and both men were much noted as stylists by their peers. For Story's last year in England the responsibility for his supervision was taken on by the literary scholar Helen Gardner, later Dame Gardner, then known for her work on the poet T.S. Eliot and a critical edition of the poetry of John Donne.[19] Story edited William Alabaster's sonnets as a B.Litt thesis, to which he added a biography of Alabaster and a history of Elizabethan Catholic politics, and submitted the whole work for a D.Phil.[20] For the rest of his life he edited renaissance texts, a body of work not discussed in this book but that would have earned him the respect of his peers even if he had not produced the body of scholarship in Newfoundland studies. The study of *bibliography*, in the sense of studying printing history to determine which texts are the closest to the original, gave Story skills useful to his study of Newfoundland.

In 1954, having acquired an Oxford degree and some English affectations, both of which served him well in the then colonially minded Memorial, Story returned to teach at the Parade Street campus. His father had died while he was in England, and he moved back into his boyhood house on the South Side Road (where he was to live for the rest of his life). Now back in St John's at a moment of great change, Story met Edgar Ronald Seary, the recently appointed head of the four-faculty-member Department of English. Seary was to become a research collaborator and a lifelong friend. Given Story's training at Oxford, Seary assigned him to teach freshman courses and courses in old English, Chaucer, and the history of language. The curricula of Memorial University College had been fairly standard liberal arts, the only Newfoundland studies at the college was in history, and that was mostly political history. Story and Seary talked about what they might do that would be fresh and interesting, and they soon set out an agenda for the study of Newfoundland that included the study of language, literature, place names, family names, folklore, history, and biography of important men.[21]

Seary was an unlikely man to be a godfather to this broad set of Newfoundland studies. When he and Story met, he was a recent arrival in Newfoundland, having been born in Sheffield, England, in 1908. He felt disdain for the educational background of Newfoundland undergraduates and the idea that there was an American (let alone Canadian or Newfoundland!) literature worth studying. Seary had studied English literature at the Honours School of English Language and Literature, a school that then had three faculty members, one of whom was a German-trained philologist. It was an unusual subject in British literature departments between the First and Second World Wars, but Seary's early exposure to philology influenced his interests.

He received a PhD in 1933 for a dissertation on the early nineteenth-century, Sheffield-area poet Ebenezer Elliott. After teaching English as a second language in Germany between 1933 and 1935, Seary took up an appointment at Rhodes University College in South Africa. During the sixteen years he taught in that country (excepting five years military service as an officer in the South African Army), he prepared a typescript bibliography of South African English-language writers with biographical notes on the authors. Such a compilation would not have required him to read any of the literature, only to catalogue it, and it reveals much about his mind. He had created a bibliography that could be a foundation for further scholarship.

In 1951 Seary left South Africa for a position as the English chair at a college in Baghdad, Iraq, before moving to Memorial to become a

1.1. Department of English Language and Literature faculty, 1961, (front, l–r) Helena Frecker, Ronald Seary, Allison O'Reilly Feder, David G. Pitt; (back, l–r) Alastair Macdonald, George Story, William Kirwin. (From the S.J. Carew Collection, Special Archives and Collection Division, QEII Library, Memorial University of Newfoundland.)

professor of English in 1953. At the age of forty-five he was older and more experienced than his colleagues, so the following year he was appointed Chair of Memorial's very small Department of English, a position he held until 1970.[22] Seary was thus in a position to be a mentor to a couple of generations of younger scholars, beginning with Story, and to set the departmental agenda. His relationship with younger colleagues was paternalistic, in both the positive and the negative senses of the word, and academic governance of Memorial in the 1950s was both intimate and hierarchical, allowing him great influence over such things as recommending whom to hire.

"Situated as we are, here," Seary commented, "it's well to do the ordinary things of an English Department, but I felt we had a special obligation to develop these hitherto undeveloped areas" of dialect study and folklore.[23] He thought it was a waste that so much linguistic evidence in Newfoundland went unstudied while scholars travelled to distant places for research. Seary and Story's focus on research on Newfoundland language makes sense given their training and the opportunity living in Newfoundland in the 1950s presented. Both men were students of the nineteenth-century European tradition of tracing the derivation of words and textual variants, a scholarly vocation that in the eighteenth century had been related to the effort to correct biblical translation based on comparing texts and in the nineteenth century to establishing canons of national literature. These methods of critical textual comparison had been important in the development of history as a discipline as well as the study of language.

The demonstration that modern languages had a common ancestor in "Indo-European" had been a turning point in philology – away from the earlier nationalistic notion that the German language exemplified the essence of German people and French the essence of France, and towards understanding linguistic change. Seary believed that critical scholarship on language could break free of the nationalism of the local amateur. In a presentation to the Conference of Atlantic Universities in 1966, titled "Regional Humanism," Seary articulated his view of the professional study of language, folklore, and social history.

> All these studies, in speech, dialect vocabulary, family names and place names are then essential to, and in part integral elements of, local history; but for the most part they have received only the attention of enthusiastic amateurs ... It is time, I think, that these studies should become subject to the rigours of academic discipline – that no statement should go unverified, that all evidence should be given chapter and verse; and the imposition of that discipline is the responsibility of our universities.[24]

"Local history," he went on to suggest, was something not much studied at universities in the English-speaking world, with the exceptions of the French Canadians, the Irish, and the Newfoundlanders. He did not observe it, but each of these cases is an example of people using history to support a modern nationalist ideology. But part of the appeal of the study of place names, for Seary, was that it corrected the nationalist teleological bias of political history through philology. Names of places in Newfoundland and Labrador that were derived from the Beothuk (potentially), Mi'kmaq, French, Basque, Portuguese, Spanish, and English were evidence of various people's interactions with the landscape.

Seary's interest in Newfoundland place names was more archival than contemporary. That his interest was in *language* not literature, something that was unusual in either British or Canadian English departments of the day, bears attention. There had been a few Newfoundland poets (including E.J. Pratt, whom Pitt was working to popularize in the province) and a couple of novelists, but studying Newfoundland creative writing would not have seemed auspicious to a man who had a low regard for American literature, let alone the literary output of the province.

The small university in St John's would also have had a difficult time competing for funding and prestige with established universities in the study of the British literary canon. But Newfoundland's linguistic variety on Memorial's doorstep gave the department an opportunity to move into an area in which it would have a comparative advantage. When Seary attended the 1955 meeting of the Canadian Linguistics Association (of which he was a founder) in Toronto, the association, at his request, devoted a session to a discussion of his ideas for a research agenda for Newfoundland. The proposal included the study of place names and vocabulary, but also phonetic transcriptions of recorded samples and the preparation of a linguistic atlas.[25] Seary later published an article arguing that all English departments in Canadian universities did too little to study language.[26]

During this era, faculty members routinely reported on their travel to Memorial's president, Raymond Gushue, and on receiving the report from Seary, Gushue asked Seary to prepare a case for developing language studies that Memorial might take to one of the research foundations for development funds. Gushue had a long and illustrious career. Born in Whitbourne, Newfoundland, in 1900, he had studied at Dalhousie University in Nova Scotia and had been called to both the Nova Scotia and Newfoundland bars. His legal career had led to appointments to government boards, such as the Newfoundland Fisheries Board and the Woods Labour Board, and international committees. He chaired the Fisheries Product Committee of Combined Food Board in Washington, DC, and was a member of the Food and Agriculture Organization of the United Nations.[27]

He had been a member of the board of both Dalhousie University and Memorial College, and Premier Smallwood hoped to take advantage of Gushue's international connections to have the international fisheries board located in St John's. That did not materialize, but Gushue served as Memorial's president between 1952 and 1966. His support of research on Newfoundland language had precedents. The university undertook an effort to establish historical scholarship, discussed in the next chapter, and Gushue was aware that as early as 1953, the auditor and antiquarian Nimshi Crewe had suggested to make sound recordings of Newfoundland dialects as part of a broader strategy of collecting history and folklore.[28]

Gushue's request prompted Seary to set out his thinking in more detail.[29] Seary argued that Newfoundland English was a virgin field for research, but that with the influence of the radio and easier communications the local dialects were disappearing. The idea that speech was becoming more homogenous with modernity was nearly universally accepted by observers in the post-war era. The impetus to salvage a record of minority languages before they were swamped existed in many parts of the English-speaking world, and the Newfoundland dictionary was only one of many regional and national dictionaries created in the second half of the twentieth century.

Seary advocated tape-recording local speakers and ultimately creating a linguistic atlas showing the distribution of dialects. Story had already begun to prepare a "Dictionary of Newfoundland Usage," he reported to Gushue, and Seary suggested hiring specialists in phonetics and philology to aid in that project. He described his own work on Newfoundland place names and stated that he needed financial aid to travel to European and American archives to continue it.[30]

Running in tandem with this effort to document the language before it eroded was Seary's case for the university to encourage such change among its students. He argued that "the quality of the English spoken by many of our students is unworthy of the products of a university" and advocated hiring one, or preferably two, experts in phonetics who would teach courses in phonetics, spoken English, philology, and grammar. This faculty member, or members, would work inside the classroom to change the way that students spoke, while outside of the classroom he or she would carry out the research into the language that was being changed.[31] Seary and Story co-authored a textbook that they used to introduce students to "reading English," which they meant in the British sense of "reading" as in making it one's major area of concentration for the degree. Majoring in English, they wrote, using the words of literary critic Matthew Arnold, enabled the student to read "'the best of what has been thought and said' which is the purpose and reward of literary studies."[32]

On 23 April 1957, Gushue, Seary, and Story – as well as Sadie Organ, university librarian; A.C. Hunter, dean of the Faculty of Arts and Science; Gordon O. Rothney, professor of history; and Michael Harrington, lecturer in English – met to discuss what projects might be supported by the newly formed Canada Council. In addition to requesting support for the dialect dictionary, a dictionary of biography, publications, linguistic atlas, and place name studies, they discussed a wide range of proposals. Hunter, Organ, and Story favoured developing programs in art, music, and drama and suggested establishing an art gallery that would exhibit high-quality work of Newfoundland artists. They also hoped to establish visiting lectureships and money for travel and fellowships, all which could help overcome the university's isolation from wider intellectual life. Rothney suggested archaeological studies of such things as tombstones to supplement the scarce historical records and "studies of life in local communities, the structure of society, beliefs and influences governing behaviour, and the effect of geography on local life and character." All of those attending the meeting agreed that the work at Memorial had national significance and had an intrinsic importance.

> It is recognized that the [Canada] Council will have to develop a *national* policy in fulfilling its functions. Most of the above suggestions are *regional* in character, and necessarily so. It is, of course, realized that the proper investigation of, say, Newfoundland history, or language or folklore, is of direct relevance to similar work elsewhere in Canada; such projects should everywhere be encouraged. At the same time it must be made clear that in its history, its language, its culture, Newfoundland forms a separate unit in a sense not true of most other parts of the Dominion. It therefore provides a legitimate field for independent research.[33]

Memorial moved each of these agendas forward. In its first year of its operation, the Canada Council awarded $8300 in support of linguistic and historical studies of Newfoundland.[34]

Memorial bet that the language research could, in Gushue's words, "make a real contribution to learning and to the prestige of the University both here and abroad."[35] In 1957 Story presented a paper titled

"Research in the Language and Place Names of Newfoundland" to the Canadian Linguistic Association in the hope of attracting Canadian skills and funding to support Memorial's research. He discovered that while Canadian scholars expressed a lively interest in studying Newfoundland speech, they had little practical aid to offer. As Story declared, "in no other English-speaking region of Canada is work as advanced in these fields as it is in Newfoundland, and in no other region is it being pursued so vigorously." As one of the Canadian linguists remarked to him "If you in Newfoundland lead the way, it may stir sufficient interest in the rest of English-speaking Canada for us to gain the support we need to follow." The Canadian linguists encouraged their Memorial colleagues to ask for Canada Council support, and Story was gratified that he had "the support of our mainland colleagues in making our a case for the preminent [sic] claim of Newfoundland for attention" and pleased that "the University is being recognized as a centre of research in linguistics and toponymy, a field in which Newfoundland is of peculiar importance in North America."[36]

Story's collection of Newfoundland vocabulary captured many people's imagination, but the beginnings of the Newfoundland dictionary were modest. Story had his collection of words and their definitions that he had made as a student, but in the late 1950s his efforts remained unstructured. Nothing in his training taught him how to compile a dictionary, and the then small library at Memorial had few dialect dictionaries in its collection that he might have used as a model. In the early years he had not "given much thought to the form of publication and consequently made little attempt to note such things as the distribution of items, the age group or social level of users" nor had he considered "defining the limits of my subject."[37] That, of course, became a key conceptual question, since most words in the Newfoundland lexicon overlapped with those of English speakers in other parts of the world.

Story became aware of these issues in those first years at Memorial as he was teaching the history of the English language. He ended the course with three lectures on local speech. Between 1955 and 1958 he also handed out to his students copies of the Devine glossary and index cards. He had the students, many of whom were adults who had taught in various parts of the island and were back at Memorial to upgrade their qualifications, note which words from Devine's list they knew and list any words that they thought Devine had missed. The students taking the mandatory English courses, whether young or mature, embodied a significant degree of linguistic variation. This method of

collecting was soon supplemented by Story's reading published materials to excerpt words and examples of how they had been used. As he
put it:

> I soon became aware that there was more in print on Nfld. speech than
> I had first supposed ... But as late as 1956 I still thought that a search of
> printed materials would not be worth the trouble. I must also confess
> that, at the time, I was still rather vaguely of the belief that a Dial[ect]
> Dict[ionary] should not overlap with an historical dict such as OED. But
> partly as the result of a growing interest in Nfld. social history, I began to
> read the relevant printed literature, and my files of citations grew stead-
> ily. It is this that has taken up most of my time during the past four or
> five years. The printed material is so diverse that it is useless to attempt
> to describe it. But I can't remember taking up many Nfld. books with-
> out finding something in them to excerpt. The slips from the very early
> works – 16th and 17th centuries deal largely with technical terms for the
> Newfoundland fishery; but by the 18th century a pretty clear "general"
> local vocabulary emerges; by the early 19th century sub-regional vocabu-
> laries emerge. So rewarding has documentary material become in collect-
> ing that I have already broken a determination to avoid mss.[38]

Story had started with a method closely aligned with his fellow dialect lexicographers – collecting words from his contemporaries through
questionnaires and interviews. Only later did his interest in social history lead him to use the traditional method used by those who compiled dictionaries along historical principles. The cardinal example of
the latter type of dictionary was the *Oxford English Dictionary*, which
was a "historical dictionary" in three ways. It organized features such
as spelling and meanings in chronological order, so readers could see
how the language had evolved over time, and it included words that
had been used in the past but had gone out of use. Along with these
characteristics was the effort to find the earliest example of a word
being used in print, which made such dictionaries excellent scholarly
tools but poor as descriptions of how people spoke.[39] A constraint that
lexicographers face is having to decide on a corpus, or a set of publications from which they excerpt quotations. A biased corpus will
result in some words being missed or whole areas of the lexicon being
under-represented. Story's decision to only excerpt words from sources
printed before the year 1850 reflected his belief, during the 1950s, that
older sources would be richer in dialect words, but he later extended

DNE-cit

Squid   **PRINTED ITEM**

> 1578 PARKHURST, [Hakluyt Society, 2d Ser., No. 76, p. 130]
> also a fish like a Smelt which commeth on shore, and another that hath the like propertie, called a Squid: ....
>
> [OED, 1613]
> For the Squid, whose nature is to come by night as well as by day, I tell them I set him a candle to see his way, with which he is much delighted, or els commeth to wonder at it, as doe our fresh water fish, ~~the other commeth also in the night~~

W. J. KIRWIN

OCT 5 1965

1.2. The earliest citation of "Squid" in the *DNE* files. (From the files of the English Language Research Centre, Memorial University of Newfoundland.)

his collecting to the present day when he noticed previously uncollected words being used in contemporary newspapers and magazines.

From Seary's collection of place names and Story's glossary grew a research program that became "a distinguishing feature of the [English] department." It was an ambitious scheme, perhaps more ambitious than the two men then knew, and they enticed many of the faculty members hired in the 1950s and 1960s and hundreds of students to join them. The broader Newfoundland studies agenda undertaken at Memorial, in which the work in the Department of English Language and Literature was a catalyst, reflected the commitment of administrators and faculty. The underlying assumption was that Newfoundland's oral culture was being eroded by the modern media and economic changes and needed to be recorded before it was gone. The efforts to modernize provoked a reaction. As Story later commented, "it is hard now to convey a sense of the urgency we felt about this matter during the decade following confederation when Newfoundland seemed hellbent on jettisoning its inheritance for the newfound delights of a new era."[40] For all the enthusiasm for the economic and social change of the 1950s, it was also a time of reawakening of interest in heritage both at the university and more generally.

> When I first came home to teach in Newfoundland – that was in 1950, and home for good three or four years later – what we call heritage work was barely begun, the very consciousness of it barely discernible. We'd just had some legislation of the first Smallwood administration reestablishing the Newfoundland museum, and attempting to control the export of historic artifacts. At the new Memorial University a course in Newfoundland history ... had been reintroduced by Gordon Rothney; a MA programme in history was being planned; a start was soon to be made on establishing a Newfoundland Archives Division, as well as the great bibliographical enterprise of Agnes O'Dea and her assistants ... I suppose, looking back on it all, that one of the things behind it was a consciousness that we were living at something like the end of an age in Newfoundland, and that change was in the air, a sharper than usual sense of "time present and time past," and the real possibility of an irreparable breach between them.[41]

Story started working more systematically on what he initially called the "Newfoundland Dialect Dictionary" "solely because of the interest and enjoyment to be derived from it," but found that it soon "developed into a large-scale investigation which transcends the personal interest of the compiler without losing any of its pleasure." He soon came to believe that the project had the potential to be important in the international study of English. It could, in his view, contribute "to the integration of English and American linguistic research into a more complete history of the nature and development of language."[42] In a 1956 speech to the Humanities Association in St John's, he also clarified that the dictionary could be an intervention in the culture at a crucial time:

> The investigation [of language] illuminates, as much as anything else does, the nature of the Newfoundland temperament, and the experience of living on this Island. This is the last chance we have to record this language before it disappears. But I would like to think that the Newfoundland Dialect Dictionary will be more than an instrument of scholarly research, and more than a record of the past. I hope also that it will be a storehouse from which we may continue to draw for that variety which has always been a characteristic of our popular speech – a variety which is the spice of language.[43]

In a paper for the Canadian Linguistics Association the following year, he set out the methodological innovations of the project and again proposed an intervention in the spoken language. Story revealed that they were using tape recorders to make a permanent record of the various dialects that made up Newfoundland speech – a technology that was then relatively novel among linguists. That would not only, he said, allow for close study and eventual compilation of an atlas showing the geographic distribution of various dialects, but it might make it "possible to work out a system which might serve for the teaching of a Standard Newfoundland Speech in our schools."[44]

What he meant by a "standard Newfoundland speech" might not be immediately clear. In a lecture to a class in 1958, he argued that in whatever country one examined, there was a tension between educated speech and popular speech and that he valued the linguistic variety of popular speech. But the development within the school system of an educated standard Newfoundland speech, which would coexist alongside the dialect diversity of popular speech, could provide a means for improved communication among Newfoundlanders from different geographic areas and make education easier.[45] In an interesting parallel to Memorial's effort to change rural people's speech, some American educators of the era advocated bi-dialectalism – an educational program of training African-Americans to accept the way they spoke as legitimate but also be able to shift their speech into talking like middle-class whites when they entered the workforce.[46]

Most mid-twentieth-century linguists were descriptive, not prescriptive, in their attitude towards linguistic variation. They attempted to understand the mechanisms of speech, not establish what the correct grammar or pronunciation should be, while English teachers tried to teach "correct" grammar, spelling, and sometimes pronunciation. Story was aware of the tension between his role at the university, that of a Dr Jekyll teaching students "certain standards of correctness, taking as the desirable model the language as it is used in cultivated speech and literary expression,"[47] while at the same time he behaved as a Mr Hyde when he pursued his interest in non-standard speech. He also saw his project as having the potential to legitimize the popular. In a speech to the Rotary Club in St John's in 1957, Story made a case for the existence of a Newfoundland English analogous to American English or British English:

One can even speak of Newfoundland English in the sense that as a people we share common speech habits which distinguish us as a linguistic

group. Had I time, it might prove of interest to speak of the common qualities in the speech of all Newfoundlanders, regardless of their education,
occupation or geographic situation. This is not to say that we all speak the
same dialect. On the contrary, there is probably a greater variety of speech
in Newfoundland than in any other English-speaking region of Canada.
My subject, however, is what we call, very loosely, "popular speech."
By this is meant those varieties of speech which are grouped together in
contrast to a standard (or educated) Newfoundland speech, the essential
difference being that they live and change and develop free from the conditions and restrictions which are imposed on any standard, written language, with its received vocabulary neatly packaged in dictionaries, and
its obligatory grammar codified in books.[48]

Even though the people of both the United States and Great Britain,
for example, have a variety of dialects, the speakers in both countries
also share common characteristics with each other that they do not
share with the people of other countries.[49] There is some irony in this.
Story worked to describe a language that was not codified by dictionaries and grammar books or legislated by an academy, and the act of
description would encourage the survival of linguistic variation by
giving people a dictionary to turn to when they wanted to establish
that a word was real. Yet codifying the Newfoundland lexicon could
change the dynamic character that was one of the factors that made
Newfoundland English what it was.

Not everyone thought it was a good idea to legitimize Newfoundland pronunciation and grammatical features as an acceptable way to
speak. While Story reported that many of his contemporaries in the
1950s saw his interest in what they saw as an archaic vocabulary as a
"harmless pastime," his "suggestion that dialect sounds and syntax are
also legitimate interests had not infrequently been greeted as a scarcely
sane threat to literacy in Newfoundland."[50] As he told a class in 1958:

My first misgiving [about talking about Newfoundland English] comes
from the reaction to the subject of many people – not only "foreigners"
from the mainland, but also from Newfoundlanders themselves. The less
they know about language, the more violent the reaction. Whenever I have
said or written anything for a wider audience than specialists the reaction has been curious – and rather depressing. Some people think of the
subject as rather "quaint" – how sweet those Newfoundland words are!
Others have been puzzled: "What in God's name is anybody interested

in *that* subject for." ... On one occasion, when I had remarked on a television interview that I saw no reason why, by and large, Newfoundlanders should change their pronunciation of words, I received *four* abusive, and *one* threatening letter.[51]

The view that non-standard grammar, or popular dialect, was a sign of backwardness, and a lack of education and sophistication, was widespread. To suggest, as Story did, that there was nothing wrong with using Newfoundland words, pronunciation, and grammar seemed crazy to those who believed there was something inferior about doing so. Some people saw the suggestion that there was value in the old and the local as heretical. This was not just a Newfoundland phenomenon; the publications of dictionaries in the United States often provoked passions among those who advocated that dictionaries be prescriptive and those who felt they should be descriptive.[52] Many Newfoundlanders tried to eliminate features of their speech that had become emblematic of their low status because they believed that adopting a high-prestige dialect would help them achieve economic success. Some of Story's critics believed that encouraging "incorrect" speech would harm the province's aspirations for economic well-being.

Many other Newfoundlanders were pleased when they learned that the university would be publishing dictionaries of dialect and nomenclature. "That is the kind of thing we would expect the university to produce" wrote the *Daily News* commentator A.B. Perlin, "In a sense, it is a national institution even if we have ceased to be a sovereign country. It has the duty of preserving our cultural heritage as well as adding to it."[53] At the competing paper, the *Evening Telegram*, Harold Horwood approved of the growing attention to Newfoundland research: "Important studies are going on in the field of Newfoundland history, and even in the English department there is a growing awareness of Newfoundland life. The same department which, a few years ago, was so out of touch with reality as to immerse its students full fathom five in a sea of Ruskin, is today doing a serious study of Newfoundland dialects. Even the non academic intellect must applaud."[54]

Story believed that there was a "'Newfoundland Regional Speech' – the sum of these *shared* features which distinguish [a] Nflder from a New Englander, a Scot, an Australian, or someone from Nova Scotia" of which few Newfoundlanders would have been conscious, and presumably no one could be hostile towards linguistic features of which they were unaware or those which had not become an emblem of backwardness. As Story suggested, there were also regional dialects, or varieties of "popular speech" within Newfoundland which many "people who should know better" mistake as "arbitrary departures from some 'correct' standard English."[55]

Story's political stance was not confined to quietly making a case for the legitimacy of Newfoundland English to fellow academics and students; in 1969 he publically criticized the pejorative stereotypes of Newfoundlanders then common in Canada. In a speech to the Kiwanis Club Convention in St John's he commented that he did not need to expound on the qualities of Newfoundlanders, even though he admitted that there were some people who doubted that there was an "ethos" of the Newfoundland people. Story suggested that the two decades of social science research and the frequent appearance of books about Newfoundland in the catalogues of Canadian and American publishing houses were evidence enough that there was something unique about Newfoundlanders. Even "the large corpus of 'Newfie jokes,' whatever else it may signify" he suggested, "is a kind of inverted recognition of a new and distinct people within the framework of Confederation."[56] Story lectured:

Over the years, I have detected in Mainland sources three principal stereotypes of the Newfoundlander ... The first is that we are inarticulate halfwits. The second presents the Newfoundlander as a destructive and brutal killer of nearly everything that walks, flies or swims. The third image presents us as kindly, gentle, hospitable, law-abiding, cheerful, and hardy ... Speaking now as a student of language (and not simply as an inarticulate half-wit) I find in my fellow countrymen, especially the unlettered ones, a sophistication and a richness in the art of expression which cultivated Western societies might envy. It is part of an astonishing inheritance of oral tradition, lore and technique which pre-dates the age of print, and puts to shame the *anemic* verbal achievement of the electronic age. If anyone believes that a Newfoundlander without formal schooling lacks an adequate vocabulary, he should consider the ways in which the Islander might call him a weak-minded fool. He might, for example, call him a *gomeril*, a *joskin*, an *omadawn*, an *ownshook*, a *scoopendike*, or a *scrumpshy* ... What the stereotypes, true and false alike, indicate, in fact, is the existence in Newfoundland of a distinctive, homogeneous cultural entity, possibly, as [folk song collector] Kenneth Peacock suggests, the only true English-speaking *nation* left in North America ... And, it must be added, [it is] now in direct cultural confrontation with the manifold and ubiquitous forces of the Continental economy and society. I don't mean to imply by the term *confrontation* a hostile clash ... But it would be dishonest to pretend that the processes of change now at work in Newfoundland are the simple examples of unmixed blessing and progress we are daily invited to admire and applaud. What is undeniable is that the past few decades have seen the creation of a fresh dynamic in Newfoundland society. It is one which has yet to reach a new repose and equilibrium. What stereotypes will emerge to express that repose it would be idle to predict. One suspects that the quality of stubborn endurance, the endowment of so many centuries of struggle, will see to it that they will reflect some characteristic amalgam of the traditional brew.[57]

The emerging study of English at Memorial was bolstered when in 1958 the National Museum of Canada contracted Seary to do an ethnolinguistic study of the Avalon Peninsula, which the museum hoped would be a pilot study of an English-speaking region that could then be extended to other parts of Canada. To work on the project Seary brought in Story and fellow Department of English member Patrick Drysdale (MA Oxford). Drysdale had come to Newfoundland in 1955 while working with the London Theatre Company and had decided to stay and teach linguistics.[58] The three used the opportunity to pursue their own research agenda of place names, vocabulary, and speech. This required they work out some methods, designing and testing before applying on a large scale, a dialect questionnaire and method of recording speech.[59] Drysdale's departure from Memorial in 1959 to work for a Toronto-based publisher (of dictionaries, among other books) prompted Seary to hire a more highly qualified phonologist.

William J. Kirwin proved to be a significant contributor to linguistic scholarship at Memorial over more than a half century, not the least as one of the editors of the dictionary. Born in Newport, Rhode Island, in 1925, the son of a civilian employee of the United States Navy, Kirwin was determined to go to college, even after the attack on Pearl Harbor encouraged many of his classmates to enlist. That had to wait, for the draft board assigned Kirwin to the US Army Engineer Corps, in which he served between 1943 and 1945 (including duty in Northern Europe). Military service entitled him to financial aid under the GI Bill, enabling him to study at an elite liberal arts college, Bowdoin College, in Maine. Bowdoin was, in his view, "a very upper middle classish school" that "issues forth very many financial, insurance, executive, stock market individuals" and "the comfortable business climate I experienced there was not attractive for a carpenter's son."[60]

Having read a *Time* magazine article on the exciting things happening at the University of Chicago, he went on to that first-rank research university, which was much more to his liking. Kirwin had originally started graduate work in literature but disliked the sort of literary criticism practised at the time. Under the mentorship of James Sledd, a Southerner then teaching English at Chicago and the author of books on Dr Johnson's dictionary and on grammar, Kirwin focused on the study of linguistics. Kirwin later worked under the supervision of Raven I. McDavid, an accomplished dialect fieldworker and prominent dialect geographer who was working on the dialect atlas of North America project. At Chicago they designed a program of studies in linguistics specifically for Kirwin, giving him an up-to-date training in American structuralist linguistic theory. His education also included, by chance, one course in lexicography taught by Mitford McLeod Mathews, the author of *A Dictionary of Americanisms on Historical Principles*, although Kirwin had no idea that he would later work in that field. Kirwin took his MA in 1951, and over the next few years he taught at a preparatory school in Massachusetts, the University of Nebraska, and at Ripon College in Wisconsin before joining Memorial in September 1959. Kirwin was recommended for the job by McDavid.[61]

Seary assigned Kirwin to teach freshman English, phonology, and the history of English, and he expected him to both write a doctoral thesis and start gathering phonological and lexical data on the speech of the Avalon Peninsula. When Drysdale learned that Kirwin had started work on St John's dialects by surveying the speech of Memorial's students, he warned him that the capital city was "a hodge podge of corrupted dialects" and suggested that "the real linguistic riches of the island are in the outports."[62] Kirwin recognized the professional opportunity presented by the great linguistic variation on the island of Newfoundland and its potential for team research. There were "fascinating problems, real conundrums, hundreds of neatly delimited little social groups abound for the analyst to survey and describe" and, he continued, "My stay here for a few years certainly will be most gratifying just because the material to work on is so luxuriant and handily accessible."[63] But he worried that linguistic research had not caught on.

One thing is sure – there is no lack of practically illiterate, talkative, unspoiled people whose forbears go back direct to the seventeenth and eighteenth centuries, often on the same property of a settlement ... The future of this study does not look bright, Our chairman and dean are earnest for dialect study, but no university students are attracted by the field, graduate students from elsewhere would not consider this exotic territory for their fieldwork, and professionals do not consider Memorial as a post.[64]

While teaching a full load of undergraduate courses, Kirwin worked on his doctoral dissertation (a structural analysis of English in the works of Chaucer for which he was granted a PhD in 1964), spent his summers doing fieldwork on Newfoundland dialects, and made trips to the United States for holidays and consultations with his advisors.

Despite his hard work, Kirwin confided in McDavid that he faced challenges as a fieldworker. His field technique as a linguist was effective, he elicited speakers to pronounce the speech items that were the object of his study, and he could hear them and transcribe them with speed and accuracy, but he faced difficulty getting informants to cooperate.

The frustration, within a radius of twenty miles of this capital, has been the rarity of informants. The middle-aged fishermen are actively earning their annual income now. The older people (ol'flas) are all hidden away in their box houses. And the people recommended by name, as authoritative or talkative, sometimes refuse outright out of distrust or assert they don't know anything, others know much more. Then a little more substantial opposition appeared in a clergyman's advice that "the people" are sick of being put on parade, that I would find them uncooperative in his community. (I translated this to mean, "No. I won't suggest to you any typical older fisherman at leisure in my settlement.") Can Newfoundland be so different from the thousands of communities visited in Europe and North America, so that informants *could* be found by earlier workers, but have to be sought more strenuously, sometimes unavailingly, in this special society?[65]

Perhaps as early as the 1960s some people were starting to feel fatigue at being the object of social science inquiry, and certainly many working men would not have interrupted their busy workday during the short summer fishing season to work their way through an interview designed to elicit words in their common vocabulary. And McDavid confirmed Kirwin's suspicion that other fieldworkers experienced the same frustrations when searching for informants. McDavid replied that he had depended on his father's professional contacts as informants and used intermediaries who knew the communities and were able to introduce him to people to study. Even then, he commented that, "certain kinds of talent scouts I've found almost worthless – teachers, librarians, clergymen ... people in these rackets tend to be self-consciously respectable, aware that they have risen above the folk, and (being somewhat patronizing themselves) are likely to suspect you of patronizing 'the people' and indirectly patronizing them."[66]

Structural linguistics in the United States differed from the historically oriented tradition of philology in England that Seary and Story had internalized – phonologists such as Kirwin sought to uncover different phonemes, the small differences in utterances that conveyed meaning in a given language (the difference between the sounds that produce the word *bit* rather than the word *pit*, for example). Such traits could be mapped to show linguistic variation across geography or across social class. Kirwin's training thus added a different perspective to Memorial's emergent study of language than the lexical emphasis of Story and Seary. In his classes and his research, like his mentor, McDavid, Kirwin strongly believed that the discipline should be descriptive not prescriptive – that his job was to record and analyse the way that people did speak, not try to impose some arbitrary dialect as the correct one. (His own Rhode Island pronunciation remained easily discernable throughout his life.)

The tension between those who favoured teaching students to speak an "educated speech" and those who believed that regional dialects had value, the tension between prescription and description, parallels the larger role the university played in encouraging a desire for the new and "modern" and an erosion of respect for the cultural inheritance. Educational institutions and the mass media helped homogenize and standardize speech, although the effect was less than critics had feared or advocates had hoped. To take the obvious example of intentional efforts to change language habits in Newfoundland, for many years the university had mandatory "speech" classes for rural Newfoundland students who wanted to be teachers. The course, titled Speech, was intended to teach practical public speaking techniques suitable for the classroom, but those who taught it viewed the standardization of grammar and pronunciation as equally important goals. They hoped that students would return to the outports as conscious agents of language change, although I have no evidence to judge the effectiveness of the speech classes.

Not everyone at Memorial was equally committed to eradicating popular speech. As Story told a class of folklore students in 1972, much of his own effort had been devoted to countering the work the province's schools were doing to erode local speech patterns, which many teachers wrongly accepted as incorrect ways of speaking. He reported having "had great disputes with colleagues about this – not only instructors of "speech classes" but also [instructors of] English composition classes."[67] To be fair to those who taught "speech," some rural students spoke dialects that were nearly mutually unintelligible and would have been ineffectual teachers when working in any communities other than their home towns. Rural students whose dialects were fairly close to "standard" English were often excused from the speech course. Story promoted the idea that Newfoundland English was a legitimate variety of English like the others throughout the world, and he and his colleagues raced to record it before it disappeared.

> A good deal of time in school is spent in (vainly) trying to wipe out traces of local speech in the silly belief that there is something improper or wrong about popular speech. The *implicit* aim is usually cultural or social, not linguistic at all. So for a good many years, those of us who are students of Nfld. speech have had to work pretty hard to establish the credentials of our subject and to make sure, though in a time of considerable change, the traditional speech of Nflders gets recorded.[68]

As he saw it, the educational agenda was one of making people conform to an imagined North American standard in their speech, so that they would fit into the modern labour force and would not be seen as socially inferior. In Kirwin's phrase, "a stigma of ignorance or the rustic is attached" to some elements of popular speech.[69] Story and Kirwin believed that all the world's varieties of English were equal, and no one group of speakers should be stigmatized. When the Memorial folklorist Herbert Halpert enlisted his students to act as field collectors of oral culture, including recording the Newfoundland lexicon, it ran counter to the role most university students played in bringing new cultural elements into their rural communities. That was not only, in Kirwin's view, on more solid epistemological ground, but could benefit the people who were the subject of inquiry. As he put in a draft of a letter seeking government aid in finding informants, "accurate fact in published work can do much to correct unflattering stereotypes and misinterpretations, and to supply present and future generations with a true picture of their heritage they can be proud of."[70]

After the whole university moved from Parade Street to a new campus on Elizabeth Avenue in 1961, the Department of English had a linguistic laboratory with modern equipment for both teaching and research. In 1962 Seary, Story, and Kirwin submitted the manuscript of *The Avalon Peninsula of Newfoundland: An Ethno-linguistic Study*, which the museum published in 1968.[71] The slender book was divided into three sections, covering descriptions and place names (for which Seary took primary responsibility), a social history of the settlement and development of the region (drafted by Story), and a survey of the dialects (Kirwin's contribution). Kirwin's pioneering phonology fieldwork allowed him to describe four dialects on the peninsula – that of the southern shore, the northern shore, Bay Roberts, and St John's. Prior to this publication, it was broadly assumed, by scholars and non-scholars alike, that geographic isolation had been responsible for both the preservation of linguistic elements in Newfoundland that had passed out of general use in the United Kingdom and Ireland and the contemporary variation from one community to the next. The persistence and variation brought about by the assumed isolation, according to the common-sense view, were what made Newfoundland language worth studying. Contrary to that, Kirwin, Story, and Seary found that "perhaps too much has been made of the 'isolated communities.'"[72] Indeed, roads were relatively recent in some communities, but transportation by sea was frequent and there were many forces at play to introduce speakers to words and pronunciations from other areas.

There was no master plan or joint research applications in the linguistic research; the collaboration on the *DNE* of Story, Kirwin, and, later, Widdowson arose fortuitously. As Story commented about the early collaborations on the dictionary: "we drifted into it, in a way, by doing the sorts of things we were interested in, in our own time, in our own way, with our own materials, without funding, without grant applications, or grants, for years."[73] Seary, Story, and Kirwin continued to build research momentum. In the summer of 1961, McDavid visited St John's and endorsed Seary's view "that in an era of rapid change, no time should be lost in making as intensive an investigation of the subject as possible by an international body of qualified dialectologists."

Seary had a commitment for aid from McDavid, and hoped for financial support from the university, the Newfoundland government, and the Canada Council to support bringing into the province a team of qualified fieldworkers during the following summer.[74] No such international effort materialized, but in 1962 considerable progress was being made. Seary continued to look for financial aid to entice graduate students at Chicago and Michigan (in linguistics) and Indiana and Laval (in folklore) to come to Newfoundland for fieldwork. One day, he hoped, Memorial could develop a doctoral program of its own in those areas, but in the meantime it would entice graduate students from other universities to do fieldwork in the province. The hoped-for large team of American linguists scouring the outports did not materialize, but the doctoral students who were supported by the university's Institute of Social and Economic Research and the addition to the Department of English faculty of John Widdowson and Herbert Halpert enabled the collection of an impressive amount of oral culture beginning during the summer of 1962.[75]

John Widdowson, a British-born folklorist and linguist, had a career on both sides of the Atlantic and contributed significantly to Newfoundland language studies. Born in Sheffield in 1935, Widdowson took an Oxford BA in English language and literature in 1959, upgraded to an MA in 1963. He had been teaching in the British school system and working on a study of a local dialect under Harold Orton for a degree at the University of Leeds. Seary had contacted Orton looking for an English instructor and someone who could collect dialect, and Orton recommended Widdowson for the job. Widdowson and his wife crossed the Atlantic on one of the last voyages of the Furnis Withy line, landing among rotten wharves and ramshackle buildings that bore little resemblance to the North America they knew from the movies.[76] Almost immediately upon beginning to teach English at Memorial in 1962, he started contributing tape recordings of Newfoundland speech to the emergent collaboration on dialect. As Kirwin put it in a Festschrift for Widdowson, he "became immediately involved with my activities in linguistics and local language varieties, and as student and colleague he experienced the strain of harmonizing [his] solid British phonetic training with [my] American structuralism – the phoneme, and all that. We both survived many disagreements."[77]

Although they shared a lifelong respect and friendship, and both fell within the orbit of Story's charisma, there was also a creative tension between the two. Widdowson had similar notions of correct grammar to most of the faculty at Memorial, and initially he had a more prescriptive attitude towards language than did Kirwin. As the two men shared interests and co-taught courses, Widdowson learned from Kirwin, and the arguments continued after they left the classroom for the office they shared. There were also methodological differences in their collection of data. Kirwin was pleased to have a colleague collecting dialect and was confident the two could work together, but he did not want to spend his time purchasing and maintaining recording equipment that by training and temperament he did not want to use in his own research. He reported to Seary:

> Clearly there are differences in the methods of dialect study espoused by the English (Orton-Ellis) and the Americans (Kurath-McDavid) … In other words, Mr Widdowson's plans and proposals suit his specific studies and his ideal of analysis of speech. I believe field-workers with an improved questionnaire have to talk with hundreds of Newfoundlanders and transcribe on the spot the minimum amount of speech useful for phonological and vocabulary studies. He prefers taping the speakers selected around the Island and then exhaustively transcribing the minute details that can be heard through elaborate electronic equipment. (I do not know if he has any interest in interviewing Newfoundlanders.) Colleagues must have diverse approaches and attitudes; it is discoveries and published results which count in the end. But for your guidance I want to express my interest in expanding my field interviews and accumulating many more, comparable worksheets, and using the lab facilities only incidentally.[78]

To Kirwin's credit, he also recognized that he was learning a great deal about British methods in phonetics from Widdowson.[79] Teaching and field collecting in Newfoundland had whetted Widdowson's interest in the language, and prepared him to teach linguistics, but Canadian law required people to leave the county or apply for permanent residence after two years. Orton suggested that he apply for a job teaching linguistics and English at the University of Sheffield, a job that Widdowson was awarded. It did not mean an end to his work at Memorial, his commitment to Newfoundland studies over the next fifty years was perhaps greater than if he had continued to live in St John's. As we will see, his work on the *DNE* and in Newfoundland folklore was critical to its development. And Widdowson developed English folklore and linguistics at Sheffield along the lines that had emerged at Memorial.[80]

In December 1963 Raymond Gushue took an ambitious integrated proposal to the Canada Council. He made a case for the timeliness of the work, suggesting that to "the linguist and to the folklorist, the Island at present provides examples of 'fossilized' communities of a kind unusual, if not unique" and the only possible parallel was the Appalachian region of the United States. Starting fieldwork was, he argued, urgent, since

> [t]he entry of Newfoundland into Confederation with Canada in 1949, after four centuries of isolation and independence, initiated a process of rapid change. Even today much of the Island is in an entirely pre-industrial state; but, with increasing momentum, the process of development and change, which elsewhere has taken decades, is being crowded into years. Roads, schools, local councils, the mass media of radio and television are transforming Newfoundland with bewildering speed. Settlements which had been isolated for centuries are being either abandoned or linked for the first time directly with neighbors. There exists, therefore, not only an opportunity of studying the dialects, toponymy and folklore of one of the largest pre-industrialized communities in the English-speaking world, but also an opportunity, unlikely to occur again, of studying and documenting the process of profound linguistic and cultural change from a rural, popular folk-society to the more characteristic forms of the mid-twentieth century.[81]

Gushue was correct; Memorial quickly established a reputation for its academic study of folk culture, but he exaggerated the isolation. The notion that Newfoundland had been isolated and independent for four centuries was inaccurate. Newfoundlanders had been highly mobile, as would be expected from people who produced and exchanged a commodity on the international market. Similarly, the characterization of the society as "fossilized" missed the significant cultural change that had always occurred. Granted, there was continuity over time in production methods and the rhythm of rural life, but the anthropologists' and folklore collectors' bias towards what they conceived of as primitive and the ancient blinded them to collecting evidence of change and invention. The idea that 1949 was a cultural as well as constitutional turning point was also frequently cited, despite the fact that there had never been a time without change, nor had there been a time that the society was closed off from participating in Western civilization.

The president saw this initiative as an opportunity to establish research at Memorial that would lead the country. Gushue asked the Canada Council for $40,000 per year over five years "to transform what have been individual, part time investigations into a systematic, coordinated, and an interdisciplinary programme of research; and to go still further in making the University a centre, unique in English-speaking Canada, for the study, at all levels, of dialectology, toponomy and folklore."[82] The money would fund six research students from other universities because, at the still-young university, there were no Newfoundland students far enough along in their training to take the positions. It would also cover the expenses of linguistic and folklore fieldwork, the publication of specialist studies, and the expansion of the library holdings in areas relevant to the study of oral culture.

Unfortunately, the proposal was too ambitious. The director of the Canada Council, A.W. Truman, seemed shocked that Memorial had asked for such a large portion of the council's total budget and for a multi-year commitment, so he authorized a more modest sum for the current year only, 1964–65. A $10,000 grant could be drawn upon to support three, not six, research fellows and their fieldwork expenses.[83] It was too late to recruit competent graduate students and have them conduct the fieldwork within that year, so Gushue got permission to redirect the grant to fund staff members' fieldwork, subsidizing the publication of a book (*Christmas Mumming*, which will be discussed in a later chapter), and purchases to build the library's holdings.[84]

It bears remembering that while the group was intensely collecting linguistic data, and of course teaching swelling numbers of under-graduates, Story was also continuing his work in English renaissance literature. He took his first sabbatical in 1964–65, using the opportunity to return to Oxford and write a study of the sermons of Lancelot Andrewes. The trip to England did not get him entirely away from duty to Memorial. Moses (pronounced Mose) Morgan, the dean of arts and science, asked Story to help fill faculty vacancies at the university. Story searched for, informally interviewed, and then recommended several English students, each of whom he imagined fitting within the New-foundland studies agenda. And even while working on Andrewes, Story's mind was never very far from his Newfoundland glossary. He met with Widdowson at Sheffield, who, Story reported, had the idea of producing word lists for the glossary from the folklore and dialect tapes he had been collecting.

Over the next few years Widdowson transcribed more than five hundred tapes, excerpting out lexical information. Surprisingly, it was not until the spring of 1965 that Story considered noting the earliest occurrence of each word and adding cross references to other dic-tionaries. He was now thinking beyond the glossary to the eventual publication of a dictionary.[85] As he reported in a letter to Kirwin, he had conversations with British lexicographers, who pointed out that to include a seventeenth-century word without reference to the context from which it was collected might inaccurately imply that the word was still being used. Second, cross references to "British and American dictionaries would underline the unusual interest of the Newfoundland vocabulary as a kind of mid-Atlantic station." He had considered both of these points about a year earlier, and his meetings with the English lexicographers had confirmed that these were good ideas. He also now foresaw the culmination of the project as a hardcover book, which was not something he had considered earlier.[86] He returned to St John's with a renewed excitement for the prospect of Newfoundland scholarship.

Just as Story's sabbatical had been important in the gestation of the *DNE*, Kirwin's sabbatical leave in 1966–67 was pivotal in his and Widdowson's careers. In 1965 Kirwin was an American working in Newfoundland, and he still thought that he might one day return to the US. That year he had declined a job offer from an American college, stating "I still feel I am too deeply involved in this interesting land and the possibilities of study here to move back to the United States, at least right away."[87] The year away from St John's solidified his personal attachment to his adopted home and marked a turning point in his research. Kirwin used his sabbatical to study the contemporary speech of the people in the areas of Ireland and the West of England from which Newfoundland settlers had originated, and he conducted historical research into "ways of life and material culture (especially related to the sea and fishing) that are reflected in the speech."[88] He returned to Memorial "more firmly committed to field work, research and writing on the linguistic side of Newfoundland studies."[89]

The depth of his commitment can be seen in his decision to name the Public Libraries Board as the beneficiary for his life insurance, stipulating that the money be used to purchase books related to Newfoundland, archival preservation, and the editing and publishing of editions of rare Newfoundland items.[90] Over the next few years Kirwin engaged less and less in rigorous phonological fieldwork and devoted more and more of his effort to collaborating with Story in the "descriptive and historical study of the English language and its varieties as planted in Newfoundland in the sixteenth and seventeenth centuries."[91] He had practised the techniques of American dialect geography and administered an adaptation of the questionnaire of the Linguistic Atlas of the United States and Canada, which he hoped would "uncover useful historical traits preserved here and theoretical points about language change and innovations."[92]

Meanwhile, Widdowson completed his MA in phonetics and dialectology in 1966 and returned to Memorial for a year to organize the Folklore and Language Archive. That same year the Department of English Language and Literature at Memorial introduced a doctoral program; it initially focused on dialect studies and folklore, and Widdowson was one of the first to enrol. Being supervised by Story and Halpert and collaborating with the two as well, Widdowson soon played a liaison role; dialect material collected by folklorists was copied for colleagues in the Department of English while those working in English would copy any material of interest to the folklorists and send it along.[93] As Kirwin put it in 1970, "All the people here, John Widdowson, Professor Story, and so on, have taken as a basic premise that it is one area – social history studies, [or] cultural history of Newfoundland ... we don't feel that there's a division at all between these kinds of study."[94]

Seary and Story had started their study of language in the 1950s using their training in philology and bibliography – two approaches that endeavoured to find the older form or the more authentic variant or the root. Seary's work remained philological. The older man attempted to trace the etymology of place names on the island. The *DNE*, however, did not directly discuss the etymology of words. It showed changes in meaning, and sometimes spelling, over time through its citations and its cross references to other dictionaries to show where some words in Newfoundland English came from. But the modest amount of lexical data made etymology difficult. Kirwin had worked on the Irish language and found it difficult to draw definite conclusions about some Newfoundland words that were popularly believed to have Irish origins. He was sceptical of so called folk-etymologizing; he believed that many of the *post facto* explanations of the derivation of words were fanciful and not consistent with the evidence or scholarly rigour. Kirwin also believed that "folk" rarely self-consciously thought about their speech and that only middle-class commentators speculated on the derivation of words. When Kirwin did speculate on etymology, as he did with the word *squid* (which seems to have entered English first in Newfoundland), he did so based upon his knowledge of phonology.[95]

The cooperation continued after Widdowson returned to live in the United Kingdom, where he established the Survey of Language and Folklore, an institution that in many ways paralleled the folklore archive at Memorial that he had helped to found. While concern for his family in England dissuaded him from immigrating to Newfoundland, in letters to Kirwin, Story, and Halpert, Widdowson often expressed a disillusionment with academic life in the United Kingdom, "especially in the present academic climate which regards both linguistics and folklore as highly unacademic."[96]

These frustrations contrasted with his warm memories of the collaborations with his friends at Memorial, and he was anxious, once his dissertation was finished, to get back to his commitments to helping with the dictionary and working with Halpert on a volume of Newfoundland folktales. While he thought it best to remain in the United Kingdom, he proposed making a "permanent pattern of research visits" to Memorial each summer.[97] In 1973 his thesis, "Aspects of Traditional Verbal Control: Threats and Threatening Figures in Newfoundland Folklore" was approved.[98] Each summer he returned to the island to continue his contributions to the DNE and a range of folk culture studies. He had been a protégé of Orton, who had been a founder of the Survey of English Dialects, and Widdowson devoted much of his considerable energy to the development and completion of a dialect atlas of the UK. While Widdowson's publications on Newfoundland dialect and folklore over the next half century would be the envy of many scholars, he also established himself as a leading dialectologist in Britain. The British dialect atlas, like its counterpart in Newfoundland, had been motivated by Orton's belief that post-war changes in the UK were erasing English dialects.

While Kirwin had been away, folklore and linguistics, two of the fields initially promoted by Seary, broke from the Department of English. A Department of Folklore was founded under Halpert's leadership, the centrepiece of which was the Folklore and Language Archive, which would house the evidence collected by the university's fieldworkers. Chapter 3 will discuss the development of folklore, but we can address linguistics here. John Hewson, a linguist who worked in the tradition of Gustave Guillaume and was a member of the Department of French, organized a Department of Linguistics, and as its first head shaped its research and teaching agenda. Kirwin had supported establishing the new department, but after a year of introspection he chose to remain in the Department of English Language and Literature so he could continue to work on Newfoundland English.[99] As he became older, he found phonological fieldwork taxing, and in consultation with Widdowson he came to believe that working from transcriptions was not dependable. He was now firmly committed to teaching English literature and language and to working with Story on the dictionary.

Lexicographers and linguists throughout the English-speaking world had drifted further apart in the 1960s, as the latter increasingly focused on the transformational grammar pioneered by Noam Chomsky, a body of theory that seemed to have little to offer to those who wrote dictionaries.[100] Kirwin had been trained before Chomsky's work had been published, and he recognized that to participate in the debates in the linguistics journals would have meant working within a theoretical framework of which he was sceptical.

As was perhaps inevitable given the nature of academic politics and the tendency for disciplines to distinguish themselves by specializing, the two new departments soon took their own directions in research and teaching, but it left Kirwin and Widdowson disappointed at the lack of interdisciplinary cooperation. Kirwin abandoned his hope to one day compile a dialect atlas; he reconciled himself to the fact that it would not be possible for him to put together a team as had the charismatic leaders who led dialect surveys in the United States and Britain. A former student of Kirwin's, Harold Paddock, was appointed in the Department of Linguistics, and Paddock took up research towards his own dialect atlas. But Paddock's project focused on a small number of speech features that he took as representative of dialects within New-foundland English, while Kirwin, Story, and Widdowson had come to believe that dialect variation within Newfoundland English was super-ficial. Paddock administered his own questionnaires and did not draw much on the data of his colleagues. The prospect of a broad cooperative study of Newfoundland oral culture was receding even as the univer-sity was continuing to grow.[101] The drift away from arduous fieldwork towards working with books made sense for a middle-aged man such as Kirwin, and the decision to work as a lexicographer rather than a phonetician meant he could contribute something to scholarship with-out dealing with the Chomskian juggernaut.

By 1968 Story, Kirwin, and Widdowson had planned the overall shape of the *DNE*, and funds from Memorial and the Canada Council enabled them to establish the Newfoundland Dictionary Centre as a place to conduct the work.[102] Story's funding application justified the value of the dictionary.

> The theoretical significance of the Newfoundland dictionary is that it will attempt to represent the thoroughly interwoven fabric of standard and dialectical usage which forms one continuous scale of usage in New-foundland. The dictionary will be an experiment in lexicography along

the lines of the *Dictionary of Jamaican English* by F.G. Cassidy and R.B. Le Page (1967). Its practical importance is that it will describe, with unusual fullness, the English language in a regional form of exceptional age, variety and interest.[103]

The American dialect lexicographer Frederic Gomes Cassidy was a referee for the *DNE*, as were Seary and Orton.[104] Since the 1950s Story had been corresponding about dictionaries with Cassidy, who was to become the principal editor of the *Dictionary of American Regional English*. Cassidy's *DJE* was the closest parallel to the *DNE* of which Story, Kirwin, and Widdowson were aware, in large part because it drew upon both oral and printed sources. Both the Newfoundland and the Jamaican dictionaries documented the oral culture of islands, and colonies, but Jamaica had a radically different linguistic history than Newfoundland. Jamaica's white population spoke a variant of standard British English while the descendants of former slaves spoke a "creole" heavily inflected with the substrate of African languages. There were no such sharp racial divisions within Newfoundland, and the class differences in language were comparatively less.

Readers used dictionaries, of course, as authorities on language, and historically their authors had drawn mostly upon elite and literary sources to provide illustrations of the words in use. Doing so in either Jamaica or Newfoundland would have excluded much of popular language. The *DJE* used oral evidence from Jamaicans of African ancestry and the working class, and Cassidy and LePage had decided to use capitals to indicate headwords that were collected from printed sources and lower-case letters to indicate those collected from oral sources. That had the effect of highlighting the racial and class divisions within the speech community. The Newfoundland team adopted the same typographic convention in 1965, but in 1973 reversed this decision, deciding to not present evidence collected from oral sources differently than that collected from written sources.[105] This presented practical problems. The identities of oral sources were disguised in the entries of the draft of the letter D, which they circulated to get suggestions, but Story confided to the historian Leslie (Les) Harris: "this has always troubled me somewhat since I myself think that "oral" informants are of equal authority to printed sources; but there are problems of tact involved here which John Widdowson seems especially sensitive to." He asked Harris, "Do you see anything in the quotations which anyone would really be embarrassed to see expressly attributed to him in print?"[106]

1.3. Kirwin and Story excerpting for the dictionary, 1977. (From the files of the English Language Research Centre, Memorial University of Newfoundland.)

A division of labour evolved between the three men and their research assistant, Joan Halley, whom they hired in 1969 out of their Canada Council grant. Story coordinated the project and both he and Kirwin collected words from the textual records. Widdowson, now visiting St John's each summer for work on the dictionary and continued work on folktales with Halpert, collected words from the tapes. In all, they collected more than 80,000 examples of words in use. Story and Kirwin recorded the spelling variants they found in texts, and Widdowson rendered the pronunciations on the tapes in the International Phonetic Alphabet (IPA). A reader of the *DNE* who is familiar with the IPA will note that he discriminated a large number of subtle variations in the pronunciation of some items. The authors of the dictionary were aware that readers turn to dictionaries to see how a word is spelled or pronounced. A reader would find either Widdowson's renderings into IPA or the variants of spelling collected from texts. Despite the common use of dictionaries as authorities on correctness, Story, Kirwin, and Widdowson did not want to assert *correct* spellings or pronunciations, but to report as completely as possible all the evidence they were able to collect.

To take one, admittedly not typical, example, the first edition of the *DNE* reports twenty-five different spellings and five pronunciations of the word *ballicatter*, and the dictionary's files contain eighty-nine uses of the word and editorial notes.[107] Further variants of the word came to light after the book went to press. The authors made no claims that any of these were the standard, only that they collected evidence of each of these varied spellings and pronunciations. Inevitably they had to confront the dilemma that they had to choose one of the variants to be the headword in the entry, and in a few cases they had found no examples of the word in print so the authors had no choice but to make up a spelling based on the arbitrary English language conventions of spelling. They were conscious of the danger that readers would likely take the headword to be the standard or most common form, although that was often not the case.[108]

Defining the corpus of a speech community is never easy. The English spoken in Newfoundland is not a different language from that spoken in Canada as Basque is a different language than Spanish. Most words Newfoundlanders used were common to English speakers throughout the world. The criteria for inclusion in the dictionary are therefore important.

> Rather than attempting to define a "Newfoundlandism" our guiding principles in collecting have been to look for words which appear to have entered the language in Newfoundland or to have been recorded first, or solely, in books about Newfoundland; words which are characteristically Newfoundland by having continued in use here after they died out or declined elsewhere, or by having acquired a different form or developed a different meaning, or by having a distinctly higher or more general degree of use.[109]

The word *boat* is common to all English speakers, but it has several senses in the Newfoundland speech community that are not used by others; these are therefore in the *DNE*. Sorting through the lexical evidence to discern the difference senses in which people use a word is a difficult part of the process. "Anyone who works in lexicography will tell you that a spelling, and a phonetic representation and a definition is only the beginning" Widdowson commented, "the nuances of usage are often slipping between one or two of the illustrative quotations."[110]

The dictionary is not a description of the lexicon of Newfoundlanders; it is a selection. Even the least verbose Newfoundlander would have a vocabulary several multiples of the number of headwords in the dictionary, and not one would know all of the words recovered by Story, Kirwin, and Widdowson. They wanted "to establish the lexical record for Newfoundlanders themselves and their descendants, and for readers and scholars who need to know about the speech and material culture of the region."[111] It is, above all, a reference tool to the language, not a description. Words that a reader could find in the *OED* or other dialect dictionaries, because Newfoundlanders used a word that was also used by another speech community, were not included even if its use in Newfoundland was unique among North Americans.

The collecting for the dictionary was admirable in its breadth and inclusiveness, especially given the limited resources for collecting. Like many lexicographers, Story was fond of quoting Dr Johnson, who had recognized that his dictionary was limited by his being unable to go into coal mines, for example, to collect the specialized miner's vocabulary. Story, Kirwin, and Widdowson did what they could to collect words from a range of occupations, and by using the survey of first- and second-year university students were able to gather a sample of words across a great swathe of varied communities. They had identified significant areas in Newfoundlanders' lives, such as lumbering and farming, and designed specialized questionnaires to fill gaps that had been left in the general collecting. The accomplishment of such a small team is admirable, and they recognized that the work was not complete. Who they were affected the vocabulary they gleaned, of course. Informants may have self-censored vulgar terms, for example, when speaking to men from the university; Story was a well-educated St John's man, Kirwin an American, and Widdowson English. Had one of the principal authors been female, to invent a hypothetical fieldworker, and devoted to collecting the language of women active in their churches, hooking rugs, aiding in the birth of babies, knitting, and the hundreds of other tasks that made up women's lives, the corpus of words that made up Newfoundland English might have looked different. Joan Halley was able to bring her life experience and knowledge of the culture to bear on her work and that contribution was valuable, but she had been hired to do clerical work – not fieldwork.[112]

Story and Kirwin typed on index cards the excerpts from the texts that demonstrated the meaning of the words and illustrated how the meaning of some terms evolved over time. This was the way that dictionary editors had long worked. Story wanted a dictionary organized along historical principles, such as the *Oxford English Dictionary*, and Widdowson had been making extensive field recordings of speakers, and he took the responsibility of collecting vocabulary from the recordings. That was not something dictionary editors had traditionally done but had been developed among those who did dialect dictionaries (such as Cassidy) on both sides of the Atlantic. Story and Kirwin also solicited contributions to the collection from a range of experts, such as ornithologists who were able to identify various Newfoundland names for birds and their Latin scientific names, for example, as well as everyday speakers.[113] The *DNE* was thus a combination of two kinds of dictionaries, the historical and the dialect dictionary. It was also unusual among dictionaries in another way: most dictionaries are created by two separate teams. In the late nineteenth and early twentieth centuries, the *OED* had recruited hundreds of volunteers to comb through literary texts to find quotations that illustrated the use of words, a practice that at the time I write this is often called "crowd sourcing," and then had professional editors who wrote the entries. But in the case of the *DNE* the three men took on both aspects of the task. By doing all the excerpting from the printed sources themselves, Story and Kirwin were able to achieve a quality and uniformity of collection that would have been impossible had they relied on volunteers or hired students to comb through the material. And Widdowson was a phonetician of rare skill; his collection from the tapes, many of which he had recorded himself, was more precise than if he had farmed out part of the task.

By 1971 the collecting for the dictionary was progressing in high gear, and they were working out how the entries were to be written. The law of diminishing returns had set in on the excerpting from the published texts, although additional evidence continued to turn up even after the book had gone to the printer, and Story and Kirwin's forays into never published archival texts proved to be a "gold mine." Story told Widdowson:

> The gleanings are very rich: plenty of supporting evidence for items in our file, material for an indication of geographic distribution, interesting items we have missed elsewhere, and above all a fascinating sense, absent in the printed sources, that the dialect vocabulary is coming to us with a

minimum of screening. It's adding a new dimension to our collection ...
With the tape excerpts we are going to be able to give us a remarkable
picture of the Newfoundland vocabulary. W.K. has also been plugging
away, and we are to have a session soon to work out some ideas of a test
editing of a letter of the alphabet, which we hope, will show up some of
the problems we will have to solve (this was, you will recall, your idea,
and Bill is enthusiastic about it.)[114]

As we have seen, the *DNE* editors were methodologically innovative in combining oral collecting with the traditional (and conservative)
method of dictionary compilation – combing through printed sources
to find examples of how words were used. While dictionary compil-
ers generally work by selecting a corpus of books (and disproportion-
ately from high-prestige authors), Story and Kirwin read *all* the printed
sources that they believed would have examples of oral culture; they
excerpted from books, periodicals, printed song collections, and a
range of ephemera. A book by an outside author who had not visited
the county would, they judged, be unlikely to have included words
from the Newfoundland lexicon, and such books would be unlikely
to repay the effort of reading. They became adept at quickly judging
whether or not a book would have Newfoundland words. It was only
with the surge of local publications of the 1960s that the volume of
material became too great to read everything, and Story had to be especially careful to catch publications that would likely have lexical evidence. And they were now combing through unpublished texts as well.

Even casting their net widely, a dictionary of a living language could
never be complete. As Story put it: "completeness is, of course, an ideal
beyond the reach of the collecting process, perhaps even in the specific
sources we have described ... That is to say, we expect to leave something for our successors to do."[115] The Newfoundland lexicographers
were well in advance of the methods used by the editors of the *Dictionary of Canadianisms*, however, and were not shy of pointing out a
number of errors and concluded that the problem was that the editors

place themselves clearly in the "well-established tradition" of *The Oxford
English Dictionary*, *A Dictionary of American English*, and *A Dictionary of
Americanisms* in relying only on printed sources. It must be said that tradition is not, now, good enough; that a lexicographer who relies only on
printed sources for his data imposes on himself a crippling disability for
the execution of his task; and that to concern himself with items from oral

evidence only when these are substantiated in printed sources is to fly in the face of nearly every lesson that modern linguistic science has to teach.[116]

Around 1974 their emphasis shifted from collecting the citations to writing the entries. Fewer and fewer old books and periodicals that had not already been excerpted turned up, and more and more often words and examples of usages they collected just repeated evidence they had previously collected.[117] But many technical questions about how the entries and references were to be written remained to be worked out, and they also continued to consult widely to fill gaps in the collection both by bringing additional contributors on to the project and by consulting friends and colleagues. A colleague in the Department of English, Robert Hilliard, helped proofread the entries, and they consulted specialists from geology to botany about names. At a time when the faculty was modest in numbers and occupied only a few buildings, many faculty members, students, and staff shared coffee in the third floor Arts Building Common Room and exchanged ideas with little regard for departments or rank. As Story reported "The morning coffee break at a table with Les Harris continues to yield the usual rich information."[118] The anthropologists Robert Paine and Thomas Nemec, both of whom were sensitive to the nuances of local culture, looked at drafts of many entries, and Story described them as "very impressed by this way of viewing the universe through Newfoundland eyes."[119]

Their Canada Council funding was nearing an end, decisions about forms for entries were being made, and drafts of some of the letters had been completed. In a handwritten exchange typical of the notes the two men left for each other about matters of editing, Kirwin brought Walter Ong's then recently published essay on the "audience" to Story's attention, and he reflected on how the "form and content" of the dictionary would affect its readers.[120] This prompted Story to comment on the nature of the *DNE* and the uses that readers would make of the various types of entries:

There will be a "tension" in *DNE*: many cit[ation]s will be, Hemingway-like, inviting the reader to become comrade-in-arms of the native-speaker; other "visiting" glosses cited are outside views looking in. *Most* of our *definitions* seem to be objective and scientific; but we occasionally cast them in the idiom we are documenting and describing, Where this is deliberate, the use of quotes is necessary (I am the one who usually forgets this!).

We should remember that all our *Nfld*. readers under 40 yrs of age will come to *DNE* as, in part, *strangers*. The ideal that grows on me is a dictionary which moves at ease, and as necessary, inside and outside the culture, getting it "in the round" as a classical lexicographer would *if he could*, capture, say, the idiom of Homer and Aristotle, Virgil and Horace, Chaucer and Shakespeare and their ages. By the time we have edited, say, half the cards we will know exactly the form and content our different audiences need.[121]

They were also thinking of the ways that the *DNE* generally, and individual definitions and examples of the words in use, could reveal social structures if the entries were written with care and readers were attentive to the nuances revealed in clusters of related words. While Story was working on the entries for the word *cod*, he reflected on how the introduction should make clear that Newfoundland speakers made careful distinctions between technologies and these distinctions had social and economic implications. As he put it in an editorial memo to Kirwin:

> *Cod-jigging* is usually done from a small boat with 1, 2, or 3 men aboard. *Cod-seines* are enormous nets requiring the use of one or two boats and 6 or more men, with a high degree of specialization (e.g., a "seine-master"). So too with a cod-trap. The fish taken by these different techniques differ in size. The season of the operation may vary from one to another. The organization may differ – e.g. a hook-and-line man will probably be "his own man," but the use of the trap or the seine will imply a "skipper" and his "shareman." Maybe, to convey all this, is more than a mere dictionary can achieve! And maybe ... some of our defining practices, esp of Attrib, comb, cpds, will look too fussy and cumbersome. Still, with some of them (e.g. *Cod-seine crew, cod-trap crew*) it seems worth trying to indicate things like number of men habitually involved, the "share" practice, the presence of a "skipper" or "seine master" and so on. Sometimes, of course, the cites do the work for us, but not always.[122]

As the writing of entries and cross-referencing proceeded, Story and Kirwin also began to think about the public reaction to the book. Some social divisions led to words with pejorative connotations, one of which prompted the polite Kirwin, who perhaps remained aware of his outsider status, to wonder about giving offence. "Are we cautious about using *bayman* in cites?" he asked. Among some urban dwellers, especially in St John's, the word *bayman* referred to a person who came from a rural community, but it also connoted someone who lacked sophistication.

1.4. Presenting the *DNE* to the lieutenant governor, 1982; (l–r) Kirwin, Story,
Anthony Paddon, Leslie Harris. (From the files of the English Language
Research Centre, Memorial University of Newfoundland.)

"We should not be cautious, but present the facts of Nfld. usage," Story
replied, "No doubt we will get into trouble with some of our readers –
but we don't mind that. Doing the entry on *bayman* etc. will be interesting."[123] Most vulgarities were rejected by the editors, not because
of prudery but because the words were common to the international
word stock.

The *Dictionary of Newfoundland English* was published to widespread
acclaim in 1982. Its publication merited a story on *The National*, the CBC
flagship evening news program, and both local and national newspaper coverage. Some of that coverage had a "man bites dog" quality that
emphasized the quaint words or saw humour in the idea that something of low social prestige, such as Newfoundland speech, merited the
high-prestige treatment it had gotten. Professional lexicographers and
many other reviewers, on the other hand, admired the accomplishment.

These reactions may have been expected, but Kirwin and Story had not imagined the tremendous popular success of the book, with its early printings selling out by the pallet-load. They had thought the book would find an audience among those Newfoundlanders interested in culture and history, but they had not imagined that the book would be purchased more broadly and by people who had no particular interest in the world of letters.

It was apparent to readers that the *DNE* not only revealed the meanings of archaic words (although the editors scrupulously avoided classifying any words as archaic), it mapped out the mental universe of Newfoundlanders in their words and the cross references. An excellent illustration of this was revealed in an interview the anthropologist Robert Paine did with Story and Kirwin shortly after the dictionary was published. Paine, who had begun his career learning the Saami language as a precursor to his ethnographic fieldwork in Norway, was alert to the ways that the language itself is the culture and to the ways that the dictionary revealed associations in people's cognitive universe:

PAINE: In the *Oxford English Dictionary* it [cod] is simply a "well-known sea-fish which inhabits the Atlantic and its connected seas" but in the *DNE* the entry runs to several pages, invites extensive cross-referencing and includes this pearl among the historical citations: "The central object in an allegorical picture which symbolized Newfoundland would be the cod-fish, and around it would be grouped its favourite bait the herring, the caplin ... and the squid."

STORY: Well, the complex of entries themselves, COD and the associated fishes, tell us centrally important things, historically, about Newfoundland. They tell us what brought Englishmen and Irishmen over here; they tell us why they were migratory fishermen, seasonal workers, rather than farmers or townsmen; and you learn more if you follow, in the Dictionary, the cross-references which spread out from COD. From COD to FISH, for example. The fact that fish is the regional synonym for cod explains that elegant little sentence you cited – cod is so massively important that we don't call it that, we simply call it FISH. And those other species (HERRING, CAPLIN, SQUID) were economically important, until recent times, *only* because they functioned as a means of catching FISH (you can add sea birds to that list too). So they reflect this massive concentration on a single species and all that implies for its processing and marketing, and I suppose really for the whole round of economic activity of the communities.[124]

Paine was intrigued by the ways in which the dictionary revealed differences in power in society. He wondered if the entries referring to females, for example, revealed a patriarchal culture and asked if the editors had, through their selection of quotations, shown language being used differently by those who had different roles in the society. Kirwin was sceptical that the various entries revealed that women were valued less than men, while Story agreed with Paine, that social divisions were evident in the dictionary. Story reported that they had deliberately made juxtapositions in the entries that revealed social positions:

> We've gone from an official report to a merchant's comment and on to something else. You can see it nicely illustrated in entries for types of fish ... here you get the government inspector defining the nature of the grade, and the fishermen watching (and you can sometimes hear them) the CULLER dividing the fish upon which their livelihood depends; then there are the songs about it and the stories.[125]

"A dictionary is really a book" Story commented to Widdowson, "consisting of nothing but elaborate notes the 'argument' of which has to be inferred from the pieces themselves."[126] That argument is implicit not only in the definitions but in the citations and cross references. One can see in the *DNE* the evolution of a term over time, as material conditions changed and as it was used by people in different social strata. Some words seem to go out of use, and in other cases the dictionary shows words being collected from eighteenth-century texts and the nineteenth-century published corpus to being collected from the lips of Story, Kirwin, and Widdowson's contemporaries.[127] This seamless integration of textual and oral evidence displays a remarkable continuity of culture over time. The argument about the language also flows from the cross references. Cross references to other dialect dictionaries clarify the relationship of Newfoundland English to the English of our ancestors and of the people with whom Newfoundlanders traded. The cross references to entries within the dictionary, as suggested, reveal the conceptual links between elements of the culture.

For Story, the *DNE* was both a labour of love and a project that had to be treated with the utmost of respect. As he wrote to an old classmate from his Memorial College days who had congratulated him on the volume:

> [Y]ou picked out so beautifully what we worked hardest to do: to write a book which would pay the subject the compliment of very deep, very

serious, and sustained attention. I can't pretend that I would have been able to do this for *any* variety of the English language, being less a pure scholar in some ways than my dauntless New England and Yorkshire colleagues, and the beautiful vitality of the subject always seemed to me to more than rise to the rigours of this kind of scholarship, so that the often facile folksiness about Newfoundland of many Mainland Canadians (and their imitators among our fellow-countrymen!) had to be avoided at all costs.[128]

As a study of the language of one part of the world, Story saw the *DNE* as providing a piece to the puzzle that would one day culminate in a dictionary of all the world's varieties of English. In that sense, he saw it not as a local study but as part of a larger collegial enterprise. He took an interest in other etymological projects, despite his self-deprecating comment that he was only working on Newfoundland English. Story made frequent references to his "fellow countrymen" among his personal correspondence, an endearment that reveals something of his nationalist sentiment and, like many other Newfoundlanders, bristled at the "facile folksiness." It is not possible to read Story's work without being impressed by the fact that he paid Newfoundland oral culture the compliment of being treated seriously. His example made it easier for younger scholars at Memorial to do so in their fields.

Reflecting on the publication of the first edition, Kirwin thought that the *DNE* would "establish an authority; by that I mean it will build a kind of respect – for language – in the people who consult it." He also thought that it "may do interesting things in the schools because words which were only in speech before are now there in print and this means they can be pronounced and used by people respectfully."[129] As we have seen, the editors did not want to prescribe spellings for the words that they had collected orally or establish standardized spellings of those words for which there was no consensus in print sources, but Kirwin subsequently reflected that if authors and editors used the *DNE* as an authority on spelling, it would have that effect.[130] He also had a view of how it should be used in schools:

> The guide for teachers should emphasize that Newfoundland English is organically related to other varieties in the British Isles, the Maritimes and the rest of mainland Canada, and to New England and the rest of the United States. I feel it is an error to give the impression that Newfoundland English is special, because chauvinism is not a good educational tactic and can lead to distorted opinions of the province's culture.[131]

While Kirwin emphasized the role the dictionary could have in schools, Story hoped to have the dictionary used creatively by students and scholars: "I'd like to see them use it in precisely the way that we mean when we call it *one* of the indexes to the regional culture – this one happens to be alphabetical ... I'd particularly like to see people in the social sciences going to work on this and making something of it – making *their* books out of it."[132] His emphasis on the *DNE* as a tool of scholarship does not mean that Story was unaware of the nationalistic uses of dictionaries in the evolution from colony to nation. "National dictionaries have almost always been compiled at a surprising distance in time from the attainment by daughter countries of political independence, and even longer after the emergence into common notice of their new linguistic features."[133]

That the ways of speaking of some half a million people in an economically depressed region of Canada should be dignified in a publication of a major Canadian academic press was not obvious to everyone. A few non-standard grammatical constructions, and some ways of pronouncing words that sounded unfamiliar to Canadian and American ears, had in the years since the Second World War become a sign of being a rube. Lacking a different skin colour or religion, Newfoundlanders' speech defined them as a socially inferior other. The diminutive "Newfie" seems to have been popularized by United States servicemen during the Second World War, and after Newfoundland became a Canadian province it was picked up with enthusiasm by those Canadians who wanted to denigrate their new citizens.

The ways of speaking of rural people are often taken by many as an index of their being stupid and unsophisticated, and many urban Newfoundlanders internalized these pejorative attitudes towards Newfoundland speech. The rural and rustic associations of the accent and vocabulary also connoted the quaint and archaic – making it possible for the provincial government to build a tourism strategy around folklore and local vocabulary that encouraged the perception among tourists that they were experiencing authentic traditions from an earlier time.[134] While the education system attempted to stamp out distinctive Newfoundland speech, the tourism department and local businesses commodified the speech.[135]

Many Newfoundlanders tried to "correct" their speech and embraced the ethnic jokes that were being told about them. That might be seen as self-deprecating or as a way of pleading an individual's case for belonging to the socially desirable group – telling the jokes or making fun of the accent became a way of saying "I'm not like those Newfies. I can laugh at them. I'm like you." In the face of this disdain for Newfoundland speech, Story, Kirwin, and Widdowson took what was being used as the marker of Newfoundlanders' inferiority – their language – and made it the subject of their scholarship. In doing so, they legitimized it as a *language* rather than collaborating in the condescension that Newfoundlanders spoke the way that they did because they did not know how to speak properly or because they were a living vestige of a premodern era.

Story and Kirwin's labour did not end with the dictionary's publication. Story put his feelings in a letter to Widdowson:

> I've got a long baggage train of old plans (and some new ones) to examine for feasibility, and also to see if I still find them interesting. I don't anticipate another dictionary! *That* work now seems already "gone away"; I don't feel quite like Dr Johnson, dismissing his book "with frigid indifference," but it is out of our hands now and will have to take its chances in a busy and naughty world. One thing, though: it's as good a work as three good scholars could make it.[136]

Story and Kirwin helped launch a new academic journal, *Newfoundland Studies*, the publication costs of which they provided when they signed over the royalties from the first edition of the *DNE* to the university. Story served on the journal's editorial board, while Kirwin and his colleague Richard Buehler were co-editors for the first few issues. The journal provided a venue for the publication of scholarship on the culture and society – an important step in the developing Newfoundland studies agenda.

But words still called out to them. Soon the two wondered about "what has been happening with the Newfoundland language since 1982 when our dictionary came out,"[137] and they almost immediately began to compile additional evidence for a supplement. Story characterized the task as a "peaceful, daily struggle with mere words: and much enjoyment."[138] By 1988 the three authors agreed to prepare a supplementary edition that would re-evaluate the old evidence and incorporate some of the evidence they had accumulated since the first edition had appeared. The second edition, which appeared in 1990, provided earlier examples or different usages of words than had been included in the first edition, as well as some revised definitions and some words that had not been previously collected. After the first edition came out,

Kirwin reported, they sheepishly realized they had missed the many Newfoundland uses of the verb *to be*. That they missed collecting one of the most commonly used verbs in the language likely reflects that in their search for the Newfoundland lexicon they had captured many nouns, which reflected the material lives of the people, but a verb of general usage slipped by. The second edition remedied that lacuna.[139]

When the work on the first edition had begun, they believed extinction of many of the words was imminent, but close attention to usage in the period between the publication of the two volumes now led the editors to conclude "that we find little evidence of the retreat of the traditional vocabulary which is so often predicted and that many regional writers are actively extending the metaphoric uses of the Newfoundland vocabulary."[140] Despite robust sales of the *DNE*, it likely had marginal influence in shaping the day-to-day usage of Newfoundlanders. Dictionaries generally have little effect on spoken language. The economic changes in the previous thirty years, such as the decline of the seal fishery, made the use of many terms related to that harvesting rare. The existence of the dictionary, however, even for those who don't consult it, may have sometimes encouraged speakers to use words that they knew to be particular to the Newfoundland vocabulary. The lexicon also became a commodity: Entrepreneurs reproduced entries on T-shirts and coffee mugs, which circulated individual words as symbols of Newfoundland that were taken out of any semantic or historical context. The dictionary's effect on speech may have been slight, but its effect on text was greater and easier to measure. Story, Kirwin, and Widdowson had hoped that scholars would use the dictionary as a basis for their own studies, which indeed occurred. The American anthropologist Gerald Sider, to take a notable example, had used the *DNE* to great effect in his study of Newfoundland culture.[141] Many Newfoundland historians have cited the dictionary, and creative writers drew heavily upon the local vernacular. Story, Kirwin, and Widdowson could not have guessed that Newfoundland poets such as Mary Dalton or American novelists such as Annie Proulx would find such inspiration in the *DNE*.[142]

Reflecting on origins of Newfoundland studies from the vantage point of 1983, at the height of a nationalist resurgence during the premiership of Brian Peckford and at a time when offshore oil promised great economic changes, Story saw "comparatively little change" in the 1950s but a great deal in the 1960s and 1970s.[143] At the beginning of his career George Story felt that he had to justify his personal interest in

popular speech as a subject worthy of scholarship rather than as something to be embarrassed about. In many respects Newfoundland was
still being integrated into the Canadian political structure, and people
were abandoning the "traditional" and embracing the modern. Late in
his career, he contemplated the changes that occurred in Newfoundland, and perhaps his own role in those changes:

> It has often occurred to me as I've lectured on the literature and society
> of Elizabethan England that a modest parallel could be drawn between
> that Newfoundland experience and early Tudor England in the opening
> decades of the sixteenth-century; that poignant historic moment between
> the collapse of medieval society, culture and institutions, and the gradual,
> painfully slow emergence of what we now call Elizabethan England. The
> real precursors of that English movement were the scholars, antiquaries,
> collectors, local historians, rescuers of old documents, the contents of looted
> monasteries and abbeys, transcribers of old medieval inscriptions, genealo-
> gists ... it can almost be said that the most brilliant discovery of a brilliant
> age was the discovery of the English past by English men and women.[144]

The first generation of the members of the Newfoundland studies
movement continued their work as long as they were able. Story succeeded Seary in the Henrietta Harvey professorship, which served as a
cap to his career, and in 1993 he turned 65 – then the age of mandatory
retirement at the university. He "reflected on this with a certain natural
ambivalence" in light of his ongoing projects. He requested a one year
extension of his appointment to continue to work on "important unfin-
ished business," including completion of the editing of the *Reminiscences of JP Howley 1868–1911* (which he was working on with Kirwin),
the preparation of *The Adages of Desiderius Erasmus* (for which he had
signed a contract with the University of Toronto Press in 1992), a *Dictionary of Newfoundland Proverbs and Phrases*, and an edition of Walter
Raleigh's *History of the World*. He was also helping Kirwin and Robert
Hollett continue the place name study they had continued after Seary's
death, and he was the director of the newly formed J.R. Smallwood
Centre for Newfoundland Studies.[145]

Story, to use a cliché, was a renaissance man in the sense of working in many fields. His work on Newfoundland straddled academic
disciplines from ethnomusicology to history and from lexicography to
biography; he was also a renaissance man in the sense that he worked
on early modern European texts. He was aware of the parallel between

the Renaissance, in which Europeans made a new culture through the recovery of models from the ancient world, and the cultural rebirth in Newfoundland based on recovering past culture. He was part of a tradition of humanist scholarship that stretched back to the Italian Renaissance. The first generation of humanists believed in the "connection between style and content, truth and words," so they had to establish the words and thoughts of ancient authors. To do so they invented philology and textual editing as techniques to reintegrate "those shards of the fragmentary heritage of the ancient world that had fortunately survived."[146] Story did that for Newfoundland. Memorial granted the extension of his professorship, but he did not live to see the completion of any of these projects. After a brief illness, he died on 9 May, 1994, days before the university marked his accomplishments with an honorary degree. The loss was keenly felt, not only among his family, friends, colleagues, and former students but among all those who cared about Newfoundland scholarship. No one could replace him; the university was too large and diverse for any one person to establish the sort of role as mentor that Story had grown into during his forty-year career.

His long-standing collaborator, William Kirwin, took early retirement in 1984, hoping to devote greater time to research and writing about Newfoundland culture. As Kirwin wrote to the then head of the Department of English:

There is one overriding reason guiding my plans. Years, many years, of collecting for and writing the dictionary taught me many things about my capabilities that I had not known in graduate school and in my teaching posts since 1951.The steady, organized routine of the project released energies, acumen, sensitivity and critical courage that I had never experience before. Writing and editing turned out to be not a chore producing an unsatisfying product, but the creation of a large, complex structure which critically was sound and worthwhile for other scholars to read. The idea grew within me that I should exploit this new source of ability and write and edit some of the works that I felt should be written in the field of Newfoundland studies. Even one of these extended projects could not be carried out unless I entered a new phase of a career, one that left all university teaching and my contributions to the running of the institution behind. With early retirement at 58 or 59, perhaps I could complete some of the projects which no one else seemed to be undertaking ... My plans are to live permanently in my present house, and do research in the various public collections in St John's.[147]

Kirwin was appointed professor emeritus in 1986, and indeed continued to live in that house and work on the projects that he, Story, and Seary had started. Robert Hollett and Kirwin revised and published Seary's *Place Names of the Northern Peninsula*, which had originally seen only limited distribution in a draft form. Kirwin and Patrick O'Flaherty prepared an excerpt of the Howley journal for publication and in 2010 the online publication of the whole text by Memorial's Digital Archives Initiative. The *DNE* was also made available online in 1998, and as I write this the whole of the collection is being digitized. In 2013 an online Dialect Atlas of Newfoundland was launched. Illness in 2012 prevented Kirwin from continuing to walk to his office, ending his daily labour on the language and history of his adopted home. Despite Story's earlier hope for renewal, the Department of English Language and Literature by then no longer had anyone studying Newfoundland language.

That the publication of the first edition of the *DNE* in 1982 was a sensation, the first printing nearly immediately sold out in St John's, reveals something of the nationalist revival that had occurred. The book-buying public in Newfoundland had embraced the volume, and indeed many people who rarely purchased books, and especially relatively expensive hardback books written by academics, embraced the *DNE*. As Story put it: "to an extent which is difficult to exaggerate, the *DNE* has become a regional *icon*: children and grandchildren buy it to present to their elders on birthdays and at Christmas – or are presented with it by their elders – at a price they would normally never have dreamt of paying for a book." As he continued, the book was used as a frequent presentation gift for official visitors, and there was a new generation that had come of age since the appearance of the book that now constituted a new market.[148]

The cluster of scholars studying and publishing on language in Newfoundland defies simple characterization. As we have seen, there was continuity with the earlier generation of nationalist intellectuals such as Howley and Devine, who had compiled place names, folk songs, glossaries of words peculiar to the island, etc. The nationalist impulse to study Newfoundland oral culture after Confederation took a slightly different shape than its predecessor because of the perception that post-war and post-Confederation economic changes and mass media were quickly eroding oral culture. For some Newfoundlanders, and Canadians, it was good riddance to a backward culture. Nationalist intellectuals always have faith that a scientific study will objectively prove the existence of the nation.

More than a half century of studying vocabulary and syntax on the part of Story and his successors has amassed significant evidence of a high degree of homogeneity in Newfoundland English and a significant divergence between it and Canadian and American English. That was a *fact* despite the existence of great dialect variation within Newfoundland. There was also a long-held self-awareness among Newfoundlanders that their speech was unique. The existence of the *DNE* provided legitimacy to the language. As Premier Peckford once put it, with a broadening of his accent, "if you don't like the way I talks, I'll make up me own dictionary." Kirwin, however, believed that neither dictionaries, nor other efforts on the part of would-be cultural interveners, would preserve elements of speech that were changing. "Dialects cannot be 'preserved' because no institutions can prevent groups of people from changing their relations, especially economic, with the rest of society" he believed, "and language follows status and location." Furthermore, he cautioned, the "use of superficial dialect in various mediums is not preservation."[149]

As one commentator put it, "Languages declare their independence by creating dictionaries."[150] At the beginning of the nineteenth century the first dictionary of a regional English within the United Kingdom appeared; the dictionary of the Scottish Language (1808) was part of an emerging trend for modern languages to be identified with emerging nationalist movements. It also reflected concern that unique Scottish uses were declining. The early nineteenth-century patriot Noah Webster created the first of his several American English dictionaries with the intention of fostering an American English different from that of Britain. Not only did he document "American" words that were not part of British usage, but he took it upon himself to rationalize an American spelling. By the late nineteenth century individuals in many parts of the British Empire were collecting local usages, a phenomenon that came to Canadian nationhood relatively late.

The historian Steve High has written of a Canadian "dictionary movement" of the 1950s and 1960s, in which many of Story's contemporaries created dictionaries of Canadian English that endeavoured to create a Canadian English separate from the colonial past as symbolized by British spelling. During the period between the Massey Commission report of 1951 and the Canadian centenary, Canadian dictionary editors often favoured American spelling, and after 1967 (perhaps because anxiety about American cultural influence outweighed the lingering resentment of the British connection) favoured British spelling.

The dictionaries represented "much more than a reference book for words and their meanings; it was an assertion of a linguistic community," complete with a prescriptive attempt to establish a Canadian spelling. In High's words, "Canada was thus part of a post colonial rush to compile national dictionaries."[151] The broader movement to create national dictionaries that could establish a national culture with historical roots included, in his list, the *Dictionary of American English on Historical Principles* (1944), the *Dictionary of Americanisms on Historical Principles* (1951), the *Dictionary of Jamaican English* (1967), *A Dictionary of South African English on Historical Principles* (1978), *The Macquarie Dictionary of Australian English* (1981) and the *Dictionary of Bahamian English* (1982).

I am not suggesting that the evidence of a distinct Newfoundland English collected by Story, Kirwin, and Widdowson was an artefact of their ideology. Seary had dismissed M.F. Howley's work as nationalistic, but he was likely unaware of the implicit assumptions of the project to study a national language that he had helped found. The new generations of scholars, such as Seary and Story, defined themselves as professionals by their adherence to new standards of scientific rigour that were unavailable to earlier nationalist intellectuals. Not that the post-war interest in the language was exclusive to those working at the university – Nimshi Crewe had been independently compiling notes on lexicography and pronunciation, and starting in 1962 he contributed to the *DNE*.[152]

Kirwin and Widdowson both developed a commitment to Newfoundland scholarship, and it's impossible to disentangle their professional interest in the work from caring about the community they worked in – but neither of them were primarily motivated by nationalism. Webster had created his dictionaries to create an American culture, but Story, Kirwin, and Widdowson were not trying to prescribe Newfoundland use or create a Newfoundland culture, they created a research tool for scholars who were studying Newfoundland. If the *DNE* created a self-awareness and confidence in Newfoundland speakers and writers, those were unintended and incidental effects.

If the agenda of studying Newfoundland language assumed *a priori* that a national language existed that just needed to be described, many of the key people in these studies would not have seen themselves as engaged in a nationalistic project. Seary, Kirwin, and Widdowson came to have an affection and identification with the place as adults pursuing their careers. Except for Widdowson, they were also fully trained scholars before they first encountered Newfoundland, and even Widdowson was no neophyte when he first started working at Memorial. They were motivated by the career and scholarly opportunities presented by work in a place that had been little studied, not by a pre-existing engagement in Newfoundland culture.

The *Dictionary of Newfoundland English* was the fortuitous collaboration of three scholars – each of whom brought different backgrounds to the project and skills to bear. Story worked from a position of someone who grew up within the culture and had been trained in working with texts. "I don't think," he reflected, "that I could have made my contribution to the Newfoundland dictionary if I hadn't been a trained bibliographer and editor, textual editor of Renaissance texts."[153] His work evolved from his time as a student keeping a list to supplement Devine's pamphlet, through his conception on it as the "Newfoundland Dialect Dictionary" to its form as a dictionary of historical principles.

He was still a young man when he returned to Memorial, and the interdisciplinary nature of much of the Newfoundland scholarship encouraged a change in his work. In his interaction with colleagues he retrained himself as a social scientist. The other two, Kirwin and Widdowson, were outsiders to the culture, which gave them a perspective different from Story, and each brought their own training and educational backgrounds. Kirwin, as we have seen, was slightly older than Story and a New Englander. He brought a solid training in linguistics to the project and had been influenced by both McDavid's belief that scholarship should be descriptive and his experience with fieldwork. Kirwin was also able to draw on familiarity with a range of American dialect dictionaries and dictionaries on historical principles. The third collaborator, Widdowson, was the youngest of the three and an Englishman. He was the least active in the writing of definitions, but he contributed much of the work on pronunciation and proofread the whole of the work.

Story and Kirwin excerpted words and quotations from as many published texts about Newfoundland as two men were able, in addition to consulting many unpublished texts and at least one epigraph on a tombstone. With Widdowson they also collected words and usages from living speakers through questionnaires, consultations with scholars in specialist fields, and broad oral collecting from various regions. Newfoundland's modest body of published works made it possible to excerpt from a larger portion of the total corpus of published work than could have been accomplished by even a much larger team in any other country. The perception, or recognition, of Newfoundland as a unique oral culture that persisted and yet was threatened with extinction in the age of textual culture had been the impetus for the *DNE* in the first place.

Some dictionary editors are motivated by wanting to intervene in a positive way in a literate culture – dictionaries are primarily aids to reading and writing. As we have seen, Story started with the assumption that little would be learned from the formal words in print and that the language was vernacular and existed on people's lips. Conversations and questionnaires, and then recordings, were the ways to record the ephemeral speech before it faded. The editor's decision to not label any of the words in the *DNE* as "archaic" or "obsolete" reveals something important. The editors maintained that they refrained from doing so because they were often surprised to hear a word spoken by one of their contemporaries that they had previously only encountered in older texts and had assumed was no longer in use.[154] Caution discouraged them from assigning to words the stigma of being archaic, and they had started from the premise that all Newfoundland words were in danger of becoming archaic because of the rapid linguistic change they saw occurring. They might have chosen to title the book the "Dictionary of Newfoundland Archaic Words" or "Newfoundland Dialect Dictionary." But they left open the possibility that the *DNE* could encourage the revival of the usage of a word. The common notion that dialects are deviant forms of languages would have reinforced the notion that Newfoundland speech was a lesser form had they titled their dictionary with the word "dialect."

Users turn to dictionaries as authorities on language because of their completeness and exclusiveness, but they are less aware of the choices made than are dictionary editors. Story, Kirwin, and Widdowson knew they would not capture all of the words in Newfoundland English, and they had excluded many words because they lacked evidence for their use or because they were words shared with other English speakers. They were also aware that dictionaries get used by people to adjudicate what is and is not a legitimate word. That users can be confident that the *DNE* does not contain, to the best of the authors' efforts, ephemeral slang or idiosyncratic uses of words makes it an authority on what is and is not a legitimate word.

Newfoundland English speakers could now feel confident in their use of a word that was no longer in common use. It could extend the life of a word that was being used less and less often or potentially reintroduce a word into use that had ceased to be used. Given the dialect variation and social variation within Newfoundland, a person on the south coast who consulted the dictionary would learn words that had only been used on the northeast coast or vice versa. Lexicographers wrote dictionaries of dead languages, such as Sanscrit or middle English, or of dying languages, such as Scots, not to preserve them as speech but to provide a key for scholars to unlock the meaning of past texts. Newfoundland lacked a classical literature, such as Cicero or Shakespeare, that could be kept accessible to new generations through a glossary, but as the next two chapters show, it had historical texts and an oral culture for which the *DNE* would be a key research tool.

As Frickle and Gross suggest, intellectual movements either examine a previously undiscussed topic or argue for a new method to examine an established topic.[155] Story, Kirwin, and Widdowson's collection of Newfoundland words, and their criticism of dictionaries that relied solely on literary sources, qualify in both ways. The collaborations of Seary and Story, and more importantly of Story, Kirwin, and Widdowson, gave birth to the Newfoundland studies movement. Their belief that Newfoundland oral culture deserved as much attention by scholars as written texts was the very thing that inspired others to study the culture. Story was the public face of the dictionary, explicitly arguing that Newfoundland speech need not be abandoned in the drive to become Canadians. But their central goal was the documentation of the language, the creation of a scholarly research tool, and the circulation of those ideas within the intellectual community.

Chapter Two

Writing History

This can be a living, exciting project, and one which will result in the story of Newfoundland being told in a vivid fashion. It can also, in my opinion, help to establish the University as a seat of research in the social sciences and give it standing and prestige in Newfoundland and outside.[1]

As Story and Seary embarked on their studies into the province's linguistic heritage and diversity, Memorial's Department of History built the infrastructure that would allow for documentary research. The historians had an advantage over their counterparts who were studying language: The writing of Newfoundland history was a relatively old and rich field. Many Newfoundlanders, and others, had written on the past of their island and Labrador. Starting with Chief Justice John Reeves in the eighteenth century, judges, clergymen, and journalists had written histories of Newfoundland, which culminated in Judge D.W. Prowse at the end of the nineteenth century.

Prowse was familiar with contemporary American and British methods of historical writing, and he wrote a comprehensive narrative based on imperial, foreign, and colonial records. His peers were journalists, civil servants, and such men as the geologist James P. Howley, who used oral history, archaeology, and archival research to compile everything known of the Beothuk.

There continued to be a local cohort of experts in Newfoundland history in the first half of the twentieth century, despite the absence of a centre of academic training in history. It included the future premier J.R. Smallwood, whose historical and folklore publications and radio broadcasts during the 1930s and 1940s prompted him to boast that he was the only person to ever make a living out of Newfoundland history.[2]

As their colleagues worried about the loss of linguistic diversity, the historians felt the absence of archival resources and bibliographic tools. Newfoundland history (more precisely Newfoundland constitutional and political history) was also the only area of Newfoundland studies that had a place in the curriculum at Memorial College during the 1940s. That should not be a surprise; many historians of that era followed the oft-quoted dictum that history is past politics. Smallwood would have agreed with the corollary, that present politics was future history.

Local interest in the past is not surprising, but it was not only Newfoundlanders who were interested in the island's history. In the 1930s a few professionally trained historians in Britain, especially at the University of London, wrote on Newfoundland's past because they saw it as part of the history of the empire and because, exceptionally, it was a self-governing dominion that had slipped back to something like crown-colony status. So when faculty members and administrators at Memorial wanted to professionalize the study of Newfoundland history, they had an imperial framework within which to fit the subject and the ability to hire English-trained scholars to establish local work.

The writing of history and nationalism are often intertwined: The modern development of historical methods in Europe occurred at the same time that the nation state was emerging as the dominant form. Newfoundland developed a national historiography as its state developed a greater measure of control over the country, but that took an abrupt turn when the island suspended self-government in 1934 and joined Canada as a province in 1949. As Newfoundland was incorporated into the Confederation, the old slipped away – the study of the past of the colony could provide a salve, or salt, to wounded nationalist pride among the nearly half the population who had voted against it.

A historiographer of India, by way of comparison, observed that in the nineteenth century there was "a growing 'hunger for history' among the Indian intelligentsia so that history became a way of recovering one's dignity as well as 'a way of talking about the collective self, and bringing it into existence.'"[3] A similar appetite for discussing the past existed in Newfoundland in the half century after Confederation. Many people on both sides of that debate believed that the new province needed a source-based study of Newfoundland history. This chapter shows how academic administrators encouraged the *professional* writing of history and the development of an archive as a strategy to establish Memorial as a research university while responding to the sense of loss now that Newfoundland was no longer on the path towards being an independent nation. It also highlights some of the tensions that existed between those who used history for nationalist and anti-nationalist purposes.

In the 1950s Memorial developed a history research group that embarked on a program of archival acquisition, bibliography, and historical research. The group created an archive, research tools, and a series of studies that were intended to one day prepare the ground for a history of Newfoundland. The lack of a repository for local records, and the difficulty of research in St John's when most documents were held in imperial centres, encouraged the Department of History to imagine itself as rescuing the historical record from oblivion in much the same way that their peers were documenting language variety. The historians' research program also included the compilation of a bibliography, preparing and publishing monographs in history, and encouraging a new generation to start graduate work in the field.

As Canadian historians professionalized by basing their writing on empirical foundations and through their "boundary work," so too the Newfoundland historians at Memorial during the 1950s and 1960s established distinctions between their professional activities and the methods and attitudes of the amateur historians.[4] While three men did most of the work on the *DNE*, the two strands of the professionalization, or modernization, of history had been knit by the Department of History at Memorial and the provincial government.

Premier Smallwood, himself a self-taught historian, reopened the Newfoundland Museum in 1957, passed legislation to protect the province's historic records, and took over the archive that the university had founded. Most importantly for our story here, his government had made the two-year junior college into a four-year undergraduate university that would undertake the study of Newfoundland.

In the absence of a civil service with specialized skills, Memorial took on many of the roles governments played in other provinces, and, as the historian Melvin Baker has shown, one such vacuum filled by the university was the creation of a provincial archive. The university hired professionals from Canada and drew on the American-based philanthropic institutions, such as the Carnegie Foundation, and the Dominion of Canada's Canada Council to underwrite the capital costs of Newfoundland historical research. The creation of a research infrastructure and the writing of history seemed, to those who undertook these tasks, as a new beginning.[5] Despite the writing of Newfoundland history having begun in the eighteenth century, a case can be made that the *Newfoundland Royal Commission 1933 Report* was the single most influential document in Newfoundland's twentieth-century historiography. Known as the *Amulree Report*, after Lord Amulree, who chaired the Royal Commission, it investigated the financial difficulties of the Newfoundland government and made recommendations as to how to put the country on a sound footing. In justifying the suspension of responsible government in 1934, it established a long-lasting interpretation of the country's political and economic history and a compelling description of rural life. The British government decided responsible government in Newfoundland was going to be suspended and that it would provide financial aid. The officials agreed that it was impossible to ask the British taxpayer to foot the bill without the exchequer having control over the purse strings, so with the conclusion decided upon, Amulree devised a rationale. Describing the financial position and cataloguing the resources of the country was a matter of accounting, but justifying the end of democratic government required finding people morally unable to govern themselves. That was a job for history.

Much of the prose of the report may have come from the pen of the commission's secretary, Peter Alexander Clutterbuck.[6] The then thirty-five-year-old career public servant had studied at Pembroke College, Cambridge, and had served in the Coldstream Guards in the First World War. Much of what the *Amulree Report* said was a repetition of things the commission heard in its hearings, so despite the sentiment of subsequent generations that the report was unduly harsh, it reflected widely held views of its day.

It started with a thirty-two-page "History of Newfoundland since the Grant of Responsible Government." This is not just a preamble before the presentation of the economic data. The "history" justifies the report's conclusion that people had been too weak to maintain financial discipline. The grant of responsible government in 1832, the report concluded, coincided with a revival of the economy and the introduction of telegraphic and steam communications. In a phrase that reveals something of the commissioners' view of Newfoundland history, this represented a "triumph over the past."[7] Responsible government was followed by a period of prosperity, but "it was not long before the country received a series of sharp reminders that its prosperity depended primarily upon the bounty of Nature."[8] Economic misfortunes took a toll, "the people, long tired, would seem almost to have lost heart."[9] Then there was cause for hope. Copper was discovered, the trans-Atlantic cable laid, steamship communication with Britain established, and sectarian election violence put to rest by dividing government patronage among the denominations. A return to prosperity coincided with the confederation of the British North American colonies, which, despite the author's seeming approval, was dashed when the electorate turned the pro-Confederation government out of office. The report attributed the defeat of Confederation in 1869 to people's failure to consider it as a "national rather than party question."[10] To justify their decision to not join Canada, the report continued, people embraced an ambitious program of railway construction. Once more, success was dashed, this time by the 1894 bank crash, precipitating a crisis that encouraged the country to seek aid from first Britain and then union with Canada.

There is a subtext running through the report that Confederation with Canada would be best and that short-term prosperity, partisanship, and "the lack of statesmanship" foiled those chances.[11] The report concurred with Prowse's judgment that the bank crash exposed the root cause of much of Newfoundland's economic trouble – the truck system.[12] It suggested that the people's morale was permanently changed by the bank crash and that educated and uneducated alike lost faith in investing in their country. The history then set out in some detail a misguided binge of railway construction and inept negotiations, brought to an end only by the 1900 election of Robert Bond. Here the account relied on the oral testimony that the commission collected, which supported an account of a golden age that preceded the fall:

> [Bond] left behind him a reputation of farsighted devotion to the interests of the Island and is generally regarded as the most statesmanlike figure in the line of Newfoundland Prime Ministers. Today, a disillusioned people, looking back on the past, single out the years of his Premiership as a period of orthodox finance and sane government when the fortunes of the island were at their zenith; there was almost universal agreement among witnesses that the present period of misfortune might be regarded as having originated with his fall from power in 1908.[13]

There was hope, the report implied, as represented by Canadian capital, which opened the Bell Island iron ore mine, British capital, which opened the Grand Falls paper mill, and the settlement of the French Shore dispute with France, so now the country was "free to concentrate on schemes of internal development."[14]

Once again hope was dashed, this time with the election of Sir Edward Morris as premier. Morris wrecked sound management by reducing taxes on fishing people while improving education grants and instituting old age pensions. In effect, Morris's efforts to ensure electoral success were too generous to the voters. Even more ruinous was the construction of railway branch lines, which both added to the government deficit and eroded people's work ethic as "men were lured away from the fishery by regular and less arduous employment."[15]

Newfoundland's contribution to the First World War received praise, largely from an extended quotation from the *Cambridge History of the British Empire*, but the effects on public morality of the "easy money" available during the wartime boom are noted.[16] A paper mill in Corner Brook was built in 1923, and the 1927 decision of the Judicial Committee of the British Privy Council confirmed Newfoundland sovereignty over much of the Labrador Peninsula, but "unfortunately, the benefits which the Island derived from these favourable turns of the wheel of fortune were almost wholly discounted, as we shall show, by a reckless disregard of the dictates of financial prudence."[17] The people's desire to live like North Americans was identified as a root cause of unsustainable government expenditure.

> A new era of industrial expansion, easy money and profitable contact with the rich American Continent was looked for and was deemed in part to have arrived. In the prevailing optimism, the resources of the Exchequer were believed to be limitless ... the people misled into the acceptance of false standards; and the country sunk in waste and extravagance. The onset of the world depression found the Island with no reserves, its primary industry neglected and its credit exhausted. At the first wind of adversity, its elaborate pretensions collapsed like a house of cards. The glowing visions of a new Utopia were dispelled with a cruel suddenness by the cold realities of national insolvency, and today a disillusioned and bewildered people, deprived in many parts of the country of all hope of earning a livelihood, are haunted by the grim specters of pauperism and starvation.[18]

Previous histories of Newfoundland, such as that of Prowse, had conformed to the nineteenth-century notion of liberal progress, in which

Newfoundlanders overcame obstacles to achieve self-government and embark on a progressive era.[19] The highest form of government was the British constitution, and improvements in technology and industry promised a prosperous future. But as useful as it found Prowse's *History*, the *Amulree Report* opined the British constitution not suited to the people of Newfoundland. And while industry and communications were of course good things, they led Newfoundlanders to want things that they were incapable of sustaining. This was no Whiggish story of the evolution of a better and better political system. Liberal, and anti-liberal, interpretations of the past and a sense of a unique path thus predated any professional historians based in the colony, and Prowse and Amulree served both as guides and a foil to subsequent scholars. The metaphors employed were of cycles of boom and bust that are outside the country's control, wheels of fortune, and falls from grace. Ideas that had been prevalent for decades – the harmful effects of the truck system and the resultant degeneracy of the people – were codified by the objectivity of a British-appointed Royal Commission.

Allan Fraser, for many years the sole historian on staff at Memorial, established research into Newfoundland history at the college, and his work was consistent within the historical outline of the *Amulree Report*. A native of Inverness, Scotland, he was hired in 1928, at the age of twenty-two, with an MA in history from the University of Edinburgh.[20] During the next couple of decades Fraser taught courses in political science, both modern and ancient history, and a course in Newfoundland's constitutional history. He was also a public intellectual; he hosted a news program on the government-owned radio station, VONF, for example.

As the sole professor teaching history and politics during the 1930s, Fraser was the local expert on Newfoundland to whom foreign academics and the Commission of Government turned. In 1937, for example, he published an essay on the Commission of Government in cooperation with two prominent University of Toronto scholars, the historian Harold Adams Innis and the economist A.F.W. Plumptre.[21] Innis was the most prominent Canadian to write on Newfoundland and had conducted fieldwork on the island and Labrador in 1930.[22] His *The Cod Fisheries* was a dense study of an international industry that examined both the production and marketing of Newfoundland's staple. For the remainder of the twentieth century Newfoundland historians often turned to his materialist, but not Marxist, account of the development of the fishery. Innis and Plumptre scorned Amulree's conclusion that Newfoundland could not be allowed to default on its debt. As Plumptre put it:

> It is difficult to see in this crucial part of the thesis of the *Report* anything much more substantial than scare-mongering ... Singularly nauseous is the suggestion that the honour and prosperity of the British Empire should, or indeed could, be maintained by satisfying Newfoundland's creditors; that is by inflicting further economic hardships or political indignities upon the already destitute population. Moreover, even the pretense of an argument at this point is palpably specious. It was based upon the commissioners' boast that no British country had ever defaulted. A blessing on short memories![23]

Ironically, these two Canadians were passionate in their criticism of the British decision to suspend democracy in Newfoundland, and more critical of the historical analysis that justified the decision, than public officials in Newfoundland were. A long-time St John's resident, Fraser lacked Innis's or Plumptre's scepticism about British policy. The dispassionate tone of his writing and absence of criticism of the Commission of Government may have made Fraser a safe choice when, in 1939, the British secretary of state for dominion affairs asked each dominion to start collecting material for an official history of the war. The commissioner of home affairs and education, H.A. Winter, believed that public opinion would "ultimately demand" an official history of the war and in 1942 commissioned Fraser to write it. Although Fraser prepared a typescript, his "History of Newfoundland's Participation in World War II" was not published.[24]

The war encouraged a renewed interest in Newfoundland affairs among both Canadian government officials, who began to look to securing Canada's strategic interests by offering to make Newfoundland a province, and a few Canadian intellectuals who discovered an interest in their neighbours to the east. In this case, too, Fraser was in the right place at the right time. His participation in the Newfoundland branch of the Royal Institute of International Affairs led to him being invited to membership in a British and Canadian research committee on Newfoundland. Ultimately the committee assembled a book on Newfoundland's economic and strategic positions edited by Dalhousie University political scientist R.A. MacKay.[25]

The Second World War had not only proven the island of Newfoundland to have renewed strategic importance to both the British and

North Americans, but contemporary relevance encouraged historians to have a new look at the history of the island as well. The Commission of Government gave copies of the MacKay book to the newly elected members of the National Convention in 1946 as material that would inform their discussions of Newfoundland constitutional future. Once more, a historical text was part of an intervention into fundamental political debate.

Fraser wrote sections for the MacKay volume on the diplomatic relations of Newfoundland, France's treaty rights to the island's west coast, negotiations over the fishery with the United States, and relations with Canada. These were his most substantive historiographic contributions, and, not surprisingly, these topics remained of perennial interest in Newfoundland history. MacKay privately told Sir Campbell Stuart that Fraser's contribution to the book was "very mediocre" and that "The quality of the material is not objective: it is entirely a chronicle based on diplomatic documents, accurately synopsized and quoted, I have no doubt, but taken entirely at their face value; it is written in a vacuum without reference to economic and social developments in the Island or to the events and trends in the world outside."[26]

Besides publishing in good company, Fraser made a couple of abortive attempts to strengthen his academic credentials. In 1945 he inquired about sending his portion of the MacKay book to Edinburgh as a doctoral thesis.[27] The stakes were raised when the college became a university; Fraser was given an ultimatum that unless he completed a PhD by 1956 he would be downgraded from professor to "acting professor" with a loss of both prestige and pay.[28] He consequently took leave from teaching during the 1952–53 academic year to work on a PhD at Columbia University in New York. His effort to have Columbia accept his previously published book chapters in lieu of an original dissertation also failed, so, under the guidance of J.B. Brebner, he embarked on work on a thesis on Newfoundland during the period from the end of responsible government to union with Canada. Brebner, who had just written an influential book on the diplomatic relations between Canada, the United States, and Britain, may have been attracted by Fraser's emphasis on Newfoundland as part of the "North Atlantic Triangle."[29]

The reawakening of interest in *professional* history at Memorial had exposed Fraser, with his lack of a research degree, to embarrassment, but he had a sympathetic ear in Premier Smallwood. Except for his tenure as premier, 1949–1971, Smallwood had devoted much of his life to writing history and biography of important Newfoundlanders and collecting and popularizing folk culture. In 1937, for example, he had edited *The Book of Newfoundland*, a two-volume collection of essays that ranged over history and geography, social description, and oral culture.[30] Even while premier he found time to serve as president of the Newfoundland Historical Society. Having done more than any other individual to bring Newfoundland into Canada (his autobiography immodestly proclaimed *I Chose Canada*), it now fell to his government to integrate Newfoundlanders into their new country. Smallwood embarked on a two-pronged strategy: ensure that Newfoundland received the maximum benefit possible from federal government programs, and modernize the Newfoundland economy and society. Memorial University would serve as one of the institutions that would train Newfoundlanders for the new economy, but Smallwood also hoped that Memorial would preserve a record of the culture and history of Newfoundland.

No one would have been surprised by Smallwood's ongoing interest in Newfoundland history. During the National Convention's debate on a motion about making the college into a degree-granting university, Smallwood had recommended that "the university become a dynamo, a powerhouse, in the inculcation and dissemination and encouragement of a distinctly Newfoundland culture." In the event of Confederation with Canada, he continued, "it will be more important than ever to see to it that our Newfoundland culture is preserved and encouraged and fostered and developed, and in no way can that be done better than through the creation of a Newfoundland university."[31]

Although he was the leading proponent of political union with Canada, Smallwood did not see joining the Confederation as inconsistent with the continuation of Newfoundland culture. He worried that becoming a province would create pressures that would erode Newfoundland culture, but he hoped that the enhanced economic means brought about by union with Canada could counter those factors. In the 1949 debate on the Memorial University Act in the provincial legislature, Smallwood repeated his call for a university that would preserve Newfoundland culture. "There will be an increasing tendency over the years ahead for the sharp definition of our culture and consciousness to become dull" he said, and admitted that such change "perhaps is inevitable, and perhaps not too regretted."[32]

Newfoundlanders' outlook would become broader and more Canadian, he thought, which made it all the more important that the university ensure that "our distinctive Newfoundland culture and consciousness do not disappear and are preserved and maintained down to many generations in the future."[33] His anticipation of change provoked by Canadianization was not the only factor that encouraged his sense that the university should record and preserve the culture. Half his speech advocated reconstituting the Newfoundland Museum, which during the 1930s had been closed and had its collections scattered by the British-appointed Commission of Government as a cost-saving measure. Smallwood, like many others with a passion for history, had seen this as an act of vandalism, and now that Newfoundlanders were in charge in their country again, he saw an opportunity to redress the previous government's disdain for history.

Smallwood's interest in history had been nurtured during the 1930s by his friend Nimshi Crewe. A native of Bunyan's Cove, Bonavista Bay, Crewe was an accomplished antiquarian and antique collector.[34] "A tall, craggy Bonavista man with a brilliant mind who, like most gifted Newfoundlanders of his generation, never found a true outlet for his talents," Crewe was "a Fabian socialist, he made a living as an accountant ... and turned his intellectual energy towards local Newfoundland history, relentlessly mining those inexhaustible lodes of anecdotes, family and folklore, that, rather than any recital of dates and Prime Ministers, are the real story of Newfoundland."[35]

Taking advantage of his longtime friend now having power, in 1951 Crewe wrote to Smallwood with a proposal for heritage and historical preservation. He believed that private collectors were unable to preserve the mass of documents, oral tradition, and material culture scattered about, so he suggested the government create a "Newfoundland Historical Records Commission" to collect, preserve, and display historical records. For the collection and preservation of material culture, Crewe argued for the reopening of the Newfoundland Museum. The Records Commission, he imagined, could collect oral history from the numerous outports, which he justified in romantic rhetoric:

No British colony existed so long with so haphazard governmental authority, no English-speaking communities have so long kept their quaintness, their original family textures and their quiet, moral tone, no other colony was founded and has lived so long on that most unhurried ... of callings, fishing.[36]

Not only did his romantic view inform what he thought deserved to be documented, archival preservation would be a reaction to the county's new status as a Canadian province. His proposed program of describing and publicizing Newfoundland's history would, in Crewe's view, encourage an understanding and "pride in *the type of people* our forbears were, and in their vocations, without apology for the characteristic simplicity and lowliness – (this stance is the more needed now we are part of a larger and harsher people)."[37] When Crewe learned, in 1953, that Memorial's president, Raymond Gushue, was seeking support from the Carnegie Foundation to begin archival collection and research into Newfoundland history he sent Gushue a copy of his earlier proposal to Smallwood.[38]

In 1950 Fraser had been joined by a new colleague at the Parade Street campus, Moses O. Morgan. "Mose" Morgan had spent his childhood in several outports and had boarded at Bishop Feild College in St John's for his high school years; he could fit in with those from town and bay. As a student at Memorial College he had specialized in classics, and in 1935 finished the two years that were then available in St John's. He took his BA at Dalhousie University in 1939 and postponed taking up the Rhodes Scholarship he had been awarded to serve overseas in the Canadian infantry. He earned an MA in classics from Dalhousie in 1946 while waiting to be demobilized. Only then did he take up residence at New College, Oxford, where his tutor advised him against taking a doctorate but to get an "education" by doing a BA in politics, philosophy, and economics. Many of the dons thought a doctorate was not essential, the Rhodes Trust favoured a two-year bachelor's degree, and many of the prominent British historians of the day, for example, did not have research degrees. Morgan finished his studies in 1948, just as his countrymen were deciding their constitutional future within the empire.[39]

Morgan returned to Dalhousie, this time to teach Latin rather than as a student, and he wrote to Memorial looking for a job. His chance came in 1950, when Gushue hired Morgan to teach political science and economics. Morgan was not content to teach such a broad set of courses; he soon campaigned for the creation of two departments, history (Fraser) and social sciences (himself), and later the appointment of an economist so that he would be free to teach political theory. In the early 1950s it was only possible to "major" in two areas in the Arts Faculty – classics or English. Morgan was one of the voices in the faculty council and university senate who called for a broadening of options to include other fields.

Over the next three decades, with the number of faculty members and students increasing rapidly, the ambitious Newfoundlander, war veteran, and Rhodes Scholar rose quickly in the university's administration. In 1956 he was appointed assistant dean of arts and science and became dean the following year.[40] He subsequently became vice president, served as interim president for a year (1966–67), and then as president (1973–81).

The historian Leslie (Les) Harris, who worked closely with Morgan, felt he was cool and reserved, careful in his management of the university's budget and the "walking embodiment of protestant ethic."[41] Harris also reported that Morgan did most administrative details himself, delegated with reluctance, was shrewd in the art of internal politics, and cultivated a network of people to keep him informed. One of the people in that network was George Story, who served as a sounding board for Morgan. As an adept bureaucratic tactician with loyalty to his cohort of Newfoundlanders, especially his friends from the days that the university was on Parade Street, Morgan was well placed to promote the study of Newfoundland within the university. Devoting his attention to administration, Morgan wrote little about Newfoundland himself, but his commitment and contribution to the establishment of Newfoundland studies were crucial.

Joining Morgan in establishing both a broader curriculum and Newfoundland scholarship was Gordon Oliver Rothney. Rothney filled in as professor of history during Fraser's leave to attend Columbia and had made a good impression. An anglophone born in 1912 in Richmond, Quebec, Rothney's experience teaching school in Labrador as a young man encouraged an early interest in the colony's history. He took a BA at Bishop's College in Lennoxville, where his father taught, and wrote two graduate theses at the University of London. The first examined the place of the Newfoundland fisheries in Anglo-French relations, and the second the place of the Newfoundland fishery in Anglo-American relations.

A couple of graduate theses that discussed Newfoundland had been written at American universities, but the University of London was from the 1930s to the 1960s the leading institution in the study of Newfoundland history or, one might say, the study of Newfoundland's place in imperial history. The Rhodes Professor of Imperial History A.P. Newton, and his successor Gerald S. Graham, encouraged several graduate students to work on Newfoundland topics, including Agnes Field, Alexander Hale McLintock, and Rothney. The Canadian-born Graham had been trained at Harvard and Cambridge and had taught at Queen's University in Ontario. Graham had been a contributor to the MacKay volume and supervised several doctoral theses in

Newfoundland history. A 1941 essay of Graham's on the "Fisheries and Sea Power" had questioned the long-standing view that Newfoundland had been an important source of trained seamen during wartime. That knocked one of the blocks out from under historians' view that the colony had an important role in imperial history.[42] In 1949 he was appointed Newton's successor and established himself as a leading imperial historian.

Each student of Newton's, and later Graham's, took a period and wrote a narrative that explained the island's history within the framework of the empire. Among the first of these was the New Zealand–born McLintock, whose 1938 PhD was published in 1941. McLintock helped to set the tone of subsequent studies when he judged works of Newfoundland history by the "light they throw upon the general colonial policy of Britain."[43] His book was also perhaps the most explicitly "constitutional" of the theses written in the 1930s and 1940s, and his narrative culminated in the "gift of representative government" to Newfoundland in 1832. While constitutionalism and the idea that Newfoundland's history was driven by the conflict between pro- and anti-settlement factions were at the core of his book, like Rothney, McLintock saw the seeds of the failure of the 1930s in the policies of the late eighteenth century.

The near avoidance of bankruptcy of the Newfoundland government in 1933, the *Amulree Report*, and the suspension of responsible government had a great influence on McLintock's view of the period between 1783 and 1832. Rather than write a Whiggish narrative of fishery to colony (then favoured by many Canadian historians when writing their own history), he used a derogatory metaphor: "the peculiar maritime system of the island government and a unique judicature developed, like rank and poisonous weeds, to choke and wellnigh overwhelm an unwanted colony which defied the legislation of Great Britain to crush it."[44] McLintock could not blame the genetic stock for the "degeneration" Amulree described as responsible for the financial failure – so it was the result of isolation. As Calvin Hollett has pointed out, McLintock transposed the bleak picture of social life during the Great Depression back onto the early nineteenth century, and in doing so had a lasting effect on the historiography.[45] McLintock returned to New Zealand for the rest of his career, while Rothney brought the influence of the University of London historians to Newfoundland.

Rothney's graduate work in London gave him a familiarity with British archival sources related to Newfoundland and imperial history.

Having returned to Canada, he taught at Sir George Williams University, giving him teaching experience and credibility when he arrived at Memorial. In 1946 while in Montreal, he had been the only anglophone to be appointed as a director of the Institut d'histoire de l'Amérique française – an association that was intended to professionalize the writing of local history by making it more "scientific."[46]

Rothney's Newfoundland scholarship, like that of many of the other British, American, and Canadian historians of the day, including Fraser, was strongest in its emphasis on the Newfoundland fishery as a pawn in great power diplomacy and war. As Keith Matthews later pointed out, much of the work on Newfoundland by British-based historians was not very good at understanding the history of the people in Newfoundland itself. These British-trained historians had explained the island's unique pattern of development by emphasizing the conflict over settlement. Matthews blamed Agnes Field for bringing that interpretation from Prowse into the academic literature, and he suggested that Field and Rothney were uninterested in Newfoundland itself and apologetic about working on the history of the colony, which by the twentieth century was no longer important.[47] Rothney objected to Matthews lumping the historians at the University of London, including himself, with the nineteenth-century amateur historians. What Matthews had perceived as apology, Rothney argued, was just a survey of the field and a statement of the problem "for the benefit of our examiners."[48]

> Miss Field was the first person to challenge some of the historical myths created by Prowse, myths which go on being repeated in some Canadian school textbooks to this day. Professor A.P. Newton of the University of London, and editor of the *Cambridge History of the British Empire*, was the man [in] back of the attempt to rewrite the history of Newfoundland on a more objective and rational basis. In volume VIII he incorporated Miss Field's discoveries into a chapter which he wrote himself. His comment on Prowse was that "the references are very imperfect and the historical judgements unreliable."[49]

Such considerations would not have occurred to anyone in St John's in the 1950s; Memorial University's priority was to hire professional faculty, and Rothney, who could place Newfoundland within imperial and Atlantic world (although they would not have used the term) perspectives, was attractive.

Rothney was energetic and forward-thinking. During his year at Memorial he prepared a memorandum for the dean of arts and science that set out his recommendations for curriculum and faculty development. Morgan, as the sole faculty member in political science and economics, was unable to offer an adequate range of courses, Rothney believed, and an economist should be hired. As to his own field, he advocated hiring a second historian and making the curriculum broader at the introductory level while more specialized at the advanced level. He thought that non-European countries would dominate world affairs during his students' lifetimes, so young Newfoundlanders should take specialized courses in the histories of the United States, the Soviet Union, China, Japan, India, and Pakistan. He also believed that the history of Newfoundland should be restored to the curriculum (it had lapsed).

> The teaching of history in school should begin with local history, and teachers are not likely to have much opportunity to obtain a scientific approach to the history of their own province unless it is obtainable in the University. Moreover, if further research is to be carried on into Newfoundland History, the provincial university should provide some opportunity for Newfoundland students who wish to do so, to begin some specialization in this field as undergraduates. It is customary in Canadian Universities to offer courses in local regional history.[50]

He could not have known it, but he was soon to be in a position to put his ideas into practice.

The historical scholarship about Newfoundland received another boost – this time from an unlikely direction. The British-born economic historian Charles Ryle Fay had developed an interest in Newfoundland while working at the University of Toronto with his friend Harold Innis. After Fay retired from teaching economic history at Cambridge University, an acquaintance who had served in the Dominions Office commented to him that now that Newfoundland was no longer a British colony people in the United Kingdom had lost interest in knowing about the place. Fay resolved to do something about that and began contacting people on both sides of the Atlantic about the availability of business and economic records relating to Newfoundland. Gushue learned of Fay's intention to write on Newfoundland economic history and in September 1952 encouraged him to visit Newfoundland.

Another person Fay contacted was George Story, then a student at Oxford. The historian Peter Ludlow suggests that a meeting between Fay and Story prompted Story to suggest to Gushue that they begin copying British archival sources on Newfoundland history for Memorial. Fay travelled to Newfoundland in the summer of 1952 to see the places he was writing about. Archival acquisition acquired a higher public profile when Fay presented a series of twelve lectures at Memorial in the fall of 1953. He made a case for local archival preservation and "stressed the need for Newfoundlanders to assume intellectual control of their past."[51] The lectures were later published, and Fay frequently sought out and arranged for copying of Newfoundland related archival material for St John's.[52] Although the content of the lectures did little to advance knowledge of the history of Newfoundland, they showed a broad range of archival documents could be brought to bear and that a scholar from the United Kingdom viewed Newfoundland as an important subject.[53]

In June 1953 Morgan set out a proposal for research into the social, economic, and political history of Newfoundland in a memo to Gushue. He had been thinking of ways to encourage research on Newfoundland and had met with Fay, Fraser, Rothney, and H. Bertram Mayo (a Newfoundlander, a Rhodes Scholar, and a political scientist) at the Learned Societies Congress in London, Ontario.[54] Morgan concluded that the absence of research degrees at Memorial held back the study of Newfoundland history, and during a lunch the group discussed ways they might encourage graduates of McGill University and the University of Toronto to go to the University of London to work on Newfoundland topics. Unlike some of the others present, Morgan preferred that Memorial control the research agenda rather than allow the University of London to determine what topics were pursued, and he recommended that Gushue hire a research team consisting of a historian, a political scientist, and an economist. Under the direction of a mature historian – he recommended Rothney for the job – the three would be regular teaching faculty members during the bulk of the year and conduct research on Newfoundland history during the summers. Morgan did not use the phrase, but he envisioned an interdisciplinary research team. Further, he imagined publishing results of the research in a series of monographs and offering MA degrees on Newfoundland history topics. Thus younger scholars would do the spadework of uncovering topics that had laid fallow. Lastly, Morgan suggested building up the library holdings on material relevant to Newfoundland and beginning the systemic collection of relevant documents.[55]

2.1. Department of History faculty, 1961; (l–r) George Schwarz, William
Dobell, Gordon Rothney, Gerald Panting, Frederick Hagar. (From the S.J. Carew
Collection, Special Archives and Collection Division, QEII Library, Memorial
University of Newfoundland.)

Rothney and Morgan proposed an archive that would make available local historical records and copies of records held in foreign repositories. They envisioned it would be administered by the university and
would enable what Rothney saw as the scientific study of the province's pre-Confederation history. His view, common among his generation of professional historians, embodied both a desire to be objective,
rather than writing history as a set of moralizing lessons and nationalist narratives, and an emphasis on research in original sources. The
nineteenth-century historical tradition of the amateur scholar, Rothney
hoped, would give way to professional scholars like himself. Prowse,
Rothney judged, had made "little attempt to explain or put them [the

facts] together in a critical manner ... The book is of value only as the precursor of some more scientific study."[56]

It's not surprising, therefore, that the creation of a Newfoundland archive appealed to both nationalists, such as Crewe and Smallwood, as much as it did to historians who imagined their subject as a dispassionate and scientific discipline. Morgan met with Smallwood and reported the premier's "deep interest" in the project. Attempting to capitalize on that, Gushue requested a special grant from the province to acquire microfilm copies of British Colonial Office records related to Newfoundland. Gushue told Smallwood he was putting a research team in place and hoped to one day have postgraduate students work in history, economics, and political science. Such research, he continued, would be "preparatory to the writing of a definitive history of Newfoundland."[57] Morgan and Rothney also advocated creating a bibliography of published works relating to Newfoundland and undertaking original research and publication in Newfoundland history. Work on Newfoundland history would, they planned, focus upon several areas: Newfoundland in Anglo-French and Anglo-American relations, constitutional history, and social and economic history. Rothney believed that the Carnegie philanthropic foundation of New York might underwrite the costs of such a program and wanted the research in England to be coordinated closely with established British historians.[58]

Fraser had been the university's first professional historian, and Gushue and Morgan had worked to foster historical research, but it was Rothney who laid the foundation for archival collection, teaching, and research. Fraser abandoned his work on a dissertation at Columbia and resigned from Memorial for his successful bid for a seat in the House of Commons in the election of 1953. Gushue seized the opportunity to hire Rothney on a permanent basis. At Gushue's request, Morgan and Rothney then used the June 1954 "Learned Societies" meetings in Winnipeg to consult with Canadian archivists and a representative of the Carnegie Corporation. Based on the information they gathered, Gushue applied to Carnegie for support for the study of Newfoundland history, basing his application on a claim that Newfoundland's past was significant to understanding American history. He repeated Rothney's sentiment that a "complete history of Newfoundland based upon scientific research has never been written and could not even now be written, simply because the materials on which alone a work of this nature should be based have never been collected and collated."[59] Memorial hoped to avoid the foundation's reticence over funding a provincial archive, which the Carnegie people felt should be the responsibility of the provincial government, by portraying it as a short-term investment in providing the tools for long-term research. In the correspondence with Carnegie, the three areas for research were to be the origins and distribution of settlement, constitutional development, and the role of Newfoundland in the American Revolution.

Newfoundland intellectuals had long been interested in history, and several of them publically expressed their enthusiasm for a scientific history when, in January of 1955, they learned that Carnegie approved a $30,000 grant over a three-year period for archival collection and historical research. (Memorial was one of only three Canadian universities to get Carnegie money that year.) A St John's newspaper had raised the idea of creating an archive to house local records as early as 1879, but the long-standing interest in Newfoundland history took on new dimensions during this period.[60]

The celebration of the centenary of responsible government, in 1955, reminded people, not the least Smallwood, of the achievement of earlier generations of statesmen and, indirectly, of the indignities to their national aspirations of the Commission of Government. The six years since Confederation had also been long enough for the disadvantages of union to become as evident as the benefits, and mainland newspapers sometimes provoked a nationalist reaction in the province by comments such as referring to Newfoundland as a parasite on Canada.

History is often an itch that nationalists cannot help but scratch, and reviewing the triumphs and indignities of the past is common. The news that faculty members were to write a source-based history was cheered. The editor of the *Daily News*, who was also the local representative of the National Historic Sites Division, C.E.A. Jeffery, applauded the Carnegie Foundation's contribution but remarked with chagrin that "it is not much to our credit that we have not attempted to do more on our own initiative."[61] The former school teacher and recently appointed curator of the Newfoundland museum, L.E.F. English, made specific suggestions. He advocated a search for documents in a range of continental European archives, such as French and Portuguese repositories as well as those in Britain and Ireland, and the archaeological and linguistic study of the Beothuk and the study of folklore.[62] English was a self-taught historian who had published a school textbook on the history of Newfoundland, as well as collections of history, folklore, and language.

Such commentators not only had broad notions of what constituted material relevant to the history of Newfoundland, they also had a notion of how the subject should be approached. "The real story of Newfoundland has never been told," the highly regarded newspaper columnist Albert Perlin commented, "that is the story of the people. What we want is not merely a political history but a social history, a history that will endeavour to trace the origins of permanent settlement and follow these early settlers in their daily lives."[63] Perlin was a student of history and a collector of Newfoundland books who frequently used his column to discuss historical topics. He was also the author of a history of the country that fit well within the tradition of using history to advertise resources.[64] He not only advocated what he saw as social history, but in a later column he proposed "a new popular history of Newfoundland" written at a professional standard but that would serve a civic agenda:

> No history that we have read deals adequately with the struggle for responsible government and the political events that followed immediately upon its successful conclusion. Prowse is at all times rambling and therefore confusing. There is no proper organization of his material ... The preparation of a new history involves necessarily a great deal of patient research. The official records of the day and the files of the newspapers as well as a great array of other documents will have to be studied and analyzed as a foundation for an authentic work. Yet this must some day be undertaken. We need it for a proper understanding of our present circumstances and for the inspirational value to be found in a proper presentation of the efforts of statesmen of the second half of the nineteenth century to overcome the terrific problems with which they were confronted.'[65]

Perlin's interest in examining history as a way of engaging in contemporary political discourse was not new. The announcement of the historical research group also prompted the lawyer George Rex Renouf, a member of the Newfoundland Historical Society (which had been formed in 1905), to recommend hiring at least one Newfoundlander and of employing a research student or two to ensure continuity in the project into the future.[66]

Gushue invited Jeffery, Perlin, and Renouf, as well as Crewe and the journalist and sometime lecturer in English Michael Harrington, to join a local advisory group to the university's Historical Research Committee. Their passion for history was genuine, but for men such as Harrington and Perlin, both of whom had only a few years earlier argued against Confederation, the dispassionate study of history could answer the question of whether the Newfoundland state had been viable.

As early as May 1944, Perlin had called for an "objective" history of responsible government in Newfoundland, which would set the record straight as the emergent debate over Newfoundland's constitutional future turned in part on whether responsible government had in the past been a success or not.[67] The National Convention, of which Harrington had been a member, had been mandated to investigate the state of the country before making constitutional recommendations. He believed that Smallwood's 1946 motion to seek terms of union from Ottawa had sabotaged the Convention's inquiry, so for him the professional study of Newfoundland history could answer questions that should have been answered before Confederation.

From its beginning, the Historical Research Committee included members from a range of personal and disciplinary backgrounds. Morgan and Rothney were joined by Murray Young, a Canadian-born historian who had written a study of the Colonial Office at the University of London. Memorial also added to the committee the Newfoundland-born and British-trained geographer Harold Goodridge and economists Gordon Groundrey and Parzival Copes. Story, the sociologist Donald Willmott, and university librarians Sadie Organ and Agnes O'Dea also joined them. In addition to the Memorial staff and the local advisory board, Gushue asked several prominent international archivists and historians, including G.S. Graham, to serve on an advisory committee. His request to the British historian Lewis Namier, for example, reveals the extent to which the agenda of the research committee was based on Rothney's interests.

A complete history of Newfoundland based upon scientific research has never been written and could not even now be written, simply because the materials on which work of this nature should be based have never been collected and collated ... a definitive history of this province may ultimately be written ... In the interim, however, there are certain fields or aspects of Newfoundland history within which it is hoped that publications can be made: a: the origins of the Newfoundland people and the distribution and settlement of the population. b: the constitutional development of Newfoundland. c: The effect of Newfoundland and its fisheries upon the outbreak and course of the American Revolution.[68]

Namier, who had an interest in members of Parliament from the West of England, consented to serving on the committee.

While the Historical Research Committee began copying archival collections relevant to Newfoundland and Labrador, it also acquired organizational expertise. Young was dispatched to the United Kingdom to start identifying archival records to be copied, and Morgan did the same in Nova Scotia, as did Rothney in Ottawa and New England. The committee also sought a librarian and an archivist to organize the material. The first appointment was possible to fill locally.

The Newfoundland-born Agnes O'Dea was one of the province's first professional librarians. She had earned a diploma in library science from the University of Toronto in 1932 and worked in St John's at the Gosling Public Library, which then had the best collection of Newfoundland books in public hands.[69] She returned to Toronto for a BA in 1939 and worked within the Ontario library system before becoming the reference librarian at Memorial in 1952.[70] O'Dea worked hard to get treated as a professional and as a partner of the male faculty engaged in the research. After some negotiation over her terms of employment, in 1956 she began compiling a card index of all the printed works relating to Newfoundland history in public and private collections and, ultimately, collections in other countries. Some sense of the method and scale of the task can be gleaned from her description of her method:

> The nucleus of the bibliography was the Gosling Memorial Library collection, the only public local history collection. Every item in this collection was examined and every footnote and bibliography in them as well ... Private collectors gladly discovered many a pamphlet, government document, and society publication that a more casual collector would have consigned to the garbage heap to be lost forever. The search continued with visits to government departments, archives, and other public institutions looking for buried reports and papers. I searched booksellers' catalogues and corresponded with many libraries and institutions around the world whose valuable collections were known to have an early Americana or a maritime connection.[71]

It is difficult to imagine conducting Newfoundland-related research in the days prior to O'Dea beginning her labour. No bibliographic tools existed, and as Memorial's report on the work put it, "Hitherto scholars in the humanities, arts and social sciences have not known where to look in order to discover what material exists in this field, or where

2.2. Agnes O'Dea. (Photographic Services Collection, QEII Library, Memorial University of Newfoundland.)

it is to be found."[72] After 1964 her bibliographic work ran parallel to her building the research collection of printed works related to Newfoundland, and her bibliography provided a guide for the acquisition of older items.

Few libraries then, or since, embarked on a policy of collecting copies of *every* published item related to a particular region or country, but the Centre for Newfoundland Studies (CNS), as it became known in 1964, did just that. That policy exemplifies the degree to which the librarians saw their role as both rescuing rare printed material and providing the basis for research. As for the bibliography itself, when O'Dea retired in 1976 she, and her co-workers, prepared it for publication. The rapidly increasing number of items published in Newfoundland studies each year made it difficult to keep up, prompting O'Dea and her editor, Anne Alexander (wife of the historian David Alexander), to organize the bibliography in chronological order, with a separate subject and author index. That decision made the book a valuable record of the history of publications; a scholar can see the evolution of Newfoundland book history. The two-volume set, published by the University of Toronto Press in 1986, contained as near as possible a complete record of the books and pamphlets published before 1975.[73] Along with the *DNE*, the *Bibliography of Newfoundland* was a foundational research tool for Newfoundland studies.

Memorial's efforts to hire an "Archivist-Historian," house the newly gathered documents, and provide legislative support for the transfer of government records to the archive were all more difficult than finding a professional librarian. As archivist they selected Harvey Mitchell, a graduate of the University of Manitoba, the University of Minnesota, and the University of London. Mitchell had studied under the British historian of France Alfred Cobban, and his lack of experience as an archivist was compensated, in the committee's view, by his experience as a researcher in both British and French archives.[74]

They also found temporary storage space at the university for both private and public records, examined the legislation in other provinces, and drafted an archives act, which they sent to the provincial government to enact.[75] Rothney envisioned Newfoundland copying the arrangement in Saskatchewan, in which a historian at the university also doubled as provincial archivist – thus ensuring close cooperation in the two branches of historical work. Such integration did not materialize. The Carnegie grant was for three years and specified that the archive was to be handed over to the government.

Fraser had been elected as a Liberal in what would normally have been a safe seat for the Conservatives because the vote had been split between two "conservative" candidates, but he lost his seat in Parliament in the 1957 election. Perhaps motivated by partisanship more than compassion, the provincial government appointed Fraser as provincial archivist.[76] That ended Rothney's hope that Memorial's historians would run the archive and ensure coordination between the two institutions. In 1958, when the Carnegie money had run out, Gushue, Morgan, and Rothney successfully applied to the Canada Council for money to continue collecting material for the study of Newfoundland history.[77] Mitchell was replaced by William Whiteley as archivist/historian that year. In June 1960 the provincial government formally took possession of the archival collection and announced it would be moved to the Colonial Building, the former site of the legislature, now that the House of Assembly was moving to a new building.[78]

The original scheme for historical research also included the recruitment of graduate students who would tackle historical topics. The three Canadians – Rothney, Young, and Mitchell, who had all studied at the University of London – launched Memorial's first MA seminar in history.

Rothney's interest in Newfoundland's political history long predated his moving to St John's; in the introduction to his MA thesis on eighteenth-century Newfoundland he had commented on the reason that it stood out among the history of the dominions: "It is the first and, so far, the only British dominion to surrender the right of responsible government, becoming what might be called 'a dominion is suspense.' A study of the developments which have produced such a unique state of affairs will be not only of great interest, but of much practical value."[79]

The foundation for the scientific study of the past, he believed, had been set out by himself and his fellow students at the University of London. Agnes Field and Judith Patterson had written on the periods 1638–1713 and 1713–1763 respectively, and Rothney had set out an account of the years between 1754 and 1783. He hoped that these studies would form the basis of a comprehensive history of the island.[80] Now that Rothney could assign his own students topics, he set many of them periods of nineteenth-century political history. The first two theses were undertaken by John Feltham (a Newfoundlander with a BA from Mount Allison), who wrote on development of the Fishermen's Protective Union, and Les Harris (also a Newfoundlander, but with a BA from Memorial), who studied the first nine years of representative government.

Political history was the most popular area among those doing graduate work at Memorial in the 1950s and early 1960s, closely followed in numbers by the development of various churches in Newfoundland. But even then, as Hollett observed, historians of religion in Newfoundland tended to focus on how it "aided or hindered politics."[81] The outlier in many respects was a woman from the Netherlands, Dirkje Laurentius, who used her Canada Council grant to work in Canada to write a history of the Dutch participation in the Newfoundland fish trade.

Not everyone shared Rothney's interest in diplomatic and political history; E.R. Seary, for example, had a different goal for historical research. He suggested the creation of a "Dictionary of Newfoundland Biography" and a series of publications (under an imprint such as the Cabot Society of Newfoundland) of rare and previously unpublished documents that would be distributed to subscribers, similar to a South African series with which he was familiar.[82]

Gushue thought that Seary's proposed biographical dictionary fell within the logical purview of the historians, not the faculty of the Department of English. Seary retorted that "we have no evidence of any interest other than our own in such a piece of work ... the *Dictionary of National Biography* for example, was done under the editorship of Sir Leslie Stephen, a man of letters."[83] Seary expressed regret that Newfoundland's historians had "almost all been political historians, happy to drag their muck rakes through elections, governments, administrations, attempts at Confederation, riots at Harbour Grace, the French Shore question – matters of that sort." As an alternative, he called for increased study of the oral tradition, since "in an age of rapid and violent change the need to preserve these traditions is of paramount importance if our heritage is not to be forgotten."[84] He also advocated the study of tools and physical structures and proposed that Atlantic Canadian universities sponsor museums of material culture. The last of his list of reasons for promoting "regional studies" were that it brought academics from a range of academic disciplines together to work on the same project and that they all benefitted from the interaction.

Seary was not the only person to criticize Rothney's agenda for the study of Newfoundland history. The Canadian Historical Association published a pamphlet by Rothney that provided a very brief (twenty-seven pages) account of Newfoundland history – an account that provoked public controversy.[85] Rothney used the pamphlet to dismiss what he saw as historical myths, such as Cabot's discovery of the island. Furthermore, "on the basis of Gilbert's visit, some school textbooks refer to Newfoundland as 'Britain's oldest colony,'" he wrote, "This expression is very misleading: firstly, because it overlooks Ireland; secondly, because Gilbert founded no colony; and thirdly, because the event did not make even St John's an English possession ... His visit made no difference whatsoever to the history either of Newfoundland or the British Empire."[86]

Each of these points was reasonable, but his account hit dyspeptic notes. He contrasted the success of Canada in the eighteenth century with the degradation of Newfoundland, and despite his word limits found space to repeat Joseph Banks's 1766 comment that "For dirt and filth of all kinds St John's may in my opinion reign unequaled."[87] His repeated references to Lord Baltimore's "Mansion House" were always in inverted quotes – perhaps Rothney was trying to signal irony and his belief that seventeenth-century Newfoundland could not have had a house that might have genuinely been described as a mansion. (Twenty-first-century archaeological investigation of the site show that seventeenth-century descriptions of a "pretty street" were apt.)

Despite Rothney's efforts to establish his superiority over amateur Newfoundland historians, his account was conventional. It hit the usual notes: France's rights to the west coast of the island held back the area's development by Newfoundlanders, the English government's hostility to settlement had prevented population growth, the naval surrogates use of flogging had been the catalyst for demands for a local legislature. These were all nationalist shibboleths in the twentieth century. The novelty was in his conclusion. While the Newfoundland-born historians had examined their history with an implicit comparison with other British colonies in mind and nursed a resentment born of adversity, Rothney used the pamphlet to make a point about international politics. Europe, he suggested, had been evolving in the direction of one government, but that trend had been interrupted by the warfare that was prompted by competition for colonies. Newfoundland's problems were a result of conflict preventing the development of a state, and now that it had joined Canada it had taken the first step towards unity with the larger world. "Unfortunately it is still a hungry and disorderly world. It is a world whose peoples, including Americans, Russians, British, and Chinese, are badly in need of a Leviathan 'to keep them all in awe,' just as the people of Newfoundland were themselves during those long years when, through lack of government on the one hand and the competition of governments on the other, they were forced to suffer so much violence and poverty upon the shores of their own ragged island."[88]

Rothney's idealistic appeal for a world government attracted little attention from anyone, and some of the same public intellectuals who had earlier applauded the professionalization of history now took exception to his account. Perlin, for example, found it difficult to understand Rothney's "gratuitousness" in challenging the "pride [Newfoundlanders] may have in the tradition that Britain's first overseas possession." Rothney's argument that Ireland, not Newfoundland, was England's first overseas English colony while true, seemed to Perlin "to be argumentative to no particular good."[89] Rothney stood by the accuracy of his judgments and insisted that "The important thing to get across to the people of Canada [in the CHR booklet] is that if our public services are backward, it is partly because Newfoundland was not allowed to become a British colony until long after other parts of eastern Canada."[90]

With a modest-sized graduate program in Newfoundland history underway, Rothney's own research interests shifted to the history of India. His former student, Les Harris, remembered Rothney as a socialist (in 1944 he had run for election as a member of the Bloc populaire canadien, and he was a candidate for the New Democratic Party in 1965 and 1968), an iconoclast (Perlin had also noted his iconoclasm in his seeming to take pleasure in challenging myths), and an idealist. Early in his time at Memorial, Rothney had great hope for the Soviet Union, Harris commented, then became captivated by the example for the world presented by Gandhi and Nehru and believed that "the new India" represented "the ideal that he had been working for all his life [that] of social democracy."[91]

He also believed that the Department of History at Memorial should find an area other than Newfoundland studies upon which to build its reputation, and he promoted an interest in the history of India among his Newfoundland students. He thought it would be difficult for Memorial's Department of History to compete with other Canadian universities in American or Chinese history, for example, but since few Canadians then specialized on the history of India, it could be a successful area for the department. Rothney used his sabbatical in 1959–60 to travel to India, to develop his new interests (which led to a disillusionment with the country as a social democratic model), and in 1960 he hired a Harvard-trained historian of India – F.A. Hagar.[92] A Canada Council grant enabled Memorial's library to purchase books on Indian history, and Rothney was pleased by the enrolment of an MA student from India, whom he optimistically characterized as "the first Asian student to undertake graduate studies in history at this University."[93] Rothney also encouraged Edward Moulton, a Newfoundlander who had written his MA on Newfoundland's political history between 1861 and 1878, to study India for a doctorate.

The most noteworthy of Rothney's students for long-term development of Newfoundland studies was Harris, whose early career exemplifies both research fields at Memorial. Born in St Joseph's, Placentia Bay, in 1929, his father was an accomplished mariner who was at sea for most of the year; his mother was a former schoolteacher, and the family maintained a genteel lifestyle during the Depression by supplementing his father's income through subsistence agriculture. His family's life was one of long hours of hard physical work (for indolence was sinful) relieved by reading and reciting poetry and setting a table for tea each day. With reading material supplemented by the Commission of Government's travelling library program, he was exposed to a variety of literature but, as was the case for many of his generation, the King James Bible left its impression on his literary sensibility: "What I really loved was the language," he reflected, "its splendor, its balance, its beautifully juxtaposed clauses, its imagery, its power, its evocation of awe, and wonder, and mystery – and yes, of piety even in me who was very far from being pious."[94]

Rather than take up a life at sea like the other men in his family, Harris became a teacher upon graduating from high school at the age of sixteen. Like many students from outports, he taught long enough to save enough money to attend Memorial for a while and then returned to teaching. He finished his education degree with a major in history in 1956, and he then started an MA on Newfoundland's political history in 1957. Under Rothney's influence, and having read Kipling as a boy, Harris worked on the history of British policy in the northwest frontier of India for a PhD at the School of Oriental and African Studies at the University of London.[95]

He was in the United Kingdom between October 1958 and July 1960, and like many Newfoundlanders of his generation who grew up with British literature and British school texts, London seemed like home in some respects the very first time he saw it. After his time in Britain he was hired to create an Asian Studies program at a consortium of colleges in Virginia. When Rothney resigned from Memorial to become dean of arts at Lakehead University in Ontario, he recommended his former student as his replacement. Harris had been comfortable working in the United States but had wanted to return home. Gushue appointed Harris to the Department of History in 1963, but he delayed appointing him head of department for a year as he got some local experience. (Seary filled in as head of history for that year.) Harris maintained an active hand in Newfoundland history, writing, in 1968, a widely used school textbook on the subject, for example.[96] But his largest contribution to Newfoundland studies was through university administration.

Harris's career seemed hitched to Morgan's, and the two worked tirelessly to promote Newfoundland studies. When Morgan became vice president of the university in 1966, Harris was promoted to dean of arts and science. When Morgan became president in 1973, Harris took on the position of vice president academic with the "special assignment ... to strengthen and improve the quality of teaching and research and to develop ... centres of strength in relation to Newfoundland problems and policies."[97] Upon Morgan's retirement in 1981, Harris became president of the university.[98] The two men were at the apex of a small group of Newfoundlanders who ran the university (the fact that a few people would quip that they were the "Newfoundland mafia" reflects both how the tight-knit the group was and the fact that academics from other places felt there was something noteworthy about Newfoundlanders in positions of power in their own university).

Morgan, Harris, and their cohort who had studied at the Parade Street campus went to Britain for their graduate degrees and gained teaching experience somewhere else before returning to Newfoundland. They had great influence, but their career advancement was not automatic. When Premier Smallwood became frustrated with Gushue's caution in expanding the university, he decided to appoint the next university president himself, and in 1967 selected a British Labour peer, Lord Steven Taylor. Morgan felt the job should have been his, and he concentrated as much power in the office of vice president (academic) as he was able and waited for Taylor's term to end so he could move into the presidency. Harris felt that the Englishman was erratic, and that while Taylor was president in name – Morgan was president in effect.[99]

Morgan and Harris hired people to work on Newfoundland studies from the 1950s to the 1970s, but with the departure in the mid-1960s of Rothney, Young, Groundrey (who had left the university to direct research for the provincial government and later returned), Copes, and Willmott, the original interdisciplinary Newfoundland history research team had dissipated. Morgan felt betrayed by those who left, undoing much of his hard work in building up expertise.[100] Replacing it was not easy. Harris was now supervising MA degrees in Newfoundland history, but his career was on an administrative track. The department needed another Newfoundland historian as badly as it had a decade earlier, so Morgan and Harris were hopeful when a British historian with an interest in the island appeared on the horizon.

Born in 1937, Gillian Townsend had grown up near Liverpool during the Second World War. She had wanted to attend Oxford or Cambridge, but her family was concerned about an unmarried girl moving so far from home. She enrolled at the University of Liverpool, where she took a required course in British constitutional history taught by the historian of the age of exploration and settlement, David Beers Quinn, who became one of Britain's pre-eminent historians of exploration. Quinn had emphasized working with documents in the seminar, which had a lasting effect on her approach. Although Townsend then wanted to work on eighteenth-century United States history, the American historian then at Liverpool specialized on the nineteenth and twentieth centuries. She chose to work with Quinn for her "special subject," and he suggested she work on Newfoundland.

After completing her undergraduate thesis on the Newfoundland fishery and cartography in the years before settlement, Quinn encouraged her to do graduate work. She planned to write a comparative study of the French and English fisheries but abandoned that when another opportunity came along. Quinn had received a letter from the widow of a geographer who had been transcribing the Willougby papers but who had died before having prepared them for publication. Quinn was too busy with other projects to edit the papers himself, so he passed it to Townsend, who, since undergraduates at Liverpool were required to take a course in paleography, had the skills to prepare transcriptions. Quinn also brought his students to London over the Christmas break, and Townsend started research at the Public Record Office (PRO) in London. Quinn arranged for her to do a seminar with G.S. Graham in London, where she met her future husband, Jack Cell.

After Gillian Cell, as she became known after her marriage, finished her two-year fellowship at the Institute of Historical Research in London, Quinn recommended she apply for a Commonwealth fellowship and work at the University of Toronto, McGill University, or Queen's University. She was awarded the fellowship and was assigned to work at Memorial in 1961 but worried that it did not have a good library, and Rothney, citing a family crisis, had not encouraged her to move to St John's. Instead of taking up the Commonwealth, she moved to North Carolina with her husband. Even with the Atlantic between them, Quinn supported her career. As she finished her dissertation in 1964, Quinn introduced her to the Harvard historian Theodore Rabb, who invited her to present a paper to a session of the American Historical Association. The University of North Carolina, which would not interview her at home, sent someone to the AHA to have a look at her. They hired her at the rank of lecturer, despite her having finished her PhD, published some *Dictionary of Canadian Biography* entries, and an article in the prestigious *William and Mary Quarterly*. Quinn also brought her dissertation to the attention of the University of Toronto Press, which later brought it out under the title *English Enterprise*.[101]

Gillian Cell's graduate work on Newfoundland prompted Memorial to offer her an appointment, and even a promise to find something for her husband to teach. Having established her family in the United States, she declined the offer, leaving Memorial to find someone else to take up teaching Newfoundland history.[102] The rest of Cell's career was devoted to academic administration and to preparing a volume of seventeenth-century documents for publication that she had been working on since her days in London. *Newfoundland Discovered* is a fine example of the British tradition of scholarly editing, but it was out of step with North American academic fashion when it came out.[103]

Had Cell accepted the job, Memorial's Department of History might have taken a turn towards editing texts, but during the 1970s it was economic and political history that predominated. In the 1950s and 1960s the study of Newfoundland history, by chance as much as by design, was dominated by those trained in London, Oxford, and Cambridge, and those places trained the next generation of historians rather than any Canadian or American university. The Rothermere Fellowship (for a Memorial graduate taking up a graduate degree in the United Kingdom), the Rhodes, and the Commonwealth Fellowships all provided for Newfoundland students to travel east rather than west. The fact that their mentors at Memorial were often English-trained and lacked social connections in such places as Toronto, Queen's, or Chicago, also played a role in ensuring that Newfoundland history fit into British models rather than American ones. Some of those who had childhood memories of Newfoundland before Confederation may also have seen attending a British university as a fairly natural decision. Morgan and Harris kept tabs on the careers of promising young Newfoundland men. Story mentored several talented students who went on to do graduate work in England, and he kept in touch with them as a way of encouraging them to ultimately return to Memorial.

Morgan identified a couple of bright students who might teach political science, George Perlin, the son of Albert Perlin, and S.J.R Noel, who Morgan unsuccessfully hoped to entice back to St John's. Noel had studied political science from Morgan, and literature from Story, before being awarded a Rhodes Scholarship. When Noel discussed possible research topics with his tutor, one of which was Newfoundland politics, he was sent to A.F. "Freddy" Madden, a historian of the empire

(Graham was later the external examiner on Noel's thesis). With Madden's encouragement, Noel wrote on Newfoundland politics during the period between 1904 and 1934 – an era of Newfoundland's political history that was then largely unexamined except by the historical account contained in the *Amulree Report*.

That period was key to understanding why Newfoundland was an exception to the "colony to nation" interpretation then influential among Canadian historians. Social interactions were likely as important as the lectures. As he began his research in the archives in London, he frequently met with a group of young Newfoundlanders then studying in England: English literature student Patrick O'Flaherty and the history postgraduate student Peter Neary. They also sometimes met with Jim Devereux, a graduate of Memorial who was slightly older than the others and shared Story's interests in renaissance literature.[104] The conversation sometimes turned to discussing home, but Noel later reflected that none of them worked exclusively on Newfoundland topics, all had broad interests, and that they did not see themselves as provincial intellectuals.[105]

Noel initially wanted to return to Memorial, which Morgan supported, but he thought Morgan was a micromanager and did not relish being his colleague in a political science department of two.[106] While still writing his thesis, the University of Western Ontario hired Noel, but it did not end his involvement in Newfoundland history. Little had been written on Newfoundland's twentieth-century political history, so Noel extended the thesis to cover the period up to the Smallwood administration. The resulting book, *Politics in Newfoundland*, was influential among Newfoundland scholars because it was the first readable and reliable history of twentieth-century Newfoundland politics.[107]

Political scientists of the 1960s fell somewhere on a continuum between the study of institutions and the statistical study of the aggregate, or between the case study and the comparative. Noel thought that a comparative approach was the best way of understanding differences and similarities among a set of cases. He believed that adopting a theoretical approach (such as the various Marxist approaches that were popular among social scientists during the era) would force the data into a Procrustean bed. *Politics in Newfoundland* did not draw on social science jargon, nor did it draw any explicit conclusions for other countries, but it was historical in narrative style and analysis. He later reported that a few readers outside Memorial, particularly members of the St John's elite families who read unflattering portraits of the behaviour of their ancestors in it, liked the book less than his professional peers did. But the book established a dependable narrative, and it embodied his best effort to accurately tell what had happened based on the few sources that were available to him.

Under the "thirty year rule" of classified documents, it was only in the 1960s that the British government records from the 1930s became available to historians. His book was, he reported many years later, in his own conception a study in modernization. While another political scientist might have focused on the constitutional structure, which might have encouraged synchronic analysis, he was interested in the actual ways in which people worked within the structures, and that required him to adopt a historical analysis.[108] For Noel, the collapse of responsible government in 1934 was a failure of leadership rather than a structural flaw in the constitution. And the decision to join Canada was not, as some Newfoundlanders of his generation believed, a failure, but in Noel's view, the right decision. Nationalism had little appeal for him. He felt that nationalism was rarely a positive force anywhere in the world.[109]

In addition to Cell's *English Enterprise* and Noel's *Politics in Newfoundland*, there were a couple of other studies written at universities other than Memorial in the 1960s that became foundational texts. Frederic F. Thompson, who had been a student at Oxford, reflected the emerging post-war consensus about imperial history in Britain, emphasizing the way that conflict at the margins of the empire affected the agenda in London in his *French Shore Problem in Newfoundland: An Imperial Study*.[110] If problems in Newfoundland affected the imperial priorities, internal politics also merited attention. There was another book in that era that attempted to account for Newfoundland's exceptional constitutional path from colony to self-government to dependant status – that of the Canadian-born Gertrude Gunn. The nineteenth-century Newfoundland constitution had been similar to that of other British North American colonies, so that seemed to not be a fruitful avenue of inquiry if one wanted to find what had gone wrong in Newfoundland. Gunn had no connection with Memorial, but under the supervision of Graham at the University of London had in 1956 completed a PhD on the political history of Newfoundland between 1832 and 1864.[111] Gunn's answer to the failure of responsible government, given the constitutional commonalities in British North America, was to find Newfoundland unsuited to democracy because of the large number of Irish resident in the colony.

Clergymen, such as the Irish-born Bishop Michael Fleming, had, in her view, undermined good government in their quest for power.

The first generation of Canadian-born historians had left Memorial, and, with the exception of Harris, the Newfoundland-born historians who had taken graduate degrees in Britain had not returned. Both Gunn and Noel pursued other career interests, and Noel's contemporary and friend, Peter Neary, became a political historian as well. A Bell Island native, Neary had intended to go to medical school, but under the influence of those working on Newfoundland studies switched to history. His Memorial MA thesis, written under Rothney's supervision, had taken up the French Shore dispute – the most long-standing aspect of Newfoundland's place in French and British diplomatic history. He too went to England for a doctorate, wrote on imperial history, and took a job teaching history at the University of Western Ontario. Neary continued to work on Newfoundland history for the whole of his career, which culminated in a comprehensive history of the politics and diplomatic history of the Commission of Government period. Having lived his whole adult life outside of Newfoundland, he empathized with the view of British, Canadian, and American officials when writing Newfoundland history.

Cell had declined the job offer – which opened the opportunity for a renewal of the approach to history at Memorial even as it represented a loss of momentum. Once again, Story played an important role in creating the conditions for a rebirth of Newfoundland studies. Indeed, Story's role in shaping the social sciences and humanities at Memorial was as great as it was discreet. He declined opportunities to put his name forward as head of the Department of English or as dean of arts, although he did not shirk from serving on university committees such as the one that established regulations for graduate work at the university. Throughout his career he had the ear of Morgan and Harris, the high regard and friendship of many of his contemporaries, and a network of younger scholars who saw him as a mentor.

In the fall of 1964 Morgan, then dean of arts and science, wrote to Story, who was then in Oxford taking his first sabbatical from teaching. Morgan complained to his friend that several faculty members had abandoned Newfoundland for higher salaries elsewhere and sent a list of positions at Memorial that needed to be filled. He asked Story to "keep his ear to the ground" for possible faculty members.[112] Story took the opportunity to hire young people who would collect Newfoundland-related archival and oral cultural material for the university, and he favoured recruiting in Britain rather than in Canada since much Newfoundland-related archival material remained in British repositories. "There's enough material over here to keep a dozen hard-working scholars going full time simply collecting material" he thought.[113]

Story was disappointed, however, that most "English academics are petrified in conventional studies" and there were few "students of the kind I would like to see coming to Newfoundland."[114] Few British scholars then worked in the interdisciplinary or oral culture methods that Story and his collaborators in St John's were developing. But there was some cause for optimism. He believed that using personal connections to select promising scholars would result in hiring better faculty members than would general job advertisements. If young, bright scholars became part of an exciting research community at Memorial, Story believed, they would also be less likely to leave for a higher salary in another province.

Story recommended several people for appointments to the faculty and research fellowships. He met the economic historian H.C. Mui, for example, to whom he provided a list of West Country mercantile houses involved in the fishery in hopes of enticing him to take up the subject. (Mui had a productive career at Memorial, but he did not take up Newfoundland-related research.) Story also talked with James Hiller, encouraging the young student to attend Memorial for an MA in history. By chance, the British-born Hiller had worked with the Moravian mission in Labrador for a year and a half between high school and university, and it made a lasting impression on the boy from the London suburbs.[115] Having completed his BA at Oxford, he earned a Canadian Rhodes Scholar's Foundation scholarship to work at a Canadian university and was interested in writing on the early decades of the mission. Story convinced Hiller to do so at Memorial, where he wrote a thesis on the foundations of the Moravian mission under the supervision of Harris. Hiller supplemented his fellowship with teaching a first-year section and was paid to organize the microfilm copying of Moriavian records in London.[116]

Story also met Keith Matthews, then about to take the exams for his BA, and enticed him to write a study of the West of England Newfoundland fishery as a graduate project. Memorial's Institute of Social and Economic Research would fund Matthews, who would also identify archival collections that could be copied while doing his research and move to Newfoundland to take up a teaching appointment. Matthews had come from a humble family; as a physically small boy from a poor family in a middle-class neighbourhood during the harsh war and post-war economic times, he developed a great ambition and work ethic. He quit school at the age of fifteen for a career as a jazz pianist in London, and that was interrupted when he was drafted into the British Army. He spent most of three years stationed in Cyprus, where he was assigned as a company clerk after doing well in the standard IQ test. An officer saw promise in him and encouraged the young man to finish school.

Once he was discharged from the army, Matthews attended Ruskin College, Oxford, which was not a degree-granting institution but catered to working-class students who lacked the qualifications to get into university. Success at Ruskin enabled him to write exams for a BA at Jesus College, Oxford, and to feel secure enough to marry. He had planned to study the National Health Service for a graduate degree but abandoned that and committed to moving to St John's after meeting Story. It's little wonder that he accepted the £1200 ISER fellowship (when Nuffield and St Anthony's colleges were offering between £850 and £900).[117] The offer from Memorial gave him economic security and allowed him to study the heritage of Devon (which he cared about). In what must have appealed to the boy from Plympton, it allowed him to earn a living studying ships. The conversations with Story, an elegant and erudite man, were also enough for Matthews to realize that moving to Newfoundland would give him a chance to distinguish himself.[118]

Matthews noted that the fellowship that Story offered him funded two years of study while the task would require longer, which prompted Story to recommend that Morgan offer a third year teaching in St John's. Story had not at that point told Matthews that he hoped the young man would identify records that could be microfilmed for the provincial archives while researching his thesis.[119] Matthews may not have realized it, but he was being hired as an archival collector as much as a teacher. Morgan offered Matthews the fellowship and ISER provided research funds to aid him in copying documents for Newfoundland.[120] There would also be a "lightened teaching load to enable him to complete this rather important project."[121]

Matthews's graduate supervision was taken on by Madden, who maintained the tradition of constitutional history in Oxford of the 1960s at a time when most other imperial historians wrote on the dependent empire rather than the Commonwealth. He encouraged Matthews to select "constitutional" documents on Newfoundland history for inclusion in his own publications, even though, Matthews reported,

2.3. Keith Matthews. (Photographic Services Collection, QEII Library, Memorial University of Newfoundland.)

the emphasis among Oxford scholars was then on Africa and Asia in the nineteenth and twentieth centuries and "even the word 'Empire' seems to have sinister undertones."[122] For Madden, the history of the Commonwealth continued to be important since it both informed British history and united historians working in various countries.[123] Constitutional historians had something to say that seemed particularly relevant to those interested in Newfoundland – a colony that developed representative institutions later than most other parts of British North America and had abandoned responsible government in 1934. Matthews shared his supervisor's view that adopting an overarching explanation trapped historians into reproducing the conclusions of others, and he believed that the key to being a great historian was to have conclusions rise inductively from reading all the empirical evidence. History at Oxford during the 1960s also included well-developed specialties, such as economic history and demography, which provided alternate bodies of evidence to the public records of the crown and Parliament and new ways of constructing an argument that owed as much to the social sciences as the humanities. In the period after 1945 Britain was losing its empire, and many British historians were examining local circumstances in the various parts of the empire and exploring economic factors rather than forms of government.[124] Too often, perhaps, the significance of the colonial story was measured by the effect on the imperial centre, but at least the constituent parts of the empire were being studied. Furthermore, Herbert Butterfield's criticism of the Whig tradition had been internalized as a matter of faith for those who saw themselves as professional.[125]

For the many historians working on political history in the tradition of Namier, "constitutionalism spelled innocence: a failure to see that politics did not work like that."[126] From the constitutionalists Matthews gained a narrative framework of the Commonwealth, and the new imperial historians made it possible to study the effect the periphery of the empire had on the centre, which enabled Matthews to avoid the teleology of constitutionalism. Namier encouraged a critical outlook on the public face of politics, a sentiment that supported Matthews's scepticism.[127] He shared a suspicion that the real history did not consist solely of stringing together royal proclamations and charters. The economic historians had provided an explanation of history that was an alternative to changes in legal regimes resulting from the struggle of Whigs and Tories (similar to what Matthews later dubbed the conflict thesis in the Newfoundland historiography).

It would be easy to exaggerate the influence of British historians on Matthews. The Oxford graduate experience was one of independent study, and his wife, Kay Matthews, did not remember him attending lectures but immersing himself in the archival record day and night, weekdays and weekends. He was also copying documents for the Newfoundland archives and being reimbursed for the expenses, even as he was writing his thesis. His thesis cited few other historians and lacked the explicit engagement with interpretation that is the hallmark of graduate theses of more recent generations of North American scholars, but it showed a wide range of reading in the documentary record.

As a younger colleague put it: "for a long time the British training drew scholars toward political history and imperial relations, and away from American model building and social theorizing; but that same training, demanding inductive reasoning from new empirical foundations, enabled Keith Matthews to demolish the myths of illegal settlement, eighteenth century anarchy, and ruthless fishing admirals."[128]

After fulfilling his two-year residency requirement at Nuffield College, in July 1967 Matthews and his family moved to St John's for him to take up a position as lecturer in the Department of History and finish writing his thesis.[129] The young Englishman soon developed an affection for his adopted homeland and a desire to show that a study of the history of the West Country fishery was important "as a study in English national history."[130] The thesis itself is more conventional than those aware of his historiographic contribution might assume. As each of his predecessors had done, Matthews sketched British policy, the effects of war and peace, and changes provoked by events such as the American Revolution. "A History of the West of England – Newfoundland Fishery" is primarily a political narrative history of the fish trade based on a reading of the same colonial office records that each of the other historians of Newfoundland had used.[131] Matthews divided his narrative into the common periods of British history, such as "Newfoundland under the Restoration" or by pivotal international milestones, such as the chapter titled "1763–1775."

Perhaps, like graduate students everywhere, he had to justify his topic to a supervisor (who in his case was a constitutionalist historian of the empire), although Newfoundland was indeed profoundly affected by warfare and diplomacy. He examined planters, ship owners, and merchants, and his narrative shares more with the histories written by his predecessors than he would have admitted. As another colleague suggested, it was a testament to Matthews's intellect that in the course of his archival research he realized the logical fallacy in the idea that government policies had been effective in discouraging settlement.[132] The evidence presented doesn't directly speak to that question, but he induced from his reading that despite anti-settlement rhetoric there had been no conflict between economic groups and ultimately realized that anti-settlement government policies had been ineffective.

Matthews not only continued to collect archival records after he moved to St John's, but his research fit into the pattern of Newfoundland studies then underway in the Departments of English and Folklore as well. Much as Seary was doing in English, studying place names and family names, Matthews began to collect files of personal names. Seary's family name study showed where the ancestors of Newfoundlanders (contained in the 1955 census) may have originated based on where those names occurred in England and Ireland. Matthews's name files on the other hand contained both the surname and first name of each person mentioned in historical records and the citation to the source. The name files could be used to reconstruct the settlement of a community or the transition of a family from participants in the migratory fishery to settlers. Matthews also began to collect Newfoundland business records and to reconstruct the merchant families in a study that he hoped might shed much light on the economic history of the fishery.

Just as Herbert Halpert, who will be discussed in the next chapter, was using students to collect oral culture, Matthews had undergraduate students write histories of their home communities. He hoped that the large amount of spadework by those students would turn up data that might be the foundation for a synthesis. Matthews, Harris, and Gerald Panting also planned a "Newfoundland Documentary Study" that would "use political documents to pose questions and the ancillary documents to suggest the answer or answers to the questions."[133] (Panting had come to Memorial from the University of Winnipeg in 1959, where he and his colleagues had resigned en masse to defend the principle of academic freedom after the university had fired a faculty member.) The Canada Council funded the documentary history project, but it was never completed, in part because Harris's time was taken up with academic administration, and Panting and Matthews, with their colleague David Alexander, embarked on a massive project of archival salvage and quantitative research.

Alexander had joined the Department of History the same year that Matthews had, and with Panting the three sought to establish the department as a centre of economic history. A native of British Columbia, Alexander had done graduate work in Seattle, where he developed a scepticism about American materialism and a dislike of American foreign policy. A deepening interest in Marxism led him to study the industrial revolution at the London School of Economics, after which he accepted the job offer in St John's. He taught economic history and finished a book on retailing in Britain during the Industrial Revolution, but soon after arriving in St John's, a friend remembered, he lost interest in English economic history. Alexander's interests were affected by wide-ranging friendships ranging from Story and Morgan, who were of an older generation, and colleagues such as Matthews to graduate students in the Department of Folklore. A developing affection for the place also meant that he wanted to help cause a positive change in his adoptive home and encouraged a new enthusiasm for writing in Alexander.[134]

Matthews had learned that the PRO in London was soon to dispose of the vast majority of the "Agreement and Account of Crew and Official Logbooks for British Empire Vessels, 1863–1938 and 1951–1976." Although many British historians objected to the records' destruction, the PRO's decision is tangible evidence that in the late 1960s Britain did not value the empire as had earlier generations. In part it reflected a turning inwards in the face of decolonization and the rise of social history. Imperial and diplomatic history seemed old-fashioned, especially in the ways they had been practised. With the aid of a Canada Council grant, Matthews and Panting spent from May to September of 1969 in London selecting records to be shipped to Memorial.[135] The Newfoundland university acquired a source that made it the largest archive of its kind in the world. Much of Matthew's effort over the next few years became devoted to managing the archive, and he and Alexander put together the Maritime History Group (MHG) to study the history of shipping in Atlantic Canada. It's worth emphasizing that their collaboration established Newfoundland history on a footing separate and different from the constitutional and imperial/diplomatic tracks its historians had travelled within. Many North American historians were discovering the computer as a tool to analyse large data sets, and the historians at Memorial saw this as a fruitful area.

As Matthews and Alexander arrived in St John's from England, there were changes happening in Canada that affected the writing of Newfoundland history. The celebration of the Canadian centenary of 1967 encouraged a resurgence of Canadian nationalism, and many historians were part of that movement. While some Canadian historians focused their attention on defining the *national* narrative, others realized that the "limited identities" (of region, class, gender, etc.) were the key to understanding Canada.

Perhaps a childhood in British Columbia, and time spent in graduate school in the United States and then in Britain, encouraged his empathy with those who were outsiders to the Central-Canadian narrative. And his leftist politics predisposed him to be a champion for the economic underdogs in Atlantic Canada. Certainly dissatisfaction with the national history found in the pages of the *Canadian Historical Review* prompted a young generation of historians to create specialized

2.4. David Alexander examining a Crew Agreement. (Photographic Services Collection, QEII Library, Memorial University of Newfoundland).

journals for such fields as women's history and working-class history, and in 1971 a journal of the history of the Atlantic provinces – *Acadiensis*. Historians living in the Maritime provinces of Nova Scotia, New Brunswick, and Prince Edward Island rebelled against the economic and social marginalization of their provinces and the assumptions on the part of Ontario-based historians that Maritimers were conservative and backward. Collectively the historians in the Maritimes hoped that discovering the roots of regional economic disparities and exposing how the Canadian government had been implicated in favouring the centre of the country over the periphery would result in the federal government adopting more equitable policies. Alexander was an early supporter of *Acadiensis*, and in his essays on the history of Newfoundland, its economic history became a microcosm for the history of Canada and an argument for state policies that would redress the disadvantages faced by the poorer regions. His study of the export of salt cod, *The Decay of Trade*, highlighted the responsibility he felt the state had to organize marketing. As long as the federal government fixated on its economic relationship with the United States (a continental outlook), it would not develop policies that reflected the Atlantic (and Pacific) orientation. While Matthews was not much interested in either Marxism or classical economic theory, Alexander brought both to the study of Newfoundland's history.

Alexander engaged with prevailing debates about modernization within the province and the international literature that considered economically depressed areas as an effect of capitalist development rather than a failure of the people of those regions. Several social factors encouraged Alexander to take up Newfoundland studies in the 1970s. The optimism and rapid economic growth of the 1950s and 1960s had been replaced with a malaise brought on by a realization that economic disparities were more intractable than the state planners had imagined. Alexander empathized with working people and those excluded from power at a time that the mainstream economics profession was trying to make itself more scientific by becoming more mathematical. Furthermore, neither the American technocrats administering the Vietnam war, nor the Canadian bureaucrats running the federal Department of Fisheries, seemed to him to have the best interest of the peasant or the fisher in mind. Friendships with Story, the anthropologist Robert Paine, and many young faculty members and graduate students in different departments also encouraged him to not only study Newfoundland, but to involve himself in critically appraising contemporary government policy. Alexander's essays looked for factors that impeded modernization, but he placed much of the blame on the state rather than the people who were the objects of the policies.

Alexander turned his attention to the question of why Newfoundland was relatively underdeveloped compared to its neighbouring provinces and why it had suffered the setback along the path of self-determination of the Commission of Government. Perhaps being Canadian, then a rarity among those who studied Newfoundland, encouraged him to take a comparative approach. While imperial and political history had long dominated the work of the Department of

History, Alexander encouraged a Canadian comparison both because he wrote within a tradition of political economy that owed much to the staples thesis of Innis and because he explicitly called for historians of Atlantic Canada to "bridge the Cabot Strait" and compare Newfoundland with the Maritime provinces. He found that Newfoundland's path had allowed a greater measure of economic growth than those provinces that had joined the Confederation, but that it suffered from a crippling public debt that would have been avoided if the country had joined Canada in 1867. The Maritime provinces were poor compared to their western neighbours, but Confederation had allowed them a "shabby dignity" denied Newfoundland during the Great Depression.[136] The island's failure was not, as Amulree once had it, a moral failure on the part of the people, but an economic reality faced by a small country aspiring to a North American standard of living but which relied heavily on exporting a single staple to the poorer regions of the world. Newfoundland's political leaders had failed it in not being of higher quality, but also in having tried to mimic the development strategies of Canada. While most federal and provincial officials saw the salt cod industry as an anachronism that should be replaced by fresh-frozen exports to the United States as soon as possible, Alexander worried about becoming dependent on the American market. Like other intellectuals, he tackled the question of development but questioned the notion that there was one path to modernization.

Alexander worked in the tradition of Harold Innis, who, although he had died in 1952, remained one of Canada's most influential historians for his wide-ranging studies of various natural resource "staples" (fur, timber, fish) and transportation systems. By the 1970s Innis was out of fashion among the leftist social historians who came on the scene in Canada; they saw him as an economic determinist who did not recognize the importance of human agency. Matthews commented that Innis's reliance on secondary sources "inevitably left him dependent upon the researches of others and his general theory of metropolitan-outport conflicts certainly predisposed him to accept their [his predecessors] conclusions regarding Newfoundland."[137] By lumping Innis with nineteenth-century amateur historians, Matthews encouraged readers to assume that Innis was obsolete. Alexander also dismissed Innis – seeing him as one of a group of historians who "imply that the stagnation of Atlantic Canada was the outcome of technological changes that left its endowment marginal to the pattern of growth in twentieth century North America."[138]

Alexander addressed the question of Newfoundland's economic development, and the political and diplomatic emphasis of the earlier generations receded in importance. Colleagues at Memorial, and the universities in the Maritime provinces, recognized the strength of his work, but most Canadian historians west of New Brunswick were unaware of the broad implications of his writings, perhaps because they assumed work such as Alexander's history of salt cod marketing was too specialized for them to read. Although the historiographies of Newfoundland and the Maritime provinces remained separate, *Acadiensis* provided an outlet for Newfoundland scholars and the historians in other provinces provided vindication that Newfoundland history had value on its own merits, not just for the effects it had on such things as Anglo-French diplomatic history.

The principal question taken up by Alexander, Panting, and Matthews in their Atlantic Canada Shipping Project (ACSP) was an important one. Why had the colonies of Nova Scotia and New Brunswick once owned one of the largest fleets of cargo vessels in the world, in the mid-nineteenth century, but divested themselves of most of that tonnage by the end of the century? The ACSP reflected the enthusiasms of the profession of the day: As a team they could take on ambitious questions that would have been beyond the ability of a single scholar.[139] In the early 1970s Alexander believed that quantitative methods and computing technology were the methods of the future for historians. Thanks to significant support from Memorial and the Canada Council, they employed a large team of researchers, including several postdoctoral fellows. This is not the place to evaluate the ACSP, except to note that it took much of the focus of the faculty's efforts and the university's funds and space in a different direction than the Newfoundland studies emphasis of the Department of History of the 1950s and 1960s. Story had once praised Matthews's tireless collecting of archival records, and Matthews now took primary responsibility for the acquisition of documents for the group, returning to Britain many times to survey archives and arrange for the copying of records.

In the summer of 1970, Head of Department Gerry Panting reported on what the twelve members of the Department of History were doing. The study of Newfoundland history had recovered from the crisis provoked by the departure of the original Historical Research Committee. Alexander was working on Newfoundland economic history, and William Whiteley, who had returned to the department in 1969, was writing on James Cook and eighteenth-century English policy towards

Newfoundland. Matthews was then in England selecting archival records to be copied.[140] The department also hoped, Panting wrote, to work with the Newfoundland Historical Society to identify local records, create a record-collecting group among chartered accountants who were interested in business history, and liaise with the Department of Folklore in developing oral history. Several MA students at Memorial were engaged in Newfoundland research, as were faculty members James Hiller and Ian McDonald, whose doctoral work on Newfoundland topics at British universities were being supported by ISER fellowships.[141]

While working on his MA thesis, and teaching in the department, Hiller had impressed people with the quality of his work.[142] ISER funded him for a PhD, and after working on a biography of the medical missionary Wilfred Grenfell, he switched to write on late nineteenth-century political history. Canadian historians had emphasized the national over the imperial, but not so the British-trained historians of Newfoundland, who, as we have seen, thought of Newfoundland history as a theme in imperial relations. "It is hardly surprising" Hiller wrote, "that most historians dealing with Newfoundland have concentrated on that part of its history with the greatest imperial importance."[143]

His doctoral thesis continued in the traditions of imperial history. It was based on the same Colonial Office correspondence and politicians' papers that his predecessors had used, and it provided "a general survey of the colony's history in the second half of the nineteenth century, filling the gap between the studies published by Gunn and Noel."[144] While he provided an effective account of local politics, he never lost sight of the perspective of London. In keeping with the writing of imperial history at Cambridge at the time, the thesis examined the interplay of St John's politics and British relations with France.

While his MA thesis had shown an interest in the lives of the Inuit and Moravians, and that was at a time when many British historians were embracing social history, Hiller's doctorate was political history. He chose to not embark on the sorts of social history then emerging in the Departments of English, Anthropology, and Folklore at Memorial, nor was he part of the ACSP. Hiller continued to work within a proven tradition of the study of the relationship between the colonies and the imperial government, and he branched out into the history of railway policy and the development of the province's paper industry.

He tried to understand why Newfoundland's political leaders made the choices they did, which required understanding the economic context and the imperial relationship, but primarily necessitated reconstructing something of Newfoundlanders' psychology. Key to understanding Newfoundland, he asserted, was remembering that it was an *island* near the mainland of North America. "Newfoundlanders" he suggested, "developed a strong sense of independence and a distinct local identity, but they were – and are – ever conscious of the greater wealth and sophistication of the mainland."[145] He thus found it reasonable that Newfoundlanders would want to replicate the economic policies of their nineteenth-century neighbours, even if those policies were ill suited to a small country.

Thus railway building and bait diplomacy were at the same time acts of economic desperation, defiant assertions of independence, and ambitious attempts to copy the continent off which the island is anchored. Success would have given the colony the substance with which to make its status a reality; but so long as it remained small and weak it could never claim equality with the other future dominions, and its interests would have to be placed after those of Canada. The attempt to throw off the limitations imposed by size, poverty and geographical position failed; and it is perhaps to the colony's credit that, after Bond's premiership ended in 1908, these limitations were accepted. Reciprocity was no longer a possibility, the French Shore question was settled, and no Premier tried again to achieve a position of imperial importance for himself or his country. Newfoundland did not achieve independent membership of the League of Nations and when, in the 1920s South Africa and Canada began to press for a definition of dominion status on the basis of equality with Britain, it stated that it did not desire any such change. Officially Newfoundland had adopted the title of Dominion in 1918; but its inhabitants still preferred to think of their country as "Britain's oldest colony."[146]

The political narratives of most former colonies, such as Canada, consisted of several stages: a settler past, growing national self-awareness among the colonists, followed by the achievement of higher and higher degrees of autonomy. But Newfoundland's historians had to account for a country that suspended responsible government and then joined a larger country. The studies of political history, Gunn, Hiller, and Noel implicitly accounted for Newfoundland's failure to follow the *normal* pattern of political modernization, and in this they owed something to McLintock and Amulree. Ian Macdonald, the other young historian working on Newfoundland, was a Montreal native who came to

Memorial; he had completed a University of London doctoral thesis on William Coaker and the Fishermen's Protective Union (FPU) in 1971, also under the supervision of Graham.[147] The FPU was an interesting social movement, which aimed at a broad reform agenda and included its own business and political arms, and had also been the subject of one of the first MA theses at Memorial. McDonald saw the failure of the union in the political career of its leader. In doing so, he reflected the interests in political history of those under whom he had trained. McDonald also took up an appointment at Memorial.[148]

While McDonald and Hiller broke new ground in political history in the 1970s, Mathews and Alexander broke with the historiography in a dramatic way that was exemplified in an essay Matthews presented to the Canadian Historical Association meeting in St John's in the spring of 1971. He published it in 1978 in the *Newfoundland Quarterly*, a literary and historical magazine that had been published since the beginning of the century, and posthumously it was corrected and republished in the academic periodical *Newfoundland Studies*. The foundations of a historical mythology, Matthews suggested in "Historical Fence Building: A Critique of the Historiography of Newfoundland," had been laid by two groups. Nineteenth-century Newfoundlanders created the myths of illegal settlement and English oppression, and twentieth-century professional historians in Britain, Canada, and the United States wrote within that mythological framework.

The author of Newfoundland's first book-length history, John Reeves, had in 1793 proposed that conflict between those who favoured settlement and those who opposed it had shaped the history of the island.[149] Nineteenth-century historians followed Reeves in assuming the conflict had determined the pace of development, and it became the dominant interpretation among twentieth-century academic historians. Matthews argued that historians had attributed Newfoundland's particular path to an assumed conflict between groups within the fishery, such as planters versus ship owners, or fishing ship owners versus sack ship owners.

The second element of his argument was that professional historians uncritically worked within the conflict thesis because they were not looking at Newfoundland for its own sake, but only as an illustration of some other theme in imperial history. These errors reached a high point in the work of McLintock, who implicitly compared Newfoundland to other colonies and decided that the arrival of representative political institutions later than other British North American colonies showed that Newfoundland's constitutional development was "retarded" by the conflict. To explain this, McLintock worked backwards from the inception of representative government in 1832 to examine the island's constitutional history. Like others, he accepted that conflict between groups that favoured settlement and those who opposed it had been responsible for the pattern of development.

Matthews concluded that history became, in the hands of several generations of historians, a set of political eruptions and constitutional acts. The statutes, charters, and judicial decisions that made up the political-legal interpretation became fenceposts, and historians stretched a narrative between them like so much wire. This emphasis on the political-legal narrative in the work of imperial historians was not surprising.

> The basic problem is that the whole interpretation of retarded development as being due to group conflict rested upon a set of assumptions which have never been tested. The theory gives primary attention to politics and legislation as factors in economic development, having assumed but not proved a material conflict of interest centered on the fishery. Newfoundland's development was, supposedly, retarded as a result of legislation passed either at the behest of an interest group or by a dogmatic government. To show that the government enacted legislation inimical to the growth of population, culture or government does not measure its effect upon that growth, for the legislation must be shown to be effective. The historians mentioned above did not prove the effectiveness of legislation and, in fact, the evidence indicates massive evasion of the law.[150]

Matthews's analysis owes a debt to Alexander, who had read a draft of the essay and commented to Matthews that

> Your predecessors have all, in fact, been historical materialists and it is an assumption of economic interests which find expression in politics and legislation, that is of primary importance. Their error was to assume the substructure and write about the superstructure ... Now, in addition, it could (theoretically) be quite conceivable that there was such a conflict of interest that resulted in legislation and which the British government attempted to enforce, but that all of this had not one jot of importance in the matter of the slow build up of settlement in Newfoundland. That is, that everyone was tilting at windmills (which is not unusual) and that the real reason for slow build-up of settlement is the reasonable one you

suggest. That is, what I am trying to say is that even if your predecessors "proved" all their theories, that in itself would not disprove yours.[151]

As a metaphor, "Fence Building" is a critique of the historical practice among both native-born and British-trained historians of Newfoundland. He too had been educated in the "constitutional" paradigm, but his professional practice in the archive had led him to test the hypothesis underlying the established historical narrative.

> By training and inclination these historians relied heavily upon constitutional documents – those which concentrate mainly upon political issues and which are written, in the main, by politicians and civil servants. Interested mainly in examining the evolution of Newfoundland ... into a colony, they used as a basis for comparison the evolution of other parts of the Empire. In this light Newfoundland was viewed as a deviation from some norm. It was "normal" for colonies to become self contained and independent, therefore Newfoundland was "deviant." Thus the historians began with two basic assumptions: that Newfoundland's colonial development is best measured by reference to colonial development elsewhere; and that Newfoundland's different development (its "retardation"!) was due to political and human factors. This alone can explain the lack of interest in the multitude of other factors – climactic, geographic, cultural and economic – which may also have shaped Newfoundland's "retardation."[152]

The essay was immediately influential among many scholars at Memorial, not only historians, and when read alongside C. Grant Head's 1971 PhD thesis, it established an economic rather than conflict-based explanation of Newfoundland's past. Head independently arrived at similar conclusions to those of Matthews. A historical geographer, Head had come at the problem of Newfoundland settlement patterns by looking at available resources and trade rather than imperial policy. "Newfoundland in past centuries," Head began in the 1976 published version of his thesis, "held a position of importance far beyond that which it holds today."[153]

The tenuous nature of Newfoundland's development meant that few archival records survived on the island itself, encouraging him to use the records of the places that had contact with Newfoundland to reconstruct its history. Head's first-hand knowledge of Newfoundland resources gained from fieldwork on the island and his evidence of settlement from his archival research on both sides of the Atlantic made obvious the error in the traditional idea that settlements were scattered along the coast because of a prohibition on settlement. People had settled, he realized, at places where there were resources, rather than, as legend had it, places where the Royal Navy could not find them.

But *Eighteenth Century Newfoundland* was not only an argument against the "folk myth" of the illegality of settlement, it was also a response to the historians in the same way that Matthews's essay had been. While historians of Newfoundland had focused on the political realm, Head looked for "the perceptions of the common man as much as those of the elite."[154] He also handled the evidence differently than did the historians of the 1960s. Matthews had written a narrative that spanned several centuries and sketched in the large trends, but he had not examined settlement in various bays with as fine a lens as had Head.

With the publications of Matthews and Head, the paradigm for the study of early Newfoundland history had shifted. But there was one dissenting voice. Rothney, one of those whom Matthews had criticized, wrote a statement of "defense against the charge." Rothney thought Matthews's claim that historians had assumed an unchanging group conflict between 1610 and 1832 was an exaggeration. Rothney pled innocent to the accusation that he had held a "timeless view of group conflict" and commented that "Matthews himself supplied ample evidence that all the writers to whom he refers, except Prowse and McLintock, were very much aware of the changing character of group conflicts between 1610 and 1832."[155] The essence of Matthews's argument, Rothney pointed out, was the claim that historians took legislative acts as their subject and assumed that nothing happened during periods that policy remained unchanged. Rothney denied that charge.

Matthews had overlooked another London thesis, that of Janet Patterson, he pointed out, which covered the period between 1713 and 1763, an era between the fenceposts. Rothney maintained that the period he chose for his own study was not dictated by any of the fenceposts Matthews had identified and that his own motives for studying Newfoundland history "had nothing to do with the subject of retarded colonization and the struggle for self-government." Rothney saw no examples of "group conflicts as a 'theory of causation'" in his own work and pointed out that he had attributed government anti-settlement policy in the late eighteenth century to the navy, not to conflict among merchants involved in trade and fishing.

Rothney insisted that Matthews's characterization of him and other authors (Prowse and McLintock excepted) as having "an interpretation of Newfoundland development, based on unchanging group conflicts" was inaccurate.[156] He did concede that historians had not distinguished between mercantile opposition to government and opposition to settlement, which he accepted was an important and innovative point. Rothney indeed assigned blame for the slow pace of settlement to the navy, and while he repeated the claim that West Country merchants had advocated the removal of settlers, that statement is incidental to the narratives developed in both his MA and PhD theses.[157] Far more explicit than conflict in his work is his observation that Newfoundland was "the only British dominion to surrender the right of responsible government" (which had happened the year he wrote his MA thesis) and his suggestion that his study of the eighteenth century might "explain the present peculiar position of the ancient island Dominion."[158]

Matthews also argued that local nationalist historians had portrayed the political reform movement that resulted in the advent of representative government in 1832 as "a struggle for liberty between Newfoundlanders, and an alliance between the Imperial Government and a reactionary band of West of England fishing merchants who opposed the growth of settlement and government on the Island."[159] He suggested that the reform campaign was a local manifestation of the desire for greater autonomy shared by colonial elites throughout the empire. The irony was that the reformers, who did so much to foster Newfoundland nationalism, were not natives of the island. "Since the St John's elite were in Newfoundland and not somewhere else, their demands were for colonial freedom," he wrote "had they been in Tasmania, Canada or any other part of the empire they would have been patriots of those regions."[160] The reformers mobilized opinion to support their personal ambitions by popularizing the interpretation of history that saw Newfoundland as having been held back by West of England interests and the Crown. The myth "that Newfoundland was impoverished and aggrieved solely because of an imperfect constitution and the indifference, even the hostility of the Imperial Government" was at the root of the error he had exposed in "Fence Building."[161]

Matthews had identified the underlying theme of conflict in the work of his predecessors, but their work ranged more widely than he had implied. Field, whom Matthews blamed for bringing the conflict thesis of the nineteenth-century historiography to twentieth-century scholars, indeed argued that the crucial factor in Newfoundland history was the duel to the death between (West of England) fishing captains and (London and Bristol based) sack ship men.[162] On the other hand, her thesis,

"Government of Newfoundland," was a broader survey of the economic history of the fishery than the title indicates. The American historian Ralph Greenlee Lounsbury also accepted that conflict between groups ran through the entire period of his study, 1634–1763. The Canadian-born historian W.L. Morton based his study on government records and, as Matthews identified, was interested in Newfoundland primarily as an example of imperial relations in the aftermath of the American Revolution.[163] It's also true that Morton proposed that "the historic conflict which for centuries disturbed British policy in Newfoundland" was indeed "the ship fishermen and by-boat keepers of Devon and Dorset [who] fought a losing battle with the resident fishery of Newfoundland, supported by the traders of London and Bristol."[164] Despite these caveats, Matthews swatted aside two centuries of historical scholarship and made a case for a new history that would be based on social and economic forces.

Both Matthews and Head found flaws in the historiography and established new questions, but they were not collaborators. In fact, Matthews recommended against the publication of Head's book, arguing that when explaining settlement it relied too heavily on factors that were internal to Newfoundland, such as his calculations of the yield of fish per boat and the availability of carbohydrates. Matthews believed that Head had given insufficient weight to external factors such as warfare and the English government's Navigation Acts. He also suggested that Head had erred in using data collected by the convoy commanders (the ranking Royal Navy admiral on the Newfoundland Station each summer), which Matthews claimed had been rejected as unreliable by observers in the eighteenth century and certainly should not be used by twentieth-century scholars.[165] Despite Matthews's reservations, Head's book was published, and in it he responded to the questions of the reliability of the data:

> From time to time these statistics have been attacked by students of Newfoundland as unreliable. Yet the same students go on to use compilations built from these detailed statistics, or quote statements or perceptions of authorities formulated from the data of the statistics. Our basic philosophy has been to get back as close to the original detail as the evidence allows, to graph it over time and space, and to see the *trends*. We have treated the statistical trends as *perceptions* of the reporter, not as hard factual statistical data, and have compared the perceptions successive independent observers. So handled, we have a data source for eighteenth

century Newfoundland better than we have for much of the nineteenth and twentieth centuries, when censuses became much less frequent and spatially so precise.[166]

As a graduate student in geography in the 1960s, Head had studied the distribution of people and resources at a time at which the government was resettling the population of remote coves and islands to "growth centres." That led to an interest in the history of settlement. Starting from a different disciplinary emphasis than Matthews, and having examined the resource endowment of rural Newfoundland, Head arrived at an environmental and economic explanation of settlement patterns. Head cited Matthews's point that the opposition to settlement was short-lived, but his analysis was little influenced by Matthews.[167] Head also criticized the "traditional Newfoundland Historiography" for asserting that the scattered nature of settlement was a reflection of the illegality of settlement, "a questionable fact in itself," and argued ecological factors explained the distribution of the population rather than government oppression.[168]

[I]t has been popular to assert that the present scattered distribution of population around the island can be attributed to illegality of permanent settlement, and the consequent scattering of people to small settlements strung along 6,000 miles of coastline in order to escape detection by British naval officers and migratory fishing vessels. This is a folk-myth and has not been dispelled by the scholars.[169]

Head concluded that "the supposed illegality of permanent settlement ... was an illusion ... even when law on paper, it had little impact upon the actual state of settlement."[170] While Head had started with a different methodology and set of evidence and reached conclusions different from his historian predecessors, Matthews started with the same methodology and read the same documents that everyone else had – but along the way had an epiphany that his predecessors shared an assumption that was unsupported by the evidence.

Story and Morgan had recruited Matthews to replace Rothney, not only for what he might write but thinking that "his spade-work on the British sources might be one way for us to get our hands on primary material for the Library and/or Provincial Archives."[171] Matthews's and Head's work began a new phase in the writing of early Newfoundland history. Head was a pioneer in environmental history, while

Matthews's legacy as a collector and founder of the Maritime History Archive had an important role in Newfoundland scholarship.

The publication of "Fence Building" was tardy, and it appeared in a magazine rather than a peer-reviewed journal, despite it having been accepted for publication, because he did not revise it. There are several instances in which he put his efforts into other things, rather than bringing his work into publishable shape. His most widely circulated writing was a 1973 series of thirty CBC school broadcasts that was available for several years as a bound photocopy and published posthumously as *Lectures on the History of Newfoundland 1500–1830*.[172] The *Lectures* brought his view of the history of Newfoundland to students in an accessible form but without scholarly apparatus or the discussion of the work of other historians. Professors often assigned the *Lectures* to students as a textbook for the course Newfoundland to 1815.

Subsequent academic historians also found frustrating that his work, which had convinced specialists, had not put to rest popular myths such as the illegality of settlement. Matthews correctly identified these historians as repeating the conflict thesis without looking for evidence and of being interested in Newfoundland primarily as a case to test ideas in other historiographic traditions. The persuasiveness of "Fence Building" should not blind us to the similarities in structure and sources between Matthews's 1968 thesis and the earlier historians. His thesis shares the same fenceposts, sources, and political narrative as his predecessors. It fit within the constitutionalist frame of imperial history and the older narratives of the history of Newfoundland more than is commonly recognized because the later essay so persuasively set out where his predecessors had been wrong. Revisiting "Fence Building" also shows that Matthews had moved past his own training to criticize the tradition within which he had been working. It is too easy to read back into his thesis the radical break with the historical literature in his later essay. For the sake of clarity, we can consider his historiographic contribution as having two elements. In his 1968 thesis, Matthews made the intuitive leap that there had been no "division between 'settlers' and 'fishermen.'"[173]

Head's, Matthews's, and Alexander's work became a starting place for the study of Newfoundland economic history. Subsequent authors, such as O'Flaherty, made effective use of Matthews's historiographic argument, although he later had reservations about Matthews's dismissal of the efficacy of the legal prohibitions on settlement.[174] The preponderance of professional opinion favours Matthews's view that any ban on settlement was short-lived and ineffectual. His conclusions have also held up well to subsequent inquiries. While many of his contemporaries in Britain and North America engaged more explicitly with theories and tested them against evidence, Matthews remained an inductive historian. While Alexander embraced quantitative history – computer analysis and team projects were, for him, the new history – Matthews's mind worked differently. He hoped that he would be able to induce what had happened in the past from the documents.

Morgan and Rothney had once hoped to establish a scientific history of Newfoundland, but with the historical profession developing into a range of topics, methods, and theories, the overarching, single explanation of a national history became more elusive, not less. Rather than attempt the synthesis that Rothney had once envisioned, the new historians compiled a collection of essays – *Newfoundland in the Nineteenth and Twentieth Centuries: Essays in Interpretation*. The initiative for this came from Neary, who enlisted Hiller as a co-editor. The book exemplified the work of the generation of Memorial historians working in the 1970s – providing key works of young faculty members and graduate students.

In addition to the historians already discussed, the book featured Shannon Ryan, a Newfoundlander who wrote an MA under Matthews's supervision before doing a PhD at the University of London. Ryan took as his life's work the study of the codfishery and seal fishery after 1815 (the year that Matthews's study of the fishery ended).[175] The collection had no pretensions to being definitive, but it was implicitly unified by the same question that had been posed by so many of their predecessors: Why had Newfoundland's path towards greater measures of self-government and its efforts at economic diversification failed? The work was now more sophisticated and did not attempt a single narrative. Despite its obsolescence from the point of view of professional historians, however, Prowse's *History* remained influential among non-historians, in part because they liked narrative and because it fit with their nationalist sense of what history should be.[176]

Alexander's death at a young age left his colleagues with a feeling not only of personal loss but also sense of unfulfilled promise. At the end of his career, Alexander argued for cultural factors, such as entrepreneurial weakness, marketing, and low levels of literacy, to explain Newfoundland's relatively poor economic performance. The ACSP was completed by his colleagues, but Sager and Panting made clear that it would have taken different directions had Alexander completed it. His death prompted a search for an established Maritime historian who could complete the project. That search was abandoned when an opportunity to hire the Canadian historian of the working class, Greg Kealey, arose. Several members of the department shared an interest in labour history (Panting, W.J. Cherwinski, and Hugh Tuck), and through hiring Kealey, who also brought with him the journal *Labour/Le Travail*, the department became a major centre for the study of Canadian labour history. With Linda Kealey encouraging a revitalization of women's history and Greg Kealey bringing study of working-class culture, many graduate students in the Department of History became engaged in "history from the bottom up." This further encouraged the longer-term movement away from political and economic history. The structuralism popular in the social sciences also provoked a reaction. The fourth generation of scholars working on Newfoundland history tended towards microhistory and the emphasis on human agency rather than institutional structure.

In a profession that strove for objectivity even when realizing it was an unattainable ideal, the historians of Newfoundland played out with local particularities within the larger trends of British, American, and Canadian historiographies. Rothney, a father of modern historical research at Memorial, tried to establish a scientific foundation that rejected the nationalist teleology of his Newfoundland-born predecessors. He drew on Prowse directly and indirectly through the historians at the University of London, however, while using him as a foil to establish his credentials as a scientific historian. The professional agenda that emerged at Memorial in the 1950s entailed rejecting nationalist shibboleths such as Newfoundland being Britain's oldest colony and it being the great nursery of seamen, but other beliefs, such as the illegality of settlement, were not questioned. Rothney and many of the others of the Historical Research Committee left Memorial but had laid foundations in the form of a provincial archive, a bibliography, and a series of post-graduate theses.

Nineteenth-century historians wrote history as the development of nations. Twentieth-century historians, such as Rothney, were critical of the idea that Newfoundland was a feasible nation but still worked with the category of nation while working towards an international future.[177] Morgan and Harris devoted most of their efforts to administration, and despite writing little, count among the key figures in promoting the Newfoundland studies movement. Both were outport-born and educated at Memorial and in Britain. Their British connections, and their friendship with Story, provided recruitment opportunities to revitalize the study of history. And Story's interest in a social history encouraged him to look beyond the imperial outlook when seeking new faculty members. The informal policy of sending promising students to the United Kingdom for postgraduate work and expecting them to get teaching experience at another university did not work as hoped. Many young academics such as Neary and Noel settled into lives elsewhere and could not be enticed back with the modest salaries Memorial was able to offer. The University of London had been the closest thing to a centre for Newfoundland history until Memorial's Department of History established itself, and the British scholars there and at Cambridge and Oxford had a constitutional and diplomatic bias that was difficult to move beyond. Both non-academic Newfoundland historians and those working in other departments, such as Seary and Story, criticized the political history emphasis and argued for a social history of everyday life.

Matthews and Alexander, Neary and Hiller, and MacDonald and Ryan reinterpreted the island's past in significant ways. Several of the Newfoundland historians of the 1970s died young, forcing another transition. Alexander's last essay on Newfoundland economic history was completed by friends after his death in 1980. Matthews suffered from a spine condition that required several surgeries and left him in considerable pain during the last five years of his life, and he died at forty-six years old, just twenty years after Story suggested to him that he study the West of England fishery. Hiller and Neary continued to write political history into the twenty-first century, and Ryan completed important studies of the marketing of salted cod and the seal fishery. The collaboration between Keith Matthews and David Alexander broke with the past in significant ways and established new paradigms for Newfoundland history. Matthews recognized that the nineteenth-century Newfoundlanders and the historians at the University of London shared a belief that conflict between competing factions impeded development of the colony. But he too seemed to take it as part of his role to undermine the nationalist mythology in both his polemic against the conflict thesis and in his portrayal of the first generation of Newfoundland political reformers as motivated by the aspirations of their class, not by solidarity with the other members of the nation. Matthews felt an attachment to Newfoundland, as did Alexander, perhaps, as much as anything, in a reflection of their instinctual desire to be on the side of the underdog.

Unlike the lexicographers, the historians lacked a methodological argument with their counterparts in other communities to unite them, although both groups shared a preservationist agenda. Much more explicitly than among the linguists, the Newfoundland historians were agents of the modernization they described. By creating an archive and other research tools, by looking to other nations that got it right, and by attempting to understand the impediments to good governance and economic development, they embodied part of the larger modernization of the province's intellectual class. The collapse of responsible government and the chronic underperformance of the Newfoundland economy had to be understood in a useful way if Newfoundland was to leave the past behind.[178] For the historians of the Newfoundland studies movement, the writing of scientific history could provide a way to reject the mythologies and a guide to adopting more rational modern policies.

Chapter Three

Herbert Halpert and *Christmas Mumming* in *Newfoundland*

Our first major book on Newfoundland folklore came about because of a fortuitous circumstance. My office was on the third floor of the Arts and Administration building ... and the first four Institute [of Social and Economic Research] Fellows, young anthropologists, had their cubbyholes in an office across the floor. They visited me to use my library and also to discuss unfamiliar folklore activities they had observed in their fieldwork. All of them had been fascinated by the Newfoundland and Labrador Christmas custom of mummering or janneying.[1]

Memorial developed a Department of Folklore that made its mark in international scholarship by leveraging Newfoundland's oral culture and by using students to engage in research. As we have seen, scholars in both English and history imagined themselves as conducting scientific inquiry into the society – so too did the early folklorists. The mission to collect and preserve evidence that motivated Seary, Story, and Rothney was matched in passion by those who took up the discipline of folklore. That is not coincidental; the study of folklore at Memorial grew out of the agenda of the Department of English.

Seary built a Department of English that emphasized linguistics and folklore in the 1950s and, in the early 1960s, hired the American folklorist Herbert Halpert. In 1968 Seary and Story supported the folklorists and linguists in their bids to form separate departments. They agreed that leaving these fields within the umbrella of the Department of English would "distort" the development of the disciplines, and that of the Department of English as well.[2] The study of languages and folk culture not only became specializations for which Memorial University became widely respected, but Story's friendship with Halpert helped shift his interests further towards oral popular culture. Their collaboration resulted in their editing an interdisciplinary anthology titled *Christmas Mumming in Newfoundland*. An examination of that book reveals what Halpert described as the two ideals in Newfoundland folklore research: bringing a group of outside experts in different disciplines to bear on a phenomenon, as in the mumming book, and training a group of Newfoundland students to collect and analyse their own culture. It also shows the role that cultural capital, in this case in the form of Halpert's library, played in sustaining research.

Just as the writing of Newfoundland history had been an activity of scholars outside the academy, so too had the collection of folklore. In the late nineteenth century the study and promotion of folk culture went hand in hand with the emergence of nation states. "Many peoples," as the folklorist Carole Carpenter-Henderson put it, "have valued oral traditions as a means of recapturing and/or maintaining what they considered to be their true nature, that is, they have viewed folklore as a mode of expressing their cultural purity" in the context of foreign oppression of national aspirations.[3] Similarly, some Newfoundlanders turned to history and the collection of oral culture during the Great Depression; the period between 1934 and 1949, when Newfoundland was ruled by a British-appointed commission; the Second World War, when the country was occupied by American and Canadian troops defending the island; and after 1949, as the country was being Canadianized.

Joseph R. Smallwood, Frederick Emerson, L.E.F. English, Gerald S. Doyle, and Nimshi Crewe were all part of a nationalist movement to preserve and revive interest in Newfoundland oral culture as well as their interest in history. Foreign intellectuals had also conducted fieldwork in Newfoundland. The English folk song scholar Maude Karpeles, for example, found cooperative local people to aid her Newfoundland fieldwork, but such collectors were often motivated by a desire to search in isolated regions for the vestiges of pre-modern culture more than any desire to understand the region itself.

Once Memorial University established a research agenda in the late 1950s, it was not surprising that faculty members realized the potential resource of the oral culture at their doorstep. Canadian folk culture scholars were slower to turn their attention to Newfoundland than had been the British or Americans, but shortly after Confederation Canadians began to include Newfoundland folk culture into their corpus. Kenneth Peacock, to take the most influential example, conducted extensive fieldwork in rural Newfoundland and compiled a two-volume collection of folk songs. Such attention encouraged the perception of the island and Labrador as places that were productive for research in folk culture.

One of those at Memorial who realized that the university should be part of these studies was the first university librarian, Sadie Organ, who drafted a proposal to encourage the study of folk culture – something she felt was urgent given the social changes underway. A St John's native with a mathematics and physics degree from McGill, she taught math at Memorial, completed a library science degree, and led the university's library during the period that it was establishing its collections. In 1957 she wrote Emerson, the province's representative on the newly formed Canada Council, reporting on what was happening at Memorial and setting out her ideas.

President Gushue had hoped to have J.H. Delargy of the Irish Folklore Commission give a series of lectures on the subject, but illness prevented Delargy's visit. Organ initiated a correspondence with the Irish scholar and hoped to encourage one of his assistants to come to Newfoundland "to engage in the work of rescuing our folklore from oblivion." In writing to Emerson, she wondered if the Canada Council might fund the trip or if it might send a Newfoundlander to Ireland for training. The "active work of collecting and preserving written and spoken records" was, she felt, "urgent, because with each passing year traditions and legends are being lost and in the not so distant future effective studies in our folklore will no longer be possible."[4] Few of Organ's contemporaries would have disagreed with her urgency, or with her desire for an archival collection of oral culture that she saw as residing in the memories of older people. But progress on that front was several years away. When Memorial did start collecting folklore it was integrated more fully with teaching than that of the Irish Commission. The Irish Commission was an independent institution and not part of a university; while it collected oral culture, it did not emphasize analysis and lacked students of its own to reproduce folklore as an academic discipline.[5]

Seary and Story had launched linguistic research at Memorial, and in 1962 attempted to do the same for the study of other aspects of oral culture by hiring an established American folklorist who had experience in field recordings. Seary learned from one of his contacts in the United States that Herbert Halpert was looking for work and wrote to him with a job offer.[6]

Born to Hungarian immigrant parents in New York City in 1911, Halpert lived in public housing in midtown Manhattan, less than half a block from the East River, an ethnically diverse part of the city that included Bohemians, Czechs, and Poles.[7] After attending a public school, he graduated with a degree in English from New York University in 1934, at the nadir of the Great Depression, and was fortunate to get work with the Federal Recreation Division of the Works Progress Administration. Not all Americans were qualified for the construction jobs the WPA sponsored, so it also employed thousands of writers, musicians, and artists whose employment prospects were particularly poor. Halpert used the job as an opportunity to collect children's rhymes and songs, a collection that one of his former teachers brought to the attention of prominent anthropologist Ruth Benedict. She encouraged Halpert to enrol at Columbia University, where he trained in anthropology under the supervision of ethnomusicologist George Herzog.

Both Benedict and Herzog had been students of the founder of modern American anthropology and folklore, Franz Boas, and Columbia was, at that time, perhaps the top school in the field in the United States. Halpert's MA thesis, titled "Folk Rhymes of New York City Children," drew on his early collecting; it still was not completed after the Second World War, but it encouraged his interest in folk culture. The folk rhymes study attracted attention; the American Folklore Society wanted to publish it, but the officer in charge of providing subventions was shocked that Halpert had included rhymes that alluded to sex.[8] The experience dissuaded Halpert from publishing the rhymes, and by then he had started collecting folk songs. There was an established method in folk culture studies of historical comparative work, and Herzog had gotten Halpert interested in a functional approach to the study of the songs (not just collecting them but studying the function the songs served), by encouraging him to ask questions about the material. Rather than just noting the songs, he started asking the basic question of singers, "why do you sing these songs?"[9]

In contrast to the nineteenth-century evolutionists who saw all cultures progressing through the same stages, Boas had promoted the idea that cultures were limited by their local environment and "borrowing was the primary mechanism for cultural change."[10] Turn of the twentieth-century anthropologists had searched among isolated populations for what they believed to be degenerate versions of original myths that had survived from ancient times. The comparison of variants among those myths, it was hoped, might reveal the ancient elite culture text behind the forms and allow scholars to map the diffusion of tales and myths across space and cultures.

Following the lead of the British social anthropologists Bronislaw Malinowski and A.R. Radcliffe-Brown in the early twentieth century, many scholars in both Britain and the United States had adopted functionalism and structural functionalism – approaches that superceded the earlier interests in comparative study of the survival of ancient tales or traditions. This was the intellectual milieu within which Halpert began his work. Functionalism shifted the emphasis of fieldwork to examining how a contemporary culture, which was often assumed to be a closed system, operated. Similarly, structural functionalism started from the premises that non-modern culture tended towards equilibrium and that the function of each part of the culture was the stability of the whole.[11]

In addition to these approaches, following such scholars as Claude Lévi-Strauss, structuralism dominated the work of many folklorists and other social scientists from the 1950s to the 1970s. Structuralism emphasized the symbols and underlying structures of society over the study of the actual surface of culture (the content of things such as songs). Structuralist folklorists were less interested in the history of a particular tradition, for example, than they were in the hidden binary oppositions within aspects of culture. Anthropologists and folklorists had also shifted their attention from the description of aboriginal groups, the natives of Southeast Asia, and Africans towards the study of communities of people of European ancestry. That change reflected broader reorganizations within North American society; urbanization had created whole new social groups that might be understood using the tools of anthropology, and there were opportunities for fieldwork within the United States during the New Deal and post-war expansion of universities. The interest in the "communication of tradition among ethnic and regional groups" that Simon J. Bronner identified among American folklorists during the second half of the twentieth century gave the folklore studies of Newfoundland outports relevance for academic folk culture collectors.[12] Each of these bodies of theory also provided social scientists a way of describing to their peers what they observed during their Newfoundland fieldwork.

By 1936 Halpert was supervising the Folklore and Folksong Department of Federal One, a division of the WPA that included the Federal Music Project and the Federal Theater Project; it was a position that allowed him to conduct field collecting in the American South. He had also started fieldwork in the New Jersey Pines region, fieldwork that he continued during weekends.[13] Some of his co-workers within the WPA, such as pioneering ethnomusicologist Charles Seeger, shared his interest in collecting folk culture. They justified field collecting by hoping that such collections would one day assist in writing dramatic productions. Since they had no specific idea as to what might be useful for some hypothetical theatrical production, Halpert felt justified in collecting everything, although he continued to be most interested in folk songs at this point in his life. Like his contemporary Alan Lomax, Halpert was a pioneer in using the very early portable recording technology to conduct field recordings – travelling extensively in a former ambulance since it was one of the few vehicles capable of carrying the equipment and the discs upon which the recordings could be made.

The WPA in general, and the Federal Theater Project in particular, received a lot of attention among Republican Party members of Congress for the progressive politics of many of the creative people working for it, and many of its activities were shut down in 1939. In the 1980s, Halpert replied to a question about the ideology:

Let's put it this way. There was a terrible Depression. Any sensitive, literate person felt it was wrong to have people go hungry and ragged. Look at the marvelous Farm Security Documentary photographs. They SHOWED what things were like in America. All of us in that generation were "left" by inclination if not necessarily by party affiliation. Remember you either thought that Hoover was the Reagan of his day or you were deaf, dumb and blind. When I hitchhiked across the US in 1937, people were talking about revolution. Roosevelt stopped that by his actions – and the Republicans hated his guts. I was often invited to join the Communist party, but had a personal disinclination to have a boss tell me what to do.[14]

He was confident that many of his co-workers of the day were also leftists but thought that made little difference to their collecting, and he had worked with communists in strikes. But he never joined the Communist Party; his reasons, he told a friend, were simple: "I've always resented authoritarian figures, whether at work, or in the army, or deans and presidents at universities."[15]

While attending the 1937 meeting of the American Folklore Society, Halpert met many academic folklorists, including two members of the English Department of Albany State Teacher's College who explained to him how they had used their students to collect folklore from their home communities. That encouraged Halpert to use student collectors in his subsequent teaching. At that meeting he also met Stith Thompson of the English Department at Indiana University, who was organizing summer "institutes" that provided training in folklore collecting.

While he was studying anthropology at Columbia, he found he didn't like having to take the courses in archaeology or linguistics that were requirements for the anthropology degree. Since Halpert was not interested in anthropology and anthropologists were not interested in folk songs, Benedict, whose work was also functionalist and psychological, suggested he go to Indiana to study folklore. Thompson was at that time perhaps the only man in the United States who would supervise a thesis in folklore.[16] In 1940 Halpert started his studies in English, working under Thompson, but was interrupted by service in the US Army between 1943 and 1946. That period of his life was not a complete loss, however; he used his posting with Transport Command to collect folktales in different areas during his off-duty hours.

By chance he had visited Newfoundland during the war and found it was the easiest and most lively collecting he had done.[17] In an amusing story he liked to tell, Halpert met Smallwood while in Gander; Smallwood advised him that there was little folklore left to collect in Newfoundland – that he had collected it all during his tenure as the Barrelman. Even in his brief visits, one to Stephenville and two to Gander, Halpert recognized that Newfoundland was a great place to collect folklore but doubted he would ever have the opportunity to visit again.[18]

After the war, he finished writing his Columbia MA thesis (on the material he had collected during the 1930s) and began writing his doctoral study – "Folktales and Legends of the New Jersey Pines."[19] Even without being published in his lifetime, that later thesis became widely known among folklorists. By the time of his return to civilian life he was an experienced collector of both folk song and folktales, and he was poised to make his mark on the discipline of folklore – a field that Halpert and his contemporaries were trying to establish on a more professional basis by both creating space for it within the academy and by establishing a specific subject matter, methodology, and body of theory.

Halpert's primary interests had shifted from folk song to folktale, and working with Thompson had a lasting effect. Thompson had earlier compiled his famous *Motif-index of Folk Literature*, which compared common elements in folktales from a variety of cultures as a step towards mapping the diffusion of tales over space.[20] Halpert had read widely, and Thompson handed over to his student the task of annotating a collection. That established Halpert's reputation as someone who wrote very complete notes, and for the rest of his career he devoted much of his energy and intellect to collection, categorization, and annotation of oral culture.

> I was insecure, so I became a demon of annotation. I always stress the functional, but I always feel I have to prove myself to the historical geographers and you do that by being a better annotator than anyone else, by knowing more. So I am better known for my notes than for the theoretical things.[21]

Halpert later reflected on his training as having been "evenly divided between anthropology and English," and thus he felt able to speak to the "sharp division in our society between the anthropological folklorists and the regional folklorists."[22] The former were more likely to study the diffusion of a tale across geography, which explains his reference to "historical geographers" in the quotation above, while the latter immersed themselves in the oral culture of a particular region (often the region in which they lived). Halpert was equally at home with the third approach – the study of ballads or tales as literary texts. Despite these divisions, no real disciplinary boundary between anthropology and folklore existed; people such as Halpert were often trained in anthropology, or in English, and strove to develop folklore as its own field.

Literary-influenced scholars often disliked fieldwork, and, as he put it, "the anthropologist, preoccupied with the unwritten culture of primitive peoples, ignores the problems of Anglo-American folklore."[23] Furthermore the study of folklore had moved beyond "the now outmoded view that folklore consisted only of 'survivals'" of cultural elements from a supposed earlier evolutionary stage of culture.[24] His training and, even more so, his experience encouraged him to argue that folklorists "should not hesitate to draw freely on the techniques of anthropological, literary, musical and historical research."[25] He also emphasized recording the context of the folk culture collection, such as noting the name of the informant and publishing information about the performance, during an era in which many scholars ignored the informant and fetishized the tale.

By the late 1950s Halpert had a reputation as a field collector and had published widely. After returning to civilian life he was elected president of the American Folklore Society and, based on his extensive CV, was hired as head of the English Department and division head at Murray State College in Kentucky, where, much as Story was then starting to do in St John's for the Newfoundland lexicon, Halpert recruited students to collect oral culture from their families and neighbours.[26] "This has been my major thing," Halpert later commented, "making students collect."[27] He believed that people from within a culture were better able to collect folklore because they understood it – but they had to be taught folkloristic method and perspective. For that reason, he spent a lot of time with individual students questioning them about the meaning of various things and, in the process, raised their awareness of their culture.

Kentucky had been wonderful for collecting folklore, but he felt the college was intellectually stagnant. Early career success as an administrator and the marginal status of folklore within the academy hurt him; he found that moving to another university was difficult since he was a professor and head of department and no one wanted to hire him at that salary. To get out of Kentucky he took a job as dean of English and sociology at Blackburn College in Illinois between 1956 and 1960, despite feeling "deaned to death by deanish piddlings" and having little interest in administrative work.[28] In Illinois he taught folklore and anthropology, but he had little opportunity to collect and as a lifelong one-finger typist, he was frustrated by the university's unwillingness to allow him the use of student labour to type for him. No one would hire him to work as a folklorist. "When I was Dean at Blackburn College in Illinois," he later wrote, "it became obvious that I had a bleak future ahead of me in which people would expect me to become president of some small college, probably one located in Jerkwater Junction."[29]

He was offered a visiting professorship in folklore at the University of Arkansas, but the president of Blackburn would not give him leave so he had to resign to take the folklore job. While in Arkansas, his wife, Violetta (Letty) Maloney Halpert, wrote more than a hundred letters seeking a job for him, resulting in a one year appointment as visiting professor of English in New Paltz, New York (a liberal arts college half way between Albany and New York City).[30] Letty was born in 1919 in Pennsylvania and had taken an English degree from Wilson College and an MA at the University of Indiana, where she met her future husband. She was among the first ranks of women to enlist in the US Navy during the war and was promoted to the rank of lieutenant before being discharged in 1951.

These administrative appointments at US regional colleges were the only work Herbert could get. It is possible that his progressive politics and experience working at the WPA before the war made him undesirable to many university presidents during the McCarthy era.[31] Folk singers such as Pete Seeger, who Halpert had met in 1939 at his father Charles Seeger's house, had kept alive the association between folk song and protest music. Federal One had employed leftists, including the radical folklorist Benjamin Botkin, whom Halpert liked, and had been shut down after being investigated by the House Committee on Un-American Activities.[32] Even if folklore had not had the taint of communism in some people's eyes, the subject matter seemed inappropriate to many scholars of the top-rank universities of the day.

Only a couple of universities had programs in folklore, and Halpert was one of the generation of scholars who saw themselves as folklorists and not anthropologists. Folklorists had to shed their history of intervening in the culture and remake themselves as social scientists, before they could find acceptance in American universities, and that was not easy to do.[33] There were no appointments available for him in the United States that would have given him the opportunity to shape a program in folklore.[34] Something of his vision for the field can be seen in his presidential address to the American Folklore Society in 1955. He made a case for attention to context and function:

> We are underdeveloped in that we do not have enough studies on the meaning of folklore in communities by those who have studied them over a long period of time ... Some of us have talked about studying folklore in its setting, but most of us are only "visiting firemen" in the folk regions where we collect. For most of us it would be difficult to gain a thorough knowledge of the folklore of a region ... by living therefore many years or settling for life. Perhaps the best solution in this undeveloped area is to train more students from rich folklore regions and send them back home to do the kind of complete functional study that only someone born to or completely accepted by a regional culture can do.[35]

Halpert had the opportunity to design just such a program when Memorial called. He initially turned down the offer. He had only visited the military bases of Stephenville and Gander during wintertime, and Newfoundland seemed both remote and unappealing, and he was still hoping that an American university might offer him a position. Seary telephoned again, increasing the pay offer and offering to pay to move his substantial personal library. Halpert and Letty remained reluctant about moving the family to Newfoundland but ultimately accepted the appointment. As Herbert said: "They wanted me to start a folklore department, no one had ever wanted me to start a folklore department."[36] Canadian universities had not experienced the McCarthy period of purging leftists from universities, and many Americans with leftist credentials found work in Canada, but more to the point, no one would have imagined studying rural Newfoundland culture had much revolutionary potential.

His decision to leave the United States to relocate to a small and relatively new university in Newfoundland reflects several factors. He would have known of Newfoundland's potential from the fieldwork that American folklore collectors such as McEdwards Leach had done. He would also have been aware of the advantages of fieldwork in a largely unstudied area that his contemporaries viewed as a bit of an El Dorado. The faculty appointment in St John's gave him a chance to train (and use) students and to shape the field of folklore on a different basis than his contemporary and rival Richard Dorson was then doing in Indiana. Dorson insisted his students research the historical background of tales and songs, an approach that Halpert thought was nonsense. Halpert wanted to encourage his students to collect folklore – the armchair work of comparing folk cultures could be done by scholars at a later date.

Although he accepted students from other countries, he especially wanted to have local students. To start, most of the rural Newfoundlanders, even those in their early twenties, had, in his view, "witnessed modernization." The students had seen dramatic changes in communications and transportation and could be made into excellent collectors when trained to make them aware of their own culture (rather than taking it for granted as normal). But Halpert would spend a significant amount of time discussing the context and significance of each item of folk culture with the students, and he encouraged them to publish material they had collected. Students were much more than field collectors. They were, in meaningful ways, collaborators. Students could not do the comparative work, in his view, but they could collect material, aid in its interpretation, and get academic credit for doing so.[37] Perhaps more immediately important – he had no other job offers.

In a wide-ranging interview with the folklorist Carole Henderson Carpenter, Halpert described his two approaches to the field. The Christmas mumming book, which will be discussed below, represented one kind of research ideal, he said, that of having outside experts examine a phenomenon from as many angles as possible. The other approach to folklore was to train Newfoundland students to examine their own culture. They would study a little geography, a bit of anthropology, and some history and then become exposed to as many genres of folklore as possible. That would enable the Newfoundland student to become "a well-trained, detached native." He or she would then recognize elements of his or her own culture that are never made explicit within folk communities (people never speak openly about things they take for granted that everyone knows). But unlike an outsider to the culture, the Newfoundlander would have immediate insight into what the culture meant to the people practising it. "I've been leading up to this my whole life" Halpert said. His aim was that the research theses written by the students would be published. "The Newfoundland student should be the one to interpret the Newfoundland material – his own material," Halpert argued, "not present it to the archive and have some outsider then try to do it."[38]

When first teaching at Memorial, Halpert asked for term papers from students but was dissatisfied with the results, so adopted a method used by a former colleague in Arkansas who didn't take attendance in classes but required students to submit a card that had some item of folk culture on it to be counted as present for each class.[39] Halpert's cards were large to encourage students to be expansive in their description of material, and much of it was short items such as riddles, proverbs, or folk beliefs. The cards also recorded the name, sex, occupation, and home of the informant and the name of the collector – so researchers could reconstruct much of the context of the items. One half of their grade was based on these submissions.

The method raises the question of the power differential between Halpert and his student collectors. He believed that the activity of collecting and of reflecting on their own culture was an effective way of teaching the discipline, and not just a way of using them as unpaid labour to collect data from their friends and families. Some students may have felt otherwise. Students voted with their feet, and most chose to take other classes. Only four students took Halpert's folklore course in its first year, and only five in the second, but the number of student collectors grew. Halpert had been an early user of disc recorders in the field himself, and the Department of Folklore now purchased tape recorders for student use when they went into the field. The recorders

3.1. Herbert Halpert. (Photographic Services Collection, QEII Library, Memorial University of Newfoundland.)

were free for the students to borrow, with the condition that the student deposit a copy of the tape at the folklore archive.[40] Among both graduate and undergraduate student collectors, Halpert was the person who decided what was noteworthy in the culture and what was not. While he encouraged students to collect material of all genres, he especially encouraged material that he valued. As he put it: "Obviously things I am interested in I will praise up."[41]

Upon arriving in the Department of English, Halpert enjoyed the support of administrators, such as Morgan, Seary, and colleagues whose Newfoundland studies agenda fit with his own professional goals. As he recounted on the occasion of his being made professor emeritus:

Memorial University was both new and small, but it was flexible. It was run by men who had no hesitation about doing things for the first time in English-speaking Canada. Introducing folklore as a university subject is one example, another I mention primarily because it had a direct bearing on our folklore work was the setting up of the Institute of Social and Economic Research, a daring project undertaken against the advice of several mainland universities ... Besides daring to try new ventures, a series of university administrators supported fully all individuals who showed genuine interest in studying any aspect of the Newfoundland environment, physical or human.[42]

In Story, in particular, Halpert had a colleague whom he admired and with whom he saw eye to eye. Story was at ease with the proverbs of Erasmus and in conversations with his neighbours and was, in the view of one of the students, the sort of man that Halpert wanted to be.[43] Both men were book collectors, and they shared an education in the literary canon and a common commitment to collecting a broad range of oral culture. Halpert was also an Anglophile, so joining a department that had more than its share of Englishmen and Newfoundlanders with an Oxford pedigree had its attractions. Halpert also shared Story's respect for the ways that Newfoundlanders spoke and developed a commitment to Newfoundland studies as a field. The anthropologist John Szwed recalled an incident in which a woman made a pejorative comment about Newfoundland speech, only to have Halpert give her an impromptu, but erudite, lecture upon the venerable European literary antecedents of local culture.[44]

Herbert Halpert's immediate priority upon arriving in St John's was to build up the library's collection of indexes, bibliographies, and folklore journals that would be necessary for teaching and research. As her husband's collaborator, Letty Halpert contributed much to the development of the field in Newfoundland. She was sometimes employed on a Canada Council grant, organizing archival collections, but Memorial's policy of not employing married women as faculty prevented her from taking a full-time teaching appointment. She collected folktales and published some of the material, but her major study of the folklore surrounding death was not completed.

An appointment as head of the acquisition's department of the library put Letty Halpert in a position to build the university's collection of international folklore publications and laid the basis for much of the work of others. The library started by acquiring books and journals from the United Kingdom and Ireland, since Newfoundland traditions were often of English or Irish origin, and Canadian and American sources next. The library did not need to start from nothing, in hiring Herbert the university paid for the transportation to Newfoundland of his personal collection of 10,000 volumes. (Working in American colleges that lacked research libraries had also encouraged Halpert to build up his own library.) Letty used her husband's books as bibliographies to generate lists of publications for the library to acquire, and they served as reference texts for many of Halpert's colleagues and students.[45] She also worked closely with her husband, and with Widdowson and Kirwin, in identifying books to be purchased.

Like that of Agnes O'Dea, Violetta Halpert's contribution to scholarship at the university was valued by her male contemporaries, but it was mostly confined to support for the work that men wrote. As with many couples of their generation, she devoted much of her effort to supporting her husband's career. She helped him in preparing his many publications, frequently serving as an editor whose knowledge of the literature matched his own.[46] Pay at the library was poor, especially for someone without a professional library degree, so she did not remain there for her whole career.

Herbert Halpert's interest in folklore was not based on the idealization of the folk that had motivated earlier generations of enthusiasts and some of his contemporaries. "In the nineteenth and early twentieth centuries it was traditional," he told an audience of the Bibliographic Society of Canada, "to think that folklore was found only among a mythical, uniform group called "the folk," usually thought of as isolated, rural uneducated and probably poor, almost the romantic concept of the 'natural' man."[47] American folklorists, he reported, no longer thought of "one mystically-unified 'folk,'" but understood that groups "set off from others by any principle: age, religion, education, language, ethnic origin, occupation, geographic location, etc.," shared a folklore of their own.[48] "In Newfoundland we have a unique opportunity and challenge," he explained.

> The island originally had 1300 separate communities set off from each other by geography, ethnic origin, occupation, religion, and educational

level. Any one of these characteristics would set off a folk group: here we had an unusual intensification. Each of these communities had its own rich traditions, chiefly derived from England, Ireland, Scotland or even France, but in most cases thoroughly adapted and changed to the New-foundland situation. Furthermore, because of this intensification the folk-lore found in these communities was not merely a survival, but a vigorous and integral part of the life of the community. Thus, as in nowhere else in the English-speaking world, all folk customs can still be studied as a vital part of the community's everyday living pattern.[49]

Folklore at Memorial would thus not be a quest for the most primitive tale or oldest ballad (preferably one previously collected by the Harvard Professor of English, Francis James Child), but a wide-ranging collec-tion of many aspects of folk culture and an examination of the functions of that folklore within communities. Although his early interests had been in collecting folk song, with the exception of "Newfoundland's extraordinary vigorous tradition of composing songs about local hap-penings," he wanted folklorists to concentrate on other areas.[50] Elisa-beth Greenleaf and Grace Mansfield, MacEdward Leach, Karpeles, and Peacock had all collected songs in Newfoundland. But, in keeping with the British folk song scholarship practice of valuing the ancient over the more recent, Karpeles, for example, had sought out songs that she believed were pre-modern folk compositions. The Americans Green-leaf and Mansfield, on the other hand, collected much more broadly, but academically trained collectors had neither exhausted the study of contemporary Newfoundland songs nor the other sorts of oral and material culture.

Story and Kirwin had been using dialect questionnaires for several years, and the Department of English supported Halpert and Story handing out questionnaires to Memorial students on various aspects of language and folklore, the first of which asked about proverbs and pro-verbial sayings. Halpert was gratified by the results. "Although some of the early questionnaire responses were perfunctory," he later reported, "it was a sign of Newfoundlanders' interest in their traditions that most of them were very full, carefully done, and often revealed new facets of Newfoundland folk tradition."[51] "We have used three meth-ods of collecting ... fieldwork with a tape recorder, questionnaires, and student collectors. We stress in our collecting that the traditional item itself – a story, a song, a cure – is only a beginning. We want to know for each item how and why it was learned; why when, how and where the item was told, used or practiced; how others reacted to it: in short, the entire situation."[52]

The group at Memorial also revised the questionnaire that had been designed for the Avalon Peninsula study to make it consistent with the *Linguistic Atlas of the United States and Canada*, and in 1963 extended their linguistic fieldwork outside the Avalon Peninsula for the first time. John Widdowson used the questionnaire and taped non-directed conversations in the central Newfoundland logging town of Bishop's Falls. Kirwin planned fieldwork on the Burin Peninsula and the south coast, an area that had not previously been studied, during the following summer.

In the meantime, about two thousand first-year and second-year students at Memorial were surveyed for dialect information, and the anthropologists who had been brought to Newfoundland by ISER contributed dialect information from the communities in which they were doing their fieldwork.[53] The correspondence with anthropologist James Faris reveals something about the design of the research: "The enclosed Checklist is designed so that a correspondent may interview a typical speaker in his area, preferably one of the old folks, and record his speech on the Checklist itself," Widdowson wrote, adding "the idea is that our friends and helpers should take the Checklist and ask someone who has lived in the local community all his life to give his own usage of the words listed."[54] The checklist was "experimental" and modelled on one used by dialect geographers [Frederic] Cassidy and [Walter] Avis, and also included a questionnaire on frightening figures that was based on one used by the Irish Folklore Commission.[55] The effort to interview the "old," "typical," "non mobile" speaker was standard method for linguistic and folkloric research in the 1960s. This was an impressive beginning in a short time, but collecting data was only the first step; analysis and publication were essential to the professional aspirations of everyone involved in studying Newfoundland culture.

Joining Halpert in the first systematic linguistic and folkloric fieldwork conducted by faculty at Memorial was his young colleague in the Department of English John Widdowson, a man who a few years later was to become his protégée and collaborator. The excitement in Widdowson's and Halpert's reports on their fieldwork that first summer is palpable, and Memorial remained committed to growth in the area of collecting folk culture. In December of that year Story expressed both pride and optimism about what was happening in the Department of English:

We are at last getting into our stride at Memorial, and although there are lots of weaknesses to overcome, I can't think of a more lively place to be. If all goes well, we will knock the stuffing out of our dreary Canadian colleagues during the next ten years. English studies need a good shaking up in Canada – they are just emerging from petty provincialism in many places. I was horrified at McGill which has been trying to tempt me to go there to take a new chair of English.[56]

University administrators also hoped folklore and language would become a research niche in which the small and young university could distinguish itself. As the then dean of arts and science Harris put it in 1970:

My basic interest is Newfoundland history, and in that field we are attempting to find something that is unique, something that would make the university distinctive, and something that would be a drawing card not only to students but to scholars. And I think this is true of folklore as well ... If you have a certain opportunity because of the environment in which you happen to operate to develop certain disciplines, certain areas, you obviously push those areas which are most easily developed with the resources you have at your disposal. If you have a choice between, say, linguistics and nuclear physics, well you know thousands of other people have better facilities for doing nuclear physics ... And the other reason is the desire to preserve the heritage and traditions of Newfoundland in the context of a very rapidly changing world. And I think we in Newfoundland have been subject to more rapid change than almost anyone else over the last couple of decades.[57]

That agenda dovetailed nicely with Halpert's personal vision for the discipline and his own career.

While Seary had hired Halpert and Widdowson during the same year, and the two names were ultimately to be linked in the history of Newfoundland folklore, the American and the Englishman were not initially collaborators. "In the first year he didn't know me and didn't give a damn," Halpert recalled with some hyperbole.[58] When the Halpert family arrived in St John's by car, Seary had sent Widdowson to greet them, and the two men were members of the still very small Department of English.

They initially worked independently in their fieldwork but later made research trips together, and while Widdowson wanted to capture speech and Halpert other aspects of folk culture, the two learned practical things from each other's method. They collected songs, stories, local history, and anything else that came up – there was no pressure to select since Widdowson wanted any type of speech. Halpert was primarily interested in collecting stories, although he was happy with any topic that happened to come up, especially anything that seemed rooted in tradition. He was careful to not prompt people to supply songs, since people liked singing and collecting songs was easier than collecting other kinds of material. "I don't want to get labeled as a song collector in any community because then I'll only get songs" he reported.[59] Widdowson, on the other hand, felt that collecting songs was more difficult than other sorts of material.[60]

Halpert learned from Widdowson that the fieldworker need not speak very much on the tape, but could use head nods to signal approval to the informant so that the interview would continue. He taught Widdowson to stop turning off the recording machine while asking questions, which had been Widdowson's effort to save the tape by recording only the responses. (Tape was in short supply.) While that had been fine for a linguist collecting natural speech who did not care what the speech was about, it meant that the tapes were of little use to a folklorist who wanted to collect material in context. On the other hand, since the topic of speech did not matter to the dialect scholar and since Widdowson's MA research in England was on a dialect in a fishing region, it was easy for him to discuss fishing technologies with Newfoundlanders.[61]

Halpert and Widdowson proved an effective team. Halpert's practice of talking to informants for a while before turning on the tape recorder and conducting an unstructured interview put people at ease and made for many successful interviews. Halpert had a mental checklist of the kinds of folklore he wanted to collect, and he would run through that list in a conversation until he felt he had exhausted the genres he was interested in. Widdowson did not try to solicit particular pronunciations to collect phonological data, which might have been more efficient in soliciting specific items but would have generated less information about incidental aspects of their lives, he recorded a much more natural conversation. Rather than telling people he was studying speech, which might have made them self-conscious, he asked them about their lives and recorded whatever they happened to say. Basic biographic information on informants would come out of the conversation in a natural way without them having to be asked directly.[62]

3.2. John Widdowson. (Photographic Services Collection, QEII Library, Memorial University of Newfoundland.)

Making contact with Fred Earle was particularly fortuitous for their collecting. Not long after being hired as a regional representative by MUN Extension, the Change Islands native and Lewisporte resident wrote to Widdowson to say that by chance he had seen a copy of the "checklist of Newfoundland expressions" and had taken the liberty of filling it in and submitting it.[63] Widdowson thanked him and commented that they were anxious to collect rhymes, songs, and "sections of the Mummers Play."[64] Earle was able to provide sections of the play and information about those from whom they were collected, prompting Widdowson to ask for the names of potential informants as well.[65]

Halpert and Widdowson had a few contacts in rural areas who could suggest the names of informants, and in Earle they hit pay dirt. "Newfoundland folklore is a hobby of mine," Earle replied, "and you hit my weak spot in asking for my help." He provided a list of potential inform-ants with details of what they would be able to provide and suggested that Widdowson could use Earle's name when introducing himself.[66] Earle's suggestions helped make Halpert and Widdowson's spring 1964 field collecting in the Salvage area a success, and Widdowson solicited further advice upon another trip to Fogo and Change Islands, where he hoped that Earle could suggest the best sources.[67]

That summer, and for several succeeding summers, Widdowson and Earle took research trips together. The ethnographers, who will be discussed in chapter 4, found that it took a long time to establish relationships with people that allowed for fieldwork, but Widdowson felt he could achieve effective collecting with only a brief visit. Sometimes people spoke to Earle and Widdowson and his recording device listened in. Other times, the older men that he targeted for interviews developed an immediate affection for Widdowson, and they treated him like they would a son or grandson. Their collaboration resulted in more than four hundred field tapes by 1967, which was then the largest component in the archive.[68] With Halpert setting the agenda and Widdowson and Earle collecting – Widdowson used a military metaphor:

> Please let me know if you will be free during that time, and I can then ask Herbert Halpert about a plan of campaign! It would be nice to complete our little sortie into the northern part of the Baie Verte Peninsula, and so finish off that broad sweep of the East coast area we have been covering in the last five years ... It would be worth the whole trip if we could get a bit of field work done as usual, and chalk up another success for "the old firm" of Earle and Widdowson Inc.! I have been working on some of our tapes for my present thesis and it is great to think back to the exact circumstances of their recording, and especially to the many happy times I have shared with you seeing the *real* Newfoundland.[69]

Earle collected on his own as well, making him the third largest contributor to the Archive (Widdowson was the largest collector).[70] The two men's field trips not only collected oral culture from many communities from along the coast but forged a close friendship. For Widdowson, Notre Dame Bay was "the real Newfoundland."[71]

A couple of years after the two came to St John's, chance prompted Widdowson to consult with Halpert on a question of folklore; Widdowson had collected a reference to a frightening figure, "hairy boogie," in his dialect collection in Filey, United Kingdom, and asked Halpert if he knew anything about such things. Halpert pulled out a file on frightening figures throughout the world.[72] Over the next few years, much as Kirwin had trained Widdowson in American structuralist phonetics, Halpert encouraged his young colleague's developing interests in folklore. It prompted Widdowson to enrol as the first doctoral student in the Department of English and to do a thesis on a folklore topic – the social function of frightening figures.[73] Under the joint supervision of Story and Halpert, he did the doctorate in the Department of English, since he feared a graduate degree in an upstart field such as folklore would not be accepted in the United Kingdom.

While Halpert and his collaborators laid a foundation of fieldwork and student collection, the first major publication of an aspect of Newfoundland folklore was a collection of essays on the Christmas season tradition of mumming. It happened by chance and, not surprisingly given the cooperation among many scholars working in different fields, it came out of the interdisciplinary conversations. Everything was in place for Memorial to capitalize on the idea when a young anthropologist, Melvin Firestone, presented a paper on mumming to a seminar in February 1963. As Halpert indicated in his address to convocation, a quotation from which opened this chapter, the folklore fieldwork overlapped with the community studies then being launched by the Department of Sociology and Anthropology, and especially by those working with the Institute of Social and Economic Research. The first five ISER Research Fellows living in Newfoundland outports were scheduled to visit St John's to report on their fieldwork and attend the Conference of Eastern Sociologists and Anthropologists. Firestone had just witnessed mummers, also known as *jannies*, in Savage Cove, and asked Ian Whitaker if he could prepare a paper on mummers as strangers. "The role of jany and of stranger are similar in some very significant ways," he thought, "and both serve to emphasize their opposites – an identified member of local society."[74] That Firestone became interested in folk culture is not surprising. His MA thesis had been on folklore among Sephardic Jews in Seattle, Washington, and he had published his first essay on that subject in the *Journal of American Folklore*.[75]

Firestone's paper captured the imagination of many of those in the room that day. "It was rich in interest not only to his fellow anthropologists but also to the linguists, folklorists, and other students of Newfoundland in the audience," Halpert and Story reported later, and "it was obvious, ten minutes after the paper had been delivered, that at least seven people present had heard a paper on a subject they too wanted to write about."[76] Halpert seized the opportunity to organize a conference, and over the next four years the original authors, with the later addition of Faris, prepared their essays for publication in a volume edited by Halpert and Story. The editors feared that scholarly books about Newfoundland lacked broad enough interest to be picked up by British, American, or Canadian publishers. To resolve this, the university negotiated a deal with the University of Toronto Press in which the latter would publish two series of books, one prepared by the Department of English and the other by ISER.[77]

Support from the university's administration and the Canada Council enabled Halpert and Widdowson to embark on additional fieldwork during the summer of 1964, and subsequent summers, collecting folklore and dialect.[78] They chose to not specifically solicit folk songs, since several professional collectors had already done so, but collected every aspect of folk culture they could imagine. As Halpert reported, Widdowson travelled thousands of miles by car, boat, and on foot making recordings of "folk legends, tales and anecdotes; the autobiographical reminiscences of sailors, seal hunters, woodsmen and others; and folk customs of all kinds."[79] He was sometimes accompanied by Halpert, a student, Earle, or linguist John Hewson, and hundreds of hours of "interesting descriptions were recorded on how to make and utilize a number of craft objects: boats, killicks, nets, lobster pots, and so on" as well as "childlore, riddles and folk beliefs."[80] The material could support study of many aspects of folk culture. "Perhaps the most significant and unexpected collecting of the summer field work," Halpert felt, "was the recovery of quite complete versions of mummers' plays from four informants."[81] The publication of the book on the mummers plays would be delayed, but he believed that including the plays would be "a significant addition to the corpus of mummers plays already published in Great Britain. What is equally if not more important is the fact that we have interesting details on performance ... thus putting the plays in a larger context."[82]

Halpert was a catalyst in a renewed awareness of heritage among other people. As a foreign-born social scientist with academic credentials, his expressions of interest encouraged some Newfoundlanders to value the old ways and tales. Media attention to the research into Newfoundland studies showed that many Newfoundlanders appreciated the university's efforts to preserve the ways of life that most people agreed were disappearing. The publicity encouraged increases in enrolment in folklore classes among young people who now attended to their heritage in ways they never had before.

The government's Centralization Program and Fisheries Household Resettlement Program subsidized the relocation of families from many inaccessible communities during the 1950s and 1960s. Some of the children of those families were attracted to folklore courses since they enabled them to reflect on their families' previous ways of life, and such students were cultivated by Halpert as valued informants for the insider access they had into the culture. Media coverage prompted members of the public to suggest potential informants to Halpert. That is not to suggest that he was alone in raising the profile of the past or that nostalgia was exclusively a rural phenomenon. The demolition of several older buildings in St John's, such as the city's General Post Office, provoked a preservation movement; Story, and many others at the university, pressured the government to save the city's built heritage.[83]

Although their concerns were rooted in the local, Newfoundlanders who were interested in their heritage were participating in a worldwide trend. The protest folk song movement in the United States, from Woody Guthrie and Pete Seeger in the 1940s and 1950s to Joan Baez and Bob Dylan in the 1960s, found fans in Newfoundland. American music encouraged an awareness of the value of Newfoundland traditional music while providing alternatives to it. Halpert and Widdowson's activities, as had that of earlier folk song collectors, signalled to Newfoundlanders that people from outside the community saw value in older local cultural forms.[84]

Others were also interested in the systematic collection of oral history before it disappeared. In November 1965, the Canadian-born author Farley Mowat sent to Premier Smallwood an "Outline for a Historical Reclamation Project in Newfoundland" written by himself and Harold Horwood. It suggested a program to record oral history. "There really isn't much time left to collect outport material," he wrote, "nor do I feel that the spasmodic efforts of the University people are able to meet the need."[85] Soon young urban Newfoundlanders who were excited by the American folk song movement began to visit Newfoundland outports to collect folk material themselves.

Scholars' collection and celebration of folklore validated the rural culture among young urban Newfoundlanders, but there was another aspect to the attention of a foreigner – academically trained scholars understood the culture through categories of analysis that had been created by social scientists working in other contexts. Halpert pointed out that faculty members at Memorial who were *of* the culture could be enroled as informants as much as rural residents, especially if they were natives who had learned the culture "traditionally," by which he meant through oral transmission rather than through books.

Professor Leslie Harris, acting head of the history department, a native Newfoundlander, turned out to have a great personal interest in and memory for riddles. These he had learned traditionally. In a taped interview he was able to give a valuable description of how riddles function in a Newfoundland outport community. When we have time for another recording session, I believe we will have the data needed for the first study of the function of riddles in an English-speaking area. Such studies have been made by anthropologists working with native tribes in Africa, but have never been attempted for English-speaking areas.[86]

At this early stage Halpert may have underestimated how much Newfoundlanders learned popular culture through printed material and radio broadcasting rather than direct oral transmission. For many collectors of oral culture, the vector through which the riddle passed from the lips of the folk, through a native who had listened to it and committed it to memory, to the social scientist who could record it and put it in the archive, established the riddle's authenticity. Halpert's parallel between his collecting in Newfoundland and anthropologists collecting in Africa reveals both his status as an outsider and a view of outports as "folk" societies even as he was intellectually aware of the dangers of romanticizing the folk.

He valued collecting folklore in Newfoundland not only for what it might teach us about the particular place but for the potential it had to address questions in international scholarship. Like the earlier generation of folklorists whose fieldwork sent them to areas they saw as remote or isolated to seek out the oldest and least educated person they could find (who would be the least tainted by modernity), Halpert and Widdowson were "working from the premise that traditions virtually unknown in England might still survive in active form in Newfoundland" and hoped to find cultural survivals from the ancestor communities in Europe.[87] "Particularly worth noting" he told Story "is the recording of two of the longer folktales scholars call *Marchen*, known popularly, though incorrectly as fairy tales ... What is important about this discovery is this" he continued, "so few *Marchen* have been recorded in England many scholars have thought that they were not known in the English tradition ... Here we have proof that the tales must have been known in England at least at the time when ancestors of the present day Newfoundlanders came over."[88] So one of the values of studying Newfoundland oral culture, in his view, was that it contained vestiges of an older culture.

Widdowson's report on his 1965 fieldwork reveals a wide range of collecting, from history to material culture and dialect to songs. Now that Firestone had raised interest in mumming, Widdowson paid particular attention to collecting variants of the mummers play, often noting its collection as "highly valuable." The diary of 17 August, for example, gives a sense of the work:

> Recorded Peter Miles at Herring Neck who also remembered a few fragments of the Play. We were unsuccessful in recording the man who is known there as the one who remembers a great deal of old stories, etc., and who is reputed to know the Play well. This was Arthur Miles, who had unfortunately been seriously ill and we were only able to call on him briefly without making a recording. This was compensated for by the recording of a substantial part of the Play, including the singing of the closing song for Hubert Watkins who ... repeated his version twice so that we have two versions to compare ... Another man, Dorman Parsons, was also interviewed here and he remembered a few fragments of the Play. This Play was probably the most significant recording of the whole trip, though no version was complete and we can only piece the Play together from the various fragments.[89]

While Widdowson collected many kinds of material, the *play* stood out as the aspect of oral culture that most excited him. The anthropologists were most interested in the function of mumming, while Widdowson, who was more in the literary tradition of folklore scholarship, wanted to document variants of the performance of the mummers play.

The fieldwork and the administration of questionnaires to university students elicited a large body of data on many aspects of oral and traditional culture, and especially information on mumming. By 1966 Halpert thought that they had collected a large enough body of material "to form the nucleus of a future extensive folklore archive" with which they could address questions about Newfoundland and the lands from which the ancestors of Newfoundlanders had immigrated.[90] People outside the university had an interest in an archive as a cultural crucible. Mowat, then living in Burgeo because he sought a place untainted by American-style consumerism, wrote Premier Smallwood to suggest the archival preservation of culture could lay the basis for a cultural revolution:

> Now the government has reached a point of achievement where all its energies are not engrossed in the economic and social battle. It has had

time to reflect on other needs and to realize the urgency of conserving the remaining fragments of Newfoundland's human story, and reconstructing these fragments so that they and the cultural renaissance which might arise from their renewal can again clothe our people in the certainty and pride which only those who know and revere their past can ever feel.[91]

Mowat suggested that the new university campus house a "Newfoundland Studies Centre" for textual archival material, published material, maps, recorded oral history, photographs and film, copies of material from foreign archives, and drafts of literary works. The centre could coordinate interdisciplinary research and provide "a working 'milieu' for MUN graduate students and for other serious students, including writers, broadcasters, film makers, academic students from other regions."[92] Mowat's ambitious scheme did not materialize, but the university's attention to oral culture did lay the basis for an urban popular culture based on rural traditional culture. As the folklorist Gerald Pocius pointed out, when the academics had asked questions about tradition, Newfoundlanders' awareness of these aspects of their culture was raised. Three of the questionnaires administered to folklore and English classes in the early 1960s focused on mumming. Many hundred students who went on to positions of leadership in the society were exposed to the idea that mumming was an element of Newfoundland culture.[93] At least this encouraged a self-awareness of practising a Newfoundland tradition among many of those who returned to their homes. For some students, having been exposed to folklore's research methodology may have altered the culture that was the object of inquiry in the first place.

"Things are beginning to pop around here," Halpert wrote to a friend. The university had approved administering a folklore questionnaire to first- and second-year students, and the material flowing into the archive was "so impressive that it has the powers that be shook up."[94] Four months were available each summer for research, and recording equipment and funding for fieldwork was not a problem. "For a folklorist," he commented "this place is pretty close to heaven."[95] Story and Halpert had "finally recognized that the questionnaire method and the development of a chain of correspondents, plus fieldwork, is the only way to make a real dent in the vast riches of Newfoundland material."[96] Meanwhile, the editorial work on the mumming book proceeded, and the university continued to increase its capacity for the teaching and study of folklore. As Halpert put it,

This past summer was almost completely shot by steady drudgery on the umpteenth revision of our mummers' book, followed up by a field trip – a wonderful one – on the South coast of Newfoundland ... This year I am teaching only folklore and folk song courses, almost for the first time in my life – barring various visiting professorships. We have the raw materials for an archive of tapes and a related archive of manuscript collections made chiefly by students. The English Dept. hired two young men with folklore training, each of whom is teaching an advanced folklore course. They, I hope, will have the energy and organizing ability to carry through the organizing of the archives very crudely begun.[97]

The "two young men" that the Department of English appointed during the 1967–68 academic year were A.E. Green, who taught folk song, and R.E. Buehler, who taught American folklore. Buehler was the editor of *Abstracts of Folklore Studies*, a publication of the American Folklore Society, and by hiring him Memorial further established its position as an emerging centre of the discipline in North America. The Department of Folklore was created in 1968, giving Halpert the opportunity to create both an undergraduate and a graduate curriculum from scratch. The department began with four MA and two PhD students. Three were Newfoundlanders, one was Nova Scotian, and two were from the United Kingdom, and each of these students documented Newfoundland oral culture.[98] Being a graduate student in the department also entailed working as cataloguers for the material Halpert and Widdowson had gathered. Archival work became a way of apprenticing another generation into the discipline.

Green left the university the following year, just as a Department of Folklore was created separate from the Department of English, prompting Halpert to hire Neil V. Rosenberg. Rosenberg was born in Seattle, Washington, in 1939, and his family moved to Berkeley, California, in 1951. While still in school Rosenberg developed a passion for folk music, and throughout his career he was both a participant in the folk music revival and a scholar of the music. While working on his doctorate, he also managed bluegrass festivals and worked as an archivist at the Archives of Traditional Music at Indiana University. By chance, Halpert met Rosenberg when he visited that archive in the summer of 1967 to get advice on how the collections at Memorial might be organized. When, a year later, Halpert learned that Rosenberg was no longer working in Indiana, he arranged for the then university president, Lord Taylor, to offer Rosenberg the job as folklore archivist at Memorial and the opportunity to teach a course in folk song. Rosenberg organized the collections of Halpert and Widdowson, the burgeoning collections of students, and established the Memorial University of Newfoundland Folklore and Language Archive, or MUNFLA (the name was Story's suggestion; it had been tentatively called the Newfoundland Folklore Archive). He did this while both undertaking his own research and supervising the graduate work of several generations of students.[99]

The initial cataloguing system at MUNFLA was not well suited to the sort of cross-referencing necessary for comparative study, and Rosenberg was able to remedy that. The archive made it possible to write a study based on its collections rather than an author going into the field. That significant accomplishment raised several dangers. There was no replacement for the intimate knowledge of the context that came from doing one's own fieldwork, and an incautious researcher mining collections for nuggets of data relevant to his or her topic would have no knowledge of the varied reliability of the archival collections being consulted. Reading a draft of a graduate thesis prompted Story to write that only Kirwin, Halpert, and himself were fully aware of the extent of that problem. "You and I are the only people who have used the collection extensively enough, and with non-Archive controls, to enable us to use it critically" he wrote to Kirwin.[100] Story suggested they write an account of their use of MUNFLA to serve as a warning. "Otherwise," he predicted, "awful things are going to get into print, and themselves beget unfortunate offspring."[101]

Rosenberg also shifted the topic matter of the department. While Halpert helped make the study of folk music in its context fashionable among folklorists, he was no longer actively involved in collecting music to the extent he had during the 1930s and 1940s. He had lost hearing in one ear while working in Kentucky, and in 1970 reported to the folklore scholar Carole Henderson Carpenter that he had become "old fashioned theoretically."[102] His collections were primarily child ballads and older local songs. Rosenberg and other younger scholars included songs adopted from phonographs and other commercial music as part of their research interest, and, Halpert recognized, Newfoundland music had been influenced by just such phenomena. MUNFLA provided a home for the collection of recorded oral material that they made and the manuscript material that was coming in fairly steadily, but its collections were not confined to Newfoundland materials. In 1969–70 they were pleased to be selected as the depository for tapes made in Ontario, McEdward Leach's collection of music from Nova

Scotia and Newfoundland and Labrador, and Carpenter's collection of interviews with Canadian folklorists made as part of her doctoral work at the University of Pennsylvania.[103]

In 1969 Story and Halpert's work in Newfoundland folklore culminated in the publication of *Christmas Mumming in Newfoundland*. Edited by the two and including the work of several other authors, it was remarkable for the range of methodologies it brought to bear on a single phenomenon. It approached mumming in three ways: the observations of five social anthropologists who had seen mumming in particular communities in the province as they conducted extensive fieldwork, a folkloristic description of the "complex" created through extensive oral interviews and survey questionnaires, and a social history of the custom in Newfoundland based on the textual and documentary records.[104] Story contributed the opening essay – a social history of the settlement and development of Newfoundland. It provided a context for understanding the communities that the anthropologists discussed in their chapters. Halpert's essay drew on examples of masking throughout the world to develop a typology of the phenomena. Story provided readers with a sense of the variety within Newfoundland culture; Halpert's classification system gave scholars a starting point from which they could discuss the similarities of disparate global phenomena. Halpert had done so from the basis of work on Newfoundland – proving the point that a local study could generate results meaningful to an international audience. He hoped his typology would also "have the merit of focusing attention on the various aspects of the Newfoundland custom, yet seeing them in some relation both to one another and to the broader body of data from some other parts of the world."[105]

Firestone's essay on the function of mumming had spawned the book. Born in 1931 in Omaha, Nebraska, he received a BA from the University of New Mexico in 1954 and worked as a research assistant at the University of Washington, where he was doing a PhD. He started his essay with the observations that masking releases people from their inhibitions and that it made mummers "strangers" to people who normally knew what to expect of each other because everyone in the small community knew each other so intimately.[106] Even before coming to Newfoundland he remarked,

Recently I have become interested in the ranges of behavior permitted in role-playing. It seems to me that the tendency in most anthropological research has been towards the construction of ideal types of behavior;

hence, normal variation is overlooked or construed as deviance. I am interested in finding out which roles in society permit greater "freedom" of action and response, and if the particular configuration of roles in which an individual participates influences the range of his permitted behavior in any or all of them.[107]

After spending a Christmas season in Savage Cove on Newfoundland's west coast, Firestone was struck by the "threat" implicit in those who disguised themselves when visiting neighbours, as the behaviour of those who were well known was no longer predictable while they were masked. He drew an analogy between the fears, and suspicion, of mummers he observed with the attitudes towards strangers that he perceived. His essay did not reflect on the ways that his role as anthropologist doing fieldwork may have coloured his subjects' reactions to him, but it assumed that people's reactions to "strangers" such as himself was an objective character of their culture. "I do not mean to imply that the people of the straits consciously feel that mummers symbolize strangers or feel that the two categories have anything in common," he wrote, "However, they are functional equivalents. They both provide individuals with socially approved means of displacing hostility."[108]

Despite admitting that mumming and the fear of strangers were unrelated, he suggested that they both served the function of displacement. Parents threatened children with harm at the hands of mummers, or strangers, he suggested, as a way of discouraging undesirable behaviour. The children would then displace their resentment towards their parents onto mythical or real figures from outside the family. Children's behaviour would thus be corrected while ensuring continued social solidarity of the family (which was the economic unit), since the children would not be aware that their parents were responsible for the potential negative implications of their behaviour (such as being taken away from the family).

Firestone's analysis was not based on any evidence of actual familial conflict, but, following Freud, he assumed that this was a universal process. Nor did he cite any evidence of hostility towards mummers or strangers. In a footnote he reported that "Janneys are the focus of much fun and merriment, and I doubt the kindness to strangers can be exceeded."[109] His analysis was based on a sort of psychoanalysis of community as if it were a person. He cited, and thanked for comments on the paper, Melford Spiro, a cultural anthropologist then teaching at the University of Washington, who had emphasized psychoanalysis in explaining behaviour. Firestone also cited other literature upon the role that shamans played in "stable" (i.e., non-modern) societies in resolving psychological conflicts between children and their parents. Even when they became adults, he believed, rural Newfoundlanders never lost their fear of strangers and mummers, and through mumming they were thus able to continue to displace the tensions within their families towards outsiders.

He could not have known it, but starting with his essay, mumming became one of the most examined topics in Newfoundland studies over subsequent decades. While folklorists and anthropologists had once started from the premise that they were salvaging vestiges of a culture from the remote past that persisted in isolated areas, Firestone showed that mumming could be analysed as a contemporary phenomenon. He also showed that mumming could be portrayed as a cultural element that had a *function* within the society. The essay's success, he reflected many years later, was that it showed what an anthropologist could do with mumming, but he did not believe that his was the only possible interpretation. He thought that there was no single approach or theoretical interpretation that provided a total explanation to phenomena.[110]

Faris, John Szwed, and Louis Chiaramonte, all American graduate students and ISER fellows, also contributed descriptions of mumming to the book. Chiaramonte, in his study of a south coast community, posited that

> The behaviour of mummers in different rural Newfoundland communities is similar in many respects. But what is especially interesting about mummering in Deep Harbour [Francois] is that the custom reflects many features of the social organization of this particular community. This correspondence between the forms that mummering takes and the social organization of a community means that mummering can be used as one of many indices for comparative studies of the social organization of Newfoundland communities.[111]

He suggested that people in Francois chose those with whom they mummered, and those with whom they drank alcohol, based on their relationships with each other. Christmas social groupings mirrored the relations people had with each other at other times. A group of men who worked together and had reciprocal social obligations would mummer together. He emphasized the fun of mumming more than the other authors did, but he concluded that its function was to reinforce work-life social bonds. Similarly, Szwed's study of the west coast noted the egalitarian nature of west coast communities, and he believed that social relations were structured by unspoken contracts of reciprocal obligations.[112] Faris, like Firestone, had studied at the University of New Mexico, but he had chosen to work on a doctorate at Cambridge, where he was thoroughly imbued with British social anthropology. He was less interested in the social function of mumming than Firestone and less cautious in seeing the position of both strangers and mummers within people's cognitive structure as the same. He admitted that his analysis was "speculative and untestable" but submitted that "they reveal a fundamental structural logic operative in 'Cat Harbour' social life."[113]

These ethnographic field studies were followed by two geographically and temporally broad descriptions of mumming, which highlighted a considerably more varied phenomenon than the anthropologists had found in the outports. Widdowson and Halpert drew on their wide-ranging field recordings and the folk culture questionnaires they had administered during the first half of the decade to describe the range of disguises mummers used. Story contributed a history of Newfoundland mumming based on published accounts. His essay surveyed evidence of the three sorts of mumming: house visits while disguised (the old practice that persisted in outports), the mummers parades (which had been practised in nineteenth-century St John's but had been legislatively prohibited), and the mummers plays that had been collected from three locales. In another chapter, Story and Halpert prepared written texts of the plays that had originally been published in St John's newspapers and collected from oral informants. They also compared these plays with similar variants in the United Kingdom and Ireland.[114]

When *Christmas Mumming* was published, both St John's newspapers, the *Daily News* and the *Evening Telegram*, noted that it was part of a boom of books related to Newfoundland then underway. The acerbic newspaper columnist Ray Guy made the connection between the increased sales of Newfoundland books and the recent "great interest on 'the mainland' these days for all kinds of material originating in Newfoundland." Typically of him, Guy expressed scepticism about being the object of social science, commenting that "some of the papers written by chaps doing postgraduate work who went to live in remote outharbours for some months are pretty deep going, especially when they get into interpretations of what drives the natives to carry on that way."[115] Similarly, the Newfoundland-born faculty member at Mount Allison University in New Brunswick, Cyril Poole, commented: "I'm not favourably impressed with the book MUN people put out on mummering – except for Story's two pieces. Sociologists can kill xmas quick. They kill everything with method."[116] The response to the book by outsiders was less sceptical than that of Guy or Poole had been. Story and Halpert must have been pleased with the vindication of their collaboration expressed in the *Journal of American Folklore*: "*Christmas Mumming in Newfoundland* is probably the most successful collaborative effort at book writing since the original publication of the King James Bible in 1611" the review opined. It went on to suggest that "it should have, if sufficient scholars attend to it, as much influence on the study of folklore as the King James Bible had on Christianity."[117]

Story and Halpert's accomplishment in *Christmas Mumming* was not just that it was a success in bringing different disciplines together to write on the same subject – those who worked in the Departments of English, Folklore, and Anthropology shared much – the book combined textual analysis with oral fieldwork, history with analysis of the contemporary phenomena, and literary with anthropological analysis. American folklorists had moved, with some debate, from the study of the text to the study of context; Halpert, his colleagues, and his students were in the forefront of that shift. More than any book before, it showed that authors could address an international scholarly audience with their feet firmly in Newfoundland. The book was also read locally, and as Pocius commented, although the authors "made no claim that mummering was anything unique to Newfoundland, [but] popular opinion thought differently, since university academics found it important enough to devote a book to it."[118] The success of the book had unintended effects on the scholarship as well. There were many other aspects of the culture, he pointed out, on which scholars might have focused their attention, but later generations of scholars drew on the book and the evidence on mumming preserved in MUNFLA as keys to understanding the whole culture. The book encouraged urban Newfoundlanders to see mumming as an emblem of their culture and social scientists to see it as the key ritual that would reveal the structure of Newfoundland society.

Halpert had been fifty-seven years old when the Department of Folklore and MUNFLA were formed and soon considered relinquishing administrative control. He had established the archive and created an academic department with its courses and degree regulations.

Christmas Mumming had been a great success, but he became concerned that when he withdrew from the day-to-day management of folklore to concentrate on his own publications, his particular vision of the field would not be realized. As Story confided to Widdowson in 1969, "As Herbert gets brooding, he becomes more and more obsessed by the difficulty of finding a fit successor who will execute his vision of Newfoundland folklore studies as part of a co-operative venture that uses the Newfoundland students as valued contributors of both material and insight in a rapidly changing society, yet does this with knowledge and awareness of European and American folkloristic, anthropological and linguistic theory."[119] A year later, Story reported: "HH still not well, damnably prolonged flu bout, and some depression over need, now to start, very reluctantly, to look for a successor who can free him to write his books at last."[120] Story's influence helped him get research chairs for some of his colleagues.

> The HH secret is that he is going to get a Henrietta Harvey Research Chair (not yet officially announced). I think it's good news, HH has his worries about the Folklore Dept., but my view is that he has simply got to have his final stint to write. He is too rare a scholar to spend his last years fiddling with paperwork. And the Department is not so complex and large that it can't be managed without him at the formal helm. The Chair is a bit of a coup. I've been pressing for a while now to have some more Research Chairs for the Humanities and Social Sciences, and am feeling very pleased about this one for Herbert, and another for Robert Paine.[121]

Widdowson remained in England for family reasons and because he did not want to abandon what he had accomplished there – not because the grass was greener at the University of Sheffield. British academics, he complained to Story, were uninterested in linguistics and folklore, while "at MUN the general atmosphere is far more conducive to such study and one is at least among people who think such a study might at least have some value. Over here it still seems to be a losing battle as far as making folklore a viable academic discipline goes."[122] He also missed the teamwork at Memorial. "The one thing I really regret about the present state of affairs" he told Story, "is being cut off from the best group of friends and colleagues I shall ever know."[123] Widdowson's collaborations continued, both long distance and during the annual trips he made to St John's each summer, and Story and Halpert hoped that he would come back to Memorial on a more permanent basis with a joint appointment in English and folklore, but the day-to-day management of the archive he had helped to found had passed to Rosenberg.

As Guy had suggested, not everyone appreciated people from St John's, or mainlanders, treating them as the subject of inquiry and wanting to collect from them. Kirwin had helped arrange for an American graduate student, Larry Youther, to tape speech in two towns, Trinity and Bonavista. Some people in both towns agreed to be interviewed, and some of them allowed themselves to be taped, but many declined. Youther reported that in Bonavista some individuals were uncooperative, and even hostile, towards him. As he put it, "I got the feeling that everybody knew I was there to study their speech, and nobody was about to do anything."[124] Story asked Youther to abandon the fieldwork and return to St John's. "These are small communities and are too easily disturbed by rumour to make it worth risking hostility" Story wrote to him, "Good will is very important to us in collecting and is not worth risking for a few more tapes."[125]

Perhaps the people of Bonavista had tired of being the subject of someone's fieldwork, but more likely Youther had offended some individuals. In an interview in 1970 Harris reported that there had not been any hostility expressed towards fieldworkers studying the culture, there had occasionally been indifference, and much encouragement, but no hostility. "There have been one or two instances when reports when published, when starkly presented, have aroused some criticism," he commented, "in part because the press have taken the more lurid examples from particular reports of customs or practices in the community and played them up."[126] The example he had in mind was the Evening Telegram having cherry-picked some of the more lurid examples of things such as witchcraft from Faris's study of Cat Harbour. That provoked an outcry among those who felt such beliefs reflected poorly on the people of the province. Widdowson's response to the public controversy was to take extra care to keep the material in his thesis confidential until he had an opportunity to prepare a suitable version for publication. As he explained to the dean of graduate studies, "it would be a betrayal of trust if some of the material given to me by so many helpful people could be presented in any other form by any unauthorized media."[127] Such difficulties were rare, however, and overall had little affect on the goodwill towards the university, perhaps, Harris thought, because Halpert's students were usually Newfoundlanders working in their own communities.

Hundreds of men and women had consented to the recording of their conversations with Widdowson, Halpert, and many others, and hundreds more had answered dialect questionnaires or took it upon themselves to write to Story or others. In large measure this was a result of generosity – fieldworkers were often taken into people's homes and fed, for example. It was also the result of some care in preparation. Halpert's method of allowing informants to talk in an unstructured way, perhaps with the tape recorder turned off for a while until the person being interviewed was comfortable, was different from the linguists' method of getting right to the heart of dialect forms. One American linguistics project, for example, had informants read a story called "Arthur the Rat," which contained all the sounds they targeted for attention, such as whether or not the speaker vocalized the R after a vowel. The more "open ended" method of Halpert and Widdowson avoided some self-consciousness about the way that people were speaking and elicited a range of history, folk belief, information about material culture, and work.

The research on oral culture paid off in an enhanced reputation for the university and its faculty; Story's growing status led to his being elected a member of the Royal Society of Canada. He was aware of how he had been shaped by an older style of textual scholarship in Britain and how he had been affected by years of collaborations and friendships with linguists, folklorists, and anthropologists. Indeed, when introducing himself to the Royal Society he emphasized that his life's work had been "working at the sorts of things that scholars have always done since the days of Aristarchus of Alexandria: text, scholia, vita, glossae – what used to be called, in a general sense now rare or obsolete, philology." But, he emphasized, he had also been engaged in "an exploration of a more directly known subject in the company of other scholars in linguistics, anthropology and folklore from whom I tried to repair the defects of an old-fashioned education."[128]

When the Canadian historian Hilda Neatby invited Story to speak to the Royal Society on a subject of his choice, he used the occasion to make a case for taking oral culture seriously as literature. His 1972 paper to the society, "Notes from a Berry Patch," became an important statement of principle for those interested in Newfoundland studies at Memorial. He took to task the work of Canadian historians generally, and the 1965 *Literary History of Canada* in particular, for failing to recognize that there had been a Newfoundland literary output worthy of scholarly attention, just because it was largely an oral rather than textual culture.[129] He advised aspiring cultural historians to turn first to folklore and anthropology rather than "conventional literary scholarship."[130] Not only would these disciplines' attention to oral evidence provide evidence of creative output, but they could reveal the role that poetry had in the lives of people, rather than bracketing off literature from the society in which it existed. Story lambasted those who did not embrace the oral culture:

> Yet this culture is customarily, and sometimes contemptuously, dismissed – often by native Newfoundlanders – as a "culture of poverty." It is true that much folk culture, here as elsewhere, grew out of societies in which physical hardship and privation were common ... The rejection of this culture by some natives of the region is certainly a phenomenon to be reckoned with. The aspiration towards social and economic mobility, especially when this must be achieved within the context of the continental urban-industrial economic and social models which have come to dominate the Island and Labrador, has frequently led native Newfoundlanders to turn away from their own traditional culture because in doing so they are turning away from the poverty with which it has been associated. This process has frequently been strengthened by other cultural and institutional influences – schools, the media, and so on – which have not often displayed notable sensitivity to the region in which they exist. The process of centralization, under federal and provincial government policies, of the rural population is not only an acute economic and social issue but has cultural implications towards which the attitude of many Newfoundlanders is ambivalent.[131]

This was as close to a political manifesto for the preservation of traditional culture as anything Story wrote. When he sent offprints of the essay to his colleagues, several of them approved of the polemic. A professor in the Education Faculty, Phillip Warren, suggested to him that it should be made required reading for all teachers in the province and added to the literature curriculum for students. Others felt that Story had vindicated Newfoundlanders: "Insecurity and feeling of inferiority in the past prevented many Newfoundland accomplishments of our people from coming to light" suggested Memorial's dean of education, William Rowe, "You and Halpert and others have done a great service to Newfoundland in promoting an awareness of so much that is good and desirable in our culture and heritage."[132] Lord Taylor, commented on Story's nationalism and the role the university had in raising Newfoundlanders' cultural level:

> I was fascinated with the conception of Newfoundland is [*sic*] an emergent *nation*. You may well be right – in the sense that Scotland and Wales – and England – are nations. I have been wondering whether this may not be the correct conception culturally. My concern has been to try to get Nfld. to set cultural standards on a national or international level – so that their achievements may make a worldwide contribution – as I believe they can. It may be that this is only possible inside a smaller "national-local" culture – just as it could be argued that Shaw and Wilde and Scott and Burns were only possible *inside* vigorous "national-local" cultures.[133]

Newfoundlanders were not the only ones impressed. The American lexicographer Frederic Cassidy wrote that the essay "does much more to arouse the imagination of what lies behind the words in a dictionary: the whole life of a people."[134]

The research paid dividends for other faculty members too. Halpert's appointment as Henrietta Harvey Professor of Folklore in 1973 freed him from much of his undergraduate teaching, and several new faculty members joined the department, including David Hufford and Richard Tallman, as well as Larry Small and Wilfred Wareham, who initially taught summer school courses in folklore. Small and Wareham were themselves from rural Newfoundland and among the first generation of outport students who had been trained as folklorists both at Memorial and in the United States. They were able to examine their own culture using social science categories of analysis and then to teach it to the next generation of students. Something of the character of the department can be gleaned from the fact that nearly the whole group, faculty and graduate students alike, decamped that year to present papers at the American Folklore Society meeting. The AFS designated Memorial as the centre to revise Stith Thompson's *Motif-Index of Folk Literature*, leading to the department sending representatives to the Folk Narrative Congress in Helsinki, Finland. As the department noted, both "staff and students are also very actively engaged in a wide range of research projects, both local and international."[135]

Hufford's departure from Memorial in 1974 prompted the department to hire another former student of Richard Dorson, Peter Narváez, who was to contribute to the transformations of the department prompted by the second generation of folklorists. He had grown up in

New Jersey of Hispanic parents and had established himself as a blues musician before entering graduate school at Indiana. Like Rosenberg before him, Narváez wanted to write on music but Dorson's idea of what constituted a proper folklore topic did not include ethnomusicology nor commercially transmitted popular culture. He was teaching as a sessional instructor at the University of Maine at Portland when he applied for the job at Memorial. Narváez had been part of the student Vietnam War protest, and the idea of work in Canada was appealing. Fortunately the Department of Folklore at Memorial had a broader view of the field than did his supervisor. After arriving in Newfoundland he became aware of labour songs being used by striking workers in the Newfoundland mining town of Buchans and decided to change his thesis topic. He wrote a thesis on the strikers' songs but was dropped from the graduate program because the thesis did not conform to what Dorson thought folklore should be. Narváez's work was later accepted by Indiana as a dissertation.[136] A broad-ranging scholar and talented musician who immediately fit into the local scene, he helped shift the department's research interests to include people's uses of the mass media.

The September 1974 meeting of the MUNFLA Archives Committee provided an opportunity to renew the folklore and language agenda. Herbert and Letty Halpert, Kirwin, Story, and Widdowson met to map out their priorities. They began by inviting two members of the next generation, linguist Harold Paddock, who was working on Newfoundland speech, and Narváez to join the committee. Story stressed that their priority should be book-length studies: the *DNE*, the Halpert and Widdowson collection of Newfoundland folktales, Letty Halpert's proposed book on customs and beliefs associated with death, and the publication of the proverbs and riddles that they had collected. Memorial and the University of Toronto Press would publish these books, the Department of English would publish articles on language in its journal *Regional Language Studies*, and MUNFLA would publish guides to the archive and a series of bibliographic compilations undertaken by graduate students in folklore. That would include Michael Taft's discography of Newfoundland recordings, Paul Mercer's index of published songs, and Wilfred Wareham's edited community history of Harbour Buffett as seen by Victor Butler. Herbert Halpert promoted the revision of the *Motif-Index of Folk-Literature*, which exemplified his professional practice of classification and annotation. *Abstracts of Folklore Studies*, which Buehler continued to edit, he argued would have "undoubtedly made the Memorial University Folklore Department better known interna-tionally."[137] But since Halpert was to soon turn 64, there was urgency to find a new head of department who would develop the archive and promote the field in English-speaking Canada.[138]

The work of the folklorists and ISER fellows proved the potential to theorize about broader issues using Newfoundland evidence. No one did so more explicitly than New York–based anthropologist Gerald Sider. His publications show how the descriptions in the ISER ethnog-raphies could be used to interpret Newfoundland culture generally. Indeed, the idea that mumming could be used as a key to understand Newfoundland reached a new international audience not directly through scholars at Memorial but though Sider's publications. Sider had come to Newfoundland by chance.

He had been working as a civil rights organizer among off-reservation indigenous people in the US South during the early 1960s, and he had tired of living with the violence of everyday life and the state oppres-sion of the poor and powerless in the region. He decided to get as far away from the South as possible and drove north until he found himself camping in Newfoundland. Renting a house in Dunville, Placentia Bay, he came to know some of his neighbours who had been resettled from nearby islands. He was struck by the contrast between the violence of the southern United States and the peacefulness of Newfoundland, as well as the fierce resistance on the part of the Natives he had worked with and what seemed to him to be the passive nature of Newfound-landers in the face of government policies of resettlement.

Sider later reported that while he was helping an older neighbour, the man described his early life on one of the islands of Placentia Bay and posed two rhetorical questions: "why did we stop mummering?" and "why did we let resettlement happen?" Sider set out to answer the first of these questions by drawing heavily on the fieldwork of Chiaramonte and Szwed (described in the next chapter), in particular, and the descriptive data in *Christmas Mumming* generally. As much as he relied on the data collected by Halpert and Story, he rejected their method. Sider's self-consciousness of his working-class background was important to his scholarship, and he perceived many of the authors of *Christmas Mumming*, and other faculty members at Memorial, as hav-ing upper-class backgrounds.

While he had friendships with many faculty members at Memorial, he worked within a Marxist tradition not shared by many of the older faculty, such as Halpert and Story, and he did not share their cautious empiricism. History could be used as a storehouse of examples that could be selected to test theories, and Sider used Newfoundland's past in that way. Many of the historians at Memorial, however, rejected such practices as cherry-picking examples from the past to illustrate theory. Not only was Sider working outside the historical method, he combined a passion for working with those who were "poor, hardworking and in need of political mobilization" with thinking about social problems at a high level of abstraction.[139] To him, *Christmas Mumming* was not theoretical enough, and its descriptive approach represented the kind of anthropology he later described as the study of the "quaint habits of the fuzzy wuzzeys."[140] Sider's first foray into the study of Newfoundland mumming was rejected by the journal *Acadiensis*, likely because its bold interpretations did not fit with peer assessors' methodological conservatism, but it was subsequently published by *Past and Present*. The latter journal's readers were more impressed by the article's contribution to social theory, and less concerned about evidence for claims about Newfoundland's culture, than were Newfoundland specialists.[141]

While many scholars at Memorial found Sider's coherent blueprint of a culture provocative, there was an immediate, widespread reaction as well. Story zeroed in on Sider's contention that the word "after" was used in reference to future encounters with people in authority. When he asked if his colleague could think of any evidence to support Sider's assertion, Kirwin replied:

> No, I can't. He should be discussing the whole *after* entry [in the *DNE*], which asserts only past action. The idiom isn't after. It is Be + after + verb + ing. Since it seems almost a perfect parallel to HAVE + just + verb + p. part., he would have to show that this standard English idiom is a future used between the poor and the dominant few. Poor Newfoundland! Suffering distortions that will have to be corrected in the future.[142]

Many people shared Kirwin's chagrin.

Sider reported that the earliest evidence of mumming in Newfoundland outports was from the start of the nineteenth century, just as the master-and-servant fishery was being replaced by the family fishery. Mumming continued, he suggested, until the middle of the twentieth century, when wage labour work replaced the family fishery. This correlation between mumming and the mode of production was not chance, in his view, since Marxist theory posited that the economic system determined the culture. So the economic organization of the family fishery, he suggested, was reproduced through the culture – in this case through mumming.

While generally thought of as a Christmastime practice, he pointed out that mumming bore little connection to Christianity and suggested that it was more of a New Year ritual. This was the season in which the previous year's tensions within the family economic unit were put into the past and men became ready to work together in the upcoming season. Once residents of outports no longer needed to reproduce the family fishing economic unit, he believed, mumming faded. The answer to his neighbour's question was that rural Newfoundlanders no longer went mumming because now that they were wage labourers they didn't need to reproduce the social relations that were once necessary for the family fishery. Sider's analysis of the function of the practice drew heavily on the fieldwork that had been conducted during the mid-1960s and published in *Christmas Mumming*. His professional responsibilities in New York enabled him to do his own fieldwork during the summers and during the month of January, but he was unable to visit Newfoundland during the Christmas season to observe mumming first hand.[143]

Sider's essay was more widely read by scholars in other countries than any piece written on Newfoundland. It helped establish Sider's international reputation and resulted in his being invited to a history and anthropology roundtable at the Max Planck Institut für Geschcte in Germany, where he presented a paper that proposed an answer to the second question his neighbour had once asked – why had people been so passive when the state relocated them.[144] The conference included such British Marxist historians as E.P. Thompson and Eric Hobsbawm, and it resulted in Sider being made part of a German working group on ordinary people's everyday history.

While his work on mumming had given his career a shot in the arm, most Newfoundland scholars were less impressed than their Canadian or European counterparts. Sider's work drew on examples from history to illustrate his argument – historians felt he was selective in his reading of history. His articles emphasized the class-based prohibitions on settlement and agriculture, for example, despite the fact that since Grant Head's and Matthews's work historians no longer believed that either had been the case. Other Newfoundland scholars saw benefit in his theories, even if they were concerned by his selective use of evidence to illustrate preconceived conclusions.[145] Story, for example, was generous; even while disagreeing with Sider's analysis, he recognized the useful role that a different perspective on the culture and history could have. As he wrote in support of Sider's promotion at City University of New York:

> I thought it was a brilliant paper and soon afterwards met the author on what was to prove the first of many occasions when he was to force us to re-examine received opinion, look again at familiar data, and engage in some of the liveliest and most creative discussions it's been my good fortune to experience. His successive papers on class and culture in Newfoundland have become indispensable documents for us here, and for many scholars elsewhere. Most of them have been presented in earlier forms at seminars here, or else have been generously shared with us after publication elsewhere, and have had a powerful influence, not least on those of us who do not share, or fully share, all of his assumptions.[146]

Few Newfoundlanders would have recognized mumming as it was described in the anthropological theory, while many international scholars read only one thing on Newfoundland culture – the article by Sider. They did so because of its relevance to debates within cultural Marxism, not because they wanted to understand Newfoundland. Within anthropology, like other social sciences, prestige accrued to those working at a high level of abstraction. Particularism, and especially knowledge of the local, was sometimes inversely proportional to the esteem with which the work was held.[147] Yet Sider's *Culture and Class in History and Anthropology: A Newfoundland Illustration* was the sort of synthesis of the ethnographies and contribution to theory that one would have hoped for.

Christmas Mumming had an effect on the scholarship and an effect on the cultural revival of the 1970s. The development of the Department of Folklore occurred at the same time as an intellectual and counter-cultural critique of modernization and a broad artistic movement in St John's that sought to find value in Newfoundland (especially rural) culture. The attention paid to mumming by scholars raised the profile of the practice as an authentic Newfoundland cultural practice (even though masking was common to many cultures). Many folklore graduate students, and faculty members such as Narváez, also played roles in the folk culture revival even as it was a subject of their academic inquiry. One of the key theatrical groups of that movement took the name "The Mummers Troupe," which encouraged the further link in some people's minds between the nation and the Christmas tradition.

The group had been founded by Chris Brookes, a native of St John's who had studied in the United States and the Toronto alternative university Rochdale before returning to Newfoundland as part of the "back to the land" movement of the late 1960s.

Reflecting on the period from the vantage point of two decades later, Brookes reported that it was "in The Bay, not in St John's, where the real essence of Newfoundland culture lies."[148] Brookes took two lessons from the Halpert and Story collection that the authors had not intended. He assumed mumming was a quintessential Newfoundland art form, glossing over its parallels in other countries, and he exaggerated its suppression at the hands of the middle class. He assumed that the academics had paid little attention to the play ("ruling class historians didn't record it") and instead focused their attention on the persistence of house visiting among rural people.[149] For Brookes, the play was the thing. Much as Halpert and Widdowson had conducted fieldwork, Brookes and his partner, Lynn Lunde, travelled throughout Newfoundland learning the oral traditions.

But Brookes and Lunde intended to revive the traditions, not preserve them in the archive. Despite Brookes's assumptions, mumming as house visiting may indeed be older, of more genuine plebeian origins, and more widespread and common than the play. Much as Halpert and Story had drawn attention to mumming among students of Newfoundland culture, the activities of the Mummers Troupe, prints of mummers by Wesleyville native and Ontario-based artist David Blackwood, and a 1970 National Film Board film on the practice had engaged the attention of the artistic community to the practice.[150] These activities, and the popularity of "The Mummers Song" by south coast musicians Bud Davidge and Sim Savoury in 1983, revived mumming as a site of nostalgia for an earlier era. But it no longer meant what it had during the 1960s; it was, in Pocius's words, now "*the* collective identity symbol for Newfoundland's nativistic movement."[151] Sider was pessimistic of its usefulness as a tool of resistance to capitalism.

> A resurrected folk culture, as an artifact rather than a way of life, be it expressed in music, dance, or in such phenomena as the recent revival of the mummers play in urban Newfoundland, with performers financed by the government, or in some form of romantic "tribalism" such as occurs in the "hippy" movement, ultimately has no significance as a political rallying point in contesting the state. The real basis of folk culture, its rootedness within the social relations of production, is gone.[152]

Evidence of the connection is circumstantial, yet without the attention being paid to the practice by Halpert and Story, it is likely that later generations would not have made mumming an icon of Newfoundland culture.

Modernization raised the stakes for those who wanted to record the folk culture before it disappeared. Such introspection about the past was common in many countries. Ian McKay's studies of the heritage movement in the nearby province of Nova Scotia suggest that efforts to preserve and popularize folk culture could be a way of imposing on others a middle class, heterosexual, white, English-speaking, view of the society.[153] Reactions to the Newfoundland cultural revival of the 1970s reveal tensions over the role scholars played in describing the culture and the ways that culture was contested. Both the writing of history and the documentation of oral culture were acts of salvage, but the desire to preserve and study folk culture were characteristic of the modern era – not reactions to it.

The aspects of the culture that social scientists selected to document reveals the things they thought unique, interesting in comparison with cultures in other regions, or embodying qualities of which they approved. The intellectuals discussed in this book were aware of the role that their work played in changing the culture they were observing. They had a professionally rigorous methodology to help them determine ephemera and slang, for example, from words that were an intrinsic part of the culture. Furthermore, folk revival is not intrinsically or necessarily politically reactionary, nor even conservative, as we are reminded by reflecting on the American tradition of Woody Guthrie, Pete Seeger, and Joan Baez.

An interest in folk culture or national history is neither always "anti-modern" nor inevitably exclusive of other ethnic traditions. The archetypal Newfoundland modernizer, Smallwood, was also a folklore collector and popularizer and a nationalist historian. He devoted his political career to making Newfoundland more like the industrial parts of North America while spending both the first half of his life – when he was a journalist, author, and radio broadcaster – and the years of his retirement, after losing the 1972 election, celebrating and fostering Newfoundland folk culture and history. Both his governmental and his intellectual work were aspects of his nationalism. The writing of history and the collection of folklore were both modern, nationalist projects. Writing a teleological narrative of the ethnic group and popularizing folktales that represented the essence of the nation were two ways of incorporating the past into the present and serving the needs of the state and civil society.

While intellectuals differed over interpretations, many students of Newfoundland culture found common cause in preservation. The cultural revival among St John's artists and the Newfoundland studies movement at the university were two aspects of a broader social phenomenon. Graduate students from other countries might find more in common with Newfoundland students of the same generation than the older generation of faculty. Michael Taft, an American who had moved to Canada as part of the protest over the Vietnam War came to Memorial to study the blues under the supervision of Rosenberg, and he soon counted himself as an enthusiast for Newfoundland culture.

In some instances the enthusiasm seems foolish. While in the 1950s some students and faculty wore tweed jackets and affected an English-sounding accent in an effort to fit into intellectual circles, in the 1970s some of the same individuals wore rubber boots to class and adopted speech mannerisms and gestures they believed displayed their working-class Newfoundland credentials. The popularization of Newfoundland artistic work encouraged people to see a future as well as a past for Newfoundland culture. Reflecting on his time in the doctoral program at Memorial, Taft perceived a difference between the attitude towards cultural change of his generation and that of its predecessors. While the first folklore scholars, such as Halpert, had preserved a record of a culture that they believed was being eroded by North American popular culture, Taft thought that the cultural revival had shown that culture's resilience. With his contemporaries, he became interested in the ways that Newfoundlanders incorporated American popular culture into their own.[154] The absence of a boundary between town and gown meant that both graduate students and younger faculty members at Memorial were part of the broader cultural movement, and that informed their choice of research topics as much as, or perhaps more than, academic considerations.

During the folk revival Halpert was no longer doing much fieldwork, and there was a clearer division between himself and the students than that of his younger colleagues. But he remained an important mentor to many scholars at Memorial. He continued to encourage the Department of Folklore's graduate students to study Newfoundland communities. Both Newfoundland-born students and those from elsewhere also supplemented their income with work on the Newfoundland collections at MUNFLA, making them familiar with the material.

Added to that was the encouragement to study Newfoundland that students received. Widdowson introduced the students to aspects of Newfoundland language, and, Taft reported, even modest publications of Newfoundland-related research by a student could result in senior scholars treating the student as having done important work.[155]

As we have seen, even as things were going well, Widdowson and Story confided in each other about their shared concern that the Department of Folklore was departing from the Newfoundland studies agenda that they had worked so hard to establish. Widdowson had organized the archive, largely because Halpert had asked him to, but in 1977 despaired that "most of those efforts dissipated in the past two or three years." University of Pennsylvania folklorist Kenneth Goldstein had been visiting the department in Newfoundland and had made it known he would be willing to become head of Memorial's Department of Folklore. Some people at Memorial saw appointing Goldstein as a coup similar to the hiring of Halpert; he was another well-established American scholar who had conducted extensive fieldwork and had a voluminous library that he was willing to move to St John's.

Hiring Goldstein would ensure that Memorial, Pennsylvania, and Indiana would be the big three folklore departments in North America. But others at the university were wary of what his appointment as head represented. Many Canadian scholars, and that included those with PhDs but no jobs, were unhappy about American-born faculty hiring other Americans. Laurel Doucette, herself a graduate of the Department of Folklore, was critical of the department's bias towards hiring men in academic appointments and of the desire to hire international scholars rather than Canadians. As she put it, "from the time of the establishment of the Folklore Department, its international appeal was founded on the availability of a province full of cultural specimens who could be viewed at will and would perform willingly. Foreign academics, gleaning a knowledge of local culture in large measure from the class assignments of their students, were willing to serve as tour guides for the experience."[156]

Widdowson watched this from afar and talked of washing his hands of the department; he felt that it was Goldstein's "circus; he is the ringmaster and it is up to him to make the progress (and take the raps)." He saw the development of the Department of Folklore along the same lines as did Goldstein, but was "almost diametrically opposed" to his views on the archive.[157] The following year, his pessimism for the prospects of Newfoundland studies seemed even deeper:

Yes, in the long term I think the future for so many of the existing developments in Newfoundland Studies looks rather bleak, mainly because younger, enthusiastic scholars, especially Newfoundlanders, seem not to want to follow where others have led the way. It will be a great watershed when HH retires and I only hope some kind of physical slot can be found for him and at least part of his library so that he can continue as a chivvier, inspirer, or even niggler, for as many years as possible.[158]

By the end of the 1970s it seemed to Widdowson that younger scholars were not taking up the work begun by Halpert, and he sensed a loss of momentum. As the cultural revival subsided so too did the passion for the study of folk culture. Widdowson was once more expressing that his "extremely strong roots in Newfoundland leave me with a continuing degree of very serious concern about the future of the Department, especially after Herbert retires." He hoped that Rosenberg would become head of the department, for that would "ensure the survival of serious Newfoundland interest and also the development of the Archive on the Halpertian model ... Any outsider who might be attracted," he felt, "would have to be more than sympathetic to Newfoundland Studies as a whole and to the crucial role played by the Department and MUNFLA in the general development of the University (not least in its liaison with the public)."[159]

Widdowson was horrified by the "exodus" of people from the Department of Folklore, particularly by the departure of Paul Mercer; he "was relying on him to carry the Newfoundland flag in the midst of the various problems of lack of commitment to Newfoundland Studies within the Department."[160] Mercer, a Newfoundlander with experience in the archive, seemed to Widdowson to be a suitable person to administer MUNFLA. Widdowson wondered if it would be possible for him to maintain some impetus to Newfoundland scholarship while still residing in the United Kingdom, perhaps by "some kind of a formal link-up which might make the white elephant of Harlow less pernicious by centering some teaching and research by MUN students either at Sheffield or at Harlow with my teaching/research involvement."[161] The Harlow campus of Memorial had been the initiative of Taylor, and it was emblematic of his view of what Newfoundland students needed. A facility north of London, Harlow provided classrooms and accommodations for Memorial's students to spend a semester taking courses in the United Kingdom and thus become exposed to the world outside of Newfoundland (which was a large part of what Taylor valued in an education). With very tight budgets in St John's, some faculty members felt that maintaining a small campus in Britain was wasteful.

Subsequent developments in the Department of Folklore show that he was unduly pessimistic about Newfoundland scholarship generally, and about the Halpertian tradition within the department in particular. The Newfoundland studies agenda within the Department of Folklore continued after Halpert's retirement, but it was no longer the only source of strength for the department. While Halpert had wanted to use Newfoundland material to build an international presence and had not encouraged Newfoundland students to work on other parts of the world, his successors were as willing to supervise graduate work or to do their own research on other locales as they were to do it on Newfoundland. Folklorists Martin Lovelace and Peter Narváez credited Rosenberg with having helped the department avoid becoming parochial and uncritical.

> [Rosenberg] found that most of those scholars who were interested in regional studies in Newfoundland "could care less about the rest of Canada." This tension between an examination and often a celebration, of Newfoundland's distinctiveness, as opposed to locating Newfoundland studies within Canadian studies, is an issue which he has addressed frequently in his teaching and writing. He never accepted that Newfoundland should not strive to have greater influence across the country, despite its situation at the geographic edge, and at the margin of the Canadian academic establishment: "There has always been this sense that Newfoundland is on the periphery ... but there's no reason why that has to be."[162]

Under Halpert's tutelage, the department had been an outpost of American folklore scholarship; there was constant cross-fertilization between Memorial and the American folklore centres as faculty members were recruited from the United States, Americans came to Memorial for graduate training, and Newfoundlanders took their final research degree from Pennsylvania or Indiana. There were no other English-language Canadian folklore departments, and Rosenberg's research in New Brunswick and his supervision of graduate students working on Canadian topics (not just Newfoundland topics, which had been Halpert's preference) reflected his commitment to the development of a *Canadian* field in which Memorial would play a key role.

Rosenberg and Narváez had also shifted the field to the study of the mass media and engaged in folklore as an approach that could yield insights from modern social interactions. Both men had parallel careers as scholars on the one hand and as musicians and impresarios on the other. They were aware of the ways that folk revitalization movements, including the ones that they had participated in, fed the interest in the scholarship, but that celebration of culture had the danger of becoming parochial and uncritical. They also saw the dangers in the romantic idealization of Newfoundland at the same time that they were part of the broader musical movement.

Folklorists at Memorial have been published in American and British journals since the 1980s, and they were engaged in an international rather than local or Canadian dialogue. That is not too surprising since they were all American, British, or Newfoundlanders (who were sent to the United States for a doctorate). The subject matter of folklore at Memorial had expanded from texts passed down through oral culture to include popular culture and the products of the mass media. Narváez and Rosenberg had also both studied under Dorson, who was known in part for his book *Fakelore*, which criticized the commercial products that seemed like genuine folk culture.[163] They rebelled against the narrow sense that their supervisor had of what appropriate topics were. Rosenberg, for example, wrote on the role that the publication of folk music had on the musical traditions, and Narváez collected recordings of radio programming published on the history of Newfoundland radio.

They were also part of the movement within folklore to shed the quest for the "folk" as an object of study and studying the folklore process among other kinds of groups. Folklore was no longer the study of the authentic traditional rural folk or an attempt to describe a regional culture that was assumed to be distinctive, and it included the study of culture of all sorts of groups.[164] Halpert's emphasis on performance had been a start in that direction, and the next generation went farther. With the work of Rosenberg and Narváez, and the work of their many graduate students, the field's subject matter expanded. Important work on Newfoundland continued through the 1970s and 1980s, but the new generation of graduate students no longer described a traditional and rural Newfoundland culture.

Halpert reached retirement age in 1976 and, with the support of people such as Story, Morgan, and Harris, was "kicked upstairs" to the position of professor emeritus with the hope that he would finish a major work on Newfoundland. It enabled him to keep his office, with its lifetime's files on a range of folklore and his library, and ultimately finish his book on Newfoundland folktales. As the éminence grise of folklore he had some influence over such things as hiring faculty and the administration of the department, and many of the younger faculty and students looked up to him, but declining health and his extensive bibliographic and annotations meant that his progress was slow – all the more so since the work was so painstaking.

Over the next two decades, Halpert and Widdowson returned to preparing for publication the longer folktales that they had collected during the 1960s and 1970s, with the addition of a few tales collected by students in the Department of Folklore. Widdowson had completed the *Linguistic Atlas of England* along with his former MA supervisor, Harold Orton, and Stewart Sanderson, and while working on the *DNE* he had developed a greater expertise than perhaps anyone in making careful transcriptions of Newfoundland speech. Fortunately Widdowson's ear for Newfoundland speech was as good as it had ever been, and his transcriptions of the tales provided the texts. Halpert's main contribution was to provide the detailed annotation to the tales – a task for which he was uniquely qualified. He identified various elements in the tales and provided references to the same elements being used in other countries.

Halpert had been at the forefront of collecting the context of the performance in the 1930s and 1940s, and the two men now raised these practices to a higher level. They identified a disjuncture between folklore theory, which held that the recorded interview should be an exact record of the performance, and the practice, in which the text was prepared for readability.[165] As they explained it:

> Folklorists often pay lip service to the ideal of the faithful recording of their informants' speech. In practice, however, this frequently results in the reinterpretation of the teller's actual words to fit the editor's and the reader's preconceptions of how a story should be presented in writing. In attempting to overcome this problem we decided to see how far it is possible to set down in written form not only the exact words of speakers but also some idea of the structure of the narrative as indicated by pauses, emphases, and other linguistic and rhetorical features. It soon became clear, however, that this form of presentation has its own shortcomings, not the least of which are the difficulties such detailed transcriptions pose for the reader who expects the normal conventions of the printed word.[166]

They did not render the transcription in the phonetic alphabet, which would have been closer to a faithful representation, because few folklorists, and even fewer general readers, were able to read that alphabet, but they made compromises between precision and accessibility. The book offered a bridge between the linguists' attention to speech and the folklorists' interests. In addition to advancing that methodology, they suggested a theoretical case as well. Halpert was renowned for his knowledge of tales from both Europe and North America and his ability to annotate and classify tales into the typology, but Halpert and Widdowson now argued that squeezing tales into static categories misrepresented them, not the least because a single performance of a single tale might borrow elements from several types and motifs. They suggested a "more dynamic" approach in which "the indexes can be utilized in a new and more functional way, by linking them to a fuller discussion of performance, context, style, and language."[167]

The tales had been collected in Newfoundland, but they were international – they matched types and motifs from throughout the world and thus demonstrated that the English tradition was similar to that of other language groups. Second, the tales were local. "In their stories and songs Newfoundlanders prove themselves to be part of a highly oral culture, rich in inventive language, colorful names, vivid proverbial sayings, ingenious riddles, and other forms of verbal art."[168] Halpert and Widdowson made a case for shifting scholars' attention from the tale towards the performance. *Folktales of Newfoundland* was not, as is so often the case, an example of someone stating a lofty goal in his or her theoretical introduction but doing something different in the application of the methodology. It provided "a more holistic and interdisciplinary approach to the study of narrative would in itself effect a rapprochement between folklorists, historians, literary scholars, linguists, other social scientists, and all those who share an interest in this perennially fascinating subject."[169] As such, when it was published in 1996, it was a culmination of many of the interdisciplinary threads that had been characteristic of the Newfoundland studies that had started in the Department of English forty years earlier.

Halpert's last few years before his death in the year 2000 at the age of eighty-nine were difficult ones; health problems made work a challenge and travel difficult. Were it not for the continuing collaboration with Widdowson and the university providing him with graduate assistants it is doubtful that the book on folktales would have been completed. Like many collectors, he guarded his life's collection of research material jealously, feeling it only fair that he have the opportunity to prepare it for publication first before making it available to others. Both he and

Widdowson were also very careful about allowing the publication of tales that they had collected but for which they had not secured permission from the original informants.

Even more explicitly than was the case with either linguistics or historical research, the development of a Department of Folklore shows the university's bid to establish itself as a research university through the study of oral culture. When they started, Seary and Story wanted to record that culture and make available to scholars. In hiring Halpert the university acquired an accomplished field collector, whose knowledge of both European and North American folklore enabled him to put Newfoundland into context, and a research library. The use of students as collaborative researchers and an interdisciplinary research agenda became hallmarks of the Newfoundland work. The methodological innovations, successes in collection, and description earned Memorial national and international respect for its research. In 1975 Halpert commented to a Swedish colleague that he saw his work as promotional:

> In Newfoundland, however, we must first convince people that folklore is respectable and scholarly, and that our folklore would be admired in other countries. Only then will they have the confidence to think it worth collecting and study. In Sweden that stage is obviously long past and you can worry about interpreting the folklorist's work to the general public.[170]

Halpert had faith that careful collecting and annotating would produce work of value. "My few articles that theorists like," he reflected near the end of his career, "came from analyzing my fieldwork data and questions stock assumptions."[171] The collection lent itself to celebration, during a period in which young Newfoundlanders were discovering the culture of their parents and grandparents, as easily as it formed the basis of social science. Halpert did not develop a cultural theory that could be exported to scholars elsewhere who wanted to understand similar societies, which limited his prestige. His professional standing rested on his fieldwork collecting, his annotations, and his library. As he hinted in the quotation that opened this chapter, the library built by Herbert and Letty Halpert was a form of cultural capital with which others at Memorial could build.

Chapter Four

Cat Harbour: Anthropologists in Outports

Nor, fortunately, did the scholars associated with ISER ever conceive of themselves as applied scientists with a mission to transform Newfoundland society. Rather, as seekers after wisdom and truth (as well as higher degrees) they took it upon themselves to understand and to describe Newfoundland society as they found it and as it had evolved. Thus, they joined forces with linguists, historians, geographers, folklorists, lexicographers and others in identifying a distinctive Newfoundland survival culture, in saving some elements of it from extinction, and in promoting a sort of damage control program aimed at conservation or even renaissance ... Not all of these outcomes were planned or in any way consciously sought; rather, the activities of sober scholars struck a responsive chord among Newfoundlanders who were, in come cases, learning for the first time where they had come from and what was their cultural lineage; and learning as well that the move to cut themselves adrift from the old holding ground and to embark upon the flood tide of 20th century "progress" had been perhaps just a little too precipitate.[1]

That was how the historian and academic administrator Les Harris reflected on the place of the community studies at the time of twenty-fifth anniversary of the formation of the Institute of Social and Economic Research (ISER). He was a humanist, able to see culture in Matthew Arnold's sense of the best that has been thought and said, and he saw intrinsic value in culture and the world of letters. Harris was also a rural Newfoundlander who had grown up during the Great Depression and the Second World War and saw the social sciences and the natural sciences as tools to make people's lives better. Newfoundland's cultural heritage could, for him, be a "holding ground" on which people could securely anchor themselves in a world adrift with change. His interest in science was genuine – he admitted to the vanity of wanting to understand geology and marine biology, for example – but his support of the movement to build a research program centred on the study of Newfoundland culture was central to his career.

The study of Newfoundland speech, history, and oral custom were all ways that people who believed they were living through a period of rapid change looked at the past. The linguists, folklorists, and historians turned over the archaic traces that survived into the present, while the anthropologists and sociologists examined in this chapter engaged more explicitly in the study of the present with an eye to the future. ISER was the unit at Memorial that most directly examined and intervened in contemporary social change. Created in 1961 and funded by both government and corporate contributions, the university envisioned ISER as an interdisciplinary research arm that would aid the government in addressing the social problems of modernization. It also had the potential to be of interest to the broader academic community. As Mose Morgan put it:

> Since 1949, however, when the province became a constitutional part of an industrialized country, the process of development which elsewhere has taken decades is being crowded almost into years. Therefore, there exists an opportunity of viewing processes normally long-term but which have occurred in a rather short period ... Unless intensive research is undertaken by trained sociologists in the near future, an unparalleled opportunity for clear analysis of different time periods will be lost.[2]

The Department of Economics and the Department of Sociology and Anthropology each began with a single faculty member in the 1950s and grew slowly, so they relied on graduate students from other universities to perform much of the research on the province. A significant body of research was produced in the 1960s and 1970s. This chapter focuses on the original seven ISER community studies since they best exemplify the university's agenda and earned the most attention among students of Newfoundland society and scholars in other countries alike. These ethnographies were widely read by anthropologists, and their descriptions of Newfoundland culture were taught to several generations of students.

As its director of sociological research from 1961 to 1964, Ian Whitaker believed that ISER should concentrate on broad, descriptive, and basic research rather than on applied studies. He believed such projects would be valuable to both government and business. While the province had many outports that were little changed from the early twentieth century and a few modern towns, Whitaker's top priority was to examine some previously isolated communities that were undergoing change. First they were to describe modernization, and subsequent projects, he hoped, would be more problem oriented. Scholars would examine, for example, "the social and economic effects of minimum wage and unemployment insurance (a team project), the social implications of full-time labour force in the woods industry (probably also a combined effort), the relative immobility of labour in Newfoundland; community studies of particular types of Newfoundland outports, the power structure of a loggers camp, problems of work-attitudes and labour turnover (another team project), and problems of assimilation and adjustment of the Native population of the Labrador."[3]

Since Memorial's faculty members were few in number and the university lacked doctoral programs in the social sciences in the 1960s, these studies were to be conducted by graduate students from other universities. The principal condition attached to the fellowships that brought research students to Newfoundland was that they each spend one year living in a rural community in the province collecting ethnographic data and a second year in residence at Memorial. These junior scholars would create a critical mass of scholars and benefit the university. "One of the purposes of our scheme," Whitaker commented, "is that we ensure in this way that we have in St John's a number of senior students from 'respectable' universities who are in touch with some of the latest thinking in our discipline, and in this way we are able to combat some of the other consequences of geographical isolation."[4] "The subsidization of research in Newfoundland is a secondary purpose of our program, but is certainly not more important that stimulating a local research atmosphere."[5] The studies examined a geographically representative sample of communities that were distant (from St John's) and relatively unknown (to academics). There was one on the south coast, one in the Codroy Valley on the west coast, one on the Northern Peninsula, one on the northeast coast, three in central Newfoundland, and one in Labrador. In all but one case that meant travel by car or by boat to a distant outport; one anthropologist worked among longshoremen in St John's.[6] This set of studies also encapsulated the society in other ways. The communities also included different Christian denominations as well as different industries.

Newfoundland was little known within the Canadian bureaucracy; the Dominion Bureau of Statistics and other Canadian government departments were late in compiling basic information about Canada's newest province and citizens. Although the Commission of Government had gathered much data with a census in 1935 and 1945, the new provincial government was hardly better informed than Ottawa about large areas of the province. That was worrisome since all observers agreed that during the 1950s and 1960s social change was both rapid and should be encouraged. Memorial tried to address the lack of information for both academic and policy reasons, but doing so presented practical challenges.

Social research had to be balanced against the university's primary mission – the education of youth. Between 1949 and roughly 1969 the shortage of faculty, and the time it took to establish graduate programs, forced the university to recruit teachers from outside Canada. The Department of English Language and Literature had a few Newfoundlanders on staff in the 1950s, but it took a generation before any local students were trained in the social sciences and available to take up faculty positions. In the absence of local scholars with the expertise, the university answered the need for social science research by combining funds from varied government departments to create fellowships that enabled postgraduate students who were attending other universities to work in Newfoundland for a period of two years.[7] By funding these graduate students, sponsoring directed research on the part of faculty members, and subsequently publishing books, conference proceedings, and research papers based on that work, ISER laid the foundation of an anthropology of Newfoundland and Labrador. It also provided a base for teaching courses on Newfoundland culture and society to subsequent generations of students and, as we saw in the case of mumming, became the foundation for more abstract work.

This examination of the ISER community studies shows the theoretical and methodological underpinning of social science research on Newfoundland. Bringing in experienced fieldworkers as faculty, and postgraduate students as field workers, rapidly expanded the knowledge. Much of that was communicated to other scholars, and to Newfoundlanders generally, in the series of ISER published ethnographies of Newfoundland outports in the 1960s. By the 1980s anthropology had changed its questions, methods, and approaches, but the body of work sponsored by ISER remains a valuable description of some Newfoundland outports on the cusp of "modernization" and a snapshot of the field of anthropology at the time. The social scientific description of Newfoundland communities conducted between 1965 and 1968 remains unmatched as an intensive examination of the province during any period.

As Harris explained it, the original ISER mandate was "to foster and undertake research into the many economic and social questions arising in Newfoundland and Labrador because of its *unique* historical, geographical, social, and economic position."[8] Don Martindale, a sociologist at the University of Minnesota whom Memorial consulted when setting up ISER, saw promise in that initiative and suggested studies of modernizing communities:

> Your project, by the way, sounds most exciting. I hope that you are planning a series of monographs on the communities. There is a perennial need for recent community studies to begin with. Moreover, since the forces of the mass society have been accelerated since World War II all the community studies prior to 1945 are quite dated. Your project could conceivably supply a basic reference point for every sociologist in North America who is concerned with the transformation of the local community by processes generated in the institutions of the mass society.[9]

On Martindale's suggestion, two Minnesota students were hired to teach sociology at Memorial (Roger Krohn and Noel Iverson), and two others were subsequently awarded research fellowships to work on the sorts of projects Martindale had envisioned.[10] It's worth making a couple of observations. In the early 1960s Morgan and Harris shared the prevailing views that pre-modern societies needed help to transition to modern societies, and the assumptions underlying that belief were the basis of both social science research and much government policy. That was what made Newfoundland outports an ideal laboratory for testing social theory.

The impetus for social science research came from Memorial, but federal and provincial governments provided the funding for community studies. The absence of a PhD program in anthropology or sociology meant that the university lacked the workforce to quickly study a range of topics, and the competition for faculty members during the 1960s made it difficult to hire established scholars who could have overseen such projects. The plain fact was that there was little known of the 1300 communities along 6000 miles of coastline, and without a description of the society the university would be unable to describe the social change, let alone intervene in it. As one anthropologist at the time put it, there was less known of Newfoundland fishing settlements than of East and West Africa.[11] The solution was to recruit graduate students at other universities to conduct fieldwork in Newfoundland by offering them funding. Each "Research Fellow" would have completed any course requirements for his or her degree before taking up the fellowship, and each topic would be approved by Memorial. When ISER's advisory council considered the program of research it decided that "one criterion to be used in selection [of communities to study] should be whether the area might be considered a typical one rather than unique. If choices were made on this basis, the conclusions from such studies would have a broader application than would otherwise be the case."[12]

Since fieldwork was a methodological cornerstone of anthropology, Newfoundland could be enticing. The British anthropologist W.H.R Rivers advocated living among "natives" and collecting data systematically. "His 'genealogical method' identified details of a people's understanding of kinship, and from these their social structure."[13] Such methods encouraged a synchronic approach and an emphasis on the function of various elements of the culture. At the beginning of the century, anthropologists in Britain had tended to work with an evolutionary model, in which they assumed cultures represented different rungs on a ladder. By studying "primitive" cultures one could see these steps, much as paleontologists revealed stratigraphic levels through the study of fossils.

Meanwhile, in the United States the German-trained anthropologist Fraz Boas represented another view – that all peoples were contemporaries and that anthropologists could reveal how cultures borrowed from each other. Both approaches emphasized the comparative, but that shifted as a new methodology emerged. Anthropologists began intensive fieldwork in which they lived within a community for an extended period. The fieldwork method took attention away from the debate between evolutionists and diffusionists and towards understanding contemporary cultures as if they were stable and closed systems. The effort to achieve a synchronic understanding of culture turned anthropologists' attention away from change over time and, in the United States, towards functionalism. By the 1930s, American anthropologists such as Ruth Benedict drew on psychology, for example, and focused on understanding the personality of a culture much as one might understand the psychology of an individual. In Scandinavia, which was to influence Newfoundland research, and in both Britain and the United States, the idealism of the 1960s and government support for research encouraged anthropologists to concern themselves with economic and social development. The development of peasant studies as an area also meant that American-trained anthropologists did not feel that they had to study aboriginal peoples but could build a career on the study of rural North American communities.[14]

The few Canadian anthropologists working in the 1950s and 1960s had emphasized the study of First Nations; the American training that young anthropologists received ensured that. When American-trained anthropologists met their British-trained colleagues at Memorial they did so in a context that encouraged community-based study. American anthropologists were trained within the four-field approach; they studied archaeology, linguistics, physical or biological anthropology, and cultural anthropology. Their British social anthropologist colleagues worked within a different tradition and were more likely to see themselves as sociologists than were their American counterparts.[15] British and American anthropologists and sociologists had been in dialogue, so differences between the two groups may be exaggerated. Like many other small universities, at Memorial the anthropologists also shared a department, and courses, with sociologists – making for a mix of approaches. By the 1950s the idea that anthropologists studied primitive peoples while sociologists studied urban ones had broken down. The boundary between anthropology and sociology in the Newfoundland fieldwork was blurred for greater reasons than their sharing an institutional department.

Ian Whitaker shaped the Newfoundland community studies. Born in Britain in 1928, he had studied at the University of St Andrews and taken an MA at Cambridge and a doctorate at the University of Oslo. From 1952 until taking up an appointment at Memorial in 1959, he was a research fellow at the School of Scottish Studies at the University of Edinburgh. He had previously conducted fieldwork among the Sami in Norway and had studied the "traditional values" of rural people in northern Scotland. In some of his earliest Newfoundland fieldwork he used funding from the Atlantic Provinces Economic Council to take some of his students "then not even half trained as social scientists" with him as he travelled along the south coast of the island in an effort to repeat the sort of study of community values he had conducted in Scotland.[16] He started with two basic assumptions: that the lack of travel and communications meant that the values of the people he surveyed had not fundamentally changed from the remote past and that he was observing a rapidly changing way of life. He interviewed older men, he said, because he felt they would respond best to him (a decision which, of course, affected his data). His method was to prepare narratives that "had to present familiar situations to which an informant might respond with some empathy," he reported, adding "Informants might then discuss them in such a way that their own values might be elicited."[17] His personal priorities affected the first generation of social scientists to study the province.

In 1965 ISER advertised doctoral fellowships in anthropology and sociology – awarding two to students from Cambridge and five to those working at American universities. The first seven fellowships went to Tom Philbrook, John Szwed, James Faris, Shmuel Ben-Dor, Melvin Firestone, Louis Chiaramonte, and Gerald Mars. Having established the context that shaped the initial community studies, we can now turn our attention to the training and field experience of each of these fellows. Philbrook, the first to be appointed, had taken a BA in 1958 and an MA in 1960, both from the University of Minnesota, and was working on a PhD in sociology there when Martindale recommended he apply to Memorial for one of the fellowships. Whitaker's instructions to Philbrook exemplify his own interests in the social changes underway and the role he imagined ISER could play in the province:

The initial appointment will be in the field of urban growth, and we have in mind sending the Associate to one of three places where there are remarkable transitions from what is almost a pre industrial society to an advanced technological or industrial centre: Tilt Cove on the Baie Verte Peninsula, Carol Lake in the Labrador, or Baie d'Espoire on the south coast, each of which is a new centre in a different stage of development ... The basic study would be descriptive with the pinpointing of certain particular problems: in the second example the difficulties of development in a one-industry "company town" would probably be the most relevant.[18]

Whitaker wanted Philbrook to study labour force mobility, changes in social values as the province industrialized, work ethic, and labour force turnover. "I believe," he wrote "a social survey of this sort would be of far wider use to the public at large than merely to the members of one department of the University."[19]

Each research fellow had to find ways of fitting into the community they were to study. Arriving in the mining town of Baie Verte, White Bay, on 20 October 1961, Philbrook fixed up the house him and his wife were to stay in, and they started meeting people in the community. His wife worked as a nurse, supplementing the family income and providing him with a social role in the community, even if it were an unusual one. "My wife, as the Nurse, is somewhat better known than I; although everybody in town knows both of us even though we don't know of them. (I'm known, by the way, as the Nurse's husband which is about as good an introduction as any.)"[20] He soon began the business of interviewing people about the changes underway. After half a year in the field, he realized that he was only getting information from men and asked for funding so that his wife could leave her nursing position and interview women while Philbrook interviewed the husbands. He pointed out that this would also fit with traditional visiting patterns.[21] Whitaker acknowledged that wives assisted the research fellows while they were in the field but did not approve the additional funding.[22]

Philbrook's contemporary at the University of Minnesota, and the second person to be appointed, Shmuel Ben-Dor, was born in Tel Aviv in 1934. Raised on a kibbutz where his father was a teacher, he had studied education and biblical studies at Hebrew University of Jerusalem between 1952 and 1957. His experience as a youth leader working with immigrants who were being assimilated into Israeli society encouraged an interest in anthropology. He attended Columbia University for one year to study that subject, and in 1958 he went to Minnesota to work towards a PhD in sociology.[23] With funding from the federal government's Department of Northern Affairs, ISER decided to have one of the students work in an Inuit community. Ben-Dor applied for that position. Whitaker wanted the study to focus on cultural assimilation or the effect of the Moravian missionaries on Inuit society. He told Ben-Dor that the study could double as a doctoral thesis and that while he would be free to address theoretical problems, the aim was to produce a "descriptive socio-ethnographic study" that along with the others would allow for a comparative study.[24]

With the aid of the Moravian mission, Makovik was selected as the place Ben-Dor would live. This posed challenges beyond transportation and communications difficulties. Makovik was segregated along cultural lines; the Inuit lived on one side of the harbour and the "settlers" (many of whom had mixed European and Inuit ancestry) lived on the other. Although the two peoples worked together when necessary, they mostly kept to themselves. Living among the Inuit initially, and later among the settlers, he was able to earn some measure of trust among both. After a few weeks on the Inuit side of the community, he reported to Whitaker:

> [I] cannot say, however, that I am fully "in." It is a slow process but some progress has been made. One of the criteria for the rate of progress is "pyak" or the locally brewed beer. When I moved from the mission to my present quarters, I had expected to witness an excessive and chronic use of alcohol (according to mission residents), but the picture was of a peaceful, amicable, undisturbed, harmonious little community. It did not last long. A week after my arrival a noticeable portion of my "pacific community" was quite drunk ... fist fighting and bleeding. Was told by two women, "We did not know who you were, but when you expressed your wishes to taste the stuff we realized you were not spying for the mission or the Mounted Police" (Must pat myself on the shoulder for a successful strategy).[25]

It was only after being invited to go on a five-day hunting trip with some Inuit hunters that he was invited to a drinking party for the first time, and then they trusted him enough that he heard complaints against the mission.

The third position was a relatively isolated fishing community on the island's south coast. It was taken up by Louis Chariamonte. Born in 1934, Chariamonte had completed a BA at Brandeis University in 1956 and enrolled in a doctoral program in anthropology at Columbia. He was interested in one of the two projects that Whitaker had suggested: a study of juvenile delinquency (which would have drawn on Chiaramonte's experience as a social worker) or a study of a fishing community.[26] Before moving to Newfoundland Chariamonte had done fieldwork in Barbados, for which he had surveyed the literature on fishing villages, so he seemed well-suited to Newfoundland fieldwork.[27] That made him attractive to Whitaker, who then warned Chiaramonte that while other fieldworkers would be stationed in places with relatively good transportation links, he "will be sent to one of the areas of the island which is not served by any road or land communication, the only contact to the outside world being by the sea."[28] Arriving in St John's in October 1962, Chiaramonte had a couple of weeks to consult with the Department of Sociology before he went to Francois, a south coast outport of about 350 people. Whitaker was willing to overlook the setback that Chiaramonte had not passed his doctoral comprehensive examination because he had faith that the gregarious young man would be able to establish a good rapport with fishermen. In fact,

Whitaker warned him "to not push things too quickly, and always to bear in mind that you are observing a community rather than changing it! Your own dominant personality is something which you should attempt to minimize in the course of your field work."[29]

The opportunity was a good one. Francois, Chiaramonte told his supervisor at Columbia, Conrad Arensberg, "comes as close as you can come to fulfilling the social scientist's dream of the ideal community"; it was relatively small, the people were friendly, and it was "self contained and relatively isolated."[30] It, in other words, was small and isolated enough to make it possible to study a community's assimilation into what Whitaker and Chiaramonte called the "urban complex." And Chiaramonte seems to have made friends in the community easily; the woman with whom he boarded helped him chart the kinship in the town, and a moose-hunting trip with some men cemented his friendships:

> My work is going along very well, rapport has reached a point where if I choose I can take pictures at will. At the moment there are more men that want to talk to me than I have the time to talk to ... I am in the process at present of getting a brief life history of all the adult males. This constitutes for the most part in getting first the age and birth of all members of each family, place of birth, when the man first started to fish, and then a history of all the jobs that he has had up to the present. The average time for this type of an interview is about two hours.[31]

But Whitaker worried that Chiaramonte was slow to find a problem to work on and felt he was in a "theoretical muddle." To impose some discipline on him, Whitaker suggested that Chiaramonte examine if different fishing methods resulted in different family structures and, subsequently, different values.[32]

The presence of American servicemen during the war and Newfoundland's union with Canada had, Chiaramonte thought, aided the diffusion of the "urban complex" of values and material culture. Following Whitaker's idea, he hypothesized that size of the vessel, and the kind of gear people used, determined how long they were away from their families, which in turn affected their social organization and their values. He proposed to study representative examples of these family types:

> One of the indicators that I will use in my analysis is the degree that the respective families have been affected by the urban complex. Families in

Francois can be placed in three categories, Traditional, Modified Traditional and Modern. The modern families incorporate more of the artifacts and values of the urban complex. The modified traditional incorporate less, while traditional tends to utilize some of the artifacts of the urban complex retaining their traditional values.[33]

Chiaramonte dutifully administered questionnaires on work and people's values, but found no support for his hypothesis. As Whitaker wrote to Arensberg:

His initial problem seems to have collapsed. You will recall that he was concentrating on what he thought were differences in values in different fishing families which he thought might be determined by the types of fishing undertaken by these families. In fact he has found there are no such correlations between ecology and values. This is a pity because it might have made a classic study but at least he is honest![34]

Much of his year in Francois had been used up, but, fortunately, he was able to write the essay on mumming and follow it up with a report on an aspect of men's interrelations for which he was awarded an MA. He subsequently revised the work for publication by ISER while working at the University of Bergen with the Norwegian anthropologist Fredrik Barth.[35]

Memorial's connection with Minnesota encouraged the appointment of two fellows from that university, and given Columbia's prominence in anthropology it's not surprising that a student from that program was hired, but that was not the only link that ISER drew on. Having a degree from Cambridge himself, Whitaker was enthusiastic about awarding fellowships to two students of that university. British social anthropologist Jack Goody recommended James Faris and Gerald Mars. At Goody's suggestion, Mars applied to conduct the study of Newfoundland loggers that Whitaker had advertised. Whitaker thought that an Englishman might find less opposition among loggers than a middle-class Newfoundlander or a Canadian.[36]

Indeed, Mars seemed better qualified for the position though his working-class background than his academic record. Born in 1933, Mars had left school at the age of sixteen after which he worked as a fairground barker in Blackpool, as well as several jobs in hotels, shops and cafes. Two years of compulsory military service aided his getting a position working for local government, during which he helped organize a civil service trade union. Night school qualified him for university entrance, and a socioeconomic study of Blackpool earned him a place at Cambridge. His tutor, Goody, suggested he go to Manchester to take a PhD in industrial anthropology and suggested the ISER fellowship as well.[37] Mars's references felt he would fit in among loggers better than he did in the public school atmosphere at Cambridge.[38]

The only Briton among the fellows, Mars was also the only one who had not been admitted to a doctoral program before being appointed, which presented the obvious problem that he had no "home" university to return to after his fieldwork. It also meant that he had to interrupt his fieldwork to fulfil a residency requirement at the University of London. But before he even arrived in Newfoundland, Whitaker had decided that the labour relations problems in the woods industry, in the aftermath of the 1959 IWA strike in which a police officer had been killed, made such a study impractical. Whitaker wondered if Mars might undertake a study of St John's longshoremen.[39] The study would be similar to that which had been planned for loggers in that it would focus on their work, their attitudes towards their lives, and their associations with each other. Here too, the labour relations climate made acceptance as a social scientist difficult. Mars found that the longshoremen knew Memorial to be the premier's special interest, and since so many government posts were patronage positions it was assumed that he was "Joey's stool." "My 'Government' appointment to enquire into the activities of longshore labour was thus regarded as firm evidence that Smallwood was aiming to extend his baleful influence into their sphere."[40]

The beginning of Mars's fieldwork was not auspicious. Whitaker was determined to "sell" the opportunity of working in Newfoundland to the fellows, Mars reflected. He remembers Whitaker picking him up at the airport – buoyant about both the project and the province. Whitaker believed it impossible to penetrate the longshoremen's community without the anthropologist becoming a member of a dockside team, but that raised difficulties. He tried to negotiate an agreement with the Longshoremen's Protective Union (LSPU) whereby Mars would work with a crew and his wages would be paid to the union so that he would not be providing free labour for the employers.[41] The union would not allow Mars to take a job away from one of its members, so he relied on drinking in the taverns that longshoremen frequented and hoping that they would talk to him. The only men willing to talk to him were not members of the union, which added to the longshoremen's view of Mars as an outsider.

Since the longshoremen initially suspected him of being a spy for the anti-union premier, Mars tried claiming he was affiliated with the University of London rather than Memorial, which was "received where it was listened to at all with at most a tolerant and usually a silent scepticism."[42] They suspected he was an investigator from Lloyd's of London looking into pilfering on the docks. As he pointed out, people's suspicions reveal what they are frightened of.[43] The dockworkers were hostile, but he adopted a new tactic. Having reconciled himself to not being able to earn the trust of regular gang members he attempted "entertaining" members of the LSPU executive. When the union president came over to Mars's apartment, Mars was able to use his union background and his knowledge of dockworkers in other cities to find common ground. Events took their own course.

An American-born literature professor at Memorial visited Mars while the union president was in the apartment, and he subsequently wrote a letter to a local newspaper calling the longshoremen Neanderthals, questioning their intelligence, suggesting they were a hundred years behind the times, and accusing them of theft. Mars was concerned that the union president would associate him with the views of the English professor and wrote an immediate rebuttal to the accusations, which was also published in the paper. This earned Mars some trust. Employers and the union had allowed Mars to attend contract negotiations, but some employers began to feel that Mars was advising the union. The employers banned Mars from the negotiating table, encouraging the rank and file to see him as one of them.[44] Mars rented an apartment near the harbour and let the word out that men could get a drink of home-brewed beer there. That enabled him to socialize and question men, but it left him without much access to women's views. Being a bachelor and a Jew also made access to the wives and daughters of longshoremen difficult, he thought, but since he was neither Roman Catholic nor Protestant he found both groups freer in their discussion of sectarian differences than they would otherwise have been.[45]

A lockout and strike caused the longshoremen to spend a lot of time in the union hall, giving Mars the opportunity to ferry beer to them and administer a survey to the members. Mars's experience as a trade unionist also encouraged him to advise the union. He suggested adopting a rotation system like that used by dockworkers in London, for example. Whitaker was angered, telling Mars that "I felt that you yourself had become an agent of change, and this fact unless brought out in your writing would invalidate much of your discussion. If brought out however it would render you open to serious criticism from your colleagues, being a gross breach of the traditional role of the social scientist. Nowadays one has come to realize more clearly that some degree of involvement of anthropologist with the peoples he is studying is inevitable."[46] Mars's supervisor, Raymond Firth, concurred: "[I]t does certainly seem as if in Mars's case it has gone so far as to imperil the scientific quality of his data."[47] Other fieldworkers became members of the communities in which they lived and empathized with the subjects of their studies, to varying degrees, but Mars presented the greatest threat to ISER's governing committee's self image as social scientists.

Melvin Firestone found the people on the Great Northern Peninsula much friendlier than Mars experienced in the city. While a student in New Mexico he had read an advertisement for the ISER fellowship, and upon getting the job he searched with little luck for publications about the island that was soon to be home. Firestone and his wife, Sharon, drove across North America, took the ferry to Port aux Basque and drove to St John's on the just-being completed Trans Canada Highway.[48] Whitaker had originally assigned Melvin to Flowers Cove, but there was no house available, so they settled in nearby Savage Cove, a smaller and less affluent community. Living conditions were rough compared to those he had experienced in Seattle, and Mel and Sharon had to rely on neighbours to teach them life skills.

> The house we live in has two floors, but we shall probably move one of the beds downstairs for the warmth. There is no running water at present, although the landlord says that he will repair the kitchen pump for us ... We are learning about country living from the ground up. How to keep a fire going in the stove is lesson one. She supplied us with some home made bread last night since none is available locally. Both they and we are conscious of our inadequacies, and we have somewhat been taken in hand. I am thinking of doing a paper entitled, "The Ethnologist as Boob."[49]

They were not only a couple in the domestic sense, including interacting in the social life of the community as man and wife, but both collected data through interviews, conversations, and participant observation.

The Firestones had arrived at a time of great change in Savage Cove. As road construction linked outports to the outside world their nature shifted, and the ISER ethnographers were there to observe the changes. Isolation is, of course, relative, and the anthropologists may have underestimated the amount of contact people had with outsiders in earlier periods – historical evidence shows a high measure of labour mobility and transportation by sea in many outports. Yet, before the arrival of the road made contact with outsiders a regular occurrence, he reported, many people feared "strangers." Some parents, he reported, even disciplined their children by threatening that strangers would take them away, including on more than one occasion a threat that "Mr Firestone" would take them if they did not behave. Despite popular wariness of people who were not known, Firestone and his wife felt they had been accepted by people of Savage Cove (who still insisted on calling him Mr Firestone though).

He admired the warmth and tolerance of his neighbours, and in 2012 he reflected that he and his wife would not have encountered similar affection in any other part of North America. Being the only Jewish person many of them had ever met was not an issue, he felt, as people told him they were never "dirty about religion."[50] But Whitaker worried about both the various fellows' sociological descriptions and their rapport with informants. "Neither he nor his wife really seems to have established a warm relationship with the people in his community, although I do not think it is a particularly 'difficult' one to stay in," Whitaker wrote to Firestone's supervisor, "I think perhaps the root cause of this is the unwillingness of both of them to face up to any rebuff, which of course is bound to come the way of any field anthropologist."[51] Whitaker recognized that Firestone's collection of folk songs was useful, but he thought it should be secondary to more orthodox anthropology. He thought the paper on mummers was interesting, "but again I look upon this rather as a sideline."[52]

Perhaps some of the formality with which people treated Mr Firestone reflected esteem they had for someone from the university or an American, rather than fear that, as an outsider, his behaviour was unpredictable. Looking back on his experience, he also reflected that many rural people were self-conscious about speaking differently than urban people, and they felt that outsiders perceived them as unsophisticated. Not only did some people from Canada express pejorative attitudes towards Newfoundlanders in that era, but some St John's residents expressed disparaging views towards outport people, and many of those whom Firestone met had internalized feelings of inferiority. After explaining the concept of cultural relativism to a person in Savage Cove one day, for example, the person replied that while that might indeed be true, it did not change the fact that "we don't talk right."[53]

Newfoundland was, for Firestone as with the others, a true terra incognita when he arrived. He was able to read only a single anthropological study that seemed relevant, an ethnography of Blanc Sablon, a community on the Quebec north shore.[54] Otherwise, each of the anthropologists started with a blank slate.

> The lack of knowledge here [of patrilocal extended family structure], as well as the dearth of information about the folk culture of Newfoundland as a whole, demonstrates that in many areas much more is known about the lives of North American aborigines than of the contemporary residents. The publication of the work that has been done by the various anthropologists who worked in other parts of Newfoundland as Research Fellows of the Institute of Social and Economic Research of the Memorial University of Newfoundland will help fill this gap.[55]

While Firestone believed that there was a potential for comparative study, he did not think that his description of Savage Cove could be generalized to all of Newfoundland. He thought that each ethnography was a portrait of a community and that each anthropologist had his own interpretation.[56]

The research fellows worked within a theoretical literature of their own choosing and wrote to satisfy their supervisory committees at their home universities. Firestone had been interested in psychological anthropology, while John Szwed, who did his fieldwork in the Codroy Valley area of the island's west coast, used the Newfoundland study to suggest an answer to a different kind of theoretical question. Szwed had studied economics and business at Marietta College in Illinois, and linguistics and communications at Ohio State University, before taking up sociology and anthropology.

By chance, he had developed an interest in Newfoundland while working as a research assistant for the Department of Motion Pictures at Ohio State. "After doing considerable research on the past uses and potential of the ethnographic film we intended to develop a number of ideas in the form of a film study of an isolated community in Newfoundland." Funding for such a film did not materialize, but he had "the benefit of reading in the history and geography of Newfoundland."[57] Many anthropologists, including Szwed, had rejected the idea that peasant societies were inherently stable and simple. Evidence from communities around the world showed peasants behaving in individualistic ways. The question, for him, then became how communities can be cohesive when there are differences between the values of the individual (the private culture) and the values of the community (the public culture).

Szwed started with the premise that Newfoundland outports had a "peasant" culture – which he defined as an intermediate stage (in which relations were contractual) between a primitive society (with kinship determining relationship) and modern society (typified by commercial relationships). This point might be emphasized. *Peasants* were not a social category used in Newfoundland; the category was deduced from a general theory and European society. He was not attempting to set out a complete ethnography but rather "to understand social relationship in a parish of Newfoundland peasants through the public imagery they employ, and through the mechanisms they employ – particularly the economic – used to support and integrate private cultures."[58] Much of this was a function of his graduate training. Fellow anthropologist Tom Nemec later pointed out that Szwed's emphasis on the role of godparents in the community, for example, was not so much a reflection of something he observed in the town as it was a result of his supervisor having written on the role of godparents in a peasant society, and thus Szwed had little choice but to include the analysis.[59]

Firestone and Szwed's contemporary James Faris wrote what became one of the most widely read, and the most controversial, of the ethnographies. It merits an extended treatment for the opportunity it presents to examine the practice of fieldwork in a Newfoundland outport in the mid-1960s. Born in Colorado in 1936, Faris grew up in the Southwestern United States and did a BSC in chemistry before switching to anthropology for graduate work. Having developed an interest in social systems organized along duolineal descent, he wrote Jack Goody to ask about one such group in Ghana. On the basis of that interest, Goody invited Faris to do a PhD at Cambridge, but as Faris was about to travel to the Sudan to start fieldwork, a coup in the region prevented him from going. Fortunately for Faris, who was "broke, discouraged, [and] disappointed," Goody had learned that ISER was offering research fellowships.[60] Goody had suggested that Faris look into "modern societies," after all, he commented to Whitaker, "who wants to spend their lives on dual descent and cross-cousin marriage?"[61] Faris agreed, but besides the practical matters of providing for his family on a student fellowship, he wondered if anthropologists encountered hostility in Newfoundland. "If the places are plagued with social workers," he commented, "a researcher may have a hard time."[62]

4.1. Upper Harbour, Lumsden North, summer 1964, general view from the water. (James Faris Collection, Special Archives and Collection Division, QEII Library, Memorial University of Newfoundland.)

Faris and his family took a steamer across the Atlantic, arriving in St John's in January 1964. ISER's directors suggested that Faris select a community on the northeast coast. The "vacancies" were Carmenville, a farming, logging, and fishing community, and Musgravetown, a similar but larger town.[63] In travelling to Wesleyville, Bonavista Bay, he met the local merchants from Lumsden North – Cyril Robbins and his wife, Naida. The Robbinses were about to move to Lumsden South, so a house large enough for the Faris family was available. Faris liked Lumsden North right way. "The place abounds with local color, so I've decided to give up the fellowship and write novels" he joked with Whitaker.[64] Formally known as Cat Harbour, Lumsden North seemed relatively isolated and "traditional," and Faris and his family were able to share the Robbins's house with them for a few weeks and then continue living in it.[65] Faris used the name Cat Harbour for his study rather than its twentieth-century name, not to disguise the community but because that was its name in much of the historical material he cited.[66] It was a typical northeast coast outport in many respects – in 1961 it had 269 people, about half of whom were less than twenty-one years of age. A three-room elementary school served younger students, and older children travelled two miles by road to high school in Lumsden South. The town had been connected to the electric power grid in 1963, just before Faris arrived, and about half the town had running water and a third had flush toilets. Since connection to the outside world by road was recent, only about half the families had vehicles. One in ten had a television.[67] Settled in the late eighteenth century, its economy had been dominated by the cod fishery, although other species, such as lobster, were harvested, and by the mid twentieth century some men travelled to other places for work.

The people of Lumsden North did not know what to make of Faris at first; he was bearded when most local men were clean shaven, he had no boat when all adult men had boats, and he seemed to not work when physical labour was nearly universal. Nearly fifty years later, Faris recounted his introduction to the people of the cove. He walked through the community a couple of times, only to have people go into their houses to avoid having to speak to him. Naida Robbins had put it out in the community that Faris was a graduate student doing a community study. That explanation was vague, and some remained suspicious that he had a hidden agenda. He had noted that during the winter about a dozen local men would gather at the largest merchant's shop, waiting their turn to do business with the merchant, or just hang out before going to their fish stores to mend nets and prepare gear for the coming season. He recounted the slow process of people becoming acclimatized to him:

I would come in, stand next to the last man leaning against the counter near the door (always facing inward – i.e., toward all the others) and simply wait. Initially all talk ceased until I finally left, so as to not disrupt their sessions any longer. After about a week of this, I came in, and the last man I was standing next to just ever so briefly nodded to me in acknowledgment – I immediately left, ran home to tell my wife, etc., in celebration. Then gradually men would continue their conversations (usually cuffers) when I came in, until finally all went back to normal, just as if I were a member of the community. I rarely talked, even to the guy I might be standing next to, and learned the appropriate slight nod of acknowledgment upon entering.[68]

4.2. Jack Melindy's shop, Lumsden North, 1964. (James Faris Collection, Special Archives and Collection Division, QEII Library, Memorial University of Newfoundland.)

Once his presence was less of an intrusion, he began more system-atic fieldwork. In the early spring he started at one end of the com-munity and proceeded to the other end, visiting each house in turn to collect the sort of genealogical data that provided a base for the study. Families knew when their turn for a visit from him was next, so they had time to prepare tea for him. Later visits to homes elicited more gossip, and the members of the Faris family started to be invited to birthday parties, weddings, and baby showers that allowed less obtru-sive data collection. By the time all of the houses had been visited the first time, Faris started visiting men in their fish stores as they worked, went hunting with them, and sometimes managed to get invited to fish with them.[69] He was especially fortunate that Cyril and Naida Robbins became friends and informants. "The rapport advantages [of having the Robbinses' aid] are immense," he reported after a few days in the town, and they were "extremely helpful and kind."[70] But the introduc-tions by the merchant family may not have reassured everyone that Faris was trustworthy. After a couple of weeks settling in, Faris wrote of his difficulty being accepted by the residents:

We are rather loosely entrenched, though people still walk over snow drifts to avoid having to meet me on the road. Everyone in town, of course has conjured up all sorts of tales regarding my purpose, etc., and our landlady is bursting with "inside" information, news, speculation and gossip on her new tenants. This has done her community image worlds of good ... Natives are friendly.[71]

As for his research question:

I have no "focus" unless perhaps you could call my interest in kinship, etc. a "problem area" – and inasmuch, my thesis will be dangerously post facto – but at least not subject to standard rural sociology biases. I'm look-ing at LN as if it were on the moon, and one is surprised to find how few of our hallowed notions of rural folk really hold up if one comes in from the bottom up. My theoretical departure then, if one wants to call it that, is simply in the methodological orientation.[72]

Each of the communities the fellows studied differed from each other, and each anthropologist drew on his own training and asked his own questions. Faris joked with Szwed about how their preconceptions determined how they perceived the people in each of their communities:

Mel [Firestone] seems to be having some trouble with a "theoretical frame-work," which to my mind is a complete delusion, but his training has oriented him toward this extremely destructive problem-focus approach – probably the greatest device ever to stimie [*sic*] intelligent research. He does have data to do a good thesis however – it appears 'tis only a mental block. Predictably, however, he found flowers/savage cove a group of prudish, repressed, drab fisherfolk, whereas LN (again, predictably) I find a wild bunch of drunken rakes (reminds me of the ian (lapps are scotch presbyterians) vs Pearson (lapps are erotic pagans).[73]

"I am interested in describing and explaining what I found," in Lumsden North, Faris noted, "by reference to the conceptualizations of social fact as abstracted by the people themselves" rather than social categories developed by theorists. But that did not mean that any of the people in Lumsden would have recognized the social categories in Faris's analysis or "to say they might have written this thesis, nor even that they would agree with its conclusions, but I am convinced that the structural logic as I outline it does have reference to the fundamental principles governing society in Lumsden, and that such society operates on such principles, even tho the actors may not specifically articulate them."[74]

Before arriving in Newfoundland Faris believed that participant observation was the way to study a culture, but he had worried that "I have never worked in communities of this sort and don't know what sort of fisherman I might make (New Mexico is a long way from much water)."[75] Faris's method of doing anthropology was, in his own words, nothing fancy – he talked to people, asked questions, and observed the community. It was not all passive observation, however. On at least one occasion he provoked a situation in which he could watch behaviour, as he did when he questioned one woman in the presence of another woman whom he knew she did not get along with. His questioning provoked a lie, which was promptly challenged by the rival.[76] While some anthropologists worked alongside those they were studying, none of the original seven ISER fellows did so. Faris mostly "stayed out of the way" as men worked and relied on interviewing people and observing behaviour for his information. Although they were unfamiliar with anthropologists and a few sometimes suspected Faris of being a Russian spy, Faris remembered that people in the community were patient with his questions, and he thought that they competed with each other to ensure that he had the right information.[77]

All of the anthropologists working on Newfoundland were men, but several of them had wives who helped with the work. Szwed's, Philbrook's, and Firestone's wives accompanied them into the field, although Ben-Dor, Chiaramonte, and Mars were on their own. Faris's whole family was in Lumsden North, blurring the line between being an informant and an observer. Faris seems to have had little difficulty gathering information from women in the community – indeed, Naida Robbins became a principal informant. It's also worth considering the ways that Faris's wife, Jennifer, and his children gathered data for him. Biographies of fieldworkers are sometimes structured by a narrative of a quest; the scientific outsider makes a solitary journey into a remote area, perhaps with the aid of a naive local informant, and discovers the significance of the local artefact that is unrecognized by the natives. Having a wife and four children provided an *entré* into relationships with many local families. As Faris later reflected:

My own kids were wonderful – they bring home gossip, tradition, child rearing practices, rumor, prejudices, etc., etc. It also "normalizes" you to have a spouse and kids in the field. Since most people in the world have them, you are not quite so strange. Maybe a witch, maybe a spy, but still a normal witch or normal spy. My wife was quite busy with little kids, of course, and I wasn't too much help domestically, as I was usually out in the community. She was a very open and friendly person, so made friends easily. Our closest friends were the merchant and his family, the wife of whom was a very socially conscious woman and found the prestige of having "Mr. Faris" living in their old house a real asset (as well as source of gossip and inside information). We got invited to their place (a new ugly ranch-style house in Lumsden South) quite often, and I could ask questions, observe appropriate/inappropriate behavior, etc., etc. I certainly would have hated to be single in the field. Kids are mini anthropologists – they just haven't the hubris, and bring home wonderful things I wouldn't have thought about, nor even knew about. Anthropology really involves no special methodologies (or not the kind of anthro I'm interested in) or secrets – just openness, curiosity, interest in other people and their lives. Kids all more or less have this, and easily make friends. My oldest started school in the one room Cat Harbour school house, so she certainly knew all the kids more or less her age. I would have had no access to children's culture, growing up models, and many attitudes without my kids as mini-anthropologists. Actually, they were less mini-anthropologists than actual informants, for they obviously wanted to blend in, be accepted, etc., so they became sort of naive mini-Cat Harbour folk. They soon filled with all the frights, prejudices, discipline experts, etc. of all the kids in the community.[78]

Observation of his own children became grist for his analysis:

Gretchen was one day playing with Maxine and trying to scare her. Gretchen is thoroughly embedded in the local mileux now, and said "I'm a stranger, I'm a stranger" trying to make a face, chasing Maxine and attempting to look fierce. This is something she has picked up, and is the local equivalent of saying "I'm a monster, or I'm the devil, etc."[79]

His family also provided many opportunities for observation that would have been difficult for a single man. On one evening, for example, two girls, aged ten and eleven, were at the Faris house (presumably to visit the Faris children) and provided him with details about a local unmarried woman who had a child in St John's.[80] Faris's wife, Jennifer, also attended all the meetings of the United Church Women and gained insights into women's lives.[81] Anthropologists long ago dismissed notions of themselves as objective outsiders describing a culture, and Faris's open-ended research method and the ways that his family became involved in social relations poses questions for the usefulness of an insider/outsider dichotomy when assessing his work.

We know something of Faris's agenda, but we know little of why people cooperated with him. They were not likely naive – and had reasons of their own for sharing information with the fieldworker. Faris perceived some informants as socially ambitious and trying to make their mark outside of Lumsden North by allying themselves to him as an outsider. Access to the Faris family, he believed, gave these people an opportunity to gain prestige in the wider world. He thought that Naida Robbins, for example, "was to some extent structurally equating me with her own role – one of the 'in' U.C. [United Church] faction – she has largely lost any concept of us as objective outsiders." On a car trip with the two of them, Cyril seemed eager to tell Faris of infrastructure improvements in Lumsden South, while Nadia seemed eager to tell him of events in the life of a local man. "Clearly they were dying to tell us the latest news," Faris noted, "they both enjoy their role as 'insider' purveyors of news."[82] Faris's attention might be sought for other reasons as well. In the context of tensions between adherents of the United Church and the Jehovah's Witness (JW), people may have had their own reasons for wanting the Faris family on their side of this divide. To avoid being perceived as part of one camp or the other, he attended both UC and JW meetings and took advantage of both opportunities to take notes on the religious aspects of people's lives.

> The U.C. reaction to my attending the J.W. assembly was mixed. The more sophisticated regarded it as a scientific venture, knowing "that I knew better." The less sophisticated didn't know what to think, and some undoubtedly thought I was being converted. Certainly the J.W.s were delighted. I am not sure to what extent they saw me as a convert, tho they clearly maximized my visit. Elmore ... is after big game, and would be delighted to nab an intellectual outsider. He told Mrs Mcdonald [the wife of the doctor at the Brookfield hospital] that "Mr Faris comes to all our meetings and you should see the notes he takes." I think Elmore knows that the notes I take are sociological, but this would indicate he doesn't, or that he is using the opportunity to best advantage.[83]

Faris's last reading of this situation was likely correct – that this is an example of a member of the community using the anthropologist's activities for his own purposes.

After fourteen months in Lumsden, save brief trips to St John's to meet with colleagues and use the library, and with a wife and four children, and another child on the way, Faris wanted to return to Cambridge as quickly as possible. All of the fellows who were married found the cost of living in St John's high when trying to get by on their fellowship. Perhaps because Whitaker had left Memorial and his successor had not yet arrived, Faris was not required to fulfil a residency in St John's as were his predecessors, so he returned to the UK to finish writing.[84]

From the vantage point of nearly fifty years later, Faris felt that his training as an anthropologist had been double-edged in its effect on his fieldwork and his publications. He knew nothing of Newfoundland when he accepted the fellowship and had read little of the then sparse literature on North Atlantic fisheries or Newfoundland – he had been preparing to go to Africa after all. Knowing little of outport culture gave him fresh eyes, but the classical anthropology he had read, and his desire to establish himself as an anthropologist rather than a sociologist, encouraged him to pay close attention to kinship. Although he reflected that even had the study of kinship not been part of what defined anthropology, he would have discovered that on his own by living in the community. His desire to establish himself as an

4.3. Newman Parsons and another loading bulk salt codfish into a truck for shipment. Lumsden North, fall 1964. (James Faris Collection, Special Archives and Collection Division, QEII Library, Memorial University of Newfoundland.)

anthropologist prompted him, he later believed, to overemphasize some of the "exotic" aspects of the culture such as witchcraft.[85] He also felt that his time in Newfoundland continued his radicalization. While a student in New Mexico and Cambridge he had been influenced by the Vietnam War protests and the emerging critique that anthropologists had been complicit in imperialism. Seeing economic exploitation in Lumsden North first-hand, learning about the history of the Fishermen's Protective Union, and reading historians such as Prowse encouraged him to move further to the left. In 2012, he also reflected that these factors may have caused him to overemphasize local resistance to economic inequality in Lumsden North.[86]

Each of the studies had required a year-long immersion in the community. Faris believed that an extended stay in a community could reveal useful sociological information and advised Colin Story (the brother of George Story and a senior civil servant) that government policy would fail if it were based on superficial knowledge of outports. "Though you are undoubtedly aware of it," he wrote, "too many projects are based on the two-day survey-type recommendations, and I can testify from experience, it took me three months to untangle the lies I got in the first two days."[87] This experience was similar to that of another anthropologist a few years later. Tom Nemec also reflected on the difficulties of relying on oral informants with whom the researcher had not established a trusting relationship. By triangulating the documentary record with what different oral informants told him and what the same informant told him at different times, Nemec felt accurate information could be gleaned.

> [F]or my first two and one-half months in the field, except for a tiny minority of trusting friends, any attempt at systematic questioning of residents was relatively unprofitable and in some instances yielded only fabrications, half-truths, laughter, ridicule or some other evasion. In time my small coterie of friends began to expand and from this group a set of useful, trusted informants precipitated out. After six months continuous participant observation (including some hard drinking at times), sufficient rapport and empathy had been achieved with select informants to permit discussion of a wide range of sensitive topics. After thirteen months in the field, including a summer "on the water" and initiation into the private world of inshore cod fishermen, I found I had gained some measure of stature in the eyes of the men of the community. Accordingly, I was finally in a position – given my newly acquired knowledge and rapport – to elicit a comprehensive portrait of the fishery, both past and present, from a variety of fishermen.[88]

Only after building relationships with informants, and working as a shareman for a season, did Nemec feel he got reliable information. Faris made many lasting friendships, but he had not worked with the local men as Nemec was to do. Faris had realized that some of what he had been told was untrue too; he had identified the *cuffer* as a popular form – people would exaggerate or fabricate stories or information for entertainment. Why did people lie to anthropologists? Testing how credulous an outsider was may have been good sport or a way of evading cooperation while not being seen to be rude. It may also have been a test in the sense of ascertaining whether one was an insider or an outsider. In a slightly different vein, Widdowson reflected on being put through a "catechism" of questions when first meeting an informant – a process in which the person established that he was not a threat to the daughters or otherwise up to something nefarious. After passing the test people were generous with their time and food, and he felt he was treated as family even though he had known them only a short while. Such testing may have also levelled the power dynamic between researcher and informant.

By 1966 the political situation in the Sudan had changed, allowing Faris to move there for the fieldwork he had originally wanted to do. As we have seen, it did not end his involvement with Newfoundland; he contributed to Story and Halpert's *Christmas Mumming*, and in 1972 he returned to Lumsden for follow-up work. While he was away, the community had been resettled to nearby Lumsden South. Some of his old friends suspected that his time living in the merchant's house (a merchant who had moved his own family to Lumsden South a couple of years earlier), and asking odd questions, was sponsored by the government, which wanted him to collect information in preparation for the move.[89] That was a reasonable inference for them to make, despite the fact that Faris maintained he had known nothing of bureaucratic agendas during his initial fieldwork. The government funded ISER research hoping to find opportunities to modernize the economy of rural areas – but that did not mean that every research project was part of some master plan.

It was one thing to conduct the fieldwork, and by 1966 the first set of ethnographies had been completed, it was another thing to disseminate the knowledge gained. Whitaker's resignation to take up a post in England left his successor to publish the ethnographies. It had long been ISER's plan to publish the work as a way of establishing the university's research profile, and Robert Paine hoped the ethnographies would be a basis for comparative work as well. After service in the Second World War, the British-born Paine read for a BA in modern history at Oxford in 1950 and began a postgraduate degree in anthropology. The next fifteen years saw him moving back and forth between fieldwork among the Sami of Norway and writing at Oxford and Bergen, Norway. His choice to work on a northern people was a significant one. British social anthropologists were nearly entirely preoccupied with Africa, and Paine believed that his work in Norway made it unlikely that he would get an academic appointment in Britain. Despite that, he had established a reputation as an ethnographer and was about to assume the headship of the Department of Anthropology in Oslo in 1965, when Memorial hired him.

M.O. Morgan asked Paine to head the Department of Anthropology and Sociology and to be sociology director of ISER. His appointment had been aided by George Story, who saw Paine as "one of the bright hopes in his field" and thought he would "see at once the possible role of the Institute, Extension, etc. in [economic] development, and although he may not himself plunge into it, he will be the kind of man who will see that academic staff are taken on and made available for contract work."[90] A brief visit to St John's was enough for Paine to recognize the research potential in his new home. Recruiting Paine also relied on assuring him that he would be able to attract colleagues, researchers, and graduate students, and he was particularly interested in recruiting people to study the Native people of Labrador.[91] For a certain kind of person, Newfoundland offered a tremendous career opportunity. "Welcome to Memorial University," Chiaramonte wrote to Paine:

> The possibilities for research come as close to satisfying an Anthropologist's dream as I have seen. It almost seems that you can decide the type of problem that you would like to explore and then looking around pick the community to satisfy your problem. What I am really saying, is that one would not expect to find so much variety in an island that appears on the surface to be so homogenous. We (the men who have done research here) are amazed at the variations to be found from one community to another.[92]

In a review of ISER's publications, Anthropologist Anthony Cohen, an ISER fellow a couple of years later, believed that under Paine's leadership the institute embodied a "Newfoundland school" in the sense of *school* as a distinctive style of scholarly work. Not that everyone at Memorial adhered to one theory or approach, but all emphasized the local ethnography and everyday politics among members of communities.[93] In 1998 Paine reflected on his excitement of building a team of scholars during the early days:

> This was certainly a new enterprise for me: setting up programmes, convening colloquia, initiating a publishing programme ("ISER Books"), directing others' research, and – what really mattered – producing a team. The key to attracting top-line persons was to arrange matters so that the

teaching department and the research institute enriched each other. So the real *coup* in those heady days was persuading the Dean of Arts (and through him the rest of the ISER Executive) to introduce faculty "joint appointments" whereby a person would alternate on an annual or semester basis between research and teaching.[94]

Story was enthusiastic about Paine helping to develop expertise on the cultures of Labrador. As Story put it in a draft of a letter to Paine, he had "been hoping for years that the university in Newfoundland would wake up to the existence of our 'overseas colony.'" A more dynamic ISER would also, Story felt, rejuvenate the Arts Faculty by building on the model used in the sciences.

> It would be worth putting the idea of a couple of research plus teaching appointments to Morgan: our scientists do it through postdoctoral fellowships. The Institute is a superb means of bringing in the social sciences. It's one way of keeping a lively current of ideas flowing and of avoiding having everyone [being] too busy with teaching.[95]

Over subsequent decades Paine himself undertook studies on political rhetoric, gossip, friendship, patronage, and other topics, but his greatest role in the faculty of arts was that of an academic entrepreneur. ISER had been established to foster work in the social sciences, and directors were appointed from different departments to oversee the work. Paine, by virtue of his energy and the fact that the secretary of ISER was in an office near the Department of Anthropology, took a greater measure of control over the organization than had Whitaker.[96] Interaction with Paine benefitted academics and students working on a range of topics. He also developed ISER Books, through which he was able to bring Newfoundland, Eastern Arctic, and North Atlantic scholarship to a broad audience. Most of the fellows were pleased to have their books published, although reflecting back on his experience, Gerald Mars, whose study was not published, thought that the ISER fellows had been exploited a little. He felt that they had been pressured into publishing their reports quickly; ISER's goal of establishing its research credentials in a hurry precluded the student's from taking their time with their studies.[97]

Paine had connections to Norwegian anthropologists that encouraged Scandinavian scholars, such as Cato Wadel and Ottar Brox, to work in Newfoundland, and Newfoundland academics to think about

Norway and Iceland as comparative examples. The comparison to other northern countries that relied on their resource base had precedents. At the opening of Newfoundland's post-war constitutional debate, R.A. MacKay had raised the example of "other small countries, notably Iceland, which in many ways resembles Newfoundland, [that] have built on a slender base of natural resources unique communities and reasonable standards of living."[98] He made clear that the choice of political independence was to opt for a standard of living similar to Northern European countries and not the standard of government services that North Americans expected in the twentieth century. As early as 1966 the university had revised ISER's constitution to allow "for comparative methodology and field research."[99] As Harris commented, "the 'unique' in Newfoundland and Labrador economy and society, in order to be understood properly, has to be measured and described in relation to certain other economies and societies."[100] The 1970 constitution provided for the ongoing research in Scandinavia and the eastern Arctic, and there was hope of expanding comparative work into Appalachia and the West Indies. Appalachia is a choice that reveals something of the thinking among ISER's directors, since as an "isolated" and "traditional" area it had been the focus of much folklore research in the early twentieth century.

While under Whitaker's direction ISER had funded ethnographies of communities because he wanted information on Newfoundland culture and cared little about what theoretical approach a student might use, Paine emphasized the study of themes rather than places. He organized international conferences in St John's, sometimes on abstract topics, such as the one on "friendship," rather than cultures or regions.[101] These brought academics from other countries to St John's to make cross-cultural comparisons. These conferences, edited collections, and publishing books on other parts to the North Atlantic litoral enhanced Memorial's reputation as a centre for anthropology. This fostered theoretical work, but, as Firestone later reflected, the changes that Paine brought to Memorial meant that the earlier outport ethnographies that had allowed for comparative studies were not followed up on.[102] The period in which most of these studies were done – between, roughly, 1964 and 1968 – became the moment in time of which we have the richest ethnographic description of outports.

In the preceding chapter, we saw how Firestone's emphasis on the "stranger" and his thoughts on mummers focused interdisciplinary attention on that phenomena, but it was Faris's book *Cat Harbour* that provoked the greatest attention of the Newfoundland ethnographies. He suggested that the harsh historical and material conditions of life required that people's cultural competence take the form of traditions that discouraged unpredictable behaviour. Predictability was important to the continued function of the community, but the observation of other anthropologists that traditions served the function of maintaining solidarity was, in his view, both trite and tautological.[103] People's culture was shaped by their history, and he believed that the community had "entered and persisted in a potentially dangerous and hostile physical and social universe" and "that a description and explanation of the ordering of this experience is sufficient to understand Cat Harbour."[104]

His suspicion of imperialism and his reading of Newfoundland historians had encouraged him to believe that the eighteenth-century Royal Navy had persecuted settlers, that the Beothuk had been hostile to early settlers, and that nineteenth-century Protestant/Catholic conflict had divided early residents – leaving a lasting suspicion of outsiders that could be still seen in Lumsden. "It appears that perhaps the *very* early history of this region," he commented to Harris, "may have more immediate bearing on current attitudes and behaviour that I had originally anticipated."[105] He consulted historical records in London and historians such as Harris and Rothney, who confirmed that settlement had been illegal (although they maintained that settlers had been deserters from the West of England merchants rather than the Royal Navy).[106] Nimshi Crewe, of the Newfoundland Archives, on the other hand, warned Faris that there was no evidence of repression on the part of the British Navy. Furthermore, he suggested, that, unlike Faris's view, kinship through female lines was important in many Newfoundland families and that he should be careful of saying that Roman Catholics had been "forced out" of Lumsden North in the absence of any proof. As for the idea that early settlers were "fugitives and pirates," Crewe advised Faris "to excise this idea completely from your mind. I have heard it a number of times in various parts of the East Coast of the Island. It is absolutely untrue generally. It has grown up in the minds of our ill-educated people, whose present recollections of their forbears here are very tenuous from what sources I can ever find."[107]

While functionalism predisposed some anthropologists to imagine communities existed in equilibrium; Faris was influenced by the anti-functionalism of British social anthropology and initially thought that the wariness expressed towards strangers had a historical basis in past conflict, rather than a "functional" role. Faris's account of life in

Lumsden North examined the words people used for material things in their lives and the idioms they used for kinship and social and economic roles. In it, Faris attempted to describe the "ethnosemantic" system of Cat Harbour in a way that one could generate predictions of behaviour based on an understanding of the rules. This generative operation made behaviour predictable to other members of the community. Faris suggested that the observer needed to understand the "dynamics of interaction" if he or she were to understand behaviour as rational:

> Subscribers to the moral order cannot articulate the dynamics of successful interaction, just as speakers of a language cannot articulate the syntactic rules of acceptable speech. In fact, in many ways the dynamics of interaction approximate the transformational rules of generative grammar (cf. Chomsky, 1968); they operate on an underlying structure composed of semantic information determined by the history and ecology of Cat Harbour, to generate potentially unique, yet predictable and appropriate behaviour in given acceptable circumstances. Like syntactic transformations, the dynamics of interaction describe processes necessary for transforming the underlying knowledge into acceptable performance.[108]

Perhaps because he had prepared to study African kinship systems and found himself in an outport, Faris's study paid great attention to the particular notions of kinship. This emphasis is, perhaps, not surprising since creating a taxonomy of kinship was integral to the formation of anthropology. As he reflected later, even without having a specific interest in kinship systems, any anthropologist would have noticed the particular features of economic and family organization in Cat Harbour. Furthermore, his book pointed out that he organized his study around categories that were arbitrary and useful for presentation, rather than idioms that people in the community would recognize.[109]

The authors of the *DNE*, folklorists, and other anthropologists were interested in Faris's attention to the lexicon. Just as scholars used mumming as a map to explore aspects of the social and economic order in outports, Faris's analysis of the role of the *cuffer*, "a tale or yarn," in particular was picked up by several other anthropologists.[110] In an article titled "Rhetoric and Political Power," for example, Paine suggested that Smallwood used the prestige that accrued to one who could tell a good story (he relied on hyperbole and repetition rather than metaphors) to emphasize his political message. Kirwin thought Paine's article interesting, but he privately expressed reservations about generalizing to all of the province's culture based on the use of a word in only a few places:

> *Cuffer* assumes a major position in Newfoundland culture studies because of Faris's outstanding dissection and interpretation. But what evidence is on record about the distribution of the word *cuffer* and the institution *cuffer* that Faris has so well treated? If, for example, *cuffer* is unknown on the Burin Peninsula, and Smallwood got good support there, how does *cuffer* explain his power? A good "Newfoundland word" is sometimes only known in a few places on the island. We don't have evidence that *scoff* [a cooked meal at sea or ashore, esp. at night and often part of an impromptu party] is a term used in the *cuffer* area of the island only. The dictionary files have 24 non-print examples of *scoff*. Only 6 of these refer to *bucking* [to purloin; to collect or gather surreptitiously] the food, *Buck* has been collected 15 times. Only Faris relates it to a scoff. How many Smallwood listeners used to observe the sequence in their community "a cuffer is followed by a scoff with bucked food"? But the Smallwood support was ubiquitous.[111]

Not everyone shared Kirwin's cautious empiricism. Faris had collected these uses of the words in one community during one period (1964–65), but some subsequent scholars drew on these idiomatic uses as if they were common throughout all outports.

The reaction of fellow scholars to Faris's work was one thing; the reaction of rural Newfoundlanders was another. Unlike archival research, the fieldwork of the anthropologists and folklorists required the trust and cooperation of people. Halpert and Widdowson had allowed people to talk about their own lives in an unstructured way, and in doing so had collected examples of language, culture, and ways of life. Many people in the 1960s, Widdowson reported many years later, were happy to talk and were very helpful. As we have seen, the anthropologists working in the mid-1960s were also welcomed into rural communities, even if they were treated with wariness for a long time. People had long been visiting the outports to buy furniture, collectibles, and jewellery at less than market value from families who were happy to have a little bit of cash. Having been taken advantage of by outsiders made it more likely that some would be suspicious of fieldworkers. Other social scientists were also intrusive in their questions, potentially raising the ire of informants.

Anthropologists of the era, for example, were often interested in constructing kinship charts that presented how each person was related to each other person. Why an outsider would be interested in such a thing might not have been apparent, but this was knowledge people in the community had at hand. "Mrs Green is a wonderful help, if I am working on the chart I bring it out on the kitchen table in the evening and start to work on it" Chiaramonte reported, "after a while she will come over, look at the chart for a while and then perhaps make a correction or give me some added information."[112]

Anthropologists also asked questions about land ownership in communities in which land had long passed from generation to generation without title being registered. Inquiries that would reveal cases of people whose mothers were unmarried and were raised by a grandmother, for example, could have raised hackles, but not as much as might questions such as who owns that garden? Despite understandable caution, Firestone, Szwed, and Faris all seem to have had tremendous cooperation on the part of the people they lived among. Knocking on doors, at a time when only salesmen and true strangers knocked, and asking who was related to whom must have seemed strange.

During the Cold War, during which television news and spy shows raised fear, each of the anthropologists encountered suspicions that they might be Russian spies. "Our Catholic status was certainly a help, for as one person confided to me 'we were certainly glad to know you were Catholics, because with a name like yours we thought you might be Communists,'" Szwed reported.[113] When the anthropologists made friends, betraying that trust was possible. Firestone felt constrained in his ethnographic description by his desire to not embarrass the people who had been so kind to him. He had noted, for example, pre-marital sex was widely practised, but he chose to not write about it.[114] Perhaps Faris was the most candid of all the anthropologists in describing things that people later felt were a betrayal of confidences and described words, such as *cunny kin*, that when published provoked embarrassment.

When he finished writing his thesis in November 1965, Faris wrote to many of his friends in Lumsden to tell them of his success, the birth of another child, and warn them that despite his disguising names in the book everyone would know whom he was talking about. "I have finally finished writing up all the cuffers and lies you told me," he joked with one friend.[115] But he knew the work might provoke a negative reaction. He had no illusion that his comments about Cyril Robbins would anger some people in Lumsden North and satisfy others and wondered if people in St John's would misuse the book. In a broad, and unwarranted, generalization, he wrote to a family in Lumsden that "St John's people consider themselves innately superior to outport folk, and see the outport as seats of inbreeding and queer customs."[116] As he wrote to Morgan:

> I am quite anxious that the "sophisticated" St John's folk not find in it material which "proves" the primitiveness of the outport – as they would, from what I gather, be wont to do. As you know, I would sooner the work be burned than used in this manner. I have tried to made sense and interpret some of the more aberrant and bizarre customs simply because these things need the most interpretation. Far, then, from calling attention to them for purposes of letting the uncritical reader exploit them, I have tried to show how, given the circumstances, they make perfectly good sense.[117]

Yet he told Paine that "it may be alright to let people in St John's see [the mimeographed report] – even students from Cat Harbour ... but I would not like it, in present form, to be gone over carefully by people in Lumsden North, for they will undoubtedly, after some study, be able to recognize themselves, others, and use it to their own ends."[118] Faris's study was published in mimeograph in 1966 and then revised in 1972. In his book he used colours as pseudonyms to protect identities, but, as he predicted, people in the community were able to tell who he was writing about. As one of his principal informants later wrote him: "Janice is having a lot of fun untangling the colours in 'Cat Harbour'"[119]

Not long after ISER mimeographed *Cat Harbour* for distribution among local scholars, the *Evening Telegram* summarized Faris's more sensational claims in a full-page article. With the subtitles "A settlement in Newfoundland where men are afraid to go into the woods because of fairies?," "Where midwives are regarded as witches?," and "Where malformed children have been 'done away with?'," the author of the article seems to have wanted to provoke indignation.[120] While he was living in England, Africa, and during a year teaching in Montreal, Faris heard little complaint about the book from his former neighbours; they assured him that they believed the newspaper had taken material from his report out of context (even if, perhaps, that was not their true feelings).[121] The *Evening Telegram* article made an impression on Widdowson, however, who asked that his doctoral dissertation on frightening figures in Newfoundland oral culture remain closed to the public because "I think it would be a betrayal of trust if some of the material given to me by so many helpful people could be presented in any other form by any unauthorized media."[122] The next year, the satirist Ray Guy criticized the ways in which Newfoundlanders were being portrayed in Canadian newspapers, the National Film Board's Fogo Films, the CBC, and Newfoundland tourist promotions. In a reference to Faris, Guy wote:

> Several years ago a sociologist came to Memorial University straight from the jungles of Borneo where he had been engaged in studying some remote tribe of cannibals. He had scarcely landed here when he lit out for a Bonavista Bay community laden down with typewriters and tape recorders to do another study of another equally colorful tribe. Our sociologist lived in that community a year (with pictures of bone-through-the-nose cannibals on the walls of his quarters), enlisted his children to eavesdrop on his neighbors, and came up with a scholarly treatise on the mores of the locals. This paper, riddled with inaccuracies and shallow as a pothole, has been published by the university and made available for study by mainland sociologists and students ... We're tired of being treated like some lost tribe with bizarre customs and ridiculous manners. We don't like to see our outport people pinned to the wall and examined by sociologists like some rare insects. There's room for science and scholarship, but also the need for a bit of respect for human dignity.[123]

Not surprisingly, some Newfoundlanders resented the suggestion that they would be the subject of the same sort of study that they associated with non-whites, while others were good natured about the implicit comparison. "Well! friends, it was surely wonderful to hear from you again, after so long," Naida Robbins joked with Faris, "I thought you must have gone under and was lost among some tribe with as many peculiarities as Nflders."[124]

Faris may have underestimated the ease with which his report would find its way back to Lumsden; several young people from the community were students at Memorial and purchased copies of the study and brought them back to their families within days of it being circulated. Faris seems to have accepted that the Robbins family would be angered, but he asked some of his friends to let him "know what some of the reactions to the book were (apart from the obvious Robbins indignation)."[125] When, in 1972, he spent a couple of months in Lumsden South to examine the effect that resettlement had on people of Lumsden North, he reported to his graduate student Ellen Antler, who was herself doing research in the area:

> The merchantile family is quite miffed at the Cat Harbour monograph – it seems as tho I underestimated how obvious were the name codes. The most of the community is delighted at having the truth told about some of the merchant brothers, certainly the merchant isn't. But in Nfld to bring this up would never be done, so the merchant family, tho somewhat cooler, are still pleasant and helpful. I should well have known that most of the youth getting to MUN would be of the mercantile families, and would thus read it and be the purveyors of information. The other thing that did not help me was the Evening Telegram's account – which head-lined stuff like fairies, the "making away" with malformed infants, and midwives as witches. One might have known that if the city folk could find some means of shitting on the outport they'd do it. I've not noticed any other real aversion to my presence tho.[126]

Perhaps politeness prevented a few people from expressing their resent-ment at having had their kindness to the Faris family rewarded with confidences being published. Certainly the insider/outsider, rural/urban, and Newfoundlander/mainlander dichotomies are unsatisfy-ing as an explanation of the reaction to his book. Faris saw himself as on the side of the people in Lumsden and defending them against the condescension of people in St John's. He had spent little time in the capital city, so he may have overestimated the portion of people with such views.

In the late nineteenth and early twentieth centuries, sociologists and anthropologists had sometimes categorized "history into two ideal-typical stages, the community-centered traditional society and the modern, differentiated, industrial society," a view "which thinned out the complex shapes of history and avoided actual historical analysis."[127] Some scholars assumed that "traditional" societies were static and that the function of culture was to encourage equilibrium, so many schol-ars were slow to see evidence of class struggle in "primitive" societies. In 2001 the historian Miriam Wright judged that the ISER community studies on the effects of the "supposed transition from 'traditional' to 'modern' society" during the 1960s and 1970s were "derived from field notes created by researchers who spent short periods of time liv-ing in these communities, [and] had a limited understanding [of] his-torical change."[128] Each of these ethnographies was a product of the anthropological theory and method of the era in which it was written and a kind of outport culture that was soon to disappear. On the first page of the first of these that was published by ISER, Tom Philbrook set out a justification for studying Newfoundland society:

> A phenomenon of increasing importance in the 20th century is the industrialization of areas of the world hitherto relatively untouched by the great revolution of the 18th and 19th centuries ... Although isolated communities are still to be found in British North America, they are a rapidly vanishing phenomena. Herein lies the special interest of outport Newfoundland. It is one of the few areas of North America still in considerable measure untouched by industrialization. As the processes of modern society penetrate this area it offers a virgin field for research in the transformation of the small community.[129]

That statement notwithstanding, the anthropologists and sociologists who studied the Newfoundland outports were aware of class conflict in both the past and the present. Faris, for example, believed that the suspicion towards outsiders he observed was rooted in a history of antagonism. People had been shaped by a history of a prohibition of settlement, oppression of the Royal Navy, and mercantile exploitation. The past and the contemporary fact that strangers were not part of the local moral economy gave Lumsden North people, for example, a suspicion of outsiders that made development difficult. It's also perhaps unfair to characterize them as having spent a short time in their respective communities. Each of them was in "the field" for approximately a year and then all but Faris spent a year in St John's. By the standards of the day, their fieldwork was intensive.

Through the first set of ISER fellowships, the university gained a set of young scholars to conduct fieldwork while drawing on the supervision of the institution in which they were enrolled. Whitaker offered them little in the way of instruction or guidance, although he insisted on each of the fellows completing a census of the community in which they lived. Firestone reported that since little was known of any Newfoundland communities, he had the impression that all description was welcome.[130] During the first year Whitaker visited each of them once to check on their progress, and all but one of them spent the second year in St John's. By spending a year living and working in an outport, each collected first-hand data of a full seasonal round of economic and social activities. Each of the fieldworkers also had the opportunity to become

4.4. Melindy crew hauling codtrap, Lumsden North, 1964. (James Faris Collection, Special Archives and Collection Division, QEII Library, Memorial University of Newfoundland.)

intimately familiar with his community and then during the year in residence at Memorial be able to write a report on the community in which they had lived. Whitaker withheld payment for the final period until each of the fellows submitted his field report.

A couple of observations may be made about the interaction of the ISER fellows. The infusion among the faculty members at Memorial of young scholars who had been trained in different traditions, at universities in the United States and Britain, and later in Norway meant that the most recent in academic fashion and approaches were brought to bear. The interdisciplinary nature of ISER, including anthropologists, sociologists, economists, geographers, and others encouraged another kind of cross-fertilization during the obligatory year in residence as well. The ethnographers discussed what they saw in their community with each other and with the permanent faculty members. While the other fellows were able to regale the faculty members with exotic stories of outports, Mars felt that few faculty members at Memorial had any interest in understanding the social life in St John's.[131] That, and the fact Mars's study was the only one not published by ISER, accounts for his being the least known of them.

The year in St John's also provided them opportunities to compare notes, and, as we have seen in an earlier chapter, each of them having spent a Christmas season in their town and then discussing their observations with each other and the faculty members at Memorial led to *Christmas Mumming*.[132] Yet this description of learning from each other may be romanticized. Firestone later reflected that since the original ISER fellows were all anthropologists with similar training they had little to learn from each other. Conversely, he also thought that since anthropology contained many different theoretical approaches, each of the anthropologists felt justified in conducting his own case study in his own way.[133] The guidance of the student's supervisory committee was welcome too. "We look upon our own role in the research as mainly that of a catalyst," Whitaker told Firestone's supervisor, "we in the Institute value close communication between a research fellow and his thesis supervisor. At no time do we wish to direct research in a contrary direction to that of a fellow's parent research."[134] Whitaker allowed each fellow's supervisory committee to shape their studies, but he wrote to various supervisors to have them apply pressure on the fellows to be more complete and systematic.

Memorial did not have the first anthropology department in Canada, nor did it have the largest number of anthropologists or sociologists of any department during the 1960s. Other Canadian departments also experienced the dialogue between British-trained social anthropologists and American anthropologists. The difference between the anthropologists working through Memorial and those at many other universities was the engagement with the modernization of outport society. In sometimes overt, and sometimes subtle and complex, ways, the ISER studies were part of the history of state intervention in rural life. British anthropology remained focused on fieldwork in Africa; in effect, there was a feeling that one's own society was too close for a scholar to view objectively, and that the "simple" societies of "primitive" people were better suited to anthropology than the complexity of the British Isles. It's not surprising, therefore, that Memorial's British-born scholars turned to Norwegian anthropologists for guidance; both Whitaker and Paine had conducted ethnographic work among the Sami.

Norwegian anthropologists and sociologists also provided Memorial's scholars with comparative studies of rural economies, politics, and social policies.[135] Paine, who had been a colleague of Fredrik Barth, encouraged a number of young Norwegians to work with ISER.

While in 1959 Whitaker thought that isolated pockets of traditional culture that had changed little from some remote time still existed and that little was known of that culture, in 1988 he believed that "modernization and resettlement have changed the social situation totally" and that thanks to ISER Newfoundland became "arguably the best-documented province of Canada."[136] As other anthropologists would have agreed, he believed that participant observation was the ideal method, but as we have seen the ISER fellows participated in only some aspects of community life. Whitaker thought that living in the community and observing and conversing with informants was a satisfactory substitute for working with people in the community; the ISER fellows, for the most part, did not fish or cut wood but observed and talked to those who did.

> Only one of our field workers can really be said at the moment to be a participant observer, and he regularly goes out fishing with one of the fishing crews. I have always found in my own field work in Scotland and elsewhere that a willingness to attempt to fulfill standardized roles is as satisfactory as actually fulfilling them ... One of our field workers was known as the "nurse's husband" since his wife was the registered nurse in the community. Although there had been no such role before in the community this was one which he was able to create.[137]

Whitaker was concerned about the rapport the fellows were able to gain, and his desire for systematic data collection that would allow for comparative work encouraged him to press for a census of each community. In several instances he was also confronted with the possibility that the fellows were changing the community they were studying. Each of the fellows was aware of that. Working in a "complex community" meant that he had to play two roles, Chiaramonte thought, "that of the social scientist and of the man living in the community."[138] As he continued:

> At first is was difficult to reconcile the two roles, but as I began to establish a "raison d'etre" in the minds of the people and my raport [sic] strengthened it became less of a problem. Regardless of how strong a man's raport

[*sic*] is he is still called upon to play a role in the community. Fortunately this is contributing to my work rather than hindering it. I can see how easily a man can become so involved in the life of the community that the scientific merit of his work would be seriously questioned.[139]

In keeping with the sense of urgency to salvage evidence of the culture before it disappeared, and the need to create basic research tools, scholars at Memorial sifted evidence with a large mesh. Chiaramonte reflected that: "Each community appears to have what might be termed a 'community personality.' One reason for the development of a community personality is that most of the communities were originally settled by one or two [families]."[140] But only a handful of communities out of the hundreds in Newfoundland were surveyed for linguistic evidence, only a few ethnographers were able to live in a community for the year it took to develop an understanding of it, and historians took the whole of the country as their unit of analysis rather than a single bay or outport. With their interest in space and the ability to represent data in an atlas, the geographers could represent regional diversity and spatial relationships, but in the end resources existed to examine only a few communities.

Among the collaborators of the Newfoundland studies movement there was none that engaged more directly with rural people, for as extended a period, as the authors of the community studies. It is more difficult to reconstruct what people thought of the anthropologists who moved into their communities than discerning something of the goals and beliefs of the anthropologists. The researchers left accounts of their work, but we lack memoirs of the people who were the subjects of the inquiry. Anthropologists may have benefitted from the prestige that came with an education, although that is by no means established. In a culture in which men valued physical prowess and skills, prestige hierarchies must have been inverted at times. They also lacked a clear social or economic role in the community, unlike the other outsiders (clergy, school teachers, police, and welfare officers) with whom rural families interacted. That encouraged speculation and suspicion that they had an agenda. People were also immensely kind to the Americans. Families that in many cases had little material wealth gave food, firewood, beds, aid, and instruction to the fieldworkers.

It's also worth emphasizing that it took a considerable time for the anthropologists to build friendships. Other field workers visited for a few hours with their surveys and tape recorders. The relationships the

ISER fellows developed gave them privileged access, but they risked betraying the trust that had made their time in outports so fruitful. In an ironic postscript to the dialogue between Faris, the university community, and the people of Lumsden, many years later a niece of Nadia and Cyril Robbins taught research ethics to students at Memorial and used *Cat Harbour* as an example of unethical methods. But in no other case was the university's goal of engaging with the modernization of a traditional society as explicit as in the ISER community studies.

The ethnographic snapshots we have of Newfoundland outports between 1961 and 1965 served as data for the *DNE* and provided a baseline for subsequent studies of the culture, not the least because ISER published them. The community studies reflected an engagement between the researcher and the subjects of the research and a dialectic between Newfoundland culture and anthropological and sociological method and theory. The agendas of federal and provincial governments that funded the fieldwork, and Ian Whitaker's research priorities, shaped the selection of outports for study and the themes examined by each of the fellows.

Chapter Five

The Peopling of Newfoundland: Mapping Cultural Transfer and Settlement

The central theme of this volume is the gradual spread of settlement in Newfoundland in the 19th century ... the inflow of migrants and settlers to different parts of Newfoundland or neighbouring areas, the establishment and growth of a permanent population and the concomitant spread of permanent settlement. There is a shared emphasis also on the source areas of the migrants, their social and economic background, and the adaptations made to a new environment as manifested by the patterns of resource use and settlement.[1]

Given the importance of the land for subsistence production, it's not surprising that Newfoundlanders developed an attachment to it. The four stanzas of Newfoundland's national anthem, the *Ode to Newfoundland*, were devoted entirely to the landscape and the weather. Other, more urban, peoples may have lived in a land of their literature, but mid-twentieth-century Newfoundlanders had a daily intimate relationship with nature. Some of the rural Newfoundlanders who resettled to St John's in the middle of the twentieth century, or who immigrated to another land, reacted with nostalgia for the outports they left behind; others never looked back. Writing in the 1970s at the height of the folk culture revival, the literary critic and historian Patrick O'Flaherty, a native of Long Beach, Conception Bay, with degrees from Memorial and a PhD from University College, London, was critical of many of his contemporaries among the university faculty. He thought some of the folklorists and anthropologists romanticized rural life and didn't appreciate the fact that the unremitting labour of life in Newfoundland left little time for appreciating nature:

It was rare to see in the inhabitants of the old outports the higher qualities which a life lived "in communion with nature" is sometimes said to
nurture – a concern for animals, for example, or a love of scenery. Such feelings were submerged beneath the brutal difficulty of making a living. The
land itself was not admired but ravaged, almost as if the people were taking revenge upon it for its miserable harvests, yielding after hard work and
painstaking weeding, fertilizing and pampering. The denuded and ragged
landscapes now seen in the vicinity of many outports, some of them spot-
ted and lined with huge rock walls, are evidence of the people's determina-
tion, but also a kind of stolid indifference, a contempt for prettiness.[2]

Setting aside the question of whether working people had the leisure
time to develop aesthetic appreciation, we need not romanticize a pastoral setting to recognize an intimate knowledge of the land. Identifying a territory as an ethnic homeland may be nearly universal. People
believe themselves to be part of a nation when they see themselves as
having a common past, a common future, and a common territory – so
urban nationalist intellectuals' attention to the land and the folk culture of peasants is not surprising. Middle-class nationalists everywhere
wrote of the people native to their land. Their writings were sometimes
as important to the development of national identity as was the writing of history of states. In the post-Confederation period, when Newfoundlanders no longer inculcated their children with loyalty to their
nation state, the desire to know the country remained. The focus among
those whose interests were spatial or geographic shifted to modernization, including conquering space through improved transportation and
communications. This chapter examines Memorial University's effort
to inventory resources, to think spatially about the people, and to use
the newly developed tools of geography to aid in modernization. Those
efforts, as the geographers worked with others of the Newfoundland
studies movement, soon turned to efforts to understand the past.

Much as anthropologists worked with the state when they established
applied fieldwork in the province, so too did the geographers examined
in this chapter. The work of neither group can be reduced solely to an
application of modernization by universities, although Memorial was
an agent of change. This chapter examines the work in economic and
historical geography as analytical research specializations (separate
from description) that developed in the 1960s and shows how it fit into
the context of Newfoundland's social and economic changes. The studies of economic and resource geography undertaken by the university,

and the focus on the challenges of social change, taught scholars things about contemporary Newfoundland. That encouraged a re-evaluation of the past of rural areas. In doing so, the Department of Geography at Memorial developed its own school of historical geography different from the work at other Canadian universities. While the geographers of Newfoundland drew on the same sources as the historians, and reached similar conclusions, their work emphasized politics and warfare as causal factors less than did their peers in the Department of History. The geographers mapped the transmission of people and culture across the Atlantic and focused attention more particularly on environmental factors. The geographers' study of Newfoundland people, resources, and landscape was less explicitly part of an imperial or nationalist ideological project than the study of history or geography had been earlier in the century. It was also more clearly an attempt to grapple with a broadly dispersed contemporary population who lived in what seemed to be a pre-modern economy.

The "New Found Lande" was the first part of northern North America to be known to Europeans, although it took about forty years for the word *Newfoundland* to settle down to refer exclusively to the island that now bears that name. The French *Terre Neuve* may have not meant this specific island until as late as 1600.[3] In the sixteenth century, the English were slower to develop their fishery in Newfoundland waters than were the French, Basque, or Portugese. While European powers developed New World settler colonies in other regions of the Americas, and based those settlements on a fur trade or agriculture, the Newfoundland fishery required neither extensive settlement nor possession of the land beyond a ribbon along the coast. Settlement of the island by Europeans was thus slow to develop relative to other regions, and British policy had been ambivalent towards the development of a colony.

After 1688 the Royal Navy dominated the island each summer, but incorporating the land within England's sphere of influence required more than occupation by settlers and defending one's claim to it vis-à-vis other powers. The flora, fauna, and terrain had to be described and mapped before the country could be imagined as part of an empire. Several seventeenth-century English investors wrote tracts describing the landscape and resources of the island of Newfoundland and gave advice to would-be settlers. As *A Discourse and Discovery of Newfoundland* by Richard Whitbourne exemplified, they sometimes combined practical information with fancy in an effort to promote the island.[4] The pattern of settlement that rose from the needs of the fishery (shore space was essential to the enterprise and thus limited the number of fishing households in any one harbour or on any one island). It resulted in thousands of people in hundreds of communities, each of which was expensive to serve and unlikely to make a transition to capital-intensive industry. The answer in the post-war period was to centralize the population, if not shift them to other provinces. As the historian David Alexander, a critic of that view, memorably put it:

> The price of being a country is willingness to bear a cross. For Germany it is the cross of beastliness; for Russia it is stolidity; the United States must rise above material wealth; and Canada is required to find a national identity. The burden which Newfoundland has carried is to justify that it should have any people. From the Western Adventurers of the seventeenth century to Canadian economists in the twentieth, there has been a continuing debate as to how many, if any, people should live in Newfoundland.[5]

Long after it had been settled by people of European ancestry who had been born on the island and knew no other home, much of the interior of the island remained terra incognita. Nineteenth-century cartographers and surveyors mapped and described the resources of the island to match the eighteenth-century charts of the coast made by the Royal Navy. To take a different example, the coast of Labrador fell within the jurisdiction of the Newfoundland governor after 1763, but, except for those engaged in the Labrador fishery it remained largely on the margin of Newfoundlanders' consciousness in the twentieth century.[6] Besides such explicit efforts to describe the colony, some of the earliest scientific research by native Newfoundlanders had been engaged in understanding the landscape and straddled the line between geography and history.

The early nineteenth-century natural scientist William Cormack had documented Beothuk life and lexicon and published an account of his trek across the island that was sometimes assigned to school children.[7] He was celebrated as the first "white man" to see the interior, setting his Mi'kmaq guide Sylvester Joe into the background of the story.[8] In the late nineteenth and early twentieth centuries, James P. Howley self-consciously walked much of the same territory as he conducted extensive geological surveys. He published a *Geography of Newfoundland* for use in schools in 1876.[9] We have already seen that his brother, M.F. Howley, had published on Newfoundland place names (James had presented many place names in his *Geography* as well) – anticipating E.R. Seary's later academic interest in onomastics. J.P. Howley carried out oral and documentary research to reconstruct the history of inter-actions with, and the ethnography of, the island's indigenous people. A labour of love, Howley had difficulty raising the money to pay for the publication of *The Beothucks or Red Indians* by Cambridge Univer-sity Press, but after its publication in 1915 it remained unmatched as a compendium of data on Newfoundland's indigenous people for nearly a century.[10] Howley also learned the names of features of the land from his Mi'kmaq guides during his fieldwork and inscribed them on maps; an act that documented an aspect of their culture and in a few cases made the Mi'kmaq names part of the English-language nomenclature.[11]

People in other parts of the empire had contributed to the descrip-tion of the Newfoundland people and landscape as well. James Cook surveyed and mapped large sections of the coast with a greater level of precision than had previously been accomplished, and in an observa-tion in 1766 determined the longitude of the island (literally putting Newfoundland in its correct place on the world map). His work, and that of his colleagues, allowed the preparation of an accurate hydro-graphic survey of the island's coastal waters, and the resulting maps made it possible for Newfoundlanders to imagine the island as a whole at a time when each outport and major bay differed from one another and when the government in St John's had infrequent direct contact with distant outports. When the fisheries of Newfoundland were an object to be fought over by European diplomats and navies, maps were weapons at the negotiating tables. Much of the interior of the island remained un-described until the major river systems were sketched in, and as late as 1895 the map included with Prowse's *History of Newfound-land* labelled areas of the island as "unknown," "desolate country," and "innumerable ponds" as well as the more hopeful "agricultural lands." Such charts and maps made it possible for nineteenth-century politicians and intellectuals in St John's to imagine Newfoundland as a coherent place even at a time when the west coast, for example, was a border zone of overlapping French and British jurisdictions. The west coast was a borderland until France relinquished its rights to the shore in 1904, but maps of the island made it possible for Newfoundlanders to imagine the island as theirs and them belonging to it. "Where do you belong to?" Newfoundlanders asked each other when they met – the answer to which would fix a person to a family, a community, and often a Christian denomination.

A few scholars from other nations conducted geographic fieldwork in Newfoundland. The French geographer Robert Perret published a geography of the island in 1913 that would be unmatched in English for a half century.[12] Similarly the German geographer Hans Schrepfer visited Newfoundland in 1932 and wrote essays in geomorphology as well as economic and historical geography. His accounts of the country included harsh commentary on political corruption and on the culture of the people, whom he viewed as lazy. The historian Gerhard Bassler, who evaluated the work, thought it "may be categorized as border-line cases of Nazi propaganda" but balanced that with the observation that "their perspectives and the evidence supporting them were based almost entirely on English-language sources."[13]

Much as twentieth century, English-trained historians had placed Newfoundland within the history of the empire, so too the earliest people we might think of as geographers were part of an imperial project. J.G. Jutes and R.H. Bonnycastle, for example, wrote books that surveyed the cultural and historical geography of the island and set out the colony's history with the goal of making it better known to the British public.[14] The first twentieth-century book about Newfoundland that carried the title "historical geography" was by John Davenport Rogers, a barrister and former fellow of University College, Oxford. That history, published in 1911, was part of a series intended to explain how the colonies had come to be part of the empire and to describe their resources. Rogers may have never visited Newfoundland, but that did not prevent him from writing a lively and imaginative narrative of the country.[15]

In the early twentieth century G.R.F. Prowse, the son of the historian, had studied Newfoundland map history, even inventing the word *cartology* for his activity. National feeling motivated the younger Prowse; he had studied early maps in an effort to prove, for example, that the explorer John Cabot's landfall had been in Newfoundland rather than Nova Scotia.[16] Others subsequently took up the study. In the second half of the twentieth century, Fabian O'Dea, a lawyer and the brother of the bibliographer Agnes O'Dea, continued the tradition of collecting and studying early maps. He eventually wrote an as-yet-unpublished manuscript on the history of eighteenth-century Newfoundland maps and bequeathed his collection to the University Library. Much was accomplished by members of the Howley family, the Prowse family, and the O'Dea family, but without an institutional home for this scholarly activity few of these nineteenth-century and early twentieth-century foundations were followed up until after 1949.

Nineteenth-century Newfoundlanders had developed a self-awareness as a people, even as they were widely dispersed along the coastline and intensely local in their sense of identity. They were aware of their distinctiveness, and, as the reactions of the Newfoundland Regiment in the First World War shows, were displeased at being confused with Canadians. Being a Newfoundlander did not preclude having a strong emotional attachment to the empire, however, or feeling that one belonged to an English culture. It was common for Newfoundlanders before Confederation to speak of the island as "the oldest colony," a practice that continued into the 1950s and 1960s and beyond. While the word *nation* was rarely used, many Newfoundlanders saw their home as a *country* in several of that word's many senses. *Country* may refer to a sovereign political unit, or it can be used in the sense of wilderness or also in the sense of a territory. In the nineteenth century, the *DNE* reports, *country born* had been used to distinguish a person born in Newfoundland from the many Irish and English immigrants residing in the colony.[17] The sense of *country* as a territory overlapped with the sense of the word that is the equivalent of *nation state*, and the two senses bled into each other in people's speech and writing.

For people who lived within sight of the sea, "going in the country" meant travelling inland to harvest resources. In the nineteenth and twentieth centuries the description of the landscape as a country was also, simultaneously, an explanation of ethnicity. Given the bourgeoning nationalism throughout the world, it's not surprising that the Newfoundland school system had paid as much attention to the geography of the island as it had the history. J.P. Howley's stated goal had been to both inform children of the geography of their country and impart "a more exalted conception of its worth."[18] Both geography and history were ways that children could come to know their country and relate it to its place in the empire, and both were part of the social studies curriculum in Newfoundland schools. "Don't sell your Country" was the Responsible Government League's anti-Confederation slogan during the referendum debates, a message that Smallwood countered with "Confederation – British Union."

The historical geography of Newfoundland that emerged in the 1960s was not only a subject matter, it was also an approach informed by their collaborations. Memorial's geographers' interests in culture transfer were shared with folklorists, their interest in names were shared with the linguists, and their concern with the past was shared with the historians. What gave the Department of Geography coherence was its members' interest in the landscape, in the ways that the landscape provided evidence of past uses and occupations, and their use of maps as research tools rather than just ways of presenting data. That might be revealed through fieldwork, or it might be revealed through documentary sources, but the key was the geographers' attention to space. While other academic disciplines had a cartographer adorn their work with a map, the geographers mapped their evidence to reveal spatial relationships that would otherwise never become apparent. While historians emphasized change over time, the geographers froze time in a map to see how areas of the world related to each other as a system.[19]

As we have seen, in the 1960s ISER was known in Newfoundland for its community studies and its role in policy, and at the same time Memorial's Department of Geography developed as large and as significant a group of historical geographers as existed at any Canadian university. The historical geographers established their own role in Newfoundland studies. Newfoundland historical geography paralleled, and was in dialogue with, the work described in the preceding chapters. Memorial created a cartography unit and described the landscape, but this chapter focuses on the three key texts that exemplify the Newfoundland school of historical geography: *Eighteenth Century Newfoundland* (1976) by the Ontario-based C. Grant Head, *The Peopling of Newfoundland* (1977) written by faculty and graduate students at Memorial and edited by John Mannion, and the plates in the three-volume *Historical Atlas of Canada*, which were authored by Newfoundland scholars. Despite their common character, *Peopling* and the *Historical Atlas* were two different sorts of enterprises. While the former explained the evidence of the past primarily in text, the atlas represented the past primarily in graphic form. That meant that the evidence was mediated not only through the minds of the geographers but also through cartographers, designers, and printers.

Despite the examples of Newfoundlanders straddling the scientific description of the landscape and attention to settlement, there were no Newfoundland geographers before Second World War. As Alan Macpherson pointed out in a history of the founders of the Department of Geography, it was largely by chance that Memorial University College hired the Cambridge-trained geographer Harold Goodridge. Goodridge had been born in Newfoundland but spent his childhood in England. He studied history at Cambridge in the 1920s before switching his interests to geography, a subject that had been taught there since 1903. His training, for which he was awarded a PhD in 1924, covered a broad range – giving him a generalist background in the discipline that was better suited to teaching than to research. During the 1920s and 1930s he taught school in England and India, and after 1942 he served as a war artist. Goodridge returned to St John's in 1944 to serve as an aide to the then governor, Humphry Walwyn, and suggested to Memorial that he teach geography and be in charge of its teaching-collection of reproductions of European art (which had been provided by a grant from the Carnegie Foundation).

His appointment at Memorial in 1946 came at a time when there were few geographers in Canadian universities. Goodridge modelled his curriculum on that of Cambridge, but he modified it because he believed that most of his students were destined to teach in the secondary school system rather than conduct research. This emphasis changed after Memorial became a degree-granting institution. In 1951 the former president of the University of Alberta Robert Newton recommended that geographic fieldwork be conducted in Newfoundland, but while Goodridge taught during the academic year, he continued to travel to Europe to paint during each summer.[20] He did little to encourage fieldwork, archival research, or the survey of resources as a prelude to economic development. Much like the teaching of history during this era, the goal of the teaching of geography was often to increase students' awareness of their county, and that is exactly the role Goodridge played. One might think of him as more of a gentleman scholar and artist than a social scientist.[21]

A kind of desk-bound geographical research at Memorial had been pioneered by E.R. Seary, who embarked on a study of Newfoundland toponymy, or place names, which he hoped would show the origins of Newfoundland names and their relationship with the language of those who had first settled and used the island. Seary and George Story had not initially evolved a clear division of labour for their linguistic and historical research, and, years later, Story reminisced about their "long afternoons, armed with a powerful hand-lens, extracting place-names from the sixteenth century maps of the Island which afford the earliest evidence of the Island nomenclature."[22] Seary suggested that the study of the origins of place names was "not only intrinsically interesting, but provide[s] one of the most valuable sources of raw material for both linguistic history and the history of exploration and settlement."[23] The relative lack of textual historical documentation of Newfoundland's early history was the very factor that made turning to oblique evidence, such as place names, so important in recovering not only the early history of international discovery and fisheries but also social history.

5.1. Harold Goodridge. (Photographic Services Collection, QEII Library, Memorial University of Newfoundland.)

While the Howley brothers' interest in the history and geography of their home was unabashedly nationalistic, Seary saw himself as part of a scientific scholarly tradition that was free of nationalism. He was one of the founders of the Canadian Linguistic Association, endeavouring to carve out a professional niche for the study of language, and criticized M.F. Howley's study of Newfoundland place names as "incomplete, capricious, [and] coloured by local patriotism."[24] That is typical of the strategy that twentieth-century professional academics used to distinguish themselves from amateur scholars. To be fair, Seary acknowledged an intellectual debt to his predecessor, since Howley's work meant that Seary did not have to go into the area blindly, but saw his own work as scientific in ways that the amateur's was not.[25]

Despite Seary's desire to distance himself from his nationalistic predecessors, the study of place names had a polemical edge in a period in which Newfoundlanders were trying to be accepted as Canadians. Tourist promotion literature drew attention to community names such as "Come by Chance," "Little Heart's Ease," and "Hearts Content," which played into the government's strategy of making the place seem picturesque to tourists. Other place names, such as Cat Harbour, Hibbs Hole, and Scilly Cove made some residents feel sensitive to the reaction they received from outsiders because of associations attached to the names, and they jettisoned eighteenth- and nineteenth-century community names in favour of Lumsden, Hibbs Cove, and Winterton. "Even place names are viewed [by outsiders] as quaint, or romantic, and they are laughing when they say it," reported Les Harris (a native of Gallows Harbour, which the parish priest had renamed St Joseph's to avoid the gruesome associations).[26] In an effort to shed their image, he continued, many Newfoundland communities abandoned ancient names and changed them to "things that were banal."[27] Harris therefore supported Seary's research, which he thought had shown "that such names were not laughable" and believed had slowed and perhaps reversed the process of renaming, not the least because Seary joined others interested in history as members of the provincial Nomenclature Board, which was formed in 1959.[28]

Nomenclature, not surprisingly, was a terrain on which ideas about cultural loss while embracing modernization was fought. The members of the board, at various points including Seary, Harris, and the historical geographer Gordon Handcock, had to approve changes to names of communities and features in the landscape, which gave them some influence over change. Seary was sensitive to people's perceptions. He reacted with anger, for example, when his publisher suggested a book title that would grab attention: "From Famish Cove to Heart's Delight." Seary worried that his work of sober scholarship would be thought trivial.

While his contemporaries among the English-trained historians emphasized the origins of English settlement, and paid attention to the French only as rivals for control of the fishery, Seary was interested in the persistence of foreign language names as evidence of people who no longer had a presence on the island. Just as Story turned to oral evidence to compensate for the paucity of documentary records on social history, Seary looked to place names on old maps to recover evidence of French, Basque, and Portugese use of the island. The sixteenth-century

Basque fishermen's use of the island, for example, left evidence in the form of place names. Seary's view was also not exclusively Eurocentric; he sought First Nations' names for the landscape on the island, finding no linguistic residue of Beothuk toponyms, and only a few names that were of Mi'kmaq origins. Compared to other areas of North America, the English borrowed little from the culture of the Beothuk, and despite the Mi'kmaq people's long presence on the island only a few of their names for the landscape were inscribed on maps.

Although a few European scholars had studied names, Seary lacked a fully developed methodology or body of theory. He had one of those minds that liked to collect and catalogue, and had he lived in another place he likely would have found something else to compile and classify. Over time his methods evolved. Although both the place names study and the family names study were exacting in their research effort, both suffered from methodological flaws that reflected Seary's source material. He worked backwards in time from Canadian topographical maps made in the 1950s, the names on which had been copied from earlier maps rather than collected from oral sources, to establish earlier versions and names for the same places. A large portion of the names with which Seary started were unknown to Newfoundlanders or were in the wrong place, and thousands of common names were not represented.[29]

Seary started with an examination of the place names of the island's Northern Peninsula, an experimental study in the sense that he wanted to work out the methodology and form of presentation for a relatively confined geographic area, but one that had a rich history of Basque, French, and English exploitation. Having worked out some of the issues of annotation and style of presentation in that study, of which a small number of copies were duplicated and distributed to people who might be able to provide informed comment, he moved next to study the place names of the Avalon Peninsula.[30] That culminated in 1971 with the appearance of his *Place Names of the Avalon Peninsula of the Island of Newfoundland*.[31] While Memorial had considered establishing its own press, the arrangement with the University of Toronto Press to publish the book made an institutional commitment to Newfoundland studies without assuming the costs of Memorial establishing its own publishing enterprise.

Seary had been keeping a list of Newfoundland family names to help him identify the origins of the names of features such as coves and rivers; he realized that this too was a sort of linguistic evidence. He was an "armchair" scholar; while serving as head of the Department of English he had little time to either conduct fieldwork to collect oral information or to go to the archives. Seary employed research assistants to comb through parish records and the questionnaires at MUNFLA, and one assistant, Sheila Lynch, became a collaborator and co-author. Their work on surnames was decidedly not genealogical, and people later consulting it would have only incidentally found clues to who settled a particular community. Yet Seary's *Family Names of the Island of Newfoundland* sold widely to a public who seemed to want to know the names of their forefathers.[32] Naming conventions, of course, obscured the line of female ancestors – ultimately making everyone seem to inherit ethnicity from only one grandparent.

While Seary painstakingly compiled lists of place names and family names, Harold Goodridge resigned from Memorial, citing both health issues and a desire to paint full time. That provided an opportunity for the university to establish geography as a research field. M.O. Morgan, always on the lookout for Newfoundlanders who had academic experience at other universities, consulted with geographers at McGill University and offered a job to William Summers. As a condition of accepting the position, Summers got a promise from Morgan that he would be able to create a real department, rather than him being a department of one person.[33] Starting in 1960, Summers not only introduced fieldwork to Memorial's students who took courses in geography but promoted the development of physical geography (as opposed to the emphasis on history and politics) within the department.

Like Goodridge, Summers was a native of St John's, born in 1919, but that's where the similarities ended. His childhood was spent in the capital, and in 1938 he began "pre-engineering" at Memorial College. With the arrival of the United States Army in St John's in 1941, Summers worked for the Americans as a cartographer as they built Fort Pepperrell. After serving in the Royal Canadian Air Force during the war, he enrolled for a geology degree at Dalhousie University in Halifax and worked during the summers for the Newfoundland government geologist as a surveyor on the island's west coast. An elective course in geography attracted Summers's interest, and he enroled in an MSc in geography at McGill (then a new field of study at that university). The same year that Newfoundland became a Canadian province, he completed his thesis, "The Physical Geography of the Avalon Peninsula." In 1950 he began teaching at McGill but continued to make summer trips to Newfoundland for fieldwork. The geographic branch of the Newfoundland government's Department of National Resources carried out fieldwork in Newfoundland, and, since there was a shortage of trained geographers, the researchers the department hired, such as Summers, were often accompanied by graduate students and undergraduates. Summers supplemented his McGill salary by working on these surveys, and in 1957 completed a PhD, "A Geographical Analysis of Population Trends in Newfoundland."[34] Long before Memorial hired him, his work thus foreshadowed the university's later role in providing expertise to the government in assessing natural resources and studying demography. He did not ignore the educational role of geographers; he wrote a textbook on the geography of the province for use in schools but founded a field research oriented department.[35] Starting in 1960, Summers built a Department of Geography with an eye to supporting the economic development of the province and worked with the federal and provincial governments in doing so. Faculty members soon worked on fisheries geography, a resource atlas of the province, and research on urban land use in St John's.[36] At a time when most anthropologists and folklorists, for example, focused on rural life, the small Department of Geography worked on urban problems as well as natural resources.

Some of the earliest fieldwork in rural Newfoundland was paid for under the government of Canada's Agricultural Rehabilitation and Rural Development Act (1961), which was later renamed the Agricultural and Rural Development Act (ARDA). ARDA was the first federal government program devoted to the development of rural areas of Canada and provided for research costs on a "special rural development area."[37] The primary function assumed by the Newfoundland ARDA administration was to carry out research on areas where there were "families with less than satisfactory income levels" and to develop programs to improve people's prospects through either resource development, or, when that seemed impractical, to assist in the resettlement of the affected population.[38]

The ARDA agreements, in 1961 and 1964, provided money for physical, social, and economic research, as long as the projects were directly relevant to rural development.[39] Nearly $7 million was allocated to Newfoundland by the 1964 agreement, and up to $12 million more was allocated for projects to address areas of "deep distress." The latter projects were funded one hundred per cent by the federal government, encouraging the province to develop such programs. One option, the provincial officials were aware, was to wait for local groups to ask for assistance and then develop projects to meet those needs.

5.2. William Summers. (Photographic Services Collection, QEII Library, Memorial University of Newfoundland.)

The university's Extension Division could help create the local groups and then help them apply for funding. The other alternative was to select depressed areas and concentrate "the full machinery of government" on solving problems.[40] Officials favoured the latter approach.

Among the early ARDA projects were surveys of soil and land use in rural Newfoundland that were carried out by faculty and students at Memorial.[41] These stand as examples of how social science research in the 1960s contributed to the reorientation of state policy. The English-trained economic geographer Allan Williams started teaching at the university in 1962 and soon became involved in applied research on agricultural resources on the island. Williams's 1963 ARDA field-work included mapping some rural communities to identify marginal agricultural land that, with government aid, could be put into production and areas that people should no longer farm.[42] In his capacity as an economic geographer, Williams worked with ISER and undertook some of the early social science and geographic research funded by ARDA, as well as teaching the people hired by the university's Extension Service who then undertook the development work in outports. He conducted a field survey of Bonavista Bay – mapping communities and resources and making observations about opportunities for economic development. The Training Course for Newfoundland Government ARDA Field Men, conducted through Extension, was led by Williams and included as instructors Parzival Copes and T.F. Wise from the Department of Economics, Ian Whitaker from the Department of Sociology and Anthropology, as well as Memorial's Extension field representatives, D.J. MacEachern and Bert Toms.[43] The following year, Williams taught a five-month course to the fieldworkers, for which he received leave from his regular teaching duties at the university.[44] Williams not only trained fieldworkers and conducted and coordinated research at the university, but he was asked by the province's ARDA Coordinating Committee to help implement the policy. He was to meet with senior government officials from various departments and decide which development projects were immediately feasible, work out costs, and prepare requests to be forwarded to Ottawa.[45]

When travelling throughout the outports, Williams found that small-garden agriculture had declined during the 1950s, and, despite government hopes to revitalize agriculture, he thought little could be done to arrest that decline. Given the poor soil on the island, he believed there was little potential for expanded commercial farming in the province and that there was "every reason why rehabilitation and development on the North East Coast should be ... first and foremost, of the relation not between man and the land, but man and the sea."[46] That study and a similar one of the Port au Port area on the island's west coast were exactly the sort of applied research on the province, rather than more theoretical or fundamental academic research, that Premier Smallwood favoured. In addition to using the money to enhance farming, as it had been intended, the provincial government used ARDA funding to help pay for studies of the modernization of the fishery and the research into resources that it thought would be required to modernize the economy. Despite his lifelong enthusiasm for farming, Smallwood's urgency to develop the province encouraged him to give priority to large-scale industrial development and to the development of an offshore fresh-frozen fishery to replace the small-boat dried salt cod fishery that had been the mainstay of the economy on the island's northeast coast.

The local shortage of skilled surveyors encouraged Summers to recruit a geographer from outside the province to undertake the ARDA field survey of the Bonavista Peninsula – something that was to have a great role to play in developing historical geography in Newfoundland. Although C. Grant Head never worked at Memorial, his work was to become influential among both Newfoundland historians and geographers. A native of Hamilton, Ontario, Head had worked briefly as a surveyor and had taken a BA in geography at McMaster University. His early education included an exposure to historical geography from R. Louis Gentilcore, who had written on settlement and land use in Antigonish, Nova Scotia. Head had also been impressed by the questions asked by the historians teaching there, which also encouraged him to take a historical approach to geographic questions.

As he was graduating, his BA supervisor, Harold Wood, offered him funding to do an MA and told Head of an opportunity to work in Newfoundland. Summers (whom Wood knew) was looking for someone with a PhD to lead a team in the field, but Wood felt that Head was capable of doing the work. After being interviewed by Williams at a conference in Montreal, Head was hired to survey resources on the Bonavista Peninsula in Newfoundland. He enjoyed the fieldwork in Newfoundland a great deal and gained a knowledge of the landscape and resources that was to shape much of his future work. In explaining why people had moved from the headlands to the bottom of bays, for example, the question of why they had settled in the headlands in the first place was obvious. That prompted him to consider historical work on the settlement of Newfoundland for his PhD.[47]

Head went to University of Wisconsin for his doctorate, where he worked with the historical geographer Andrew Clarke, who had written on the historical geography of Prince Edward Island and was then working on a similar project about Nova Scotia.[48] Although teaching in the United States, he was his generation's most prominent historical geographer of Canada.[49] In the seminar, and in his supervision of students, Clarke emphasized an exhaustive search of archival sources, a lesson that Head and his wife, who helped with his research, applied in their search for Newfoundland material in American, Canadian, Newfoundland, British, and Irish archives. Head studied both geography and history at Wisconsin and set out to write a history of the settlement of Newfoundland in the eighteenth century. Not long after starting his archival research for his doctorate, Head noted that the level of spatial information contained in the Newfoundland census was very high compared to that available in many other jurisdictions – making it an excellent region for a historical geographer to study.

Few Canadians had conducted historical or geographic research on Newfoundland since the 1930s, when Harold Innis worked on the international cod fishery, and being from Ontario shaped Head's experience. Canadian historians who wrote within their national traditions had little reason to think about Newfoundland – a place that seemed marginal to the colony-to-nation framework within which many of them worked during the 1950s. The emphasis on the social history of daily life, rather than politics, among geographers may have made it easier for Head, then a graduate student at an American university, to write about Newfoundland. While Head made friends in Newfoundland during the several months he lived in the province in 1969, he did feel like somewhat of an outsider at Memorial. Head felt that some faculty members at Memorial, such as Keith Matthews, were suspicious of a Canadian who studied Newfoundland, although many others were generous in aiding his work. British and American scholars dominated the study of Newfoundland during the 1960s, and it was not the native Newfoundlanders who felt a sense of ownership over the field. Some of the British-born faculty members at Memorial thought of themselves as Newfoundlanders rather than Canadians and saw themselves as defending Newfoundland culture against perceived Canadian slights and North American popular culture. Despite his friendships in Newfoundland, and his wife's family having roots in Newfoundland, the Englishmen and Americans who ran Newfoundland studies did not always welcome a Canadian whose work overlapped their own. Upon finishing the research in the UK, Grant Head took up a job at McMaster while writing his thesis, and he later went on to a successful career at Wilfrid Laurier University. The thesis was finished in 1971 and revised for publication in 1976.[50]

Eighteenth Century Newfoundland, which was briefly discussed in chapter 2, not only laid a foundation for a history of settlement but was based more heavily on quantitative analysis than was Matthews's doctoral thesis. There were other differences. Most historians had taken all of Newfoundland as their unit of analysis; Grant Head demonstrated that there had been considerable variation between different areas of the island. He was also, arguably, the first person to write ecological history of Newfoundland; he integrated an understanding of the environment with settlement in new ways. He worked with the rudimentary, but then up-to-date, science of the marine ecosystem. He was, for example, aware of the data that indicated there were different stocks of cod that were largely independent of each other and was ahead of his time in understanding the role overfishing may have played in the eighteenth century. He suggested that as early as 1683, people had recognized the limits of shore facilities (including resources on land and the distance from the fishing grounds) and realized that overfishing of local stocks had lowered the yield per boat. These factors, Head proposed, had encouraged people to settle in new areas.[51]

Eighteenth-century settlement, for Head, grew as a result of the confluence of several factors: ships from the West of England stopping at Irish ports for provisions provided transportation for Irish servants to move to Newfoundland, relatively high wages in Newfoundland encouraged Irish labourers to travel to Newfoundland, good prices and catches for fish in Newfoundland made the place attractive for immigrants, and agricultural surpluses in the American colonies provided the provisions necessary for life on the island of Newfoundland.[52] More than any published work had done up to that point, *Eighteenth Century Newfoundland* shifted the emphasis in historical debate from the focus on warfare and English policy to an examination of the places from which Newfoundland settlers originated.

In the 1970s the historians of Newfoundland, such as Alexander and Ryan, focused much of their attention on exports of fish, and they had paid less attention to the settlers' consumption. Export statistics were a useful proxy for economic activity in a country that relied heavily on international markets in fish, paper, and iron ore. Matthews emphasized the West of England-Newfoundland trade and was aware of the importance of the American provisions. Yet Head's education in Canada and the United States encouraged a different orientation than that of the English-trained historians.

The geographer Carl Sauer (who taught a seminar at Wisconsin while Head was a student there) had asked questions of Head such as when did Newfoundland settlers start to grow potatoes?[53] Sauer had moved away from the environmental determinism of early twentieth-century geography to emphasize the ways that people shaped their environment. The attention to such questions opened a new set of concerns for historical geographers. While Matthews had made good use of English documents, he had been unable to use American records when writing his thesis. Head used New England port records to reconstruct the trade of the thirteen colonies and bring a new focus on the Newfoundland diet, and he was able to visit English archives as well.[54] Matthews had been trained within a constitutional history tradition in Britain and lacked Head's facility with quantitative data. Head wrote his thesis within a social science department that was oriented towards model building and at a time when the enthusiasm for quantitative research was high. Head's book presented his data in graphs and tables. Despite his infrequent professional contacts with Memorial faculty members, and the fact that most of his work after 1973 was unrelated to Newfoundland, *Eighteenth Century Newfoundland* remained an important text. Head studied historic settlement patterns, at the same time that the government and university were wrestling with rural economic privation. The intellectual debate about resettlement, discussed in the next chapter, raised questions about the distribution of people across the island and the ways that they earned a living.

The greater interest at Memorial in "traditional" rural culture encouraged scholars to turn their attention to how people came to be settled in such places. That element of research in the Department of Geography was encouraged when they were joined by John Mannion – who combined an interest in cultural transfer with the demographic archival research that become one of the defining methods of Newfoundland geography. An Irish native, Mannion had trained in the study of material folk culture, an area in which few Canadians then worked. He moved to Canada and in the late 1960s was working on a PhD in geography at the University of Toronto under the supervision of Cole Harris. (Harris was to become Canada's most prominent historical geographer and was at that time working on French Canadian material culture.)[55]

For his dissertation, Mannion conducted fieldwork in three areas in which Irish immigrants had settled, Newfoundland, New Brunswick, and Ontario. His interests in folk life, material culture, and cultural diffusion were all similar in orientation to the newly emerging work in folklore at Memorial; Mannion focused on transfers of house types, tools, and farming techniques from Europe to North America. While doing his fieldwork in the St John's area, he became well known to the folklorists and geographers at Memorial, which led to Herbert Halpert hiring Mannion as a cross-appointment between the two departments in 1969. The course in folk life that Mannion initially taught at Memorial was then the only such course in Canada, but over time his involvement in folklore diminished as his work on historical geography developed.[56]

When his dissertation was published, it established his reputation as a scholar of cultural transfer and of the Irish diaspora.[57] Mannion worked in historical geography, folk life, and social history; his work both overlapped with that of his new colleagues in the Departments of English and Folklore and encouraged greater attention to the past among his colleagues and students.

Economic geographers, such as Alan Williams, had described the contemporary distribution of resources and people, and he too turned his attention to history. In that area he became an important figure in the study of geography at Memorial, despite the brevity of his appointment (he left in 1965 and returned as acting head of the department for the year 1971–72). Living in the United Kingdom did not eliminate his influence on younger colleagues and Newfoundland geography – even after leaving he remained a part of the extended family of Memorial geographers. As a native of Bristol with a doctoral degree in geography from the University of Bristol, it was not surprising that Williams's interest in his home town's historic association with Newfoundland was piqued. Williams's interest in John Guy, the Bristol-based merchant who led the first formal effort at colonization of Newfoundland in 1610, was whetted when he was introduced to the mayor of St John's, who was himself interested in the historic connections between the two cities. A 1963 field trip with a group of undergraduates to Cupids (the site of Guy's Cuper's Cove settlement) encouraged a lifelong archival research project that resulted in a posthumously published study of Guy.[58]

Most of his research in the 1960s had been in economic geography, as we have seen, but as a geographer interested in history, his example, and that of Alan Macpherson, encouraged graduate students and younger colleagues to take up historical topics. Two of his Newfoundland students who later pursued historical geography at Memorial, Gordon Handcock and Ches Sanger, recalled Williams leading a group of colleagues on a field trip to Trinity Bay with a copy of John Guy's 1612 journal in hand in an effort to match the seventeenth-century descriptions with features in the twentieth-century landscape.[59] For many geographers, walking the terrain was an important, if sometimes intangible, part of the work that was based on historical records. The historian Gillian Cell, by contrast, then the leading expert on early seventeenth-century Newfoundland settlement, had based her work on the English historical records and had only briefly visited Newfoundland. Williams's method also varied from the practice of many studies of colonization of North America in which the documentary research was in Europe and the fieldwork was in the Americas. He also conducted fieldwork in England, reconstructing the life of Guy in England by examining his houses, places of work, and the churches he had attended. Williams also wrote on John Cabot, the Venetian mariner who when sailing from Bristol had discovered the island of Newfoundland in 1497.

With Williams's departure from Memorial in 1966, William Summers articulated his desire to have the department turn from a "service unit" providing undergraduate teaching to a department that produced professional geographers and undertook research. As the only Department of Geography east of Laval University, "we now feel we are in a position to take advantage of our strategic location" to earn national and international recognition by concentrating in fisheries geography and regional studies of the North Atlantic.[60] The department proposed a Fisheries Research Centre, which would be unique in the English-speaking world. The staff in the department, and some research workers, would conduct physical, historical, economic, social, and political research into the fishery of the east coast of Canada. In addition to the publications that would be expected, the project would culminate in an atlas of the fishery.[61]

It was an ambitious scheme, combining environmental with cultural geography and economic with historical geography, and it would have advanced the knowledge of the sea at a crucial time, but funding for such an ambitious program was difficult and the principal fisheries specialist in the department left Memorial. Building such a research program necessitated developing a graduate program and some additional appointments. As part of his bid to expand the department, Summers had hired two graduate students he had gotten to know at McGill – Joyce and Alan Macpherson. Joyce was initially hired part-time and added expertise in physical geography, a developing strength in the department as in the field of geography generally, while Alan became Summers's right-hand man and later helped to establish the distinct approach to historical geography that emerged in the department in the 1970s.

A native of Scotland, Alan Macpherson had started a PhD at the University of Edinburgh, working on the history of the Jacobite estates under one of the first geographers in the United Kingdom who was interested in changing geography over time. He was teaching at McMaster University when the time limit on his doctoral program ran out. A friend recommended he enrol at McGill to take a PhD, where he met both his future wife and Bill Summers.[62] Macpherson was teaching at Rochester University when offered the job at Memorial and was attracted to Newfoundland because he was interested in working on a rural society. ISER appointed him director of geographic research to accompany his position in the teaching faculty in the Department of Geography. Over his career, he conducted Newfoundland-related research and supervised several graduate students who did important work on Newfoundland. While many North American geographers pursued fieldwork, Macpherson encouraged his students to use archival material as well. He had used parish records of births and marriages, for example, as a source, which graduate students in the department, such as Rosemary Ommer, Patricia Thornton, and Handcock, subsequently used in their research.

Another key appointment was Michael Staveley, a research fellow with ISER who had impressed Summers both with how hard working he was and with how well he fit into the department's plans. Staveley (BA, MA Reading) was working on a PhD at the University of Alberta when he came to Memorial on an ISER fellowship in 1966.[63] Even before his appointment to the faculty in 1968, he had participated in the colloquium on resettlement and an Extension Service conference on the subject. While Head had used census data to describe the growth of settlement, Staveley's interests were in population geography. Working at a more abstract level than many of his peers, he explored the changing demographic character of the population in regions as they successively became the site of immigration and settlement. Staveley served on the board of ISER, was head of the Department of Geography from 1979 to 1983, and then spent a decade as the dean of arts. In each of these capacities he supported Newfoundland studies.

Gordon Handcock's career followed a familiar path to many Newfoundland-born academics of his generation. Having been given an atlas as a boy he long had a fascination with maps and landscape, and at Memorial he studied geography, history, and other subjects from the few faculty then available. Having studied with Goodridge, Summers, Williams, and others, courses from Mannion made him familiar with the sort of cultural geography pioneered by Sauer, an approach then unknown in Britain. The arrival of large numbers of baby boomers as students at Memorial, not the least encouraged by the government's brief period of free tuition, had strained the teaching capacity of the university. Added to that, some of these students lacked the necessary preparation to thrive, which prompted Memorial to hire a group of junior division instructors to teach introductory courses. Junior division instructors were initially not expected to teach advanced courses and were hired for their teaching rather than their research abilities. In some instances, such as the case of the Department of English, "senior" and "junior" division faculty did not even meet together in department meetings.

The Department of Geography, by contrast, wanted to control hiring itself rather than leave it to the administrators of junior division.[64] With Williams's and MacPherson's encouragement, Handcock was the department's first graduate student. His MA thesis, a study of the Commission of Government's land settlement scheme of the 1930s, was clearly historical rather than a contemporary policy-related work, and it included maps and the attention to resources like the studies of Williams and Head. He was also the first of the department's graduates to be hired as a faculty member at Memorial. Handcock joined the faculty in 1970 and the next year went to England to begin a doctorate. While nominally a student at the University of Birmingham, working with Williams, he lived most of the time at the University of Exeter and learned much from the members of that university's Department of Geography. The department also hired Handcock's contemporary Ches Sanger, who had also taught school for several years after finishing his BA. Sanger wrote on the nineteenth-century seal fishery for an MA thesis, paying close attention to the environment and technology, which included both archival research and going to the ice with sealers to observe the harvest. He followed with doctoral work on the history of whaling.[65]

For his PhD, Handcock turned his attention to the origins of English settlement in Newfoundland – the area pioneered by his contemporary, Grant Head. Newfoundland historians had blamed the settlement pattern (a population dispersed in small communities along thousands of miles of coastline) for both poor economic growth compared to other colonies and the chronic underdevelopment in contemporary rural Newfoundland. And the nineteenth-century Newfoundland historians had blamed British policy, rather than economic or environmental factors, for discouraging settlement. Handcock had read widely in the history of settlement in many areas of the world, and while most work in migration history had focused on "push and pull" factors, Handcock realized that Newfoundland settlement did not fit with such models. Reading parish records in Newfoundland enabled him to identify the names and places of origin of Newfoundland inhabitants, and subsequent tracing of those names in English parish records showed that understanding the administration of the poor in Britain was necessary to understand recruitment for the Newfoundland fishery. Handcock viewed Newfoundland settlement as a side effect of the migratory fishery, rather than a process of immigration as in other regions of the new world.[66] He acknowledged his intellectual debts to Matthews and Head and had a friendly competition with Matthews to find new records. He responded to Matthews's discussion of the migratory fishery, and Head's emphasis on the environment, by examining the role merchants played in encouraging settlement. He also drew on Seary's ongoing research on family names, which had identified many of the documents on settlers on both sides of the Atlantic.[67]

Students of Handcock and Sanger's generation often gravitated to Newfoundland research, both because of the influence of their mentors and because so little had been done that Newfoundland topics were low hanging fruit. While linguists and folklorists looked first to outports as the terrain that contained the gems upon which they would build their careers, the geographers were often interested in the urban as well as rural experience. Living in St John's had an effect. George Story was developing a more intense interest in social history in the 1970s, when he became involved in community organization. Road construction threatened his neighbourhood and several historical buildings were demolished. His personal example of political activism led others to become interested in preservation, not only of individual historic buildings but of neighbourhoods. (Built heritage advocate Shane O'Dea, a colleague of Story's in the Department of English, counted Story as one of his mentors.) Story also provided intellectual underpinnings to the disparate individuals who became animated by the changes in the city; he introduced, for example, members of the recently formed Newfoundland Historic Trust to Jane Jacobs's *The Death and Life of Great American Cities*.[68]

The department had hired other geographers by 1970; appointments broadened the research and teaching. H. McCutcheon taught political and urban geography, while C. Banfield taught climatology and biography. Summers continued to work on economic development, Alister Goodlad studied the modernization of the fishery, while others conducted physical geographic fieldwork. The presence in the same department of Macpherson, Mannion, and Staveley, and a slightly more junior cohort of graduate students, provided a synergy among those whose interests were historical. At the same time, Macpherson and Staveley were mapping denominational adherence in the nineteenth and early twentieth centuries, working towards a denominational atlas. Although of the same generation as his colleagues, Mannion was soon to edit a volume that exemplified the Newfoundland approach to historical geography. During 1972–73 some of the faculty and graduate students held a series of seminars at Memorial's facility in Harlow, England. It included Mannion, Sanger, Staveley, Macpherson, and three former MA students at the university who had moved to McGill University for doctoral work, Ommer, Thornton, and Frank Remiggi. David Mills, an MA student of Mannion's who then worked with the Historical Resources Division of the provincial government, was also included. Their presentations on historical geography were later published in a volume by ISER in one of that publisher's few forays into geography.[69] *The Peopling of Newfoundland* laid a foundation for the study not only of where the Europeans who settled the island came from but traced their distribution on the island. As the Canadian historical geographer Graeme Wynn observed when looking back at the work of the group at Memorial, it was common for scholars in that era to count migrants at the port of entry, but those at Memorial used parish records, newspapers, merchant ledgers, and other records to specify both the points of origins and their destinations.[70] The book also discussed the cultural transfer across the sea and closely examined the economic structures that determined settlement. The varied essays had an admitted bias towards the northeast coast of the island and paid less attention to Irish immigrants and people on the Avalon and south coast. The hope was that the volume would provide a starting point, rather than a conclusion, for "much work remains to be done before any definitive historical geography of Newfoundland can be written."[71] In the meantime, *Peopling* provided a textbook that could be assigned to students, which was a significant step in defining the field of Newfoundland historical geography.

After being invited to reflect on the fiftieth anniversary of Memorial's Department of Geography, Wynn pointed out that in the 1970s only one other Canadian university matched Memorial for its number of historical geographers. He also believed that the geographers at Memorial shared characteristics that made them unique among geography departments. They differed from historians as well. Canadian historians often worked with a colony-to-nation framework and had a similar Constitutional emphasis to that which we have seen among the historians at Memorial. That resulted in a continental outlook in their work.

American historians, with their emphasis on the Revolutionary War as a break with the past and the frontier thesis with its claim for the exceptional nature of America, tended to look inland rather than to Europe. The migratory nature of Newfoundland's fishery, the competition for the island among European powers, and the export of fish to the old world encouraged the geographers at Memorial to emphasize the Atlantic perspective before American historians developed the approach (which in the 1980s came to be known as the Atlantic World). While Newfoundland historians such as Matthews focused nearly exclusively on the codfishery, the geographers pointed out that terrestrial resources were essential to settlement. A focus on other fisheries and economic resources is evident in the *Peopling* collection. Wynn concluded that the publication of the *Historical Atlas of Canada (HAC)* was the high water mark of Memorial's work in historical geography.[72] The *HAC* project began in the early 1970s, and while housed at the University of Toronto involved geographers from many provinces. It drew on existing research, but large gaps existed, and much of the textual evidence collected by geographers could not readily be translated into graphic form by cartographers, so a great deal of the research for each plate was new. Each required a collaboration between those who did the research, the editor of the volume, and the cartographers to decide what each plate would convey, acquire the data necessary, and then design the plate.[73]

Macpherson was one of the editors; he represented the views of several of his department members who contributed to the atlas. The plates not only conveyed an understanding of Newfoundland settlement, trade, and the fishery but did so with beauty. Cole Harris, the editor of the volume, congratulated Handcock on the plate of Trinity, which he felt was the Canadian town best covered, and the contribution of all of the Memorial geographers. "I think the Atlantic section of the volume is the most balanced," he wrote, "and, in some ways, the most original of the lot."[74] One might argue that the nature of the plates emphasized the presentation of description over explicit analysis, but even the clearest illustration of spatial relationships was built on sophisticated conceptual understandings.

The *Historical Atlas* was a continuation of the Memorial group's research into the patterns of settlement, and it was the only project that represented the culture through graphic art rather than text. The presentation of quantitative data was mediated through art. Thickness of line, colour, and direction of arrow were all choices made by the atlas's cartographers in consultation with the "authors" of the plates. Text accompanied each plate to explain relationships that could not be represented in pictures, and each plate was dense with data.[75] Having solicited the views of contributors to the atlas, one reviewer reported Mannion's comment that "the value of the project was in making the work of the Memorial University group on Newfoundland more visible to other colleagues across the country. In his words, the atlas 'made us national, as opposed to local.'"[76]

Through the balance of their careers, the historical geographers contributed to local research. Having taken a PhD at McGill, Ommer returned to Memorial, but to the Department of History rather than Geography. She worked on the ACSP in the 1970s and the codfishery of the Gaspé Peninsula in the 1980s, after which she was influential in interdisciplinary social science and natural science approaches to Newfoundland's economic life in the aftermath of the 1992 cod moratorium. Handcock's work on English settlement of the island was accompanied by more local historical research on the community of Trinity and the transcription of the diary of the prominent merchant of that town, Benjamin Lester. He also worked on place names, much as Seary had. Sanger followed his work on sealing with significant work on the history of modern whaling, a species that had not attracted much attention from historians. Mannion's exhaustive work on the Irish who immigrated to Newfoundland set a new standard for the history of immigration and balanced the study of the English in Handcock's work. Mannion's work on Irish merchants involved in the provisioning trade, for example, opened up new areas. Staveley, Macpherson, and others, such as the urban geographer Chris Sharpe, also continued to write into the new millennium. But as members of the department retired, they were replaced with people who worked in different traditions.

Intellectual movements come to an end. When Wynn surveyed the accomplishments of the department, he noted its failure to capitalize on its advantages. Its faculty members and students had developed their own approach to historical geography, but without a PhD program no cohort of young scholars emerged to replace their predecessors or spread their influence to other universities. No book-length synthesis of the many interpretative strands and local micro-studies emerged to follow up *Peopling*. Without a major statement of theory or method having been published, he suggested, its influence in Canada remained muted:[77]

> In the 1970s and 1980, scholars at MUN came close to formulating a new and powerful approach to understanding land and life in Newfoundland as they shaped a distinctive approach to Canadian historical geography. Engaged more heavily than their counterparts elsewhere in the country with demographic techniques, their work shaped to a degree unusual in Canada by concerns characteristic of earlier work on European peasant and Celtic fringe societies, and quick to recognize the value of an Atlantic perspective in history, their practice reflected both the peculiar conjuncture of influences, approaches and traditions brought together by their appointments in this place, and the particular circumstances of that place itself. Newfoundland is, of course, a place like no other ... No one has been brave enough to be bold, and engage the tantalizing possibility, suggested in *The Peopling of Newfoundland*, that outport society, unlike that in the rest of North America, simplified with time (as mercantile concentration led to the decline of domestic industries and the withdrawal of specialized artisans and commercial personnel from outlying settlements). Without such illustrations of its interpretive power, without much presence in the larger disciplinary literature, and with its few monographs tightly focused on specialized concerns, the influence of the MUN School in Canadian Historical Geography has remained muted, its power and its distinctiveness noticed by few and consigned by default to the increasingly quiet margins of Canadian historical and geographical scholarship that has moved on to other infatuations, some of which might yet benefit from greater awareness of the work reviewed here.[78]

Indeed, not long after the third and final volume of the *HAC* had been completed, historical geography at Memorial, as was the case in Canada more generally, diminished as retiring faculty members were replaced with experts in other fields and graduate students chose to work on questions of more contemporary interest. Memorial's new cohort of geographers had new specializations and methods. The sort of geography now done on the sea and land, as with Newfoundland language, culture, history, etc., is different than that done during the Newfoundland studies movement. As clearly in geography as in any other discipline discussed in this book, the Newfoundland approach rose and fell. Even as Memorial's geographers were laying the foundation of a sophisticated understanding of the historical geography of

Newfoundland, their sorts of work were already fading from fashion in geography departments. The decline of interest in historical geography and, more importantly, regional geography, occurred throughout the profession. Even as the foundational work on Newfoundland was just getting underway, professional geographers were turning away from that sort of work. As Wynn put it in a survey of the field:

Ironically, the characteristic concerns of historical geographers rapidly came to appear dated and divorced from the preoccupations of most of their colleagues in the 1960s. As the philosophical tenets of logical positivism took hold across the social sciences, many geographers turned away from the regional studies that ... [some] had regarded as the capstones of the discipline to pursue the development and identification of distinctive spacial laws ... With the much-heralded quantitative and behavioral revolutions pointing the way to a brave new world of scientific geography, the study of geographic change was dismissed as a cul-de-sac ... Inductive methodologies and the principles of historical scholarship were declared irrelevant to the task of understanding geographical change.[79]

When asked about the diminished role of historical geography with the profession, Alan Macpherson concurred that regional geography courses and texts had once provided the synthesis that tied together the various strands (cultural, economic, physical, etc.) within geography departments. But as each of the sub-disciplines became more specialized, increasingly technical, and more sophisticated, he thought, the various geographers at Memorial, like their colleagues elsewhere, found they had less in common with their colleagues in the same department. Collaborations and cumulative work became more difficult.

Ironically, regional work among geographers, including work on Newfoundland, declined as the research became richer. In the case of Memorial's department, the significant number of individuals doing historical research in regional geography were not replaced with clones of themselves as they retired. Similarly, Grant Head, who after his seminal work on Newfoundland historical geography worked on Ontario subjects for the rest of his career, saw the rise of quantitative methods overwhelm those who worked within a humanities approach. Some Canadian historical geographers reacted to their colleagues' privileging of the natural sciences by adopting neo-Marxist models, he reported, or shifted to working on environmental issues. In either case, the sort of historical empirical study that had once been so fruitful came to be seen as old fashioned by younger scholars who realized that they could not sustain a career working within the sorts of historical geographic paradigms established by himself and Memorial's historical geographers.[80]

As geographers adopted theory and method from the sciences, they abandoned the sort of historical empiricism that might have provided data useful to biologists, for example, who tried to understand long-term changes in the ecology. It was not until after the biological collapse of the northern cod stock caused the federal government to declare a moratorium on fishing for cod that biologists and many social scientists turned their attention to traditional ecological knowledge. Head had shown that historical data on fish landings could be used to address policymakers' questions about the effect of fishing effort, but few were doing that sort of work anymore.

Nineteenth- and twentieth-century Newfoundlanders developed a sense of themselves as a people who belonged to a particular place, even as their attachment to the empire remained part of their identity. The scholars examined in the preceding chapters, and many nationalist intellectuals, saw language, song, mumming, and cuffers as the essences of Newfoundland culture. Ian Whitaker saw the adoption of new consumer items as carrying with them new values, and St John's artists who were members of the nationalist revival often cited as an example of cultural loss the replacement of the handmade wooden tables and chairs with a chrome dining room set from Sears. The folklorist Gerald Pocius emphasized that the identity that is attached to belonging to a place is more important in understanding a people than are oral traditions excerpted from their context. The scholarly attention paid to artefacts, folk songs, and once-a-year cultural practices, he suggested, were a strategy that was limited to describing things that were not that important to the people whose culture was being examined.[81]

No one geographer dominated the field of Newfoundland scholarship in the way that Halpert had shaped the approach of the folklorists; the collaboration of those doing archival and fieldwork, the cultural geographers and the economic, the attention to the rural and the urban is the defining feature of geographic research. Geography also straddled the arts and sciences in a way unmatched in the other fields that made up the movement. The geographers combined physical oceanography with economics, attention to the history of technology with the ways that space was organized, and proposed integrated fisheries research. As the only Department of Geography in eastern Canada, it worked as closely with geologists as historians and housed both social scientists and natural sciences. Research and teaching expanded into environmental research, but while the department went its own way, its important role in the Arts Faculty continued. Geographers helped develop an interdisciplinary undergraduate program in Newfoundland studies as an option for those taking a BA.[82] In the 1950s Story had recognized the tension between his teaching standard English grammar and doing research on Newfoundland English, and by the 1980s it was possible for a student to specialize in the study of the society and culture of Newfoundland.

The geographer Cole Harris's characterization of the University of British Columbia's Department of Geography during the 1960s as teaching "regional geographies that owed more to inventory than analysis" would also be an apt description of Memorial's activities during this period as well.[83] Geographers and social scientists' emphasis on inventory had been encouraged by their relationships with government, but their involvement with the Resettlement Program prompted them to make a more critical appraisal of government policy. Applied research, whether community studies or surveys of resources, could whet the appetite for more fundamental scholarship.

Both Grant Head and Allan Williams were introduced to Newfoundland through their work on contemporary resources, but the efforts to understand the contemporary world encouraged them to turn their attention to the past. Head's work on the historical geography of eighteenth-century Newfoundland was one of the books that prompted a re-evaluation of the basic narrative of our past and continues to be relevant, while his fieldwork is largely forgotten because the conditions that prompted it no longer apply. Similarly, Williams's fieldwork was ephemeral – social and economic change in the province soon made it irrelevant – but his legacy in historical geography was carried forward by his students. Harold Innis had been very influential among both Canadian historians and geographers, and, as Wynn observed, historians in the 1950s turned their attention to political history and away from the way that the environment shaped history, while geographers were becoming more committed to careful archival study.[84]

Newfoundland geographers embarked on the study of history with as much enthusiasm as any in Canada, probably more than most, but Newfoundland historians did not abandon the staple thesis for political biographies, as had many Canadians. For the historical geographers of the Newfoundland studies movement, emphasis on the roles of staple products and demography remained central concerns. Geographers and historians who came to the field after the 1992 cod moratorium turned their attention less often to preceding centuries or to the process of settlement. Perhaps those questions had been answered to people's satisfaction. They were more likely to focus on environmental factors and use the methods of the natural sciences than the painstaking community reconstruction that had once seemed the goal. The unique collaborative circle that was most clearly embodied in the *Peopling of Newfoundland* lasted about twenty years: Macpherson, Mannion, Staveley, Handcock, Sanger, and others such as Sharpe all eventually retired, and the study of geography moved in new directions.

As Frickel and Gross observed, successful intellectual movements must recruit new members and frame their enterprise in ways that appeal to younger scholars.[85] The first generation trained a second, but there was no third generation to carry on their practices. Both endogenous and exogenous factors explain the growth and decline of Newfoundland studies. The unique circumstances at Memorial, with an administration that invested in the movement and faculty members who embraced it, explain its rise, just as shifts in the administrative priorities and new generations of faculty with new interests explain its decline. The shift within the discipline of geography in Canada, for example, away from the sort of empirical historical research focused on the region towards more theoretical and environmental science (and less humanistic) also explains the failure of the Newfoundland school of historical geography to have lasting influence.

In the seventeenth century, describing the resources of the island had been a way to promote settlement, just as describing settlement patterns was important in understanding the island's history in the twentieth century. Eighteenth-century naval charts provided the first precise picture of the country as a whole, and they did so at a time when most people's experience was intensely local and when the political and economic elites in St John's did not have effective sovereignty over the whole of the island. The surveys of terrestrial resources in the nineteenth and twentieth centuries were part of the state's efforts to develop the economy, and Memorial's faculty, social and natural sciences alike, did some of that work. William Summers founded a department of geography that engaged in fieldwork in the province, and Williams conducted field research for the government, trained development officers, and helped to implement policy. Research in economic geography that was integrated with state policy encouraged a turn towards historical research when Williams and Grant Head looked to the past to understand contemporary patterns. The historical geographer Alan MacPherson and the cultural geographer John Mannion then laid the groundwork for mapping change through time that involved many of their peers. The collaborations among the geographers and like-minded scholars in folklore and English gave Newfoundland historical geography its particular character.

Chapter Six

Communities in Decline: The Study of Resettlement

Newfoundland is the Canadian province which is undergoing the greatest sociological transition, and therefore offers wonderful material to the social scientist. The Institute is already providing a useful nucleus of information, and the facilities for the production of a worthwhile piece of entirely original research are expanding rapidly.[1]

"Dragging Newfoundland kicking and screaming into the twentieth century," as it was often put, is perhaps a fair characterization of Premier Joseph Smallwood's drive for progress, yet it errs by implying that Newfoundlanders resisted rather than supported the changes. Most Newfoundlanders were eager to modernize and pressured the government to provide a better living. As one of my relatives on the island of Greenspond, which lacked medical facilities, once said to me, "you only need to sit up with a sick child one night for you to want a causeway." The Resettlement Program became most associated with the drive for modernization and nearly synonymous with Smallwood's policies. The government subsidized the resettlement of rural communities to centres where services could be provided at a lower cost. This chapter discusses some of the ways that Memorial's scholars engaged with that program and how their applied research then affected their view of rural Newfoundland.

It is an instance in which the broader community reaction against Smallwood's policies shaped the Newfoundland studies movement. While many of the scholars discussed in the preceding chapters were funded by the state, they were relatively autonomous from the policies and priorities of governments. Other university-based research, such as that discussed in this chapter, was integrated with policy to a greater degree. Both the governments in Ottawa and in St John's hoped to modernize the Newfoundland economy and improve the social opportunities available to rural people, but they found the lack of information on the province impeded the development, implementation, and evaluation of policies. Meanwhile, Memorial's Institute of Social and Economic Research was eager to expand its profile by conducting applied research projects for the state. As the most striking, and ultimately the most controversial, government policy of the 1950s and 1960s, the Resettlement Program provided an opportunity for university-based scholars to do social science research in an area of political importance.

Urbanization and the disappearance of rural communities occurred nearly everywhere in the twentieth century, but starting in 1953 the provincial government hastened the process, under its Centralization Program. The Newfoundland government's Department of Public Welfare subsidized the moving costs of families willing to relocate to where it was less expensive to provide basic services, such as schools. Outports in places difficult to serve, such as islands in Bonavista Bay, were evacuated and the families settled in other fishing outports. These community relocations became more ambitious when the federal government entered into a cost-shared Fisheries Household Resettlement Program with the province in 1965. The program then became more closely aligned with efforts to modernize the fishery. The intention of this program was to shift those employed in the small boat fishery to work in capital-intensive offshore fishery or to work in other industries. From its modest beginnings, and over time, those implementing resettlement became more assertive in encouraging communities to move, lowering the threshold of community consent, for example, or even threatening to not provide a school teacher to a community – to the point that its critics viewed the program as coercive. In other cases, people who feared that they would be left behind and miss out on receiving the subsidy rushed to move, leaving the government unable to control the pace of community abandonment and straining to find the money in its budget to fund the new housing.

It's not surprising, therefore, that several of Memorial's faculty members turned their attention to the ways that Newfoundland's population was distributed, as we saw in the last chapter, and how that might be changed. When the government commissioned scholars to evaluate the Centralization and the Fisheries Household Resettlement Programs, it unintentionally embroiled the social scientists in policy debates.

This chapter examines the relationship between the government and social scientists and shows that while many faculty members and graduate students worked closely with the state, in some cases the experience turned them into critics of the policy they had helped to implement. The sociologist Ralph Matthews and the economist Parzival Copes, to take two prominent examples, both assessed policy for the provincial and federal governments and found themselves on different sides of a political debate. While the sociologists and anthropologists examined in previous chapters studied social problems and challenges to economic development, it was the studies of resettlement that most directly engaged with the political process and brought the university into partisan controversy. Sociological studies of rural Newfoundland, such as Noel Iverson and Matthews's *Communities in Crisis*, and Copes's essays on resettlement and fisheries policy, became important texts in both the political and academic arenas.

"The unlikely revolutionary," Smallwood's biographer called him. The changes in the province in the 1950s and 1960s were, in part, a revolution from above. Government resettled hundreds of small communities and provided schools and roads to hundreds of others. Smallwood enticed German businessmen to establish factories in the province, using the small financial surplus he had inherited from the Commission of Government to subsidize them. But that created few lasting businesses. Rural electrification and the replacement of a labour-intensive, small boat, inshore fishery with a capital-intensive large vessel fishery affected nearly every outport, but it could not provide full employment for the burgeoning population of young people. As these efforts had mixed results, the government looked to large-scale industrial projects such as the Churchill Falls hydroelectric generation station to kick-start economic development. Smallwood also hoped the oil refinery at Come by Chance, Placentia Bay, would act as a growth pole that would attract a plastics industry. The policies were disappointing. As Matthews put it: "The province was dominated by, that is the Smallwood government was dominated, so was the Department of Regional Economic Expansion, by theories of growth centres ... they believed they had to create these growth points, which in Newfoundland was simply large numbers of people who were characterized by unemployment."[2]

While the needs of industry and demands for services attracted much of his attention, the university played two important roles for Smallwood. An autodidact and a nationalist intellectual, Smallwood supported the university both as a force for education and as a symbol that Newfoundland was becoming modern. The official opening of the new campus in 1961 allowed him to luxuriate in the symbolism of a campus with modern buildings, a library, and laboratories. In a more practical sense, the university was also to be a tool for the social and economic transformation by training white-collar workers, while the expanded trades colleges provided blue-collar workers, and the Fisheries College professionalized those who worked at sea. Faculty members gave the children of fishermen the education that Smallwood had to acquire on his own. He was proud of every new school, mile of road, and hospital, and he frequently counted each of them as measures of progress. But Smallwood was impatient with the slowness of the university in expanding to serving new areas. Faculty members were seconded to work with government departments, and when those at the university lacked the expertise to do so Smallwood went to other sources. In his rush to develop the province he had little time for fundamental research but hoped for applied research that would solve practical problems. The university received a great deal of support from both Liberal and, after 1972, Progressive Conservative governments. Given the nature of the challenges of modernization, it's not surprising, therefore, that the government sometimes enlisted sociologists and anthropologists to address the factors that limited growth.

Many Newfoundlanders of Smallwood's generation shared his vision for the role of Memorial University – that of an agent of modernization of the province that would foster individual self-reliance. Smallwood had long admired William Coaker's Fishermen's Protective Union, and he had himself attempted to organize a cooperative on the Bonavista Peninsula during the Depression. He was a liberal who saw himself as a socialist, and he hoped cooperatives would play a role in rejuvenating rural areas while at the same time he hoped foreign industrial capital would industrialize the province.[3] Within months of being sworn in as premier, Smallwood had fostered a fishermen's union and tried to rejuvenate the cooperative movement.[4] The premier had also appointed the former cooperative fieldworker and his old ally from the confederation debates, William Keough, as minister of a combined Department of Fisheries and Cooperatives. To an extent not always remembered, because of his later high-profile mega-projects, Smallwood's economic development strategy in the first couple of years of his government included fostering cooperatives. To resolve the dilemma of having government agents trying to encourage people to help themselves, rather than look to government, Smallwood asked Memorial University to create an Extension Department.

Smallwood rarely intervened in the administration of Memorial, not because he was uninterested in what was going on at the university or because he had some principled respect for academic autonomy, but because urgent issues usually dominated his calendar. He was also a man prone to bold visions more than the details of daily administration. But at times he made his preferences known to the administrators at Memorial. The government prompted the university to hire Raymond W. Miller – a sometime instructor at the Harvard Business School, a public relations consultant, and an employee of the United Nations' Food and Agriculture Organization – to consult on the creation of an Extension Department.

Miller recommended that the government fund a university Extension Service since "experience shows that cooperatives cannot be as successfully promoted by government as by a university through extension."[5] Smallwood had even gone as far as to say that Memorial should be "an Extension Department with a university tacked onto it, not the other way round."[6] Not only was a university Extension Department a priority for Smallwood, he seemed to want Memorial to take responsibility for several areas of economic development that were the responsibility of provincial officials.[7]

With urging from Smallwood to hurry, Gushue hired S. John Colman (MA Oxford) as director in 1959. Colman brought international experience to the university; English-born, he had worked as director of extramural studies at the University of East Africa at Makere. Colman consulted extensively in Newfoundland, Canada, and the United States and drafted a policy for extension.[8] In May 1960 the board of regents endorsed Colman's view that Memorial had to employ representatives outside the capital and that Extension had to be experimental. The university's Extension representatives "will be sociologists with special training in community development. It will be their principal task to help people assess their needs in a scientific manner and to ascertain the best methods of meeting them."[9] Extension would also set up working committees on fisheries, agriculture, cooperatives, etc., to work with governments, employers, and labour groups to design programming. Colman had received the cooperation of the premier and minister of education, as well $30,000 from the province and the enthusiasm of the administration and faculty of Memorial in implementing these plans.[10]

"There must be no hesitation in trying new projects, or in abandoning activities which have manifestly failed," Colman wrote, adding, "that there will be failures and setbacks is evident to anyone familiar with the problems of organizing extension activities anywhere, quite apart from the special difficulties which arise in Newfoundland."[11] He advocated an emphasis on community development based on involving as many people as possible generating an assessment of their needs. The key to success, he felt, was to have community development specialists living in rural communities and thus in a position to encourage local volunteers to assume leadership positions: "to know intimately local people and their needs; to be accepted as a respected member of the local community rather than a suspected outsider ... [can] provide a psychological foundation for extension workers which cannot be achieved if the university keeps itself and its faculty apart, in one place."[12]

Colman also advocated offering of a range of adult education courses, taught by specialists in home economics, labour relations, and business management as well as academic subjects such as English, history, and economics. He envisioned a set of working committees at Memorial, in such areas as fisheries, agriculture, and social welfare, which would identify the needs of the community and coordinate the Extension Service activity with government development efforts. The first step in his strategy, as he outlined it in 1960, was to send teams of researchers to the Bonavista Peninsula and the west coast to study the needs of different areas. That would be followed by a program to encourage skills, talent, and leadership and the encouragement of discussion among rural people. "Helping them to think" was the goal, he said, "not telling them what to think."[13]

With a small staff in St John's, the key to Extension's community development activity was its fieldworkers. Within a couple of years it employed three: D.J. MacEachern and two women who had worked in community development, Vera Moore and Julia Morgan. The sister of then dean of arts and science M.O. Morgan, Julia Morgan, had worked with the adult education division of the government's Department of Education before Confederation. In 1953, after completing a BA and MA at the University of Wisconsin, she transferred to the Department of Public Welfare of the Newfoundland government. She and Moore, who also had an MA from Wisconsin, had worked in the central Newfoundland town of Windsor on community development. After earning a doctorate in 1960 at Wisconsin, Morgan was appointed to the Extension Service and went to Bonavista as a fieldworker. Unfortunately, illness forced her to resign after a few months.[14] MacEachern was one of the seven Nova Scotians trained at St Francis Xavier University who had been a fieldworker for the Commission of Government's division of cooperatives between 1936 and 1943. He had established "study clubs" on the island's west coast to encourage cooperation and had founded a co-op in the area. Returning to Newfoundland in 1961, he established Memorial's field office in Corner Brook.[15]

Other fieldworkers were soon added. Colman assigned Fred Earle, whose role in John Widdowson's folklore collecting has already been noted, a large area and a broad mandate:

> The purpose of your appointment is, by discussion with large and small groups, and by other methods of education, to help fishermen adopt to whatever modern methods (either of catching, processing or marketing) may be relevant to their local situation – to help them also by seeing that they are informed as fully as possible of the various governmental and other aids available to them, and that they express their local situation and needs as well as they can, and with as much knowledge as they can get, to the governments, if they wish to do so. The single ultimate purpose of all this is to help fishermen get as good a living as they can through efficient fisheries ... While your task is not necessarily concerned with encouraging the growth of efficient cooperative enterprises, the Provincial Government's Department of Cooperative Extension should be called upon for help wherever there is a chance of developing cooperative education ... For the most part you will take "community development" to mean "economic development" but as time goes on it is possible that you may be able to help fishing communities solve some of their social problems.[16]

Most North American university Extension Services seconded fieldworkers to a particular government department or had them implement government programs. Memorial's fieldworkers lived in the rural communities and had no set programs to implement. Their job was to listen to people and identify problems and local leaders whom the Extension Service could then engage in dialogue.[17]

For all their ambition to advance their careers and help the province, faculty members were few in number in the 1950s. Sharing close quarters at Parade Street and within the Department of Social Sciences, academic disciplines such as history, economics, and geography split, grew, and developed their own character. Subject matter, theory, and methodology varied among the handful of researchers within the Department of Sociology and Anthropology, and this chapter focuses on the department's effort to work on the problems of rural modernization.

In North American universities, the boundary between the disciplines of sociology and anthropology was blurred, and it is worth pausing to consider some of their common conceptual notions about society. From the 1950s to the 1970s, policymakers and social scientists alike shared many assumptions about modernization. Based on the pioneering work of Talcott Parsons and Edward Shils, American sociologists and anthropologists tried to understand the transition of what they saw as pre-modern societies to modernity. The two proposed a dichotomy between primitive and advanced societies in which "the former were based on such qualities as ascribed status, particularism, role diffuseness, and orientation toward the collective, the latter revealed values of achievement, universalism, role specificity, and orientation toward the self."[18]

Before any of the anthropologists and sociologists knew anything of the island of Newfoundland, their training established an evolutionary view of conceptualizing, organizing, and describing their observations. Once they saw the outports, with ways of life that seemed primitive compared to those in the urban centres in which they had attended college, the lack of amenities was either a welcome fieldwork opportunity or depressing. Some faculty members at Memorial left for higher salaries and more affluent regions when the opportunity presented itself, others embraced aspects of local life.

From its emergence as an academic discipline in the United States, sociology had been an applied discipline. Its practitioners were similar to social workers in that they tried to relieve social problems or believed they could help communities move forward if they were stuck at an earlier developmental stage. As one historian of sociology put it, influential "Chicago theorists believed that social progress was guaranteed in the evolutionary process but that it was incumbent upon sociologists, by observation and investigation, to discover the laws of that process and aid in its development."[19] Many policymakers throughout the world worked towards encouraging societies to develop into something much like the contemporary urban United States.

It must also be noted that many rural people in the United States and in Newfoundland were equally determined to gain road connections to the outside world, electric power, and wage labour jobs. By the 1960s, however, not all scholars were comfortable with their role in changing the society they observed. Even those social scientists who were sceptical of the loss of community values that accompanied industrialization and urbanization didn't emphasize the "modern" characteristics of pre-modern society or the "pre-modern" aspects of contemporary urban society. In the immediate post–Second World War era, modernization theory offered "a kind of 'unified field theory' for social science."[20] The interest anthropologists had in studying African kinship, for example, reflected a desire to understand the impediments to modernization in non-modern societies as much as the intrinsic interest of the exotic.

Anthropologists had benefitted from the prestige that imperial and military officials administering colonies had for their field, and many younger scholars criticized the founders of their discipline for their complicity in imperialism. The academic critique of modernization theory on the grounds that it wrongly assumed that there was only one sort of modern society, and only one path towards replicating it, was in the future when ISER began its study of outports. By the 1970s, the theory was rapidly falling out of fashion among scholars, yet the ethnographies discussed in chapter 4 were influenced by these models. Furthermore, historians of Newfoundland, such as Raymond Blake and Miriam Wright, show that the common assumptions of modernization informed government policy.[21]

One of the dangers of the binary divisions commonly used by social scientists early in the twentieth century, such as gemeinschaft/gesellschaft, primitive/civilized, traditional/modern is that scholars were discouraged from recognizing facts that didn't fit the pattern. If one assumed that outports were communities without history, social stratification, or change, then the researcher might not see the evidence of change or social tensions or might explain it away. If the assumption was that Newfoundland outport society was in stasis, then culture must serve the function of maintaining equilibrium. The question for those who wanted to develop the province was: What could be done to remove the impediments to change? That was something sociologists might be able to help with.

At its inception, sociology at Memorial University was as much a tool to help people as it was a social science. The first sociologist to work at the university, Donald Willmott, had Canadian parents, was born in China in 1925, and moved to the United States after the Second World War. He trained in Far Eastern studies and sociology at Oberlin College, University of Michigan, and Cornell, but he worried about being blacklisted during the 1950s because of his leftist politics and his interest in China.

These concerns encouraged him to apply to Memorial, which was then advertising for a sociologist to help train social workers. His application attracted the attention of Gordon Rothney, who, as we have seen, was building an interdisciplinary research team, and who had his own research interest in the Far East. Joining Memorial in 1956 at the age of 31, Willmott worked for the Newfoundland government's public welfare as research director for part of the year while teaching sociology to social workers through Memorial.[22] The government officials with whom he worked seemed unsure of what problem he should work on, beyond a desire to understand the challenge to modernization. As he wrote to one of his academic mentors, while teaching "scientific methodology to undergraduates," his research work for the state was not directed:

> The research side of my work promises to be fascinating too. Again, no one knows enough about it to interfere very much within broad outlines set by the needs of the Welfare Department. Neither the Deputy Minister nor his assistant, who are my "bosses," has a B.A. and neither has any academic training in social work. Yet both are surprisingly well informed and broad-minded, and are pleasant to work with. There is still no idea of what I should investigate – except for the vague idea that I should find "the facts" about the "outports": and for the frustrated feelings of social workers who would like to know why everyone doesn't have good middle class morals and aspirations![23]

Through his research, both survey research and participant observation, he concluded that poverty was not an individual failure but was best tacked as a social problem at the community level. Those he worked for, however, hoped for some "facts" that would enable them to understand poverty as a failure of individuals. Wilmott would have been happier to have worked on policies that addressed social structures, but his role within the bureaucracy was supplying information, not social criticism. Working for the Department of Public Welfare, which administered the Resettlement Program, also encouraged him to give the program some thought. He believed that the program could be more effective in addressing poverty if economic opportunities were spread throughout the province and the government subsidized housing. He believed that Newfoundland could be an El Dorado for research into modernization, and in 1959 he commented that "in parts of Newfoundland we might find the 'folk society' which we now understand has never existed in Quebec."[24] Willmott later reflected on the 1950s as a period in which the Smallwood government turned to Memorial for social science expertise, but he thought that soon came to an end when the premier didn't like what experts had to say and replaced them with "yes men."

Willmott had a role in creating ISER, which later became a catalyst for sociological work in the province.[25] The sociologist James Overton described the ideological origins of ISER as having its roots in academic staff members working towards modernization of the economy. A 1958 seminar of the Atlantic Provinces Economic Council at Dalhousie University, at which Willmott was one of the Newfoundland contingent, discussed a research agenda for the Atlantic provinces similar to that which was later adopted by ISER for Newfoundland.[26] The government officials and academic economists, sociologists, and political scientists who met in Halifax wondered if social research could find the factors that prevented economic development. In a summary of the discussions, Alexander Brady, of the University of Toronto, wondered out loud if "the devotion to traditional ways of life and a shunning of innovation" was in part responsible for the poor economic performance of Atlantic Canada.[27]

Willmott was soon joined on the faculty by an economist, Parzival Copes, who helped design the research institute. A native of British Columbia, born in 1924, and whose family had moved to the Netherlands when he was a boy, Copes had fought with the Dutch resistance, been captured by the Germans, escaped, and joined the Canadian Army. Degrees in political science and economics from the University of London, after the war, led to a job with the Dominion Bureau of Statistics in Ottawa, which he left in 1957 to take up a job at Memorial. Morgan asked Copes, who in addition to his teaching had begun to compile basic economic data on the province, to recommend an administrative structure for a research institution. The institute that Copes projected would allow faculty members at Memorial to combine their teaching with research while providing basic economic and social data for businesses and the government. Morgan and Raymond Gushue sought advice on the proposed institute from a range of government officials and universities in Canada before deciding that it would consist of a director of sociological research and a director of economic research and have associates who would do the bulk of the research. Initially, its efforts were devoted to providing graduate fellowships for doctoral students at other universities to work on Newfoundland so that, despite lacking PhD programs, "ISER attains, in effect, its own selective doctoral program of research."[28]

The university intended the Institute of Social and Economic Research, which launched in 1961, to aid in policy development in the context of a rapidly modernizing society.[29] Gushue informed Smallwood of its creation: "The Institute will provide fundamental information for the rational formulation of policies and measures, and in this way it will be of invaluable assistance to the Government of the Province, to the industries, as well as to the Extension Service of the University ... I might add that for the past few years the University has been building up its Department of Social Studies," Gushue wrote, "in September, we will have on our staff two Sociologists and three Economists, and it is proposed to encourage these full-time members of the staff also to concentrate their research activities on Newfoundland problems."[30] The first report on ISER's mandate set out its justification for studying the province.

> Geographical isolation, the pattern of its history, and the scattering of its population have contributed to a retardation of economic and social development in Newfoundland and Labrador. Much of the province is still in an entirely pre-industrialized state. Since 1949, however, when the province became a constitutional part of an industrialized country, the process of development which elsewhere has taken decades is being crowded almost into years. Therefore, there exists an opportunity of viewing processes normally long-term but which have occurred in a rather short period.[31]

ISER would conduct "fundamental research" as the "traditional social character of communities" was altered, and its governing board hoped that the basic data would be useful to policymakers.[32]

Premier Smallwood, who doubled as the minister of economic development, took an interest in the research at Memorial that could help with modernization generally. He personally wrote the noted economist John Kenneth Galbraith to ask him to come to Newfoundland to synthesize the ongoing social science research into Newfoundland's economy. Galbraith, who was then working in the Kennedy White House, declined but recommended that Smallwood hire one of his colleagues at Harvard, Raymond Vernon. Vernon was a highly accomplished public servant and economist. Holding a PhD in economics from Columbia, he had worked for the State Department and been a member of the Marshall Plan team. He had also helped set up both the General Agreement on Trade and Tarriffs and the International Monetary Fund. After a brief period in private business, he had joined Harvard University in 1956 to conduct a study of urban planning, and in 1965 he was directing the Multinational Enterprise Project at the Harvard Business School.[33] Smallwood's sense of urgency was palpable in his job offer to Vernon:

> Part of the ARDA scheme is for Ottawa to pay the cost of research in the Provinces concerned, and we have between 20 and 30 separate pieces of research going on at the moment. Economists, college professors, etc. etc. from other parts of Canada and from Newfoundland itself are doing this work. We will shortly begin to receive these reports and the crying need is for someone who can read and analyse them, form some conclusions, and write one overall report that would (at the very least) summarize the situation.[34]

Vernon accepted the assignment, but after reading the studies, visiting Newfoundland, and discussing the provinces' problems with public and private officials, he had a fundamental criticism of the ARDA investigations. While he did not question the contribution to knowledge of the individual research reports, he was surprised to find that the ARDA studies did not add up to a systematic study of the province's problems. He believed that the reports had value in tackling particular problems, but as a group they lacked "any tight conceptual structure."[35] Vernon argued that Newfoundland did not need another general economic study, the full implications of the existing studies of the province having not been absorbed by policymakers. The province needed, in his view, a government department "continuously to appraise, reappraise, and adjust Newfoundland's development strategy."[36]

The Inter-Departmental Committee of the provincial government overseeing ARDA accepted Vernon's report as a framework for economic development.[37] Smallwood agreed that action rather than further study was necessary. Within days, Smallwood wrote the federal government requesting that ARDA fund pilot projects that could be evaluated and then extended more broadly. While he was committed to the university's Extension Service playing an educational role in the modernization of the province, Smallwood was sceptical of the usefulness of the more general research then being done at the university.

I begin to think that research in community development cannot be effectively done by universities, nor can there be a substitute for action, wherein pilot development action projects are undertaken to assess the merits of alternative courses of action. If a broadening of the interpretation of the word research were possible, it could make relatively large amounts of ARDA funds available for continuing research, and also for a broad spectrum of extension personnel that can meet the educational needs of a local activation programme.[38]

Unfortunately for Smallwood, the federal government rejected this request, since the ARDA legislation provided for physical and social and economic research but did not envision "action projects."[39] The provincial government was not blocked from pursuing such a research strategy on its own, however; in June 1963 the province had passed legislation to provide funds for "rural development action and research projects" and funded several of them in different locations.[40] The 1964 agreement also provided for research projects that tested development programs.[41]

The Extension Service had its own strategy, which was to encourage applied research. Colman met with the premier at his residence and then let his staff know about Smallwood's preferences as well as his own view:

[L]ong drawn out fundamental academic surveys are usually not what is wanted and we shall no doubt ourselves be conducting various surveys (more like the one going on now under Williams for the Port au Port) in preparation for ARDA schemes. In order to keep us all as straight as possible on the overall planning considerations I very strongly urged that the services of the Harvard Economic Planning Institute be retained. It is obvious that the faculty at Memorial is incapable of doing this job.[42]

Despite Colman's concern that Memorial's faculty members lacked the economic development expertise needed to modernize the province, ISER combined applied with fundamental research. Individual scholars had freedom to direct their own research on their own question, even when it was funded by ARDA or another government agency, and that work could have implications for government policy.

Symbiotic relationships developed between federal and provincial government policymakers, Extension, and the scholars ISER hired to study the economy. The fact that George Story's brother Colin was the deputy minister of the Department of Economic Development, and thus the civil servant in charge of ARDA in the province, may have eased the cooperative relationship between the government and the university. The two brothers almost certainly discussed the government's research agenda and how it fit with both ISER's priorities and George's general agenda for Newfoundland research. Colin had told George of his efforts to recruit development experts, for example, prompting George, then in England on sabbatical, to report back about suitable English and Scottish experts that the government might hire. A copy of that correspondence exists among Smallwood's papers.[43]

Through more formal channels, MUN Extension and ISER invited the federal and provincial governments to turn to Memorial for aid in fostering economic and social development in rural areas. The Newfoundland government lacked economists who might recommend policies to address inefficiencies in the labour force or, to take one example, make recommendations on the number of fish plants that should be licenced. The directors of ISER were eager to fill those gaps. There were broader issues to be addressed as well. One of the prevailing ideas in the 1960s was that regions with poor economic performance suffered from a failure of entrepreneurial talent or that the population lacked a modern work ethic – in a sense, their culture was an impediment to them becoming successful workers. ISER hoped that the community studies would result in a "fundamental information for the rational formulation of policies and measures, and ... will be of invaluable assistance to the government at both levels."[44]

Despite Willmott's belief that the outports were virgin territory for the study of modernization, he left Memorial for an appointment at the University of Saskatchewan. At that point it seemed that Saskatchewan was experimenting in democratic community development, an area in which Willmott wanted to work. Donald and Elizabeth Willmott's decision to leave the province was also encouraged by the anti-union atmosphere in the province in the midst of the 1959 IWA strike. In suppressing the strike among woodsworkers, Smallwood had used anticommunist and nativist rhetoric to great success, and it seems to have had a chilling effect on leftists at the university. Leftists such as the Willmotts and Rothney found themselves being made to feel that they were outsiders who didn't have Newfoundland's interests at heart.[45]

A document that was likely written by Copes and Ian Whitaker, who replaced Willmott, illustrates their thinking on ISER's role. They sketched out a research program that would examine cultural impediments to labour force participation:

> The lack of economic diversification in the province until very recent times and the individualistic method of prosecuting the fisheries have favoured the development of idiosyncratic attitudes towards employment. These are in conflict with the industrial needs resulting from the economic development of the province. Social welfare benefits introduced at Confederation have affected work attitudes and motivation. There are major problems for employers who find labour extremely difficult to recruit in some areas, even when there is a high level of unemployment elsewhere in the province. There is often a rapid labour turnover and in many cases an irresponsible and non-cooperative attitude to the work being performed.[46]

This sort of study fit well with government efforts to "modernize" the economy, and the emerging efforts of the university's Extension Service. It's worth emphasizing that the initiative for the studies came from Memorial and that federal and provincial government departments (fisheries, agriculture, labour, etc.) funded the research.

The provincial government wanted expert advice on modernization and in 1967 appointed a Royal Commission, chaired by Gordon Pushie, to investigate the prospects of the Newfoundland economy. The Pushie Commission decided it was "important to consider the Newfoundland people's attitudes and institutions" when considering how to foster economic development, so it hired Whitaker, then working at York University in England, to report on these factors.[47] His submission, "Sociological Preconditions and Concomitants of Rapid Socio-Economic Development in Newfoundland," drew on his own experience in the province as well as the ISER community studies.[48] He thought any successful policy had to be based on an understanding of the sociological factors that stood in the way of development. The Newfoundland environment and fishery, he believed, had "bred" men prepared to face danger. They were inventive and respectful of authority, he thought, but the roulette-like prospect of return in the seal fishery affected men's attitudes towards labour. Newfoundlanders' productivity had to be raised, and that required they take a more modern attitude to work. In analysis reminiscent of the *Amulree Report*, he found that not only did people's work ethic fall short, they had been badly governed. "Every country is a prisoner of its history," and Newfoundland's "failure" to join the Canadian Confederation in 1867 had "led to Newfoundland becoming something of a Colonial backwa-ter."[49] The suspension of Dominion Status in 1934, he argued, "was the last stage in a long process of failure through inefficiency, corruption and mal-administration."[50]

Whitaker thought several social factors discouraged individuals' eco-nomic success. Rural people, he believed, were innately conservative, little travelled and poorly educated and, therefore, resisted change. Few non-Newfoundlanders lived in the province that the natives might emulate, and few mechanisms to introduce new ideas to rural people existed. He also thought that the suspicion of outsiders, which the anthropologists had perceived during the community studies, discour-aged people from changing their backward ways.

But he had hope. Improved opportunities for travel and modern com-munications, especially television, he believed, were bringing North American urban values into Newfoundland. He did not define "urban values," but he seems to have meant individualistic economic relation-ships between people, rather than the peasant-like social relations he perceived. Newfoundlanders tended to be grateful for any service they received, he reported, no matter how bad, and didn't demand any better. The traditional labour force engaged in occupational plurality and sub-sistence production, he thought, which encouraged egalitarianism and a suspicion of entrepreneurs. Differentiation of occupation was necessary for capital accumulation and improved productivity, so entrepreneurial behaviour should be promoted through such things as the Resettlement Program, which would get people out of their communities. While Whi-taker advocated cultural changes in attitudes towards work, he also con-demned the individualism in which people in the outports used local resources without regard for others. As Overton described it:

Whitaker accepted "the assumption ... that the goal of rapid social change by industrialization in the western capitalist model is essential for the province," arguing that there existed a "rural ethic" in Newfoundland and that "capital accumulation is in some sense seen as an anti-social activity," both these being barriers to social change and "inimical to development," and as such to be "deliberately changed." The tide of modernization was still riding high in the late 1960s and early 1970s and Whitaker's essay was used in W.E. Mann's Social and Cultural Change in Canada, published in 1970, a celebration of modernization in action in Canada which included the transformation of "the isolated, inbred, pre-modern fishing communi-ties of coastal Newfoundland."[51]

The Pushie Commission's report was consistent with Whitaker's submission; it recommended removing the "obstacles to growth" and "rationalizing production" while recognizing that such changes would be painful to some Newfoundlanders since they required "a disruption of the old ways of doing things and a break with existing institutions and relationships."[52] The break with the past advocated by Pushie was nearly as radical as that recommended by the 1933 Royal Commission, which had also identified a dilemma of individualism coexisting with a lack of wealth accumulation. These changes in the ways that people lived and worked were as important to development, Pushie suggested, as were capital investments.[53] The 1967 report quoted an International Bank for Reconstruction and Development's recommendations for economic development in Kenya, making explicit the comparison to what was then called the third world:

> The most important factor in the process of growth is the speed with which people adapt themselves ... to changing conditions. A bulldozer can move trees and earth but not ideas and habits. Development will not take place unless enough people and their leaders are prepared to make the changes in their habits, attitudes and thinking necessary to achieve the end.[54]

Pushie recommended increasing commodity production, resettlement of remote communities to growth centres, and an "orderly transition from the traditional semi-subsistence way of life to a modern, monetary economy should be planned and encouraged."[55] As Overton put it, the academic researchers that the government recruited to work on the Pushie Commission were "unabashedly pro-modernization" and the finished report drew on Whitaker's submission when suggesting a role for the social scientist and educator in removing those obstacles to growth.[56]

Whitaker envisioned using sociological research on Newfoundland, of which he advocated more should be done, to help the government change the culture of rural people. While he drew the lesson from the community studies that Newfoundland culture was an impediment to modernization, the fieldworkers on whose work he drew varied in how much they imagined their own work fitting into government policy. Their primary interest was furthering their academic careers, and when they came to Newfoundland it was initially just a fieldwork opportunity. But sometimes living in Newfoundland made them not only observers of the culture but advocates of change. One such example was Faris, who, seven months into his fieldwork, provided Colin Story with a detailed reconnaissance of Lumsden North and recommendations for development of the region that he was studying.

Many years later, Faris reported to me that he had little knowledge of where the ISER funding had come from or government policies, yet that does not mean that his views in the 1960s did not coincide with those of government planners or that he had not been in communication with them. He was, of course, aware of the Resettlement Program, the earliest application of which had been in other communities in Bonavista Bay a decade before Faris had arrived, and resettlement was a frequent topic of conversation throughout the province. While some residents in Lumsden suspected him of being a spy, and subsequently believed that he had foreknowledge of resettlement since the community was moved shortly after he left, Faris said he had no knowledge of government plans to resettle the community, if indeed there were any.[57] He certainly knew of the government's plans to modernize the fishery, however, and had a good working relationship with Alan Williams, who had earlier surveyed the community with an eye to development prospects. Faris knew but was unimpressed by the initial set of ARDA field representatives he had met, who were then trying to get fishermen to adopt new gear. That underlines the fact that neither the social scientists' research agendas nor policies of the state actors were entirely coherent.

Faris told Colin Story that he was willing to cooperate with government. "My final report might be utilized – I'll trade advice for information," Faris wrote, "if your department feels it best to leave the academics in their ivory towers, however that's another matter altogether and I shall, of course understand. I would naturally hold any information in strictest confidence."[58] It's plausible that Faris knew nothing of specific government policy; even a cursory examination of government policy of the day reveals that often different agencies were working at cross purposes, and the government was often reacting to events rather than implementing some grand plan. Despite perennial rumours, it's unlikely that there was ever a list of communities to be resettled. But Faris favoured the government's plans to modernize the fishery, and he privately advocated the resettlement of Lumsden North even as he studied the community.

Faris's lengthy letter to Colin Story reveals his view of the role sociological research could have in developing and implementing policy. He started with the assumption that a "scientific" appraisal would conclude that the offshore fishery would be the best way to ensure adequate incomes for the people of the area. Doing so, he concluded, would require the development of harbour facilities suitable for larger vessels than the small boats used in Lumsden North. The investment for the new wharf should, he believed, be made in Lumsden South since its shoreline was more suitable. For that reason, he advised, "no effort should be spared to centralize the population." A well-planned town could serve as a model community and of a modern fishery for other communities in the area, and that as "a showplace [it] shouldn't be another of the all-too-common 'strip' towns, strung out along the highroad." He suggested instructors from the College of Fisheries could offer courses and that building a local library would help modernize the fishing workforce, and he imagined a "boat house as the fishermen's 'intellectual' centre – a place where new items [of gear] might be introduced and explained." The physical and financial challenges could be overcome, and "needless to say," he continued, "social barriers are the only real problem in a good development's success. If it is not a well planned, articulate program with *full* cognizance of the values, ethics, and sociological organization of the community, then it, even with best intentions, will likely fail."[59]

Faris believed that intellectuals had a role in guiding social change. Sociological research through participant observation in individual communities was necessary, in his view, to provide the context of each outport before development could proceed.

> He [the researcher] (a she would be unwise at the introductory level) should be qualified, preferably (though this may reflect a bias) in sociology or social work, with a good grounding in the sociological, economic, physical and traditional setting of the community. This sort of thing my material could give him to a large degree, albeit rather theoretical and abstract. He would have to come by most of it himself, however, simply by living with the people, listening to the fishermen, and observing the dynamics of community life for a while – a few months being essential.'[60]

The people of Lumsden North could not be forced to move, he concluded, so "you must simply present a situation so well planned and attractive that they cannot afford to do otherwise."[61] His thinking was consistent with the views of many politicians and civil servants, and his letter reveals his view that social science research could have been used by governments when developing policy. In this case, Colin Story sent a copy to the premier's office, on which Smallwood's executive assistant, Edward Roberts, added the marginal note: "Premier: This strikes me as being an excellent report. Surely this is precisely the type of project ARDA should be doing – and the type of Fisheries Development Programme which Ottawa must implement."[62] It is not certain that Faris's views affected government policy, or even that Smallwood read the report.[63] But his ideas were consistent with the views of both the federal and provincial governments, and an extract from Faris's letter that commented on the qualities necessary for a community development fieldworker was incorporated into a summary of ARDA's efforts:

> He must be thoroughly consulted at all phases of the development and be able to defend or criticize the govt.'s and/or community's action at all points. He is here to *introduce* the program, not "try it out." ... The "trying out" should occur only in the planning stages – then it is not necessary to have to "bull through" the program – to shove it down throats without the people knowing what is happening. He should be able to handle the petty conflicts and jealousies which are bound to arise with the well planned program, not with the ultimate authority – by god we're going to do it and you'll be damned-type approach. He of course must be circumspect with regard to certain aspects of the program, but any decent community development worker will be aware of this and should act accordingly. He must have the confidence of the fishermen with whom he is working and they have to be able to trust him. I think it would be better if he had few loyalties in the community, for this, especially in Newfoundland, is always an area emotionally-charged, and often subject to abuse. If he has no kinship or affinal ties, no business or commercial ties, then this at least removes the development from the traditional abuses often suffered. He must make it clear who is doing what – the development can't have the Federation fighting the merchants, the Liberals fighting the Tories, or residential, religious, or social cliques arguing over participation, responsibility or credit due.[64]

A training in social science and then time living in the community, in Faris's view, were the ways a man could develop such skills.

After 1965, the province had an opportunity to engage in a more assertive effort to modernize the fishery and centralize the population – and use federal money to pay for it. Smallwood had considered developing one community as a model of a modern fishery that other outports could emulate, and Jack Pickersgill recommended Lumsden for that role (he was the MP for the district within which that community was located). Memorial was soon involved in this work as well. Colman asked Williams to "write a little survey of 'Lumsden and ARDA' as a sort of instructional field report-survey for a new class of ARDA trainees coming into the University under my direction in September."[65] Meanwhile, Ottawa wanted information on the provincial Resettlement Program now that it was entering into a cost-shared Fisheries Household Resettlement Program. In a meeting with Memorial's new director of Extension, Donald Snowden (who had replaced Colman in 1965), the federal deputy minister of fisheries indicated the department would be willing to fund a study "to determine their attitudes toward resettlement in order that checks and balances could be added to the Government's resettlement program if the research project established that changes were needed."[66] The Manitoba-born Snowden had studied at the University of Manitoba and Carleton University before joining the federal government's Department of Northern Affairs and Natural Resources. In that capacity, he had helped organize craft production and cooperatives in the eastern Arctic, giving him skills that made him attractive as director of Extension. The province had hired Snowden to conduct an ARDA-funded study of cooperatives in Newfoundland, and Smallwood offered him a job implementing his recommendations. Snowden accepted Morgan's offer of the job as director of the Extension Service, however.[67] Snowden told Robert Paine, who had replaced Whitaker as a director of ISER, that he thought it was important that this small grant generate a useful document, so that federal fisheries would be willing to give substantially larger research grants in the future.[68]

Federal officials in the Department of Fisheries asked the sociologist Noel Iverson, a University of Minnesota graduate who had just left Memorial for the University of New Brunswick, to conduct an "attitude survey" of resettled families. He was to investigate the views towards the provincial program of those who had earlier been resettled and advise how the joint federal-provincial program might be made more effective. Iverson had little knowledge of Newfoundland, so he asked the younger Matthews to help. Matthews had grown up in St John's, and his family had sent him to spend his summers in Nippers Harbour in Notre Dame Bay to lessen his chances of contracting polio. In the experience he discovered that "there was something called rural society which was rather different" than St John's. That awareness was sharpened when, as a student at Memorial between 1960 and 1964, he was "taken under his wing" by Whitaker.[69]

Having taken classes from Roger Krohn, another Minnesota-trained sociologist teaching at Memorial, Matthews went to the University of Minnesota for graduate work at the age of twenty. Matthews was flattered an older professor asked for his help, only realizing later that he was the research partner who brought essential local knowledge to the project, and as the Newfoundlander he guided much of their interactions with people. The sociologists moved into outports as a base of operations and travelled to other communities to interview 128 heads of households who had been resettled. They persuaded people to cooperate by citing the benefit that other Newfoundlanders would get from the experience and advice of those who had taken advantage of the program.

By the late 1960s public suspicion, and in some quarters antipathy, towards Smallwood had risen to a high point, something that might have dissuaded potential informants from talking to the fieldworkers. To assuage fear, the two sociologists assured the informants that, while the government funded the research, the university was conducting it. No one but the two researchers would see the record of their conversations, they assured the informants, and no particular people would be mentioned in the report.[70] Matthews's recollection was that people were happy to talk to them and that they had not yet learned the risks of cooperating with sociologists. People were, he reflected, "very open."[71]

Iverson and Matthews used a standardized questionnaire, unlike many of the anthropologists working with ISER, who had relied on an extended period living in a community. The anthropologists were sceptical that survey research would be productive, Matthews reported, since they believed "that rural Newfoundlanders would be intimidated by structured interviews and clipboards."[72] They believed that one had to earn people's trust before a productive interview could take place. That reflected their view that participant observation defined their discipline as distinct from sociology as much as their field experience did. Rural Newfoundlanders likely had their own reasons for participating in the surveys and were not always intimidated by the interviewers' social prestige. John Widdowson observed in his fieldwork that rural people would often question him on such things as historical characters from the *Royal Readers* (the books from which they had learned to read) before they would talk to him about the questions he had. He reflected that this was their way of levelling the power relationship between themselves, who had little formal education, and himself, who was a university-educated outsider.[73] Living with outport residents for an extended period of time was not feasible given the brief amount of time available for the research, Matthews and Iverson reasoned, and both of them had positions outside the province to return to. In practice they found the warnings about "intimidation" were not warranted; during a two-month period they found most people were very willing to talk about their experiences. Matthews felt that the provincial officials were not pleased to have a federal-sponsored study of administration of the province's policy, however, but they too cooperated.[74]

Iverson and Matthews had practical advice for government. Describing some of the reasons that the program had sometimes failed to provide the means for economic success in families' new home communities, they made several recommendations aimed at making the program more effective. They favoured an increase in the money given to families who were relocating, for example, so that inadequate housing in the reception communities could be brought up to a higher standard.[75] Iverson and Matthews did not, at this stage of their careers, raise objections to the desirability of the government's goals of reducing people's isolation and creating an urban workforce – but wondered if the program was benefitting the families who had been moved. Officials within the federal Department of Fisheries implemented many of these changes. Provincial and federal government officials, and the directors of ISER, were pleased with the report.

"Contrary to the popular belief that government-sponsored research reports remain unread on bureaucrats' shelves, we found an amazing willingness among federal and provincial officials to both read our reports and implement our suggestions," Matthews later commented, adding, "thus, our study of the resettlement program led to an expansion of resettlement with almost no questioning of the legitimacy of its goals."[76] As he put it, "we had identified the frictions in the resettlement program, and the government responded and made it far more efficient at doing things I didn't like ... if anything I wanted the program cancelled."[77] Edward Roberts, who had been elected to the House of Assembly in 1966, recommended that the minister of community and social development read *Communities in Crisis*, since he found it "very useful, particularly in the emphasis placed upon additional aid for housing as being a key to the success of the programme."[78] In a marginal note he added that the federal Fisheries Department was negotiating for another study to be commissioned, "but with a better research design" than that of Matthews and Iverson.[79] Meanwhile, the federal government's assistant director of the Industrial Development Service outlined to Paine that the federal government hoped to have a more up-to-date study that examined a larger pool of those who had been relocated and those who had not.[80]

The government in Ottawa wanted information that was independent of that which it received from the Smallwood government, in Paine's view, and therefore was willing to provide additional federal funding to Memorial.[81] ISER quickly followed up on Matthews and Iverson's report by organizing a colloquium for academics, bureaucrats, and politicians to discuss it. It seems that no one from the general public or people from rural communities were invited to the meeting in February of 1967, but government officials and faculty members sat together. One federal bureaucrat reported having benefitted from the discussion, and he was not only interested in resettlement but was enthusiastic about funding the sociologist Robert DeWitt to conduct a broader community study of Fogo Island after hearing him speak about his ARDA-sponsored research.[82]

A graduate of the University of New Brunswick, and then a doctoral student at the University of Toronto, the twenty-seven-year-old first arrived in Fogo in September 1966, intending to study the island's religious pluralism. Quickly realizing that their economic future was on everyone's minds, he modified his questionnaire on religious behaviour to ask questions about economic development and resettlement. DeWitt had spent a year in three communities on the island. His work was influenced by the Iverson and Matthews's study of those who had resettled and believed Fogo would be an interesting case since it was an opportunity to study a community that was likely about to choose to resettle.[83] Drawing on French sociologist Durkheim's concept of anomie, DeWitt doubted that the residents of the island, divided as they were by religious denominations and communities and without effective local government, would be able to work together to foster economic development. He therefore identified factors that made local decision making difficult. "I would consider myself remiss as an applied sociologist," DeWitt wrote, "if I were not to provide a clear statement of what action I think the Government should take on Fogo Island."[84] He recommended the government not wait until there was a petition from the residents to resettle but encourage them to ask to be moved.

DeWitt observed the communities at a point when residents felt they were facing a crisis and also during a period that Memorial University and the National Film Board (NFB) were experimenting in community development. Early in 1964 Memorial's Extension Service had sent Earle to work with the Fogo Island Development Committee. The committee was a self-selected group of pro-development community leaders that included businessmen and clergy (until sectarian resentments led to the resignation of the clergymen). Earle cajoled and supported the efforts of these local men (they excluded women from attending meetings) to work together, meeting in each of the outports on the island so no one in any community felt the committee was being dominated by another community. DeWitt sat in on each of these meetings as an observer, both affecting the discussions and writing a study of the Development Committee, which dealt in part with the university's role in community development. Earle's presence, in DeWitt's estimation, "gave new hope to all those who claimed an interest in improvements."[85] Earle rejuvenated interest in island-wide cooperation, and the people on the island felt he could provide a link with the remote government in St John's. But his efforts to be an impartial actor caused some members of the committee to suspect that rather than telling them what course of action would be best, he was not helping as part of a government plot to destroy the committee.[86]

Whitaker had thought that exposure to the values of the outside world would provoke cultural change, but DeWitt concluded that "social change never follows from the mere exposure to new ideas and techniques."[87] Local initiative and self-help were, the younger man believed, essential to successful development. That idea fit well with Extension's philosophy and with the NFB's *Challenge for Change* films. Both Colin Low, of the NFB, and Snowden were determined to do something about rural poverty after reading the 1965 Economic Council of Canada's *Report on Poverty in Canada* and settled on Fogo as a place to experiment in the use of film to motivate community action.[88] As Low put it, the Fogo Island Project "used film as a catalyst to generate local debate – to give local people a voice and even editorial control – and to provide these people with access to people in power, via film."[89] The Newfoundlanders who worked for Extension, and some of the Fogo Islanders themselves, learned both technical skills and philosophy of activist film-making from Low, but as Susan Newhook has demonstrated, the innovation of the Fogo Process was as much the result of work that the Extension fieldworkers were doing as an innovation among film-makers.[90] A series of films were shown in which local men articulated their goals and problems. Once the films were edited, the film-makers showed them to people on Fogo Island as a way of raising an awareness of the commonalities each shared and breaking down community suspicions. Extension and the NFB also realized that they could show the films to government officials, film the response of the officials, and then show those films to people in rural Newfoundland.[91]

Earle had been at the centre of both the Fogo Process and the formation of the Fogo Co-op, which provided hope that the island's communities could develop rather than resettle. He had grown up in a merchant family, had a brother who was a prominent Anglican clergyman, and worked readily with local businesses and understood their needs, to the point that a few of his colleagues criticized him for being too close to business in general.[92] An account of university Extension fieldworkers that presented them as an arm of the state, or as organized resistance to the state, would be too simple. Earle was upset about the pressure the provincial government applied when trying to encourage communities to accept resettlement. "I am afraid the type of work I am doing will become more difficult as time goes by," Earle wrote to the Norwegian social anthropologist Cato Wadel, adding "I think human beings should be treated with more respect than just use them as instruments to move because someone in power thinks it is alright to do so. I guess we must accept it. Or must we?"[93] People such as Earle could help people resist government policy, even if they were fieldworkers tasked with implementing that policy. As Earle wrote to Wadel, who taught at Memorial between 1967 and 1970:

> I am only inserting this paragraph as I think you, as a ~~socialist~~ sociologist, would appreciate it. Doubtless you have heard me express my sentiments toward fishermen from the North East Coast moving to the South Coast and taking part in the big fishing industry which our Government advocates. Of course, being in the field of education, I am supposed to supply the ideas of others and practically sit (in public) on my own ideas. During my recent film showing on Fogo Island I slipped in a film on Dragger Fishing. I will admit I selected a film taken in a severe storm where the pot of soup left the stove, men were called in the middle of the night to secure things getting loose on deck, men darning their socks, etc. The comments following the showing were interesting; – "You will never get me to go to Marystown" ... "Darning socks, that's my wife's job" ... "I rather eat [at] home where the soup pot stays on the stove" ... "You can keep your draggers" ... "All right for them fellows up there, they are used to it." I got my message across, Cato, without saying a word and I only used the materials supplied by the educators which showed the Government's million dollar investments elsewhere.[94]

The federal and provincial governments had funded research through the institute by DeWitt, Ottar Brox and Wadel, and the economists Clinton Herrick and Michael Skolnik, but politicians and bureaucrats soon became wary of the risks of hiring outsiders to study government policy.[95] The social scientists' work shifted from the question of how to make the program more effective towards asking if resettlement of communities was a good policy for rural people. Brox had trained as an agronomist before meeting Paine in his native Norway, and he had been inspired to work as an anthropologist by Paine's book on the Sami. Paine invited Brox, a critic of the Norwegian rural resettlement program, to come to St John's for a year to examine the Newfoundland policy.[96] Brox pointed out that the Newfoundland resettlement program had two goals: creating an industrial workforce for a modernized fishery and reducing the cost of providing education and health care to difficult-to-reach communities. Neither of these, he believed, were accomplished by the existing program. It generally moved people from one rural community to a nearby rural community, rather than to an urban place where there were good employment prospects. Brox also got to the heart of the matter of what role Memorial was to play in government research:

> By and large my personal opinion is that a social scientist is merely an academical parasite if he refuses to advise on policy matters. But he should always question the objectives, and try to reformulate the problems that he is supposed to help in solving; and should do this in a more radical sense than Matthews and Iverson have done.[97]

Brox put these ideas into practice, getting elected to the Norwegian legislature in 1973. DeWitt also thought it possible for a social scientist to do applied sociology on political questions and still remain "faithful to scientific objectivity."[98] He tried to avoid prescribing goals but hoped the study would aid the people of the island by encouraging government to do one of two things: either encourage resettlement or work with the local development committee to foster economic alternatives to welfare.

Governments faced the risk that the social scientists they hired would start to empathize with those whom they were studying rather than share the goals of the state. In her survey of advocacy in Newfoundland and Labrador anthropology and sociology, Barbara Neis pointed out that the early social scientists who studied resettlement, including Iverson, Matthews, and DeWitt, initially believed that they could undertake applied policy research for the government while maintaining their scholarly objectivity. "The institute has emerged," Paine commented when thinking about the experience of working with "the leviathan" on applied research, "the Institute has emerged with its scientific integrity unblemished."[99] He coordinated the publication of the research on resettlement.

Paine was impressed by the government's willingness to commission research that criticized its policy, and the prospect of collaboration between the university and the state resulting in "enlightened, ameliorative planning for the future."[100] But, Neis continued, that faith in being able to take government money and then criticize the Smallwood government was eroded when the media started to report on the research.[101] She suggested that the research results did not change the social scientists' views of their work, but media reports on their publications caused the social scientists to rethink their role. Resettlement became a lightening rod for Smallwood's critics among the political opposition and, increasingly, some of the faculty members and students at the university. Critics of the Smallwood government were quick to read the Matthews and Iverson report. At an interdepartmental committee meeting to discuss resettlement, at least one federal official resented the way that the report had been used to criticize the program in public. Despite the fact that the federal officials had gotten a report that identified problems they could remedy, he hoped that future studies would adopt the "proper perspective," which was to emphasize the economic benefits of the program.[102] Bureaucrats and elected officials favoured academic studies that would be attentive to political optics, rather than critical of policy. This highlighted differences in the goals of federal and provincial bureaucrats and politicians as well. Matthews reflected that:

> The federal officials seemed to regard the old provincial plan as a welfare program, largely irrelevant to their use of resettlement as a strategy of development. Moreover, when our final report received widespread newspaper coverage, few newspaper columnists made a distinction between the two programs. As a result, the federal officials often found themselves attacked for previous provincial failures.[103]

Provincial officials, who initially welcomed the Iverson and Matthews report, were displeased when it became fodder for the opposition

Progressive Conservative Party and for those in the media who criticized the Resettlement Program. That was not only an immediate phenomenon, it had a lasting effect on the relationship between the government and the university. As late as the 1990s, a sociologist who had been seconded to the province to work on economic development policy, J.D. House, reported that senior civil servants within the provincial government opposed the idea of contracting ISER to do social research for the province. They remembered the way that the research on resettlement in the 1960s had embarrassed the government.[104]

While many faculty members at Memorial maintained good relationships with the government, and President Morgan was careful when dealing with Smallwood, in the waning days of the Liberal government political dissent became more common. Smallwood's anti-union legislation during the IWA strike had convinced leftist faculty members that he was a reactionary, and many young Newfoundlanders had disdain for what they saw as his dictatorial style. Some young men and women watching the Vietnam War protests on television took opposition to Smallwood as a cause through which they could play out the rebellion of their American contemporaries. The North American hippie back-to-the-land movement also encouraged urban youth to see virtues in rural life, which in many cases their parents had sent them to university to avoid.

As Story and Halpert told students of the value of rural oral culture, young people questioned the cultural loss that accompanied resettlement. That change in attitude encouraged further dissatisfaction with Smallwood. Wadel and Brox developed critiques of the modernization agenda that the sociologists such as Wilmott and Whitaker had initially taken as desirable. Wadel even spoke to the Progressive Conservative Party's annual meeting at a time when that party was being rejuvenated by a broad-based feeling that Smallwood's develop-or-perish policies had failed. Some younger faculty members who had once affected ivory tower detachment now became part of the anti-Smallwood popular front and saw their work as activist, if not adversarial. Paine recollected that in his early years at Memorial the newly revitalized Progressive Conservative Party "came to us [at ISER] and acquired ideas."[105] Keeping government agencies happy had been important to Whitaker from the beginning. At the most basic level he wanted to keep the funding flowing, and that had required him to hector the academics into producing their reports in a timely fashion. Paine was particularly effective at disseminating the research results of ISER and at bringing together bright people to tackle interesting problems. The series of books and papers published by ISER was one element, and the symposia that he organized was the other. Increasingly, anthropologists questioned the goals and motives of the state, but many sociologists felt they were treated unfairly by Paine.

Many social scientists in the 1960s and 1970s were animated by the debate on modernization; there was a continuum between collaboration and resistance to the state. At different moments the sociologists, geographers, and economists at Memorial played varied roles in challenging government policy and in conducting research for government. Even those in the humanities disciplines, such as George Story and David Alexander, cared about their community and engaged in applied research on policy questions as well as their principal and historical areas of research for which they are best known. The two co-chaired a Committee on Federal Licensing Policy and Its Implications for the Newfoundland Fisheries, for example.[106] They are good examples of the general trend among faculty members to be both emotionally and ideologically on the side of the people during the countercultural movement of the late 1960s. Not all social scientists became leftists in response to the changes brought about by economic change and government policy, and some became critics of government policy from the right. While Whitaker had cultivated government funding while pursuing the goal of establishing social research at Memorial, his contemporary and ISER's co-founder, the economist Parzival Copes, pursued the applied research into problems that confronted the labour force. Brox and Matthews became vocal critics of the Resettlement Program because they felt the program went too far, while Copes became a critic of it because he viewed it as a half measure. While he worked at Memorial, and after he left for an appointment at Simon Fraser University, he conducted research for the government and was outspoken in his opposition to government policy when he felt government was not being economically rational. It put him at odds with the prevailing attitudes of most scholars at Memorial.

Copes challenged what he saw as two elements of conventional wisdom within the province: first, that Newfoundlanders should have access to the inshore fishery as a birthright, and, second, that people were an asset and that out-migration should be discouraged. The result of these assumptions, in his analysis, was an overcapacity in the fishery brought on by state subsidies and, consequently, low income for fishermen. In a brief, but sweeping, analysis of twentieth-century

Newfoundland electoral history and economics, Copes argued that
the government subsidies to the fishery were greater than the income
generated by that industry. "In a century and a half Newfoundland's
fishing industry," he wrote in 1970, "has been transformed from its sole
economic asset to its major public liability."[107]

He believed that Smallwood took advantage of the distribution of
fisher voters across rural electoral districts (which were over-represented
in the legislature) and adopted economically irrational policies because
they were politically popular. Copes thought that Smallwood encouraged workers to remain seasonally employed in the inshore fishery,
rather than move to another province for year-round work, and did
so in part for partisan gain. Only by ending the electoral influence of
those who fished, he believed, could the government stop subsidizing
an industry that was unable to provide its workers with an adequate
income. Copes concluded that the labour force in the fishery needed
to be reduced to balance the revenue it generated with the expenditure and that, given the relatively high rate of population growth in
the province, there was no prospect of lowering unemployment in the
province without outmigration. He believed that the existing resettlement program "reshuffled" the unemployed and underemployed from
one community in Newfoundland to another.[108] More than thirty years
later, when receiving an award celebrating the role of those who took
controversial stands, he explained:

I advocated higher rates of mobility assistance to Newfoundlanders willing to move to suitable jobs in mainland Canada, of which in those days
there were many. The massive subsidies and income support programs
that were enticing more workers to join the fishery and were destroying its
natural viability had to be replaced by, or at least offset by, strong incen-
tives to take jobs where they could be found, which at that time clearly
was on the mainland. Contrary to what my critics contended, I was careful
to emphasize that out-migration was to be entirely voluntary and that it
was not suitable for many Newfoundlanders who were lacking in appropriate skills or social mobility.[109]

I have noted his courage during the Second World War and his willingness to publish unpopular views, but I did not mean to imply that
he was thick skinned. He seems to have been shocked by the negative reaction to the publication of his work. He did not shrink from the
criticism – writing an angry letter to George Story, for example, when

Story questioned if Copes was an appropriate person for the Department of Fisheries and Oceans to contract for a study of joint ventures in the fishery. (Story's view was the same as many of his colleagues at Memorial, as well as the same as the position of the fishermen's union.) The two men fought on the territory of disciplinary authority. Copes asked what Story knew of his qualifications and questioned Story's own qualifications to comment on the fisheries.[110] Story struck back:

> [Y]our published views on the social and cultural context of the fishing industry in rural Newfoundland were contentious and, to me, not sympathetic ... when, as in "The Resettlement of Fishing Communities in Newfoundland," which I do not think is at all a good study, you present that economic analysis in a manner heavily laden with often crude value judgement, your work enters, with respect to those judgements, a domain in which it becomes fair comment for anyone with a serious and responsible interest in contemporary Newfoundland.[111]

Copes maintained that the Newfoundland media had unfairly attacked his reputation rather than engaged with his analysis of economic problems.[112] He later reported, relishing the controversy his work had provoked, that he had been "likened to a Nazi, slandered as a villain, and ridiculed as a fool," but "one of the meanest assaults on my character came from a pair of Memorial University professors who composed a Newfoundland folk-song in my dishonour. It called for my assassination and promised free passage through the pearly gates of heaven for my executioner."[113] "The Ode to Professor Parzival Copes," by Corner Brook–based poet and playwright Al Pittman and Memorial's English and folklore professor Pat Byrne, two artists that were part of the Newfoundland cultural revival then underway, expressed resentment over the idea of being forced to move to the mainland and joked about how satisfying it would be to shoot Copes with a muzzle-loaded gun. Part of the song ran:

Now here is the gist of his marvelous plan
To save all the livyers of this Newfoundland
Just take one half of the horrible lot
And heave them to pickle in Canada's pot

Take an uncle a daughter some sisters and brothers
And put them on barges along with the others

Bid them goodbye and say now there you go
You're going to glory in Ontario

Just shove them on board and don't make a fuss
There's not enough room here for the whole crowd of us
So two hundred thousand or so must take leave
And over such progress there's no need to grieve[114]

Regardless of the merits, or weaknesses, of Copes's analysis, both those who opposed the Resettlement Program and those who sympathized with the fishermen discounted Copes's view as an outsider's attack on the people of rural Newfoundland. While rhetoric comparing Copes to a Nazi was unfair, it is not surprising that his critics saw his argument that democracy stood in the way of the state adopting a rational economic policy as a logic similar to justifications adopted by authoritarian regimes.

It's worth emphasizing a couple of other points. Copes's argument was based on economic theory and an analysis of data and claimed to be scientific through its presentation in the clothing of reasoned prose.[115] Pittman and Byrne's response, however, was emotional and expressed through song. The two men had themselves been resettled from rural communities to urban centres, so they wrote as insiders of the culture rather than claiming objectivity. Ironically, they had the opportunities to work as intellectuals who could comment on public life in ways that they never could have had if they fished out of the islands in Placentia Bay.

Copes perceived the controversy over his view of resettlement as "extraordinary attacks on my character" by "an irresponsible press bent on sensationalizing my conclusions, and to ignorant critics who for sentimental reasons opposed change in the traditional inshore fishery, which had been reduced to the role of employer of last resort in what had become, economically, an increasingly non-viable industry."[116] His publication of such views made him persona non grata in some circles in Newfoundland, if not a folk villain, while most Newfoundlanders who favoured resettlement were more cautious in their public pronouncements. With time, tempers cooled. Many of his views were consistent with government fisheries policies in the new century, and in 2004 the university awarded him an honourary degree in recognition of his contribution – all had been forgiven.

It was not Copes's views that had political effects between 1968 and 1971, but the criticism of those who questioned Smallwood's quest to develop at all cost and the feeling among younger generations that he lacked fiscal competence. During the last years of his government, Smallwood drove many men of talent out of the Liberal caucus. He had difficulty imagining anyone filling his shoes. Changes in the relationship between government and the university also marked a turning point for Extension and ISER. Director of television for Extension, Gerald Ottenheimer, left Memorial when he was elected as a Progressive Conservative member of the House of Assembly in 1966, and the next year he became the leader of the party. With the election of Frank Moores as premier in 1972, the Resettlement and Centralization Programs were officially abandoned (although money could still be found to help communities move). The changing needs and political landscape prompted Snowden and his associate George Lee to agree that Extension should wind down. "The whole philosophy of Extension related to the arts and culture was that the university should do it as long as nobody else was doing it," Lee put it, "but our role was to get it started, to get it going, and as soon as government departments or some other agencies, community colleges or whatever wanted to take it over."[117] Some faculty members at the university continued to do research for the government and to criticize government policy, but the provincial government now had greater access to its own expertise.

This chapter has shown that the earliest generation of sociologists, anthropologists, and economists at Memorial, such as Wilmott, Whitaker, and Copes, shared with government policymakers the assumption that the state's efforts to modernize rural communities were best for the people. Policymakers too often saw social problems as individual failures rather than systemic effects. Willmott seems to have been trapped in a fact-gathering sort of research that did not fit well with his social democratic politics, and like Whitaker and Copes he left Memorial. The next generation of faculty members at Memorial, such as Ralph Matthews, who taught sociology in St John's for three years, were forced by the popular revolt against resettlement to ask themselves which side they were on (that of the state or of the people). Matthews felt himself forced out of Memorial in part because he would not toe the line.

For many residents of the province, as Neis noted, the debate over resettlement among Newfoundland intellectuals was a catalyst in their becoming sceptics of government policy, much as the Vietnam War encouraged their American counterparts to question their government. The improvements in the standard of living that accompanied

Confederation had encouraged people to leave behind rural ways of life, but some of those who had moved to urban centres romanticized their former homes. Young, urban middle-class university students also questioned the eagerness to discard rural ways of life that many of their peers expressed. *Christmas Mumming*, the community studies, the *DNE*, and the folk culture revival in St John's all encouraged faculty members and students at Memorial to take a more positive view of the culture of the outports. Smallwood seemed to personify both resettlement and failed modernization policies, and anti-Smallwood sentiment had affected some of the scholarship. Matthews became a critic of both government policy and those social scientists (like himself as a younger man) who did applied research:

> This leads directly to the issue concerning the policy researcher's responsibility to his employers and to those he studies. As he is often in the employ of policy makers, the policy researcher may find himself obtaining information from those affected by a program, which will be used against them in the battle over the program's implementation. As those most directly affected usually have no access to his findings, they are unable to protect themselves from this unfair exploitation of their goodwill. Significantly, the two issues of value freedom and political neutrality come together in the widely accepted belief that social scientists, in order to maintain their value neutrality, should be "free floating intellectuals" not allied with any power group.[118]

ISER's coordinated research on resettlement is the best-known example of social scientists at Memorial engaged in contract research for government agencies, and subsequently providing the analysis of policies that could be used to argue against those same policies. In Neis's analysis, ISER's directors believed they could maintain a division of labour between the social scientists and policymakers. "Social scientists would not confine their research to the needs of policy makers nor formulate the policy recommendations they felt were implied by their own research."[119] She thought that the founders of the institute were not aware of the contradictions between the goals of policymakers and the goals of social scientists, or the differences "between the interests of policy makers and the groups they were studying."[120] Perhaps they were initially unaware of the conflict between the government's goals and the people's goals but believed that value-free science could determine what the best policies would be. I am not sure, however, that the earliest generation of ISER directors believed that there was always such a division of labour between the research and the implementation of policy. Williams, Whitaker, and Copes conducted applied research and trained agents to implement changes in the society that government thought desirable. Neis's judgment seems sound. Both policymakers and social scientists shared the same sorts of assumptions about progress and that improved services and economic opportunities would be best.

While many of the social scientists shared the government's assumptions, they also learned a scepticism of government policy through their research. Iverson and Matthews criticized the provincial Resettlement Program in an effort to make it more effective – which encouraged the federal government to hire Iverson to do a larger study. As the example of Matthews most clearly shows, working with policymakers sometimes caused an awakening of concerns about whether the researcher was on the side of the state or the people. Matthews's study of government policy, both resettlement and economic development more generally, encouraged him to take a critical perspective. Some sociologists, such as Willmott, came from a Christian, and leftist, desire to ameliorate poverty. By the 1960s, Marxist theory and the nationalistic desire to replace American models and theory with Canadian ones encouraged sociologists such as Matthews to cast a more sceptical eye to working with the state.[121] Drawing on the international literature that saw poor regions as having been created by the nature of capitalist relations rather than areas that had been left behind by capitalism, in 1983 Matthews published a critical appraisal of government economic development policies.[122] Copes also conducted fundamental economic research sponsored by the government and became a critic of government policy. He did not believe that the policies went far enough in encouraging changes that would make the province more economically rational. In his treatment, like that of Matthews, the state unintentionally made poor regions poorer, but Copes thought government intervention had made things worse.

As this chapter has shown, the dichotomy between applied and fundamental research was not as clear as it might appear in the abstract. Those who worked directly for the state used the tools of social science to create knowledge just as they did when their work was self-directed. The sociologists and economists shared a modernist paradigm, and all worked on policy-related research that was funded by the federal and provincial governments. Federal and provincial officials shared more than they differed. Ethnographic discourse often had a direct relationship to the state, and the relationship between the two was reciprocal, but the social science discourse did not determine policy.[123]

This account of the study of resettlement suggests that there was no clear dichotomy between applied and theoretical research and that there were no firm disciplinary boundaries. One of the characteristics of the social science scholarship of the 1960s and 1970s was its variety. Harris, who as dean of arts and science was the chairman of ISER, commented that the institute had not required researchers to adopt a particular kind of analysis or belong to a "school" but emphasized that all the work was comparative and empirically based. "This rule does more than ensure social relevance in the projects undertaken," he observed, adding, "it also helps collapse the distinction between applied *contra* pure research."[124]

As we have seen in the discussion of mumming and in the examination of the community studies, Harris also valued the way scholars could "examine the meaning of any phenomenon" through cultural, economic, geographic, historical, and other contexts.[125] Much of the foundation of anthropological and sociological engagement with Newfoundland came out of a cooperative relationship with the provincial government. In the 1950s the provincial government rushed to industrialize the economy, raise the level of social services and education, and, starting in 1953, through its resettlement and fisheries policies, to encourage more rapid urbanization and centralization. Premier Smallwood was determined to make the province new. Memorial's mission was to help in that modernization, both by training teachers to go back to the outports to raise the province's education level and through the university's Extension Service helped promote economic development. The sort of client-driven social science, in which the government defined the problem and the sociologist attempted to propose a solution, was common in Canada during the period that Willmott was establishing the first courses in sociology at Memorial. Such work sometimes evolved into sponsored research, such as that conducted by Iverson and Matthews. The client's agenda was still paramount in the ISER projects, but the sociologists had greater autonomy to define the nature of the problem than did those who worked directly for the state. Lastly, the latter work of Matthews shows that advocacy research can evolve when the social scientist decides what issues are important to the community and brings to bear his or her expertise.[126]

The sociological research was the most applied of all the parts of the Newfoundland studies movement. "If there is a lesson I learned from writing *Communities in Decline*," Matthews reflected from a position more than forty years later, "it was that they don't leave reports on shelves ... they actually implement them."[127] Many social scientists throughout the world saw themselves as helping to usher in social change – whether they worked in Africa, a Native community, or a Newfoundland outport – even as many of them respected the positive qualities of the peoples whom they studied. Others worked to ameliorate the social problems created by uneven capitalist development and became critical of the state. "It is no more remarkable, or especially praiseworthy, or an expression of high morals, that a field worker ends up identifying with the community than that a person who grows up in it does so," Ottar Brox later observed, "growing up and participant observation are in both cases a kind of socialization."[128]

Conclusion

This new direction in Newfoundland studies has been evident in many disciplines: in history, of course, but also in folklore, geography, sociology, anthropology and English. This lively interest in the local milieu is a sign that the university has recognized and accepted its scholarly responsibilities to the society that supports it. It is becoming a Newfoundland university.[1]

Before the beginning of systematic work on Newfoundland studies in the 1950s, there was little in the way of *professional* scholarship on the province's culture, society, or economy. As the historian Patrick O'Flaherty put it, "a university college had, indeed, been founded in St John's in 1925, but it set about imitating the model of an English public school and was almost totally indifferent to Newfoundland studies."[2] There had been non-academic intellectuals who studied and wrote about their homeland during the nineteenth and twentieth centuries, and a history similar to this one could be written of those men and women. In its first few decades, Memorial University of Newfoundland became a research university in large measure through the study of Newfoundland. Political considerations, nationalist sentiment, and professional career aspirations led to a large intellectual output in that area over the thirty years after Newfoundland became a Canadian province, with the result that the island is now better known to scholars than many comparable areas.

"One of the most striking phenomenon of post-Confederation Newfoundland," George Story wrote, "has been the emergence of a diverse and active interest in Newfoundland studies."[3] The energizing idea of the Newfoundland studies movement – that the university had a

mission to preserve and build on the oral culture of Newfoundland –
gave it a character different from the Canadian studies movement
with which it overlapped. Newfoundland studies was not a *school*, in
the sense of an identifiable style, method, or ideological position, like
abstract expressionism or the Chicago school of economics. We may
think of the Newfoundland specialists not as a school of thought, like
Keynesianism, but as a school of activity – a group of collaborators who
worked together and influenced each other.[4]

Those working on Newfoundland studies shared an object of study
and much in theory and method, however, and their interactions and
collaborations established certain conventions that are identifiable. I
have suggested that Newfoundland studies was a scientific/intellec-
tual movement along the lines theorized by Frickel and Gross. They
posit that such movements have a coherent program of intellectual
goals, and we have seen how much lexicographers, historians, folklorists, sociologists, anthropologists, and geographers shared in both
method (enlisting students as collectors of data) and a stance (arguing
that Newfoundland oral culture merited attention and respect). The
critical attention to oral culture, for which Story and Halpert were passionate advocates, was contentious in many disciplines the 1950s, just
as Frickel and Gross describe. Faculty members at other universities
did oral culture research in the 1970s, but those in Newfoundland were
ahead of their time. The argument that rural and non-elite people had a
culture that deserved respect was, of course, inherently political among
scholars whose attention was generally devoted to written literature.
And establishing that Newfoundland studies as worthy of the attention
of Canadian, American, and British scholars was a challenge. Lastly,
the Newfoundland studies movement was profoundly collaborative –
individuals carrying out his or her research in isolation using only the
tools of a single discipline were less common.

Frickel and Gross called for systematic research into such movements.[5] They theorized that an intellectual movement is more likely to
emerge when leaders feel dissatisfied with dominant paradigms. As
this book shows, George Story, Herbert Halpert, and others argued that
oral evidence should be used by lexicographers, literary scholars should
examine oral culture, and that in the study of folklore the performance
was as important as the text. Their colleagues and students, even those
in other disciplines such as history, followed their lead and argued
for change within their fields. Yet few Newfoundland scholars saw
themselves as an opposition to dominant Canadian discourses – they

were more likely to be working within British or American theory and debates. David Alexander was part of the *Acadiensis* generation of historians who demanded Ontario-based historians treat the Atlantic region with respect, and he was at the forefront of quantitative history in Canada. Keith Matthews was an *Atlantic World* historian before that field had a name and wanted Newfoundland's importance to be understood by his British contemporaries. Newfoundland studies fits Frickel and Gross's description of a movement, and they suggest further work remains to explain why particular movements arise at the times that they do.

Young scholars saw career advantages to adopting the program of someone such as Halpert, but service to the community of Newfoundland had at least as much weight in individuals' decisions regarding adopting the research program as did career strategies. Frickel and Gross also posit that structural conditions are likely to explain when movements get the resources that make them successful. In this example, people at the university were able to mobilize political and popular support because of the community's desire to remember and preserve Newfoundland's past, now that it was a Canadian province. At the same time, the widely perceived need to grapple with impediments to modernization also ensured the state's support for the broad Newfoundland studies agenda.[6]

Frickel and Gross draw a distinction between movements that are internal to their fields of inquiry and those that are tied to broader social movements. I would characterize the Newfoundland studies movement as of the latter category. The scholars at the university, even the most erudite and most devoted to conservative methodologies and elite culture, wanted their work to have a positive effect on the people of the province. Scientific/intellectual movements are most likely to be led by high-status individuals, and Frickel and Gross theorize that autonomous intellectual movements are more likely to be led by younger scholars who have less invested in the established models and methods. Younger scholars see career advancement through the adoption of innovative practices.

One might characterize nearly everyone discussed in this book as a "younger" scholar in that way – since their status outside elite North American universities encouraged them to experiment and take chances. They did not rest on a smug confidence that they were the elite in their field. Older scholars, in Frickel and Gross's proposition, are often more methodologically and theoretically conservative since the social capital of their career is based on work they did using older methods. In the case of SIMs that are linked to social movements, they see it working in the opposite way. Younger scholars avoid risking political actions that might end their careers, while older intellectuals feel secure in making radical claims about the nature of knowledge.[7]

The Newfoundland studies movement was part of a broader social response to economic and cultural change in the thirty years after Confederation. Story, Halpert, and Paine, for example, were high-status intellectual leaders at Memorial and put little at risk in embracing the same enthusiasm for the local culture experienced by their younger collaborators. Despite their considerable methodological innovations, none were working without firm footings in well-established, indeed conservative, disciplinary norms. Young scholars of the New Left, the hippy back-to-the-land movement, and the anti-Vietnam War movement could gain social prestige by embracing alternatives to middle-class urban life. Gerald Sider, the most radical figure in Newfoundland scholarship, never studied or taught at Memorial, and he was sceptical of the folk culture revival that many Newfoundland residents embraced. Participants in the Newfoundland studies movement, as we have seen, treated Sider's work with caution, but it was very successful in highly prestigious international venues.

Newfoundland studies was affected not only by the local context in the classrooms and library, the close community life of St John's, and the cruel beauty of the island but also by the methodological and theoretical developments in the social sciences and humanities. Since Memorial developed a full undergraduate degree in only 1949 and graduate degrees came later, it recruited British-, American-, and Canadian-trained faculty members. Other Canadian universities also hired both American and British men and women, so the story told here has parallels in other Canadian institutions. The small campus in St John's became a site at which people with different American and British training and different bodies of theory and methodology mixed and learned from each other, so it can be a helpful example of processes that were repeated elsewhere. Because of its historical attachments, Newfoundland was more likely to turn to the United Kingdom than the United States to recruit faculty members and as a place to send students for their advanced degrees. Studies similar to this one on the scholarship at other Canadian universities might reveal a different mix of intellectual influences. Perhaps because it was a new university it had less inertia to overcome than some other Canadian institutions, and perhaps the administrators were less fearful of new approaches than their counterparts at older institutions.

Scholars' individual and collective efforts may be measured in the influence they had on government policy, or the extent to which their work shaped people's identities. Much of the ISER-sponsored economic and sociological work, such as the work on resettlement, had demonstrable effects on the implementation of government policy. It is impossible, unfortunately, to be precise about the ways that the study of the culture by social scientists and humanists, such as lexicographers and historians, affected the people of the province. Les Harris believed that "it is good for people to become aware that they are part of a very long tradition of which you ought not to be ashamed."[8] When commenting on the role the university played in the culture, he drew on a martial metaphor. Newfoundlanders were "besieged by a metropolitan culture which is disseminated by television and radio and schools ... and [by] the university itself, which tends to denigrate the origins or the cultural backgrounds of the people."[9] The university fought cultural homogenization through the documentation of those backgrounds. "If there were no counterattack launched against it, the end of the folk tradition would be in sight, because the folk tradition would go underground" he said, and "people would move quickly to become speakers of CBC English, or believers in the current mythologies of the metropole."[10] Memorial's research was valuable, Harris believed, because it told Newfoundlanders that they should not abandon their ways of speech or their culture.

While the social scientists tried to shape public policy, often with success, the humanists had a different audience in mind. Story, Harris, and dozens of others engaged in conversations with other men and women of letters, with learned individuals in the past, and with scholars of the future. "Write for posterity," Professor Kirwin advised me when I first embarked on writing this book. Relevance to contemporary social problems was not the yardstick by which all scholars measured their accomplishments. Even as the *DNE* collaborator least comfortable with public visibility, he believed his life's work had benefit to the broader community. When members of the public purchased and used the *DNE*, for example, Story, Kirwin, and Widdowson were gratified, and everyone wanted what was best for the people of the province, but their scholarship was written as a labour of love, not for fashion or popularity.

George Story left his fingerprints on nearly every branch of Newfoundland scholarship as an author, mentor, and collaborator. He was a central node in academic networks at the university and a pioneer in the city's heritage preservation movement. As a Newfoundlander who bridged town and gown, he was highly regarded by those in the emergent cultural community. He served as president of the Newfoundland Historic Trust from 1969 to 1971, the Newfoundland Historical Society from 1978 to 1981, and in 1980 was named the first chairman of the Newfoundland and Labrador Arts Council. A close collaborator with Halpert, Kirwin, and Seary, Story had links to nearly every historian, geographer, and anthropologist who studied Newfoundland society and culture. This book has shown that such relationships, and social context, matter in intellectual history as much as theory, method, and evidence. The researchers' interactions with each other, and with their social environment, shaped Newfoundland studies.

Most of the leaders of the Newfoundland studies movement were Newfoundland born like Story, but the vast majority of those who studied Newfoundland were newcomers to the place. Yet they embraced the culture and society of their adopted home. To take one of many possible examples, Michael Taft moved to Canada from the United States to avoid being drafted, enrolled in folklore at Memorial between 1971 and 1977, and fell in love with Newfoundland culture. As this book has argued was common, he perceived the study of the culture at the university and the engagement in that culture by artists in the city as two parts of the same phenomenon. Taft described the social environment in the university, city, and province, as keys to understanding what was happening at Memorial.[11] With a couple of exceptions, such as Halpert who was older and more reserved, many of the faculty members that Taft encountered were in their early thirties and many of the graduate students in their late twenties. A large, and constantly evolving, cohort from different departments talked before classes started in the morning, lunched together most days, and shared meals and parties many nights. It's not surprising that those who grew up in the self-governing colony of the British empire, such as Morgan, Harris, and Story, felt something had been lost in 1949, even when they welcomed the economic benefits of Confederation. Neither is it shocking that some of the British- and American-born scholars who made the province home felt it was a distinctive part of North America and developed an identification with Newfoundland.

To describe some of the foreign-born Newfoundlanders as *nationalistic* seems apt, but the use of the word requires some nuance. Seary, who had briefly worked in Germany while the Nazis were in power, thought nationalism inconsistent with scholarly objectivity, and Rothney thought it a danger to world peace, but both saw value in the study of the local. Many younger men and women embraced the cultural nationalism of the Newfoundland renaissance. The historian Keith Matthews once argued that the generation of political reformers of the 1830s had not been born in Newfoundland but took a nationalistic position in relation to the empire and those who held positions of power in the colonial society.[12] He might have been describing himself, and his cohort, in that essay. In the early 1980s he said to me that he considered himself a Newfoundlander but not a Canadian – a feeling that others living in their adopted home might have sometimes felt but never articulated. The British Columbia–born David Alexander empathized with Newfoundlanders, rather than the federal state or the Toronto-based media. As he finished his last essay, before succumbing to cancer, he wrote "Newfoundland defended – again."[13] Alexander felt both loyalty to his adoptive home and, more broadly, an intense sense of the injustice of all of those who found themselves at the periphery of power. Not only the native born were nationalistic, and nationalism was not always political. Even Smallwood, that archetypal Newfoundland nationalist intellectual, distinguished between political nationalism (which focused on the nation state) and cultural nationalism (which focused on the qualities of the people).[14]

Each of the individual efforts and the collaborations at the university had their own internal dynamics, but, while they were not directed by a central authority, they were shaped and encouraged and cajoled by administrators and academic mentors. University presidents Gushue, Morgan, and Harris not only provided money and institutional support but also recruited individuals (such as Rothney, Kirwin, Halpert, and Keith Matthews) who had specific skills and set them to working on Newfoundland studies. The university administration did not micromanage the scholars once they were hired; it more subtly shaped the research by celebrating successes and promoting the careers of those who worked on the island's culture. Kirwin, as we have seen, was recruited as a phonologist to work on Newfoundland dialects and might have worked on that independently for his whole career – his collaboration with Story on the lexicon was a chance occurrence.

Administrators did not tell faculty members what to write, although ISER worked with government and business to fund several applied studies. Whitaker insisted on the anthropologists collecting sociological description so that the community studies could be easily compared, but he gave the fellows free rein in their interpretations. Dynamic scholars such as Story and Halpert led their younger colleagues both by setting an example in their own work and by showing an interest in the efforts of the younger crowd. Taft reported that when as a graduate student in folklore he published an essay on a Newfoundland topic, he received praise, and affirmation of his value, from faculty members whom he barely knew.[15]

Story and Halpert supervised graduate students and were mentors to fellow faculty members who pursued work on oral culture. Rothney sketched out an agenda for graduate work in history that laid the foundation for a later synthesis, and when he left Memorial it provided an opportunity for a new generation to establish new priorities. Whitaker promoted the anthropologists' fieldwork in outports, as did his successor, Paine, who also developed ISER's publishing arm and brought the community studies and research papers into print. Under Paine's leadership, ISER Books became part of what made Memorial an enticing academic community for anthropologists. ISER did not impose a single methodology or an interpretation, and starting in Newfoundland it spread its interests into the Arctic and the North Atlantic litoral. The university provided institutional support for research on Newfoundland and Labrador, but as a *field of study* rather than as research institution such as a so-called think tank. There was no central coordinating body that directed priorities. Individuals and collaborative teams competed for attention, but they were united in the general goal of understanding the society around them.

Some social movements, including intellectual movements, achieve stability as they become institutionalized. The positive effects of that change may be balanced by a loss of fervour as the movement achieves its goals and becomes institutionalized. The intellectuals of the Newfoundland studies movement, historians, linguists, folkorists, anthropologists, and geographers collected evidence of Newfoundland's past and present. Story hoped to create a common research centre that would coordinate acquisition and cataloguing of publications, unpublished textual material, recordings of oral interviews, and material culture.[16] The creation of dedicated physical spaces such as laboratories and observatories were as integral to the emergence of professional science as was fieldwork.[17]

The "Dictionary Room," MUNFLA, Halpert's personal library, and the provincial archives provided the cultural capital and the space for professional research on Newfoundland culture as much as did the fieldwork. Story proposed a Centre for Newfoundland Studies that would be "the single most important step that could be taken" in furthering the research.[18] A centralized cataloguing and research centre could institutionalize collaboration that had been to that date informal. Material that should be brought together in one place was scattered among different archives, preservation was less than ideal, and no institution was able to collect systematically. The centre would take responsibility for setting priorities in acquiring materials for Newfoundland studies, coordinate major projects, raise funds for research, and award research associate positions.[19] Morgan, Harris, Halpert, Keith Matthews, Seary, and Kirwin all approved of the proposal.

After viewing the university's master plan in the fall of 1968, Halpert was disappointed that there was "no provision for a Newfoundland Studies Centre" that "would have considerable space requirements for tape and manuscript storage, for filing and processing areas, and for study and research rooms."[20] The idea did not die. A Committee on Newfoundland Studies was struck in 1973 to advise on Newfoundland scholarship, to identify areas of common interest, and the physical requirements of storing and making accessible Newfoundland research material. Meeting in 1974, the committee was encouraged by the ongoing planning for a new university library and by the possibility that the federal government would donate an archive building to the province to mark the twenty-fifth anniversary of Newfoundland joining Canada.[21] While the government allocated funds to build a new library, it was apparent in 1975 that funds would not be forthcoming for a joint university-provincial government archive, the centrepiece collection of which would be the J.R. Smallwood Papers, which the former premier had given to the university.[22] The university senate approved a Newfoundland Studies undergraduate program, ample space was set aside for Newfoundland publications in the new library, and the university had its sights set on a Newfoundland Studies Centre. That May, the board of regents of the university approved in principle the creation of such a centre, which would coordinate research, oversee archival collections, and develop academic programs.[23] Much that had started informally was codified and institutionalized, but the university was unable to fund the ambitious research institution that the movement's leaders envisioned.

This book examined the varied and important roles played by collaborations between, Seary and Story; Story, Kirwin, and Widdowson; Story and Halpert; Halpert and Widdowson; Matthews and Alexander;

and others in the study of Newfoundland culture. The sociologist Michael Farrell emphasized the dyadic relationships that develop into collaborations, which produce work that is more creative than would have resulted from any one person. Each of these chapters examined a collaborative circle. While many of the personal dynamics that Farrell found common to collaborations can be seen in the Newfoundland case, there are two exceptions to his model worth considering. His analysis suggests that collaborative circles break up in about ten to fifteen years as tensions emerge between members who seek individual prestige.

At Memorial, many of the collaborations continued until the deaths of the collaborators and, in several cases, decades beyond the deaths of the senior members. Farrell's model assumes careerist motives are uppermost in people's decisions, while I suggest that the individuals in this movement often subsumed their egos in the effort to achieve something for their community. Farrell also suggests that collaborations emerge in a "magnet place" to which ambitious scholars are drawn. St John's was not a seductive scene like Paris in the 1920s or New York in the 1950s, and Memorial was not a place that uniquely offered freedom of thought like the University of Padua during the renaissance or a prestigious university like Columbia during the early twentieth century. It might therefore seem an unlikely candidate as a magnet place.[24] Although for those who were interested in fieldwork opportunities, Newfoundland was widely known to be a place at which one might make his or her mark. The province also had a reputation as a place rich in oral culture material and as potential virgin territory for research from archaeology to zoology. A few charismatic individuals, such as Paine when he was the driving force behind ISER Books, also helped make the university a place people wanted to work.

Political support and cultural conditions in the middle of the century, and the desire to leverage local resources to build a research profile, encouraged scholars to study Newfoundland society and culture. The sociologist Neil McLaughlin identifies several factors that illuminate the successes or failures of intellectuals. He points to the cultural climate of the times and institutional prestige as factors that affect the reception of ideas. The study of Newfoundland culture seemed more relevant during the period of intense change from the 1950s to the 1970s than it did before or since, and Memorial had significant local prestige even though it was newer and smaller than many of its counterparts in Canada. Newfoundlanders looked to the university as an agent for the modernization of the province. Rural parents often saw university as the only feasible route for their children to escape a life in the fishing boat and on the flake. Faculty members had considerable social capital in the view of those eager to modernize. At an individual level, Keith Matthews's reputation was created by his appointment at Memorial and his association with the Atlantic Canada Shipping Project. While Grant Head's historiographic contribution was similar to that of Matthews, his career in Ontario put him at the periphery of a Memorial-centred field.

McLaughlin also points to the importance of personal characteristics in the establishment of an intellectual's reputation. Story was universally admired at Memorial. His publications about the Northern European renaissance and his scholarly gravitas encouraged others to believe that Newfoundland could be the subject of serious study by a world-class intellectual, and not just a subject of parochial or amateur interest. The quality of the ideas matter in their becoming widely influential, but McLaughlin finds the history of academic reputations incomprehensible without balancing sociological factors with attention to the history of orthodoxy and revision within intellectual movements. Success, or influence, he suggests, is shaped by social movements outside the university and the "loyalties and commitments that operate in the context of the fierce competition for legitimation and resources in modern universities and intellectual life."[25]

The situation at Memorial supports such an interpretation – much of the prestige enjoyed by individual faculty members and departments came from their ability to claim knowledge of Newfoundland. The Faculty of Education, ISER, and other units supported the state's agenda to modernize, while the broader community interest in the culture of Newfoundland allowed the humanists to have influence and public support in preserving and celebrating a culture that was rapidly changing.

The first couple of generations of scholars at Memorial University established foundations for the study of the culture, and those were shaped by the national traditions and disciplinary norms within which they worked. A few Canadian-trained scholars studied Newfoundland, a larger number of American-trained men and women worked in the province, but the largest number of researchers came from British universities. Administrators such as Morgan had an unofficial faculty recruitment strategy of hiring British-trained faculty members and of sending promising local students to the United Kingdom for doctoral work. The creation of the Rothermere Fellowship was a tangible example of the policy. Named after the university's first chancellor, British newspaper magnate Lord Rothermere, it provided funding for Newfoundland students to pursue doctoral work in Britain. After the development of graduate programs at Memorial, the unwritten policy until the 1970s was to not hire anyone with a graduate degree from Memorial unless they had worked at another university for a while before coming home. Motivated by a desire to not become intellectually parochial, the practice had the unintended effect of discouraging the reproduction of Newfoundland research expertise. Several of the Memorial graduates who played key roles in Newfoundland studies, such as Peter Neary and S.J.R. Noel, used their doctorates from British universities to take up appointments in Ontario. Once they had lived in England for a period and had settled into careers in Canada, they chose not to return to St John's. For a department such as folklore, which had the only PhD program in English-speaking Canada, the restrictions on hiring their own graduates made hiring Canadians, let alone Newfoundlanders, difficult. The example of the Newfoundland historical geographers is particularly striking. They developed an approach to their field that was unique and productive, but the lack of a PhD program and the decline in interest in historical geography throughout North America meant that they did not reproduce themselves. When the last of them retired, their tradition ended.

We have seen how both local and international contexts shaped the research into the society and culture of Newfoundland. In the nineteenth and twentieth centuries, academic disciplines developed in North American and Europe by splitting off from each other and coalescing around new methodology, theory, or topic matter; the fact that they often defined themselves in opposition to other disciplines discouraged interdisciplinary study. At Memorial in the 1950s and 1960s, the Department of Social Sciences split into history, economics, and a Department of Sociology and Anthropology. That last department later separated into Departments of Sociology and Anthropology, and subsequently the Anthropology Department divided into Departments of Anthropology and Archaeology. The Department of English Language and Literature spawned a Department of Folklore and eventually became a Department of English. A Department of Linguistics developed that was separate from either anthropology or any of the departments of modern languages. True to their common roots, however, and reflecting their common area of study and a common use of students as research collaborators, the various departments shared much even as they diverged. In 1970 Harris emphasized that the university had groups of collaborators who were "working on the same wavelength." Halpert's and Seary's studies of oral culture, the historical scholarship of Matthews (which included having his students write the history of their communities), the community studies of the anthropologists, and the work of the geographers, he reported, "form the nucleus of a centre for Newfoundland Studies."[26]

The culture and the description of the culture created by self-aware scholars were two different, but related, things. The crowd at the university produced description, taxonomies, maps, archives, catalogues, and analysis. Anthropologists' interest in modernization and their preoccupations with kinship predisposed them to stress facets of the culture that their subjects did not emphasize and do things like draw kinship charts. Most researchers were rigorous in applying their critical faculties to evidence and were aware of the observer's paradox inherent in participant observation. In doing research they intervened in the culture. Newfoundlanders became aware of the university's activities and self-conscious in ways that they otherwise would not have been.[27] The multiple mumming revivals in the decades that followed the publication of Halpert and Story's *Christmas Mumming* are obvious examples. David Whisnant, in a widely cited critical appraisal of cultural revivals, suggested that intellectuals may choose to work on traditional culture as a way of avoiding the more difficult work on economic and power disparities within modern society:

"Rescuing" or "preserving" or "reviving" a sanitized version of culture frequently makes for rather shallow liberal commitment: it allows a prepared consensus on the "value" of preservation or revival; its affirmations lie comfortably within the bounds of conventional secular piety; it makes minimal demands upon financial (or other) resources; and it involves little risk of opposition from vested economic or political interests. It is, in a word, the cheapest and safest way to go.[28]

Some of the intellectuals examined in this book were cultural interveners by Whisnant's definition, but all varied in their relationships to the community and their informants. Most of these scholars were suspicious of the vested interests of those with economic and political power even if they did little to challenge them directly. While a few Newfoundland intellectuals may have shared the cultural and aesthetic conservatism described by Whisnant in Appalachia and Ian McKay in

Nova Scotia, most of those who studied Newfoundland hoped that social change would empower rural people. Some of the faculty members and graduate students were members of the New Left, and there was no necessary correlation between an interest in folklore and reactionary politics. Many scholars valued the objectivity of social scientists or shared the assumptions of the state, while others developed a critical practice and endeavoured to make the material lives of Newfoundlanders better.

Were rural people's lives made better by Newfoundland studies? Most academic books attract few non-specialist readers. At most, they have only an indirect effect on the society; generally academic publications were only part of the cultural and intellectual landscape within which people lived.[29] A few books, such as the *DNE*, sold broadly to members of the general public and were displayed on shelves in homes. Others, such as *Cat Harbour*, were assigned to hundreds of undergraduate students as a standard description of "traditional" outport life. The public's interest in Newfoundland culture encouraged the scholars to continue their research, and that interest was sustained by the work at the university. Some of the scholarship on the province reached an audience well beyond the corridors of the university. While we often use the word *intellectuals* for people who earn a living through their mental labour and who work at a high level of abstraction or specialization, everyone does intellectual work when they are thinking and talking about their culture, their shared past, and their shared future. Since the nineteenth century there had been men and women who financed their intellectual work with another occupation, and that continued throughout the twentieth century. As we have seen, faculty members worked to distinguish themselves from the amateurs, but professionals' understanding of the culture was not always superior.

From its modest beginnings among of a handful of scholars studying Newfoundland culture at the Parade Street building in downtown St John's, Story estimated that by 1968 about fifty men and women on the new campus were doing research on the province. Newfoundland studies also extended beyond the university. Most Newfoundlanders embraced the social changes that followed Confederation; indeed, they demanded modernization and a higher standard of living. The quip that Smallwood "dragged Newfoundland, kicking and screaming, into the twentieth century" is an exaggeration; most people wanted to leave the past behind. The university provided students and faculty members time to focus on scholarship without having to do other sorts of labour, and some intellectuals moved back and forth between town and gown. Michael Harrington, for example, studied at Memorial University College during the Second World War, replaced Smallwood as the author and host of the Barrelman radio program in 1943, opposed Confederation as an elected delegate to the National Convention between 1946 and 1948, and taught English literature at the university in the 1950s. He was a member of the advisory committee to the Historical Research Committee and had a career as a journalist and newspaper editor from the 1960s to the 1980s. He wrote modernist poetry and books and newspaper columns of Newfoundland history.

Harrington may have been the author of the *Evening Telegram* article critical of James Faris's *Cat Harbour*, discussed earlier. In his retirement he returned to the university as a research fellow in history to edit the proceedings of the National Convention with the historian James Hiller. Others, such as Nimshi Crewe, L.E.F. English, and Alan Fraser, benefitted from the patronage of the state. Thousands of individuals whose names are forgotten did intellectual work on their society and culture, and the names of hundreds more are recorded in the MUN Folklore and Language Archive. Many members of the public bought the books produced at the university and made their own sense of them.

The efflorescence of local histories, memoirs, and community museums of the second half of the twentieth century were all vernacular intellectual efforts by Newfoundlanders who sought to preserve and engage with their heritage. The books in Newfoundland history published each year by amateurs currently outnumber those by professional historians by many orders of magnitude, and successful novelists engage with the Newfoundland past. The popular persistence of "myths," such as the illegality of settlement, decades after university academics dismissed that interpretation show that people unaffiliated with the university see their past in nationalistic ways and do not accept that the faculty members at Memorial have a monopoly on knowledge.[30] Entrepreneurs print words from the *DNE* on T-shirts and sell mummer figurines that are made in China. Many Newfoundlanders reflect on their rural heritage by purchasing framed photographs of houses being floated from one bay to another or paintings of wharves and stages. This shows that the cultural residue of the past can be made into commodities that find new resonances as badges of identity. That there have been several non-academic dictionaries of Newfoundland English published in the twenty-first century, and that there are periodic popular discussions of pronunciation and the lexicon on the radio and social media, reveal that a self-awareness of linguistic distinctiveness continues.

Newfoundland studies was, in part, an attempt to salvage a record of a world that men and women at the university saw as quickly falling into twilight. The movement was also, in Whisnant's evocative term, a *cultural intervention*. He characterized interventions as "someone (or some institution) [who] consciously and programmatically takes action within a culture with the intent of affecting it in some specific way that the intervener thinks desirable."[31] They could, he continued, "range from relatively passive (say, starting an archive or museum) to relatively active (like instituting a cultural revitalization effort)."[32]

Many of the activities described here were just those sorts of passive interventions, such as the creation of the Folklore and Language Archive, which inspired young people to document and revive elements of the culture. Newfoundland studies was a leading edge of the broader cultural movement in the province that Sandra Gwyn called the "Newfoundland Renaissance." As the British-born Robert Paine put it: "The university was perhaps in the vanguard" and "the painters, playwrights and musicians would join us later."[33] Gwyn identified the constituent parts as a folk music revival, growth of indigenous theatre, painting, literature, and the architectural preservation movement.

We can add to that list the continued interest in the province's history and culture. Many of the artists who had been born around the time of Confederation were either students at Memorial or had spent time on campus. Several of them reported being inspired by Story's example of taking oral culture seriously, even if they had not had him as a teacher.[34] The nationalist cultural resurgence to which Gwyn drew attention was initiated and sustained by many activities at the university. The folk culture revival included many people at Memorial University in leadership roles, but it was a broader movement than just university intellectuals. The artistic movement also encouraged younger faculty members and students to engage with Newfoundland culture, and intellectuals who were unconnected to the university continued to do such things as collect folk music and write history.

The musicians of Figgy Duff, for example, emulated the academic folk song collectors through their own field collecting, and then performed the music with contemporary arrangements and electric instruments, to reach new audiences. The cultural influence ran in both directions; the artistic movement in the community – such as the theatrical group the Mummers Troupe, which was influenced by the academic study of mumming – inspired the academic staff members to feel that they were participating in the culture of a living community and not just documenting a fossil. Just as artists used the cultural repertoire to build their career, the academic movement's participants also had personal motives. Scholars strove to advance their academic careers by reorienting fields of study, which they felt favoured textual over oral evidence or elite history over popular, and they benefitted from institutional support for their agenda.[35] The creative interaction of organic intellectuals and those in the academy infected many scholars with enthusiasm for Newfoundland. Although a strong case can be made for his inspirational role, Story reported having been surprised by the renaissance. In an address to the Royal Society of Canada he reflected that he had been "sort of developing the thesis that from the old forms of literature that it might be expected or it might be possible for a fine art or a sophisticated art to grow and develop."[36] The artists of the cultural revival felt that too.

In the midst of that youth movement at end of the 1960s, the older generation of intellectuals continued to work. Joseph Smallwood lost the premiership in 1972, in part signalling voters' rejection of his autocratic style, the "develop or perish" mentality, and the rush to abandon old ways as the province urbanized.[37] Memorial had contributed to the end of the Smallwood era both directly, through the criticism of his government's management, and indirectly, by educating several generations of people who assumed leadership positions in their communities. Young people were less likely to defer to the self-styled "only living father of confederation" if they had no memories of a time before Confederation. The generation born around the time of Confederation had their knowledge of Newfoundland culture shaped by the cultural renaissance and the Newfoundland studies movement, and they were the people to turn against Smallwood's hold on power.

Many of this generation's aspirations seemed embodied in Brian Peckford, a member of the cabinet in the Frank Moores government and himself premier between 1979 and 1989. Peckford was a product of Smallwood's modernization agenda. A graduate of Memorial, even while a sitting premier he published a part memoire, part manifesto in which he drew on his analysis of history, and the confidence that came from the revival of Newfoundland culture, to project a positive future. He claimed: "I have come to know not only the bare facts of our history, but have developed a deeper appreciation of our heritage and way of life ... I have come face to face with the real Newfoundland."[38]

In addition to references to Prowse, other nineteenth-century historians, and the *Amulree Report*, he drew heavily on the historical research at Memorial. Noel, Neary, Hiller, and Alexander were all cited. Peckford painted a picture of government mismanagement and asked "can we now, instead of repeating our errors, shape a realistic development philosophy which will change our dependence on others, or is our past necessarily our present and our future?"[39] Newfoundland studies, a field of which Smallwood saw himself as a pioneer and one of its greatest practitioners, played a role in the rejuvenation of the anti-Smallwood political classes. And the past was something to escape from.

In his retirement, Smallwood wrote an autobiography (political biographies and history were his favourite leisure reading) and returned to his roots as a nationalist intellectual. Just as he had worked to "make Newfoundland better known to Newfoundlanders" on his *Barrelman* radio program from 1937 to 1943, he founded and edited the first volumes of what eventually became a six-volume *Encyclopedia of Newfoundland and Labrador*. Although initially resistant to writing for it, fearing it would be amateurish or partisan, many faculty members at Memorial wrote entries on their areas of expertise. The encyclopedia staff, all graduates of Memorial, also relied on the university's research infrastructure, including the hundreds of papers written by students in courses in folklore, history, and geography. When Smallwood became ill, Mose Morgan, then retired, took over the project. Story subsequently chaired the foundation and hoped to use the position to smooth the process whereby the revenue from the encyclopedia would endow a Smallwood Centre for Newfoundland Research. Smallwood's effort to be an encyclopedist was fulfilled by those at the university of which he was so proud.

The initiatives undertaken by the first generation of Newfoundland scholars were mostly completed by the early 1980s, and the province underwent a more explicit politically nationalist phase. In 1983 a visiting sociologist, Kenneth Westhuse, asked Story what he thought about the resurgence of Newfoundland nationalism exemplified by the antagonistic relationship Premier Peckford had with the government in Ottawa. Story did not believe that Newfoundland was experiencing a phenomenon like the separatist movement in Quebec or the Irish aspiration for independence, although he admitted that some Newfoundlanders drew on both analogies when thinking about themselves. The Newfoundland variety of nationalism, he argued, was less a coherent political program and more a *recognition* of each other:

7.1. M.O. Morgan. (Photographic Services Collection, QEII Library, Memorial
University of Newfoundland.)

Nationalism in Newfoundland seems to me to be a kind of consciousness
of a shared community and to operate on that level of recognition of your
fellow countrymen – not in the sense of we are in a nation, a great nation,
but the feeling of being alike and therefore of being different. I don't think

Newfoundlanders think of themselves as a great, great people, or ever have, but there's certainly a great feeling of uniqueness which is illusory, of course, in comparative sort of terms but it is felt ... It's more a feeling of separateness ... [a] feeling of shared community, of identification and I've noticed this in all kinds of ways of meeting fellow countrymen abroad. Well, that's not uncommon for compatriots to feel that way but Newfoundlanders together, they're not self-consciously Newfoundland but they can be made to be self-conscious by the reactions of other people and this is fed and aided and abetted too within confederation by the way that Newfoundlanders are perceived. I've knocked around a bit but I'm constantly noticing, when, say, I'm on the mainland, if you're identified as coming from Newfoundland, there is a reaction to that in a way that I don't find when someone is from Saskatchewan and is identifying where he's from ... I find that Newfoundlanders are, can be, typecast and we sometimes invite it by laying it on a little bit thick, broadening the speech a bit or exaggerating weather or playing to it for fun, or sometimes ironically, I don't find that offensive at all. I find it interesting and I rather enjoy it.[40]

Story's characterization of Newfoundland nationalism as cultural self-awareness was perceptive. Awareness that the *DNE* was being compiled was itself a spark for the cultural revival. It was a book that encouraged the newfound respect for the history and culture just as the artists of the cultural movement were attempting to promote. Recognition of each other is a sort of nationalism, and one that has greater continuity within Newfoundland than the occasional nationalistic reactions to provocations. In this conception of national feeling, Story shared much with the Smallwood of the 1930s. Contrary to the anthropologist Benedict Anderson's emphasis on the dominant role of print in encouraging individuals to recognize that they belonged to a nation, Story saw Newfoundlanders' awareness of community as based on an oral culture.[41] The irony is that the publication of the *Dictionary of Newfoundland English* by a prestigious Canadian academic press was part of the broader cultural movement of renewed pride in oral and traditional culture.

In Frickel and Gross's estimation, scientific and intellectual movements succeed by having their agenda widely adopted in their discipline or by becoming an established sub-field within a larger field. It would have been naive to hope that Newfoundland studies would develop a method and theory that could have colonized history, lexicography, anthropology, and the other disciplines. Many of the scholars at Memorial were proud of their innovations, however, and aware that they were often ahead of their time. But such movements are of their time and momentum fades. The demographic bulge in the 1960s filled the classrooms with the students who became partners in the research on Newfoundland and required the hiring of new faculty members. But the declining birth rate that accompanied the higher standards of living after Confederation, and financial factors, meant that far fewer people were appointed at Memorial after the peak hiring of about 1968 to 1973, and the changing labour market meant new faculty members were less likely to have other job offers than earlier generations. They were more likely to stay in St John's even if they did not care for the work that was happening at Memorial. The mean age of the faculty rose through the 1980s and 1990s, and few younger recruits picked up the work started by the generation of the 1950s.

University administrators had once hired British-trained scholars for jobs in the humanities and social sciences, while there were few jobs in the United Kingdom and salaries there were unattractive. The Vietnam War also encouraged many Americans, especially left-leaning ones, to come to places such as Memorial. The resulting conversation about Newfoundland culture between British and American intellectual traditions had been productive. Having a university of its own after 1949, and one in which the Newfoundland environment, culture, and society were principal objects of study, meant that younger generations of Newfoundlanders could take up the movement. Newfoundland-born undergraduates and, after the 1960s, graduate students, and ultimately faculty members, carried on the work.

Opportunities diminished in the 1980s. The average age of the faculty in the 1960s was low, relative to later periods, and the faculty members were expanding in absolute numbers and in the diversity of approaches. Youth and expansion encouraged optimism on the one hand, but the construction of new buildings and the sectarianism of departments made it increasingly difficult to share enthusiasm and ideas with scholars in different departments. In the 1980s the downsizing of the faculty through attrition and financial austerity took a heavy toll on the momentum. As the generations that had sustained Newfoundland studies reached retirement, the institutional impetus was elsewhere.

When Morgan retired in 1981, Newfoundland scholarship lost one of its most steadfast supporters. He was succeeded by Harris, who was equally committed to Newfoundland cultural research, but in

1990 he too retired, and leadership at the university passed into the hands of a new generation with new priorities. While the university had once found administrators within the university and among the Newfoundland-born and Memorial-trained, a system that encouraged administrators who had a long-standing commitment to the place, as the university became more like other corporate Canadian universities it recruited leaders from outside. The labour market it hired from, and the funding sources it accessed, meant that the Newfoundland scholars did not reproduce themselves with a new generation of faculty. New faculty members moved to a province that no longer had such obvious pre-modern vestiges, and the Newfoundland-centred agenda no longer had the same appeal. It ran its course and was then succeeded by other intellectual movements. The Department of English abandoned the study of language to embrace contemporary trends. The Department of Geography shifted its emphasis towards the natural sciences and became less historical in the process. Folklorists engaged with popular culture and "folk groups" in other areas of the world. Anthropologists abandoned the extended ethnographic participant observation to adopt new methods.

The development of research universities in the nineteenth and twentieth centuries had enhanced the social prestige and autonomy of intellectual workers even as they made themselves responsible to abstract disciplinary ideals and an international community of scholars. It had also sometimes done so at the cost of alienating them from the local communities in which they lived.[42] In this case, however, there were countervailing tendencies. Many of the scholars at Memorial participated in the cultural and social movements of their day.

At the same time, leaders at the university used the examination of the local community as a strategy to earn prestige for their research in national and international circles. The discovery of the local culture also worked against the fragmentation of disciplinary boundaries prevailing in the academy. Lexicographers, historians, folklorists, anthropologists, and geographers evolved approaches that, while no single one of which was exclusive to Memorial, were at the forefront of their disciplines. Newfoundland studies prompted the university to develop new disciplinary departments, such as folklore, linguistics, anthropology, and geography, each of which were innovative. At the same time individuals in each department drew on the work of colleagues in other departments and developed similar research approaches. O'Flaherty had once described Memorial as a "Newfoundland university," but in the twenty-first century most faculty members were graduates of Canadian universities, and they replicated Canadian curriculum and research agendas.

The period from the 1960s to the 1970s was a productive era, but there are reasons to be wary of seeing it as a golden age. Paine, who arrived at Memorial near the movement's peak and embraced his new home with gusto, reflected that "both the university as a collective and the individual faculty were young in vigour and ideas as well as age."[43] James Overton, who also came to Newfoundland from England, warned that the view of the period as a golden age of scholarship should be set against the fact that some Newfoundlanders resented being the objects of study of social science meddlers.[44]

Telling lies to anthropologists, or evading their questions, may have been a way of eluding the attention without seeming rude. Kirwin sometimes had difficulties finding informants, Youther reported people didn't want to speak to him, and it had taken the anthropologists a long time to earn the trust of informants. Mars was suspected of being a spy for either Smallwood or the insurance companies, and many other fieldworkers were suspected of being Russian spies. Not everyone teaching or studying at Memorial embraced the intellectual movement or the related cultural revival. Overton took a critical view of the way that political leaders such as Peckford referenced Newfoundland culture and used nationalist rhetoric to enlist political support.[45] Overton had a leftist critique of the ways that the ideological right used nativist appeals to enlist support for policies that disadvantaged the poor. Sociologists who worked with the state, or those whom he believed supported the neo-liberal agenda, were frequent targets of his criticism. In a series of essays he used historical research into such things as poor relief to mount an attack on those who undermined the welfare state.[46]

It was also possible for those on the ideological right to mount criticism of the celebration of Newfoundland culture. Newfoundland-born philosopher F.L. Jackson thought foreign-born academics romanticized Newfoundland culture and, with their friends in the arts community, created a "Newf-cult" that bore little resemblance to the real culture.[47] Jackson was a critic of the attention Newfoundland received from the academics from outside:

I arrived at Memorial University in the mid-sixties just as the social scientific conquest of the province had begun. Formidable phalanxes of anthropologists and folklorists descended on us like gold prospectors, enthusing over the vast, untapped resource that was Newfoundland's cultural history. They commenced to mine it and their efforts have yielded much valuable ore, though not without leaving a few slag-heaps around. Up to that point Newfoundlanders had been a modest if peculiar lot who never thought of themselves as a consequential people. So it was quite startling, indeed very flattering, to be informed by our new social scientist friends that we were in fact an extraordinary, pristine breed, with a rare mint-condition, pre-industrial culture living out a version of the world-historical class struggle in the exquisite microcosm on our blighted rock.[48]

Jackson wrote of it being "impossible to swim against the Newf-cult tide at the time," and when invited to an academic conference he felt his wife and he were "not academic colleagues, but raw cultural data; not fellow observers, but specimens."[49] He didn't object to the textual scholarship of the older generation of Seary and Story, but he criticized the younger generation of academics who affected "rubber boots and salt-and-pepper cap" in celebrating a romanticized version of the rural culture. For Jackson, Newfoundlanders of the 1950s had been striving to move from primitive life to modernity, and "cultural identity and the rights of national folk-groups were ideas we associated with Nazis and Fascists, the culture-freaks of the thirties."[50] But "hippies" had discovered the "natural and primitive" in the 1960s, and by the 1970s they were working in governments and universities and now coped with the alienation of mass society by promoting "heritage-mongering." Jackson, whose father had been an outport Methodist clergyman, argued that the preservation of enclaves of backwardness was dangerous, but that change had to be accommodated with the preservation of tradition in a different way than of the "Culture-Vultures":

The preservation of traditions is all-essential in carrying out this task, not because a "traditional way of life" has some mystical value in itself, but because in traditions lie the wisdom and experience of time and place and the deeper consciousness of spiritual identity that are necessary if a people are to survive and prosper in the course of history and the challenges it presents. And when I speak of keeping traditions alive, rather than fossilized, I don't mean native or traditional exclusively, but also the one that is rarely spoken of in these multi cultural, anti-western times except in tones of implied disrespect, namely my own Anglo-Saxon, Christian tradition.[51]

Jackson's conservative critique of the cultural revival, and his hostility to the young scholars who used Marxist analysis, resonated with some people at the university, as did Overton's leftist critique.

Jackson alluded to an implied disrespect towards Christianity within the academy, and it's worth considering how scholars in this period approached the subject of religion. With the exception of historians who were interested in sectarian politics and geographers who were interested in population patterns, social scientists paid little attention to religion. In an age when secularism and modernity seemed synonymous, many social scientists were uninterested in it or saw religion as another vestigial folk belief, like the belief in witchcraft or fairies. Perhaps Newfoundland-born intellectuals, aware of how divisive sectarianism can be, also exercised care to not emphasize it in their accounts.

Sectarian bigotry had been used as a partisan weapon during the Constitutional referenda of 1948, and during the period covered by this book the province had a denominational school system in which the churches jealously guarded their prerogatives. Memorial had been founded as a non-denominational college in the aftermath of Catholics and Protestants dying side by side in trenches of the Great War, and some of its faculty and administration were careful to not do anything to provoke division. Other faculty members worked towards the abolition of the denominational school system, with its wasteful duplication of schools and practice of teaching separateness to children. The historian of Memorial University College, Malcolm MacLeod, suggested that in the 1940s history was a subject that college trustees feared could threaten the status quo. Fraser was hired as a historian because he was a Roman Catholic, and the Catholics would feel he was one of them and thus could be trusted to teach the Reformation.

In 1953 Gushue checked with the various denominations to ensure that there would be no objections to Fraser's replacement, Gordon Rothney, an Anglican.[52] Similarly, Donald Willmott reported that "an unwritten 'gentleman's agreement'" existed at the time Memorial was founded that any sociologist would be Roman Catholic. That would ensure that topics such as birth control would not be taught.[53] He faced suspicion from some Roman Catholics among the faculty members but held firm in teaching different points of view rather than toeing the anti-birth-control line. Newfoundlanders were practised at avoiding religious controversy, even if that meant maintaining separateness and the three principal denominations taking turns in civil service appointments. Some scholars may have extended this habit of taking care to not offend from their teaching into their research. We can't generalize too much about the young faculty members that arrived in St John's in the late 1960s, but many of them believed religiosity to be a characteristic of backward societies, and that secularization was an intrinsic part of modernization.

While class was an analytical category to be employed in one's work, people's religious beliefs were more likely to be considered an impediment to modernization or a source of partisan strife, and thus something that should wither and disappear. The historians were most likely to discuss religion of any of the disciplines, and then it was most often not appreciated as a vital aspect of people's lives but presented as a source of partisan dissension that prevented the colony from being governed well. We should not take the lack of engagement with religion as always a choice made by scholars. In a discussion of the Fogo films made by Memorial's Extension Service and the NFB, the professor of education Philip Warren, a lifelong critic of the Denominational School System, asked why the film-makers had not asked the religious leaders for their views. He thought it "unnatural" to discuss the power structure in Newfoundland without discussing the clergy who were the leaders in the communities. Fred Earle, who had been instrumental in making the films, defended the film-makers on the basis of them having tried to get the cooperation of clergy on Fogo Island – but, he said, the clergy would not participate.[54]

This book has described a series of productive interdisciplinary collaborations. These had tangible results, and in my conversations with scholars they freely talked about other people who had a positive effect on their research careers. When individuals disliked each other or did not cooperate, however, little trace is left to the historian, but we know that tensions between individuals occurred. ISER started as a facilitator of social and economic research but came to be dominated by anthropology in large part because Paine was a forceful figure. Some of the sociologists, for example, felt Paine had been hostile to their discipline, and that resentment was one of the factors that encouraged a split into two departments and the departure from Memorial of the Newfoundland-born sociologist Ralph Matthews. The fact that ISER published few titles in economics, history, or geography, and even fewer in folklore, may reflect tensions between faculty members and departments as well as Paine's priorities.

For this book I selected research projects on society and culture, and collaborations, that were born in the 1950s, thrived, and grew to full strength in the 1970s and 1980s and which declined in vigour and relevance in the 1990s. They have now passed into memory, although many of these books continue to be read. The metaphor of a life makes the birth, development, and death of the Newfoundland studies movement seem natural, rather than explaining history as the results of effort, choice, and chance. Individual scholars, and university administrators, accomplished nearly all of what that they set out to do, and the scholarship was a product of historical factors. Just as we might see our own state of knowledge as an apex and select scholars and publications that mark steps along the way, so we might point to projects that ended or research avenues that were not followed as failures. No one is currently working on a third edition of the *DNE*, the unique approach to historical geography that developed at Memorial was dissipated as the geographers retired, and so on. We have seen how the research projects grew in the context of Newfoundland's rapid social and cultural changes, and we now live in a different era. The urgency to document a vanishing culture, which animated the work in the first two decades after Confederation, is gone, but that is in part because the efforts to document it succeeded. Many people, notably Story and Kirwin, also came to view the culture as more resilient than they had once believed. More recently Jerry Pocius made a compelling case that culture persists even as its material trappings become "modern."[55]

During the half century after Confederation, Newfoundland lexicography, history, folklore, anthropology, and geography experienced a remarkable rise in the level of completeness and sophistication. The key texts from that era are all foundations for contemporary scholarship – just as the original authors had hoped. In the process the state of the culture of the 1960s has for many subsequent scholars seemed *traditional*, a category that assumed that there had been little change before modernization took hold. Smallwood claimed modernity itself as a blessing brought by Confederation, while others pointed to the effects of the American servicemen stationed in Newfoundland in the 1940s. Ironically, even Smallwood's critics were prone to accept his periodization of Newfoundland history as beginning its modern era in 1949 and assume a long, unchanging cultural equilibrium.

The ability to transmit the knowledge of Newfoundland improved even as the mass media made American popular culture and scientific knowledge increasingly available. To take only one example, in the 1950s Memorial's administration partnered with the University of Toronto Press to publish Newfoundland scholarship, while at the time I write this Newfoundland scholars are able to publish within the province, including the journal *Newfoundland and Labrador Studies*, and through national and international publishers. The movement at the university to record Newfoundland culture and society was bold, ambitious, and successful. Students of Newfoundland culture in 1955 had no basic research aids at hand, and most Newfoundlandia was in private libraries. By 1985 Memorial's library boasted a comprehensive research collection and bibliography, the folklore and language archive had preserved a range of oral culture, and the provincial archive provided access to the archival records. The work of librarians, most of whom were women and worked anonymously, created knowledge as did the male teaching faculty. The oral culture had been described, and the framework of history had been sketched in. The early writings in Newfoundland studies are foundational in the sense of being the first of their kind and also in the sense of providing reference points for later generations of scholars. Gushue, Rothney, Morgan, Harris, Halpert, Seary, and Story launched Memorial on its effort to describe Newfoundland.

The changes in Newfoundland during the half century after 1945 set the context for a cultural revival and scholarly intervention. When taken with the institutional history of Memorial University, the social factors fostering the movement can be seen. Psychological forces and interpersonal dynamics played a key role. Friendships and collaborations between Seary and Story; Morgan and Story; Story, Kirwin, and Widdowson; Story and Halpert; Halpert and Widdowson; and Alexander and Keith Matthews were more creative than their work as individuals might have been. These groupings, in turn, involved colleagues, staff, and students in their research programs, and the key projects this book examined transformed the work of the dozens of scholars that space has not allowed me to examine. The collaborative circles studied by Farrell generally lasted between ten and fifteen years.[56] He emphasized interpersonal factors in the life cycle of collaborative circles. Friendships among young creative people provided each other with the confidence to break with the status quo; they consolidated and institutionalized their programs, but conflict over credit led people to split from the group and strike out on their own. The Newfoundland studies movement does not conform to each of these stages exactly; most notably many of these collaborations lasted until the death of the principal investigators and beyond. Although jealousies and argument affected some relationships, what is remarkable is the way that a commitment to scholarship and a passion for the place so often kept egos in check.

The Newfoundland studies movement was shaped by both local and international factors. Memorial's engagement with rural Newfoundland shaped the careers and scholarship of many of these men and women. The mixing of American, British, and Canadian scholars, each with his or her own training and interests, also encouraged fruitful hybridization. One's country of origin, or indeed citizenship (since some faculty members took Canadian citizenship and others did not), seems to have made little difference to his or her commitment to Newfoundland scholarship. Some mainlanders, to use the Newfoundland colloquialism for those from the continent, and some British citizens adopted a loyalty to Newfoundland that included their feeling of ownership and suspicion of Canadian-based scholars as interlopers. Whether locally born or foreign-born, though, the faculty members at Memorial were not isolated from European and American academic fashion. They embarked on discipline-specific searches for empirical or scientific truth in the 1950s and shared the assumptions of functionalism, for example, of their counterparts elsewhere. Historians used to focus on the discoveries and theories of those who time has proven right and assume that our knowledge is becoming ever more complete. Starting in the 1950s, they recognized that social factors shape what questions we ask and thus what we believe to be a fact. Knowledge seemed not to be something that could be confirmed by reference to independently existing facts, but an exercise of power whereby a social group determined what the facts were. All academic fields, although the pace and scale of influence varied, moved away from a naive positivist position and embraced a multiplicity of views. In this book I have described how theory and training shaped the research on the history, culture, and society of Newfoundland and have shown how ideological changes in the world affected scholars' changing views of the island. This is consistent with the view that knowledge is socially constructed but that ideological position must be tempered. Many of these scholars were affected by their interactions with those who worked within different paradigms, but more importantly these scholars revised their theory when faced with the evidence they saw in the archive and in the field. They were not confined to confirming the assumptions that underlie their research.

This book's end date of the mid 1980s is arbitrary, but it roughly coincides with the completion of the research agenda set out in the 1950s, and by then the sense of urgency that had once animated Newfoundland studies was gone. The research described in this book remains foundational for contemporary scholarship, and therefore the construction of that knowledge merits study. My argument that the Newfoundland studies movement is a thing of the past is also arbitrary in the sense that the current generation of scholars is also working dialectally with theory and evidence, as did their predecessors.

Today there is a variety of ongoing scholarship on Newfoundland and Labrador culture and society, which of course fits with our current intellectual and material milieu rather than the priorities of the 1950s. Some day, another historian may examine the work of my generation, which took up the study of Newfoundland in the 1980s. In the meantime, we can consider what caused the end of the Newfoundland studies movement. To start our discussion, universities everywhere underwent many of the same reorientations in the second half of the twentieth century. All universities became less local and more national and international in outlook. Throughout North America, business owners who had earlier endowed universities in their cities now diversified and saw their interests less correlated with the region in which they lived, and they were consequently less interested in local philanthropy. With rising costs, tuition covered a smaller portion of their budget, and that encouraged university administrators to look outside their local community for funding. National granting agencies set national priorities, and prestigious publishers were based in a few metropolitan centres – both factors that encouraged scholars to work on topics that had no relation to any specific part of the world.

The increasing awareness of the interconnectedness of the world also encouraged scholars to see themselves as global in interest.[57] The forefront of academic work, or academic fashion, was not rooted in local communities or nations. The new left, feminism, postmodernism, etc., all encouraged a global subject matter. Since the labour market for faculty members, and academic administrators, was national and international, fewer people at universities in North America felt a commitment to the place at which they worked. Knowledge of Newfoundland, whether gained through fieldwork, archival research, or collaboration with students, was no longer such a compelling route to gain the symbolic capital that advanced one's career. Theorists working on high-prestige academic projects worked at high levels of abstraction, in which knowledge of the real world was relatively unimportant.[58]

The trendsetters among academic disciplines became more self-reflexive and valued empirical research less than had previous generations.

The men and women who created the Newfoundland studies research agenda – creating reference sources in toponym and family names, the *DNE*, the *Bibliography*, etc. – were united in their assumption that the oral culture was threatened by modernity. They also intended to make up for lost time, since the province was late in creating a research university compared to other nations, by laying a foundation of reference sources for the next generation of scholarship. The *DNE* and the *Bibliography* have served as reference sources for later scholars, and it is not an exaggeration to say that much of the research on Newfoundland oral culture had its roots in the early initiatives of Seary and Story, just as historical research builds on the foundation of Rothney. But the movement I describe was not something that existed exclusively on the Parade Street campus or only within the corridors of the Arts and Administration Building at Memorial. Rural Newfoundlanders (Earle is an outstanding example, but thousands were involved in small ways) collaborated in the study of Newfoundland oral culture, and thousands talked to anthropologists and folklorists when there was little to be gained by doing so. After spending a summer collecting geographic and economic data and experiencing "overwhelming co-operation" from rural people, Grant Head commented that "Seldom does one find a people so friendly, so helpful, so accurate and so precise."[59]

Beyond the scientific rigour they all shared, those who practised each academic field had their own methodology that they used to establish their authority. Geographers mapped the land and inventoried its resources. Anthropologists lived and worked with the people to chart their kinship and their cultural structure. Folklorists sat in kitchens and collected oral and material culture and created a canon of tales, songs, and artefacts that exemplified the more general common culture. Historians used their traditions of source criticism and archival research to trace the origins of the present in the remote past. All of these scholars categorized, classified, and described the evidence they found. Some aspects of Newfoundland's culture were thus described with a high degree of precision. The lexicon, constitutional history, folktales, mummers, outport ways of life, and settlement patterns all received attention; in doing so the scholars created social knowledge as they recorded and described the culture. Theory and tradition informed their choices of what to transcribe and document, as did aesthetic views. Historians' colourful anecdotes, folklorists' märchen, anthropologists' elegant abstractions or quaint beliefs, and lexicographers' unique words all became part of the corpus of knowledge that then informed Newfoundlanders' sense of themselves.

Faculty members at Memorial in the middle third of the twentieth century rarely employed gender or race as conceptual categories in documenting Newfoundland culture, although class was used more often. Residents of the island were nearly exclusively of European ancestry, and while anthropologists and archaeologists worked on and with aboriginal peoples most other scholars did not. Gender analysis had not fully developed in the era of the Newfoundland studies movement, and Memorial systematically discriminated against women (who were most likely to employ gender as an analytical category) in hiring decisions and forced women on the faculty to quit when they married. The women played supporting roles. Female graduate students wrote studies that became part of the synthesis in various fields, and a few of them were hired as faculty members. Agnes O'Dea and Letty Halpert both worked as librarians, and both produced bibliography and research collections that shaped knowledge. Jennifer Faris and her counterparts not only made the homes that the anthropologists lived in while working, they collected ethnographic data from other women. A few wives, such as Sharon Firestone, became anthropologists themselves. Other women accompanied husbands into archives and served as unpaid research assistants, typists, and editors. The most accomplished female anthropologist at Memorial, Jean Briggs, was renowned for her ethnographic work among the Inuit, but she did not work on Newfoundland research. Most of the scholars discussed in this book also had wives who cared for the household and hosted the faculty dinner parties that served as social lubricant among men who worked together. The desire to document a culture that they perceived to be threatened, and their efforts to aid in modernization encouraged description, taxonomy, and the construction of narratives that explained the exceptional society they found. These goals did not, in the first instance, encourage theorizing.

The texts described in this book described and circumscribed Newfoundland culture at a particular moment of history. Outports during the 1960s became codified as "traditional" or as authentic and the benchmark against which modernization or assimilation was measured. Much as Story realized would happen, soon younger Newfoundlanders were strangers to the culture that had been collected by folklorists and anthropologists. Having grown up as the son of an air

traffic controller in Gander, Newfoundland, I did not dress as a mummer, listen to folk music, or tell cuffers, mend nets, or hook rugs. As a
university student in the1980s I became conscious of Newfoundland's
cultural heritage through interactions with older friends who had been
part of the cultural revival of the 1970s and through the textbooks I
was assigned – the very books that this book has attempted to put into
context.

The energizing idea that gave the Newfoundland studies movement
its character – the drive to document Newfoundland culture before it
was forgotten – continues to echo. During the thirty years or so after the
Second World War, the expansion of the state's responsibilities encouraged social scientists to engage in an effort to encourage development
by identifying social and cultural barriers to modernization. Anthropologists, geographers, economists, and sociologists used state funding to finance their fieldwork. As we have seen, the administrators at
Memorial recruited people to bolster local research, and scholars self-
selected as well. While the academic job market was good, the turnover
of staff was high, and many of those who did not become involved
in local research went on to appointments at other universities. Those
who stayed at Memorial were likely to have made a personal commitment to the community and to have engaged in local research.

That local research was often interdisciplinary, which had its challenges. "It is much easier to talk about interdisciplinary work than to
actually do it, particularly in the contexts of small financially weak
departments who are attempting to establish themselves, their pro-
grammes, and their reputations upon a firm footing," Harris recognized, adding, "However, we now, I believe, have success within our
grasp."[60]

By many measures, the Newfoundland studies movement was a success – the administration achieved its institutional goals, the careers
of its participants were furthered, and advances were made in the
description of the culture. The crowd that documented Newfoundland
culture was a product of its era, but neither the scholarship nor creative practices were the last efforts to describe, nor participate in, the
culture. In the late twentieth century Newfoundland authors achieved
a level of success and reputation that would have pleased Story, or
Smallwood. The first generation of scholars established chronology,
genealogy, lexical indexes, taxonomies, and maps of the culture. For
some, like Harris, it was the culture of his childhood; for others it was
the culture of an adopted homeland that seemed more authentic than

mass society. Learning of their new home could take on a mystical quality. Paine, when reflecting back on the role the university had in the culture, quoted George Story: "Newfoundland was once seen as but a 'twilight world, halfway, metaphorically between Europe and the New World' [it] was now – in all its singularities of time, space and place, language and people – to be mapped, and still more important – to be honoured."[61]

Notes

Introduction

1 Les Harris, "Remarks ISER 25th Anniversary," Harris Papers, Archives and Special Collections, Queen Elizabeth II Library (ASC), MUN.

2 See Williams, *Key Words*, 208–9. A good introduction to modernization in post-war Newfoundland is Wright, *A Fishery for Modern Times*.

3 Bruneau, "Quiet Flow the Dons." See also the bibliography in that volume, pp. 382–412. For an example of the study of one discipline in one country, and only the English-speaking literature, and only a few "national" figures at that, see Berger, *The Writing of Canadian History*.

4 Camic, Gross, and Lamont, "The Study of Social Knowledge Making," in their *Social Knowledge in the Making*, 4–6.

5 On the development of Canadian historians, see Wright, *The Professionalization of History in English Canada*. For a study of Quebec historians that shows how they reflected social trends in their province, see Rudin, *Making History in Twentieth-Century Quebec*.

6 For a notable effort to bring multiple authors together to examine a common problem among many disciplines during the half century after 1945, see Steinmetz, *The Politics of Method in the Human Sciences*. For examples of such studies, although of an earlier period, see Ross, *The Origins of American Social Science*, and Shore, *The Science of Social Redemption*. Shore places the intellectual history of sociology at McGill University in both its academic and civic contexts. Smith, *The Fontana History of the Human Sciences*, 25–34, contains a helpful discussion of the writing of the history of science.

7 Said, *Orientalism*, 50.

8 Steinmetz, "A Child of the Empire."

9 Farrell, *Collaborative Circles*, 2.

10 McLaughlin, "Why Do Schools of Thought Fail?," 115.

11 Novick, *That Nobel Dream*, 3–4.

12 Camic and Gross, "The New Sociology of Ideas"; Lamont, "How to Become a Dominant French Philosopher."

13 Camic, Gross, and Lamont, "The Study of Social Knowledge Making," 6–7.

14 Thomas Kuhn, *The Structure of Scientific Revolutions*, continues to be an influential argument that social factors affect science.

15 Desmond, *Huxley*, 617–18.

16 The distinction is made in Novick, *That Nobel Dream*, 12.

17 *Crowd* n. 1. An organized, integrated group of people. 2. All or most of the people (of another community or group). Story, Kirwin, and Widdowson, *Dictionary of Newfoundland English*, 124–5.

18 Frickel and Gross, "A General Theory."

19 Frickel and Gross, "A General Theory," 204.

20 Frickel and Gross, "A General Theory," 206–8.

21 Gwyn, "The Newfoundland Renaissance."

22 Camic, "The Making of a Method," 436.

23 Novick, *That Nobel Dream*, 577.

24 Camic, "Three Departments in Search of a Discipline," 1006.

25 Camic, "Three Departments," 1011.

26 For a discussion of the fieldwork experience affecting knowledge, see Pang, *Empire and the Sun*.

27 Memo from G.M. Story to editors, St Patrick's Day [19]75, *DNE* files, English Language Research Centre (ELRC), MUN. Story attributed the quote to the English classicist and poet A.E. Housman, *The Confines of Criticism: The Cambridge Inaugural, 1911*.

28 For a discussion of the way that engagement with the city of Chicago shaped the University of Chicago, see Shils, "The University, the City, and the World." The quotation is from page 221. See also Low and Bowden, *The Chicago School Diaspora*, 12.

29 Mellin, *Newfoundland Modern*.

30 Hobsbawm and Ranger, *The Invention of Tradition*.

31 O'Flaherty, *Leaving the Past*, 38.

32 O'Flaherty, *Leaving the Past*, 39.

33 Harold Horwood, *Evening Telegram*, 11 September 1952, as cited in O'Flaherty, *The Rock Observed*, 163.

34 I thank Jerry Pocius for suggesting this to me during a conversation.

Chapter One

1 Story, Kirwin, and Widdowson, *Dictionary of Newfoundland English*.
2 Patterson, "Notes on the Dialect."
3 Anderson, *Imagined Communities*, 41–6.
4 Pope, *The Many Landfalls of John Cabot*.
5 Colton, *Newfoundland Rhapsody*.
6 Devine, *Devine's Folk Lore of Newfoundland*. See the preface by Philip Hiscock, iii–v.
7 Ayre, *Newfoundland Names*.
8 In 1956 the university librarian, Mrs. Huston Dixon, gave the cards to Story when his work on the dictionary began. Story and Kirwin, "The Dictionary of Newfoundland English," 15. The reference to the glossary club is in MacLeod, *A Bridge Built Halfway*, 119. In MacLeod's account, Hunter and the historian A.M. Fraser were the only humanists working at the college who published scholarship.
9 Story, interview with Kenneth Westhues, 2 March 1983, 5.13.033, George Story Papers, ASC, MUN, 63.
10 Story to Bill Whiteley, 2.03.019, George Story Papers, ASC, MUN.
11 Story, interview with Westhues, 2 March 1983, 5.13.033, George Story Papers, ASC, MUN, 43.
12 Story to George Ian Duthie, 24 March 1958, 2.01.003, George Story Papers, ASC, MUN.
13 Story, lecture to English 300 class, November 1958, file 1958, *DNE* files, ELRC, MUN.
14 Story, "A Critical History of Dialect Collecting," 4.
15 Johnston, "Government and University."
16 MacLeod, "Crossroads Campus," 131.
17 D.G. Pitt, interview with Malcolm MacLeod, 18 October 1982, C-5966, 82–282, Memorial University of Newfoundland Folklore and Language Archive (MUNLFA).
18 G.M. Story, "News out of Galilee," address to the Association of Canadian Archivists, 21 July 1993, 5.09.036, George Story Papers, ASC, MUN, 1–4.
19 Story to Elizabeth Epperley, 5 August 1988, 2.01.005; Story to David Frank, 6 January 1983, 5.11.007, George Story Papers, ASC, MUN.
20 Story to Bill Lebans, 25 January 1961, 2.03.010, George Story Papers, ASC, MUN.
21 George Story, interview with Carole Henderson-Carpenter, 16 March 1970, 78–57, MUNFLA.
22 Story, "Edgar Ronald Seary."

23 E.R. Seary, interview with Carole Henderson-Carpenter, 17 March 1970, C3911, accession 78–57, MUNFLA.
24 Seary, "Regional Humanism," 14–15.
25 Seary to Gushue, 15 August 1955, file 1955, *DNE* files, ELRC, MUN.
26 Seary, "The Place of Linguistics in English Studies."
27 Raymond Gushue, CV, 3.05.004, Joseph Smallwood Papers, ASC, MUN.
28 Nimshi Crewe to Joseph Smallwood, 24 April 1951, N. Crewe – 1953 Archives, C-11, President's Office, MUN, 5; Crewe to Gushue, 27 May 1953, N. Crewe – 1953 Archives, C-11, President's Papers, MUN.
29 Gushue to Seary, 2 November 1955, File 1955, *DNE* files, ELRC, MUN.
30 Seary, "Proposals for Developments."
31 Seary, "Proposals for Developments."
32 Seary and Story, *Reading English*, 85.
33 "Suggestions for The Canada Council," 23 April 1957, Canada Council 1957–1964 file, Seary Collection, ELRC, MUN.
34 A.W. Truman, Canada Council, to Seary, 11 April 1958, Canada Council file, Seary Collection, ELRC, MUN.
35 Gushue to Seary, 5 April 1957, file 1957, *DNE* files, ELRC, MUN.
36 G.M. Story, "Memo on the Relation of Newfoundland and Canadian Research in Place Names and Language," 14 July 1957, file 1957, *DNE* files, ELRC, MUN.
37 G.M. Story, "Notes on Collecting for and Editing a Newfoundland Dialect Dictionary," February 1964, *DNE* files, ELRC, MUN.
38 Story, "Notes on collecting."
39 Béjoint, *The Lexicography of English*, 101.
40 Story, "Edgar Ronald Seary," 6.
41 George Story, "Address to A Carillon for Heritage Conference," 1987, 5.09.025, George Story Papers, ASC, MUN, 1.
42 G.M. Story, "A Newfoundland Dialect Dictionary: A Survey of the Problems." Paper read before the Humanities Association of Canada, 13 April 1956, 5.09.001, George Story Papers, ASC, MUN, 14.
43 Story, "A Newfoundland Dialect Dictionary," 14.
44 G.M. Story, "Research in the Language and Place-Names of Newfoundland." Paper read before the Canadian Linguistic Association, Ottawa, 13 June 1957, 5.09.002, George Story Papers, ASC, MUN, 12.
45 George Story, second lecture to English 300 class, November 1958, file 1958, *DNE* files, ELRC, MUN.
46 Sledd, "Bi-Dialectalism."
47 G.M. Story, "Dialect and the Standard Language," Address to the St John's Rotary Club, 21 November 1957, 5.09.003, George Story Papers, Coll. 243,

ASC, MUN, 1–2. Later published in the *Journal of the Newfoundland Teachers' Association*, 49 (1957): 10–20.

48 G.M. Story, "Dialect and the Standard Language."

49 In the 1950s Story believed that there was greater dialect variety in Newfoundland than in many other countries, but by the completion of the *DNE* in 1982 he had found a greater consistency in Newfoundland English than he had once supposed. He attributed that to Newfoundland having had two founding linguistic groups (Anglo-Irish and West of England) and the mixing of language by those who engaged in the Labrador fishery, seal fishery, work in the woods, etc. Kirwin concurred and added that there was greater similarity in vocabulary than there was in pronunciation, particularly if compared to a country such as Britain. Story and Kirwin, interview with Robert Paine, 19. Excerpts of the interview were published in Robert Paine, "Dictionary of Newfoundland English: An interview with Two of Its Editors," *Newfoundland Quarterly* (Fall 1982): 46–8.

50 Story, "Dialect and the Standard Language," 5.

51 Story, lecture to English 300 class, November 1958, file 1958, *DNE* files, ELRC, MUN.

52 Consider the disproportionate antipathy to the word *ain't* among many American educators. For a witty discussion of the struggle between prescriptive and descriptive American dictionaries in this era by one of William Kirwin's mentors at Chicago, see Sledd, "Dollars and Dictionaries."

53 Wayfarer, *Daily News*, 6 June 1956, 4.

54 Harold Horwood, "Political Notebook," 15 December 1955, *Evening Telegram*.

55 Story, second lecture to English 300 class, November 1958.

56 G.M. Story, "Newfoundland: Stubborn Stereotypes." Speech to Kiwanis Convention, St John's, 1969, 5.13.002, George Story Papers, Coll. 243, ASC, MUN, 1.

57 Story "Newfoundland: Stubborn Stereotypes," 6–8.

58 *Daily News*, 13 September 1956, 7.

59 Jacques Rousseau to Seary, 29 May 1958, National Museum of Canada; Seary to Carmen Roy, National Museum of Canada, 1 May 1959; Seary to L.S. Russell, 29 December 1959, National Museum of Canada file, Seary Papers, ELRC, MUN.

60 Kirwin to Raven McDavid, 13 April 1973, file 1973, Kirwin Papers, ELRC, MUN.

61 Much of this account of Kirwin's career is based on my conversations with him, starting on 18 July 2010, as I conducted research at the English Language Research Centre. McDavid was a native of South Carolina and

had reacted to people from other regions trying to correct his speech. He went on to become an accomplished dialect fieldworker and joined the University of Chicago in 1957. He edited several works in dialect geography. See "McDavid, Raven I(oor), Jr," in McArthur, *The Oxford Companion*, 634–5.

62 Drysdale to Kirwin, 6 October 1959, file 1959, Kirwin Papers, ELRC, MUN.
63 Kirwin to H.R. Wilson, 2 February 1960, file 1960, Kirwin Papers, ELRC, MUN.
64 Kirwin to Arthur Norman, 11 April 1961, file 1961, Kirwin Papers, ELRC, MUN.
65 Kirwin to R.I. McDavid, 17 July 1960, file 1960, Kirwin Papers, ELRC, MUN.
66 McDavid to Kirwin, 28 July 1960, file 1960, Kirwin Papers, ELRC, MUN.
67 Story, second lecture to English 300 class, November 1958.
68 Notes for guest lecture in Herbert Halpert's folklore class, 1972, 4.04.005, George Story Papers, Coll. 243, ASC, MUN.
69 Kirwin, "Either for Any," 8.
70 Kirwin to Smallwood, Miles Murray, and Dr McGrath, 5 August 1960, file 1960, Kirwin Papers, ELRC, MUN. There is a marginal note indicating that the letter was not sent.
71 Seary, Story, and Kirwin, *The Avalon Peninsula*.
72 Seary et al., *Ethno-Linguistic Study*, 57.
73 Story and Kirwin, interview with Robert Paine, 4–5.
74 Seary to Dean of Arts and Science, 13 October 1961, *DNE* files, ELRC, MUN.
75 E.R. Seary, "Research in Newfoundland Linguistics, Dialect, Toponymy and Folklore," 31 October 1962, file 1962, *DNE* files, ELRC, MUN.
76 J.D.A. Widdowson, interview with the author, 13 July 2011.
77 Kirwin, "Standardization of Spelling," 19.
78 Kirwin to Seary, 11 December 1962, file 1962, Kirwin Papers, ELRC, MUN.
79 Kirwin to Arthur Norman, 29 July 1963, file 1962, Kirwin Papers, ELRC, MUN.
80 J.D.A. Widdowson interview, 13 July 2011.
81 Gushue to A.W. Truman, Canada Council, 27 December 1963, Canada Council file, Seary Collection, ELRC, MUN.
82 Gushue to Truman, Canada Council, 27 December 1963, Canada Council file, Seary Collection, ELRC, MUN.
83 Truman to Gushue, 8 June 1964, Canada Council file, Seary Collection, ELRC, MUN.
84 Gushue to Truman, 14 July 1964; Truman to Gushue, 24 August 1964, Canada Council file, Seary Collection, ELRC, MUN.

85 Story to Kirwin, 6 June 1965, file 1965, *DNE* files, ELRC, MUN. J.D.A. Widdowson, interview with the author, 13 July 2011.

86 Story to Kirwin, 2 July 1965, file 1965, *DNE* files, ELRC, MUN.

87 Kirwin to Berkely Peabody, Moorhead State College, 9 March 1965, file 1965, Kirwin Papers, ELRC, MUN.

88 Kirwin, Application for Canada Council Grant, 18 October 1965, file 1965, Kirwin Papers, ELRC, MUN.

89 Kirwin to Seary, 12 September 1967, file 1967, Kirwin files, ELRC, MUN.

90 Kirwin to Hudson, 7 May 1968, file 1968, Kirwin files, ELRC, MUN.

91 Kirwin to F.R. Léon, 19 September 1973, file 1973, Kirwin files, ELRC, MUN.

92 Kirwin to Léon, 19 September 1973, file 1973, Kirwin files, ELRC, MUN.

93 Kirwin, interview with Carole Henderson-Carpenter, 23 March 1970, C3925, 78–57, MUNFLA, MUN.

94 Kirwin, interview with Carole Henderson-Carpenter, 23 March 1970, C3925, 78–57, MUNFLA, MUN.

95 For example, "The following is tentative interpretation of the evidence about the origin of *squid* ... If the substitution, or mistake, of b d is possible, *squib* is a plausible guess as to source ... So we just have a parallel: the squirting fire of the *squib* in the sixteenth century *may* have been altered by the West Country sailors to *squid* to apply in the early seventeenth century to the squirting fish in Newfoundland. There is not strong phonetic reason why b should shift to d, but if the word is imitative or symbolic (cp *squirt*), maybe there doesn't have to be a phonetic explanation." Kirwin to R.J. Clark, Dept. of Classics, 1 May 1973, Kirwin Papers, ELRC, MUN.

96 Widdowson to Kirwin, 21 November 1968, file 1968, Kirwin Papers; Widdowson to Story, 5 January 1970, *DNE* files, ELRC, MUN.

97 Widdowson to Story, 5 January 1970, *DNE* files, ELRC, MUN.

98 J.D.A. Widdowson, Programme of oral examination, 12 January 1973; Seary to the Registrar and Secretary, University of Sheffield, 7 September 1972, J. Widdowson file, Seary Papers, ELRC, MUN.

99 Kirwin to Seary, 12 September 1967, file 1967, Kirwin files, ELRC, MUN.

100 Béjoint, *The Lexicography of English*, 264–7 and 271.

101 Widdowson to Kirwin, 27 December 1967, file 1967, Kirwin files, ELRC, MUN.

102 Story and Kirwin, "The Dictionary of Newfoundland English," 16.

103 Story application for Canada Council grant for *DNE*, April 1969, file 1969, *DNE* files, ELRC, MUN.

104 Kirwin and Story, "A Newfoundland Glossary," the American Dialect Society, 1965, file 1965, *DNE* files, ELRC, MUN. See F.G. Cassidy and

R.B. Le Page, *Dictionary of Jamaican English* (London: Cambridge University Press, 1967).
105 Editorial meeting, 22 August 1973 (Story, Kirwin, Widdowson), file 1973, *DNE* files, ELRC, MUN.
106 Story to Harris (VP Academic), 4 May 1977, file 1977, *DNE* files, ELRC, MUN.
107 *DNE*, 18–19.
108 Kirwin, "Standardization of Spelling."
109 *DNE*, xii.
110 Widdowson, interview, 13 July 2011.
111 *DNE*, xiii.
112 Kirwin to Joan Halley, 11 September 1969, file 1969, *DNE* files, ELRC, MUN.
113 *DNE*, vi.
114 Story to Widdowson, 13 May 1971, file 1971, *DNE* files, ELRC, MUN.
115 G.M. Story, W.J. Kirwin, and J.D.A. Widdowson, "Collecting for the *Dictionary of Newfoundland English*." Lecture to the International Conference on Lexicography in English, New York, 1972, file 1972, *DNE* files, ELRC, MUN.
116 Story and Kirwin, "National Dictionaries."
117 W.J. Kirwin in Story and Kirwin, interview with Robert Paine, 12.
118 Story to Widdowson, 27 January 1974, file 1974, *DNE* files, ELRC, MUN.
119 Story to Widdowson, 27 January 1974, file 1974, *DNE* files, ELRC, MUN.
120 Kirwin was referring to Walter J. Ong, "The Writer's Audience Is Always a Fiction," *PMLA* 90, no. 1 (January 1975): 9–21.
121 Note dated January 1975, file 1975, *DNE* files, ELRC, MUN.
122 Story, editorial note, 3 March 1978, file 1978, *DNE* files, ELRC, MUN.
123 Undated editorial memo, [1975], file 1975, *DNE* files, ELRC, MUN.
124 Story and Kirwin, interview with Robert Paine, 14–15. The citation Paine and Story are discussing is from the historian J.D. Rogers, *A Historical Geography of the British Colonies*, 104.
125 Story and Kirwin, interview with Robert Paine, 21–2.
126 Story to Widdowson, 3 January 1978, file 1978, *DNE* files, ELRC, MUN.
127 Terry Pratt, 11 June 2011.
128 Story to Mary Henley, n.d., 2.02.008, George Story Papers, ASC, MUN.
129 W.J. Kirwin in Story and Kirwin, interview with Robert Paine, 22–3.
130 Kirwin, "Standardization of Spelling," 23–4.
131 Kirwin to Edward A. Jones, 18 January 1984, Kirwin Papers, ELRC, MUN.
132 G.M. Story in Story and Kirwin, interview with Robert Paine, 22–3.

133 G.M. Story, "The Role of the Dictionary in Canadian English," paper presented at In Search of the Standard in Canadian English conference, Kingston, ON, October 1985, 5.09.019, George Story Papers, ASC, MUN, 4.

134 See, for example, English, *Historic Newfoundland*, and subsequent editions.

135 Clarke, *Newfoundland and Labrador English*, 134–8.

136 Story to Widdowson, 15 September 1982, file 1982, *DNE* files, ELRC, MUN.

137 Story to Widdowson, 15 September 1982, file 1982, *DNE* files, ELRC, MUN.

138 Story to Elizabeth Epperley, 19 January 1988, 2.01.005, George Story Papers, ASC, MUN.

139 *DNE*, 2nd ed., 658. Professor Kirwin pointed out the omission of *to be* to me in a conversation we had 23 February 2011.

140 *DNE*, 2nd ed., 632.

141 Sider, *Culture and Class in Anthropology and History*.

142 Mary Dalton, *Merrybegot* (St John's: Running the Goat, 2002); Annie Proulx, *The Shipping News* (New York: Scribner, 1993).

143 Story, interview with Westhues, 2 March 1983, 5.13.033, George Story Papers, ASC, MUN, 16.

144 George Story, "Address to A Carillon for Heritage Conference," 1987, 5.09.025, George Story Papers, ASC, MUN, 2.

145 Story to Head of Department, 5 January 1993, 2.06.021, George Story Papers, ASC, MUN.

146 Bartlett, *A Short History of the Italian Renaissance*, 65.

147 Kirwin to Patrick O'Flaherty, 18 February 1983, ELRC files, ELRC, MUN.

148 Story to Ronald Schoeffel, 12 November 1988, file 1988, George Story Papers, ELRC, MUN.

149 Kirwin to Kenneth Goldstein, 16 February 1978, Kirwin files, ELRC, MUN.

150 This paragraph is based on Bailey, "National and Regional Dictionaries of English." The quotation appears on page 279.

151 High, "The 'Narcissism of Small Differences,'" 90, 93, 102.

152 Story commented after Crewe's death: "I recall one winter evening when he took from a desk a series of small black notebooks and showed me the observations he had made for many years on local vocabulary, grammar and pronunciation. I often urged him to publish these, but he had so many things to occupy that powerful and curious mind that he never did. Then, in September 1962, he began to send me the first of what was to become a steady stream of memoranda on local words and phrases ... His contribution to the Newfoundland dictionary ... is a permanent and valuable legacy which we acknowledge with gratitude." Story to Editor, *The Daily News*, 23 September 1971, file 1971, *DNE* files, ELRC, MUN.

153 Story, interview with Westhues, 2 March 1983, 5.13.033, Story Papers, ASC, MUN, 66–7.
154 *DNE*, xiii.
155 Frickel and Gross, "A General Theory," 204–32.

Chapter Two

1 Raymond Gushue to J.R. Smallwood, 25 June 1953, 3.09.034, Smallwood Papers, ASC, MUN.
2 "Archives to Archives," *Evening Telegram*, 27 June 1960, 6. On Smallwood's career as a radio broadcaster, see Webb, *The Voice of Newfoundland*.
3 Iggers and Wang, *A Global History of Modern Historiography*, 103.
4 Wright, *The Professionalization of History in English Canada*, 83.
5 Much of the following section is based on Baker, "Memorial University's Role in the Establishment of a Provincial Archive." The Carnegie Foundation of New York supported Memorial University College and, after 1949, both historical research and extension work. On the college, see MacLeod, *A Bridge Built Halfway*. On the role of the foundation in Canadian education and culture, see Brison, *Rockefeller, Carnegie, and Canada*.
6 O'Flaherty reports that Clutterbuck wrote the report under the direction of Amulree and others within the civil service in London. O'Flaherty, *Lost Country*, 394.
7 Great Britain, *Newfoundland Royal Commission 1933 [Amulree Report]*, 3.
8 *Amulree Report*, 13.
9 *Amulree Report*, 13.
10 *Amulree Report*, 16.
11 *Amulree Report*, 27.
12 The "truck system" varied over time and from community to community – but essentially it meant that fishing families took provisions and supplies on credit from a merchant and paid for it in fish at the end of the season. Often, little cash changed hands.
13 *Amulree Report*, 37.
14 *Amulree Report*, 39.
15 *Amulree Report*, 40.
16 *Amulree Report*, 42.
17 *Amulree Report*, 42.
18 *Amulree Report*, 43–4.
19 Bannister, "Whigs and Nationalists."
20 Neary and Baker, "Allan Fraser's 'History,'" 40. See also Neary and Baker, "Introduction."

21 Plumptre, Fraser, and Innis, "Newfoundland, Economic and Political."
22 Webb, "The Newfoundland and Labrador Fieldwork of Harold Adams Innis."
23 Plumptre, Fraser, and Innis, "Newfoundland, Economic and Political," 66.
24 Neary and Baker, "Allan Fraser's 'History,'" 15; Neary and Baker, "Introduction," 11–12.
25 MacKay, *Newfoundland*.
26 R.A. MacKay to Campbell Stuart, 3 November 1944, B1972–0025/011 (23), Harold Innis Papers, University of Toronto Archives.
27 Fraser to McKay, 11 September 1945, B1972–0025/011 (23), Harold Innis Papers, University of Toronto Archives.
28 Neary and Baker, "Introduction," 16.
29 Brebner, *North Atlantic Triangle*.
30 Smallwood, *The Book of Newfoundland*.
31 Smallwood in National Convention, in Hiller and Harrington, *The Newfoundland National Convention*, vol. 1, 581. The National Convention was an elected deliberative body that existed to study the position of Newfoundland and make recommendations for constitutional options that would be presented to the people in a national referendum.
32 Smallwood, "Memorial University of Newfoundland," 3.
33 Smallwood, "Memorial University of Newfoundland," 3.
34 "Nimshi Crewe," *Encyclopedia of Newfoundland and Labrador*, vol. 1, 557.
35 Gwyn, *Smallwood*, 51.
36 Crewe to Smallwood, 24 April 1951, N. Crewe – 1953 Archives, C-11, President's Office, MUN.
37 Crewe to Smallwood, 24 April 1951, N. Crewe – 1953 Archives, C-11, President's Office, MUN.
38 Crewe to Gushue, 23 May 1953, Crewe to Gushue, 27 May 1953, N. Crewe – 1953 Archives, C-11, President's Office, MUN.
39 Morgan to A.G. Hatcher, 3 January 1952, Department of Political Science, 1947–65, President's Office, MUN.
40 Poole, *Mose Morgan*.
41 Leslie Harris, interview with Malcolm MacLeod, 4 July 1984, C7185, 84–221, MUNFLA.
42 Gough, "The Royal Navy and Empire," 333; Gerald S. Graham, "Fisheries and Sea-Power."
43 McLintock, *The Establishment of Constitutional Government in Newfoundland*, xii.
44 McLintock, *The Establishment of Constitutional Government in Newfoundland*, xi.
45 Hollett, *Shouting, Embracing, and Dancing with Ecstasy*, 12–15.

46 Rudin, *Making History in Twentieth-Century Quebec*, 74–6.

47 Matthews, "Historical Fence Building."

48 Gordon Rothney's "Comments of [*sic*] Keith Matthews's 'Historical Fence Building'" can be found in 5.01.092, Matthews fonds, Maritime History Archive (MHA), MUN.

49 Gordon Rothney's "Comments of [*sic*] Keith Matthews's 'Historical Fence Building.'"

50 G.O. Rothney, "Memo to the Dean of Arts and Science," 10 November 1952, Faculty of Arts History, President's Office, MUN.

51 Ludlow, "Searching for the Past," 101–2.

52 Ludlow, "Searching for the Past," 89–108; Fay, *Life and Labour in Newfoundland*.

53 That was a considerable contribution to the field, although as Ludlow later pointed out, despite his living in Belfast, he made no effort to copy any Irish records relevant to Newfoundland but concentrated his collecting on English sources. See Ludlow, "Searching for the Past," 105–6.

54 Mayo was a Newfoundlander who had been a Rhodes Scholar for 1935 and had studied politics. His dissertation was on the prospects for Newfoundland's joining the Confederation.

55 M.O. Morgan, "Memorandum to the President Regarding Research into the Social, Economic and Political History of Newfoundland," June 1953, Department of Political Science, 1947–65, President's Office, MUN.

56 Rothney, "The History of Newfoundland and Labrador," 2.

57 Gushue to Smallwood, 25 June 1953, 3.09.034; see also Crewe to Smallwood, 9 July 1953, and Gushue to Smallwood, 15 December 1954, 3.02.014, Smallwood Papers, ASC, MUN.

58 G.O. Rothney, "Proposed Program of Research in Newfoundland History," 10 November 1953, London Conference, President's Office, MUN.

59 Gushue to S.H. Stackpole, 20 October 1954, Carnegie Corporation 1954–1965, President's Office, MUN.

60 *The Temperance Journal*, 10 March 1879, cited in Larry Dohey, "The Foundation for The Rooms Provincial Archives," accessed 9 July 2015, http://archivalmoments.ca/2015/03/the-foundation-for-the-rooms-provincial-archives/.

61 *Daily News*, 2 February 1955, 6.

62 L.E.F. English, letter to editor, *Daily News*, 8 February 1955, 6.

63 Wayfarer, *Daily News*, 3 February 1955, 6.

64 Perlin, *The Story of Newfoundland*.

65 Wayfarer, *Daily News*, 19 July 1955, 6.

66 G. Rex Renouf, letter to editor, *Daily News*, 20 April 1955, 6.

67 O'Flaherty, *Leaving the Past*, 126 and note 23.

68 Gushue to Lewis Namier, 27 April 1955, Archives – History Research Committee and Correspondence 1955, M – 50, President's Office, MUN.

69 Agnes O'Dea, interview with Carole Henderson-Carpenter, 17 March 1970, C3911, Carole Henderson-Carpenter Collection Accession, MUNFLA, 78–57.

70 Hart, "Dr Agnes O'Dea, 1911–1993."

71 O'Dea, *Bibliography of Newfoundland*, vol. 1, x.

72 Gushue, Morgan, and Rothney, "Report of Newfoundland Bibliography," Canada Council, 1957–59, Box 26, President's Office, MUN.

73 O'Dea, *Bibliography of Newfoundland*.

74 Gushue to S.H. Stackpole, 22 June 1956, Archives – History Research Committee and Correspondence 1955, M – 50, President's Office, MUN.

75 Gushue to Myles Murray, Minister of Provincial Affairs, 25 January 1957; Rothney to Smallwood, 23 April 1958, 3.09.035, Smallwood Papers, ASC, MUN.

76 Account by Jack Pickersgill: Fraser "feels rather keenly that if he had not interrupted his academic career to be a Liberal candidate he would still be in the University at a considerably higher salary than he is now getting [as provincial archivist]." Pickersgill believed that "it would be unfortunate if the impression got abroad that it was likely to be a liability to be a Liberal Member" and for that reason advocated finding some way to raise his salary. See J.W. Pickersgill to Smallwood, 26 October 1963, 3.10.026, Smallwood Papers, ASC, MUN.

77 Gushue, Morgan, and Rothney to the Canada Council, 14 January 1958, Canada Council 1957–1958, Box 26, President's Office, MUN.

78 "Archives to Archives," *Evening Telegram*, 27 June 1960, 6.

79 Rothney, "The History of Newfoundland and Labrador," 1.

80 Rothney, "The History of Newfoundland and Labrador," 2.

81 Hollett, *Shouting, Embracing, and Dancing with Ecstasy*, 7.

82 Seary, "Proposals for Developments."

83 Seary to Gushue, 10 April 1957, *DNE* files, ELRC, MUN.

84 Seary, "Regional Humanism," 15.

85 Rothney, *Newfoundland*.

86 Rothney, *Newfoundland*, 4–5.

87 Rothney, *Newfoundland*, 16.

88 Rothney, *Newfoundland*, 27.

89 Wayfarer, *Daily News*, 2 June 1959, 4. On Rothney undermining myths useful for tourism, see L.E.F. English, letter to editor, *Daily News*, 5 June 1959, 4.

90 G.O. Rothney, letter to editor, *Daily News*, 8 June 1959, 4.
91 Harris, interview with Malcolm MacLeod, 28 June 1984, C7184 84–221, MUNFLA.
92 For an explanation of why Rothney thought Memorial should specialize in the history of India, see Rothney to Morgan, 1 July 1961, Canada Council 1960–61, Box 26, President's Office, MUN.
93 Rothney to Margaret Forbes, 14 December 1962, Faculty of Arts – History, President's Office, MUN.
94 Harris, *Growing Up with Verse*, 153.
95 Harris, interview with MacLeod, 4 July 1984, C7185, 84–221, MUNFLA.
96 Harris, *Newfoundland and Labrador*.
97 Helen Crewe to Harris, 19 December 1973, Harris Papers, ASC, MUN.
98 Leslie Harris, cv, in William Whitely's research notes for a history of the Department of History.
99 Harris, interview with MacLeod, 4 July 1984, C7185, 84–221, MUNFLA.
100 When he found that many faculty had been lured away by other universities he commented, "when I stop to think of the number of hours I have spent in building up the Institute of Social and Economic Research for these two gentlemen and in acquiring research monies for their grandiosement that I find it difficult not to be cynical." Morgan to Rothney, 14 October 1964, 10.02.005, M.O. Morgan Papers, Coll. 083, ASC, MUN.
101 Cell, *English Enterprise in Newfoundland 1577–1660*.
102 Gillian Cell, interview with the author, 8 May 2010.
103 Cell, *Newfoundland Discovered*.
104 Devereux, "Early Printing in Newfoundland."
105 S.J.R. Noel interview with the author, 29 August 2011.
106 Noel to Morgan, 13 September 1960, Morgan to Noel, 3 October 1960, M.O. Morgan Papers, Coll. 083, MUN.
107 Noel, "Government and Politics in Newfoundland, 1904–1934"; Noel, *Politics in Newfoundland*.
108 Noel, interview, 29 August 2011.
109 Noel, interview, 29 August 2011.
110 Korneski, "Development and Diplomacy"; Thompson, *The French Shore Problem*.
111 Gunn, "The Political History of Newfoundland, 1832–64."
112 Morgan to Story, 5 November 1964, "Report on Prospective Faculty Members – G.M. Story (at Oxford 1965)," Box F-3, President's Office, MUN.
113 Story to Morgan, 14 March 1965, "Report on Prospective Faculty Members."
114 Story to Morgan, 14 March 1965, "Report on Prospective Faculty Members."
115 Hiller, "Is Atlantic Canadian History Possible," 16.

116 J.K. Hiller to Webb, 1 November 2013, letter in the possession of the author.
117 Story to Morgan, 9 April 1965, "Dean of Arts – History Dept. 1971," Box 3, ISER files, President's Office, MUN.
118 I thank Keith Matthews Jr and Kay Matthews for discussing Keith Matthews's life and work with me.
119 Story to Morgan, 9 April 1965, "Dean of Arts – History Dept. 1971."
120 Morgan to Matthews, 25 June 1965, Dean of Arts – History Department 1971 file, Box 3, ISER files, President's Office, MUN.
121 Morgan to Story, 23 March 1965, "Report on Prospective Faculty Members."
122 Matthews to Harris, 1 June 1966, "Dean of Arts, History Dept.," Box 3, ISER files, President's Office, MUN.
123 Madden, "The Commonwealth," 22–3.
124 Louis, Introduction, 39–41.
125 Herbert Butterfield, *The Whig Interpretation of History* (1931).
126 Bentley, *Modernizing England's Past*, 22.
127 Burrow, *A History of Histories*, 472.
128 Sager, "Newfoundland's Historical Revival," 104.
129 Matthews's acceptance of the appointment read "It is with great pleasure that I accept the post as Lecturer in History and look forward to my arrival on July 20th. I can hardly wait to see an Island which I have been so closely studying for the last two years." Morgan to Matthews, 17 April 1967; Matthews to Morgan, 26 April 1967, "Matthews, Keith," Department of History files, MUN.
130 Keith Matthews, "A History of the West of England–Newfoundland Fishery," Dphil thesis, Oxford University, 1968, preface, 6.
131 I thank Jerry Bannister for bringing my attention to this point.
132 Lewis Fischer, personal communication.
133 Meeting, 7 October 1968, re "Newfoundland Documentary Study," 5.01.506, Matthews fonds, MHA, MUN.
134 Pierson, "David Alexander: A Reminiscence"; Sager, "Newfoundland's Historical Revival," 104–15.
135 Keith Matthews, "Report concerning a visit to England in the summer of 1969...," file, Faculty of Arts – History, Box PO-35, President's Office, MUN.
136 Alexander, "Economic Growth in the Atlantic Region, 1880–1940," in Alexander, *Atlantic Canada*, 74.
137 Matthews, "Historical Fence Building." 155.
138 Alexander, "Development and Dependance in Newfoundland," in Alexander, *Atlantic Canada*, 4.

139 Another team project emerged in the same period at the ACSP. Several members of the Department of History had read an award-winning biography of Huey Long, which drew on oral history, and they were prompted to collect interviews with Smallwood's associates. See T. Harry Williams, *Huey Long* (New York: Knopf, 1969). It is not uncommon for people to understand the situation in their new home with reference to models from other parts of the world, and the patronage and populism of the Smallwood government brought to mind Long's powerful political hold on Louisiana. During the final months of his premiership, the historians at Memorial sensed a historical moment of change that would one day be the subject of historical inquiry. Hiller, Ralph Pastore, Panting, William Reeves, Ryan, and Matthews formed an Oral History Group (OHG), which undertook a Provincial Election Project. The plan was to begin interviewing before the election, concentrating on candidates defeated in nomination contests and proceeding to interview those elected and party officials, etc. They felt that "the forthcoming election may well mark an end to a distinctive trend of politics" and that once sufficient time had passed to allow for a historical perspective, future historians would find the collection valuable. Unfortunately, unlike the ACSP, the Provincial Election Project did not come to fruition. See Panting to Dean of Arts and Science, 27 September 1971, Faculty of Arts, History 1970–73, President's Office, MUN, 35.

140 Gerry Panting to Dean of Arts and Science, 1 October 1970, Depts. – Summer Activities and Academic Staff 1970–72 file, Box 2, Dean of Arts and Science, President's Office, MUN.

141 Department of History to Dean of Arts and Science, 20 November 1969; History Department Budget, 14 November 1968, Plans and Proposals 1970–71 file, Box 2, Dean of Arts and Science, President's Office, MUN.

142 Hiller, "The Foundation."

143 Hiller, "A History," i.

144 Hiller, "A History," iii.

145 Hiller, "A History," 368.

146 Hiller, "A History," 368–9.

147 McDonald, "W.F. Coaker and the Fishermen's Protective Union."

148 Hiller edited McDonald's thesis for publication. McDonald, *"To Each His Own."*

149 Reeves, *History of the Government.*

150 Matthews, "Fence Building," 156.

151 David Alexander, undated comment on draft of "Fence Building," 5.01.003, Matthews fonds, MHA, MUN.

152 Matthews, "Fence Building," 161.
153 Head, *Eighteenth Century Newfoundland*, xi.
154 Head, *Eighteenth Century Newfoundland*, xiii.
155 Rothney to Matthews, 30 June 1971, 5.01.092, Matthews fonds, MHA, MUN. The reference is to D.W. Prowse, *A History of Newfoundland from the English, Colonial and Foreign Records* (London; New York: MacMillan and Co., 1895) and subsequent editions.
156 Rothney to Matthews, 30 June 1971, 5.01.092, Matthews fonds, MHA.
157 Rothney, "History of Newfoundland," 97–8; "Britain's Policy in the North American Codfisheries, with special reference to foreign competition, 1775–1819," PhD thesis, University of London, 1939.
158 Rothney, "History of Newfoundland," 1, 25.
159 Matthews, "Class of '32." An earlier version of this essay, titled "The Reformers of 1832," was presented to the Newfoundland Historical Society on 29 January 1974. A copy of his lecture can be found in 5.01.52, Matthews fonds, MHA, MUN.
160 Matthews, "Class of '32," 92.
161 Matthews, "Class of '32," 93. O'Flaherty questioned Matthews's view, suggesting that the local grievances were genuine. See Patrick O'Flaherty, "The Seeds of Reform: Newfoundland, 1800–18," *Journal of Canadian Studies* 23, no. 3 (1988): 39–59.
162 Agnes Field, "The Development of Government in Newfoundland, 1638–1713," MA thesis, University of London, 1924, 6, 21, 43, 322.
163 W.L. Morton, "Newfoundland in Colonial Policy, 1775–1793," BLit thesis, Oxford, 1935, ii.
164 Morton, "Newfoundland," 15–16, 28n3.
165 Keith Matthews, "Eighteenth Century Newfoundland: An Historical Geography" by C. Grant Head (thesis review – 2 drafts), file 5.01.018, Box 1, Series 5, Keith Matthews Collection, MHA, MUN.
166 Head, *Eighteenth Century Newfoundland*, xiii. Emphasis is in the original.
167 Head, "The Changing Geography of Newfoundland," 51–2.
168 Head, "The Changing Geography," 293–4.
169 Head, *Eighteenth Century Newfoundland*, xii.
170 Head, *Eighteenth Century Newfoundland*, 244.
171 Story to Morgan, 9 April 1965, "Dean of Arts – History Dept. 1971," Box 3, ISER Files, President's Office.
172 Matthews, *Lectures on the History of Newfoundland*.
173 Matthews, "History," 448, 521–2, 603.
174 O'Flaherty, *The Rock Observed*; O'Flaherty, *Old Newfoundland*, 40–6.
175 Ryan, "The Newfoundland Cod Fishery; Ryan, *Fish Out of Water*.

176 For a perceptive commentary on its relevance to Newfoundland nationalism, see Bannister, "Whigs and Nationalists."
177 Lorenz, "History and Theory," 32–3.
178 For Premier Brian Peckford, the past was something that persisted and
   had to be overcome. See Peckford, *The Past in the Present*. For historian
   Patrick O'Flaherty Newfoundland's intellectual elite and its would-be
   political leaders let the country down during the 1930s and 40s. In their
   rush to get financial aid, they willfully forgot why Newfoundlanders had
   argued for representative government in 1832 and responsible government in 1855. They accepted a version of their history, created locally but
   sanctified by the 1933 Royal Commission, which saw only poverty in the
   past and projected no future for an independent Newfoundland. This,
   O'Flaherty argues, explains people's willing suspension of disbelief that
   allowed them to have faith in a British sense of fair play even as the UK
   government looked out for its own interests rather than being an honest umpire in the Confederation debates. It was something that we had
   forgotten at our peril. O'Flaherty, *Leaving the Past Behind*.

Chapter Three

1 Halpert convocation address, *Gazette*, 10 June 1987.
2 Story to Harold Paddock, n.d, 2.02.016, George Story Papers, Coll. 243,
   ASC, MUN.
3 Carpenter, *Many Voices*, 164.
4 Sadie Organ, University Librarian, to F.R. Emerson, 21 November 1957,
   Canada Council, 1957–1964, Seary Papers, ELRC, MUN.
5 Dorson, "Is Folklore a Discipline?"
6 Memories of who suggested Halpert's name to Seary varied. See George
   Story, 16 March 1970, C3909; E.R. Seary, 17 March 1970, C3911, Carole
   Henderson-Carpenter Collection, Accession 78–57, MUNFLA.
7 Halpert to Joan Hall, 8 April 1998, Herbert Halpert Papers, Department of
   Folklore, MUN.
8 Halpert to June Factor, 23 August 1983, Herbert Halpert Papers, Department of Folklore, MUN.
9 Herbert Halpert, interview with Carole Henderson-Carpenter, 24 March
   1970, C3967, 78–57, MUNFLA.
10 Kuper, "Anthropology," 360.
11 Bronner, *American Folklore Studies*, 74–80.
12 Bronner, *American Folklore Studies*, 108.

13 Halpert to James Boyd, 19 March 1973, Halpert Papers, Department of Folklore, MUN.
14 Herbert Halpert to Charles Perdue, 2 October 1984, Halpert Papers, Department of Folklore, MUN.
15 Halpert to Kenneth Goldstein, 7 February 1995, Halpert Papers, Department of Folklore, MUN.
16 Halpert, interview with Henderson-Carpenter, 24 March 1970, C3967, 78–57, MUNFLA.
17 Halpert, interview with Henderson-Carpenter, 24 March 1970, C3967, 78–57, MUNFLA.
18 Halpert, interview with Henderson-Carpenter, 25–7 March 1970, C3673, 78–57, MUNFLA.
19 Halpert, "Coming into Folklore," *Journal of American Folklore*.
20 Bronner, *American Folklore Studies*, 72–3.
21 Halpert, interview with Henderson-Carpenter, 24 March 1970, C3967, 78–57, MUNFLA.
22 Halpert, "Some Underdeveloped Areas," 229.
23 Halpert, "American Regional Folklore," 360.
24 Halpert, "American Regional Folklore," 359.
25 Halpert "Some Underdeveloped Areas," 229.
26 Halpert, "Breadth versus Depth."
27 Halpert, interview with Henderson-Carpenter, 25–7 March 1970, C3673, 78–57, MUNFLA.
28 Halpert to Maurice Mook, 11 April 1960, Halpert Papers, Department of Folklore, MUN.
29 Halpert to Angus Gillespie, 19 April 1979, Halpert Papers, Department of Folklore, MUN.
30 Halpert, interview with Henderson-Carpenter, 25–7 March 1970, C3673, 78–57, MUNFLA; Halpert to Richard Tallman, 8 May 1979, Halpert Papers, Department of Folklore, MUN.
31 Michael Taft, interview with the author, 28 March 2011.
32 Michael Denning, *The Cultural Front*, 79.
33 Bendix, *In Search of Authenticity*, 153.
34 Halpert, "Coming into Folklore," in *Folklore*, 3–22.
35 Halpert, "Some Underdeveloped Areas," 304.
36 Halpert, interview with Henderson-Carpenter, 25–7 March 1970, C3673, 78–57, MUNFLA.
37 Halpert, interview with Henderson-Carpenter, 25–7 March 1970, C3673, 78–57, MUNFLA.

38 Halpert, interview with Henderson-Carpenter, 25 March 1970, C3674, 78–57, MUNFLA.
39 Halpert, interview with Henderson-Carpenter, 25–7 March 1970, C3673, 78–57, MUNFLA.
40 Neil Rosenberg, email correspondence, 15 November 2011.
41 Halpert, interview with Henderson-Carpenter, 25 March 1970, C3674, 78–57, MUNFLA.
42 Halpert convocation address, *Gazette*, 10 June 1987.
43 Michael Taft, interview with the author, 28 March 2011.
44 John Szwed, interview with the author, 16 March 2011.
45 Herbert Halpert, "Folklore and Newfoundland," 15.
46 Sandra Martin, "Violetta Halpert," *Globe and Mail*, 5 June 2009. For an example of her work in the library, see "A Report on Acquisitions of the MUN Library in support of special research in language, dialect and folklore, 1964–65 and 1965–66," Canada Council, 1965–67, PO 26, President's Office, MUN.
47 Halpert, "Folklore and Newfoundland,"17.
48 Halpert, "Folklore and Newfoundland," 18.
49 Halpert, "Folklore and Newfoundland," 19.
50 Halpert, "Folklore and Newfoundland,"18.
51 Herbert Halpert and Neil V. Rosenberg, "Folklore Studies as Memorial University: Two Reports," St John's: Department of Folklore, 1978.
52 Halpert, "Folklore and Newfoundland," 18.
53 G.M. Story, "Newfoundland Dialect Studies: Progress Report 1963," 22 December 1963, file 1963, *DNE* files, ELRC, MUN.
54 Widdowson to Faris, n.d. ca. 1964, James Faris Papers, ASC, MUN.
55 Widdowson to Faris, 23 June 1964, James Faris Papers, ASC, MUN.
56 Story to Patrick O'Flaherty, 11 December 1962, George Story Papers, 2.01.014, ASC, MUN.
57 Les Harris, interview with Carole Henderson-Carpenter, 25 March 1970, C3908, 78–57, MUNFLA.
58 Halpert, interview with Henderson-Carpenter, 25–7 March 1970, C3673, 78–57, MUNFLA.
59 Halpert, interview with Henderson-Carpenter, 25–7 March 1970, C3673, 78–57, MUNFLA.
60 John Widdowson, interview with the author, 16 July 2012.
61 Halpert, interview with Henderson-Carpenter, 25–7 March 1970, C3673, 78–57, MUNFLA.
62 John Widdowson, interview, 13 July 2011.
63 Earle to Widdowson, 28 March 1964, 2.01.057, Fred Earle Papers, ASC, MUN.
64 Widdowson to Earle, 2 April 1964, 2.01.155, Fred Earle Papers, ASC, MUN.

65 Widdowson to Earle, 8 April 1964; Widdowson to Earle, 22 May 1964, 2.01.157, Fred Earle Papers, ASC, MUN.
66 Earle to Widdowson, 25 May 1964; Earle to Widdowson, 2 June 1964; 30 June 1964, 2.01.157, Fred Earle Papers, ASC, MUN.
67 Widdowson to Earle, 25 June 1964, 2.01.157, Fred Earle Papers, ASC, MUN.
68 Widdowson to Earle, 11 September 1967, 2.01.157, Fred Earle Papers, ASC, MUN.
69 Widdowson to Earle, 3 June 1968, 2.01.157, Fred Earle Papers, ASC, MUN.
70 Halpert to Earle, 23 October 1968, 2.01.062, Fred Earle Papers, ASC, MUN.
71 Widdowson to Earle, 22 July 1965, 2.01.157, Fred Earle Papers, ASC, MUN.
72 John Widdowson, interview, 13 July 2011.
73 John Widdowson, interview, 13 July 2011.
74 Firestone to Whitaker, 9 January 1963, Firestone, ISER, President's Office, MUN.
75 Firestone, "Sephardic Folk-Curing in Seattle."
76 Halpert and Story, *Christmas Mumming in Newfoundland*, v.
77 Memorial paid the production costs and got 70% of the revenue, and committees at Memorial did all the editorial selection, while UTP handled the book design, the printing, and the distribution. Francis Halpenney, UTP, to Seary, 4 January 1965, Toronto Press, 1964–1973, Seary Papers, ELRC, MUN.
78 For a detailed description of one of the interviews, see Halpert and Widdowson, *Folktales of Newfoundland*, vol. 1, xxxix–xliv.
79 Halpert to Seary, 20 April 1965, Canada Council, Seary Papers, ELRC, MUN.
80 Halpert to Seary, 20 April 1965, Canada Council, Seary Papers, ELRC, MUN.
81 Halpert to Seary, 20 April 1965, Canada Council, Seary Papers, ELRC, MUN.
82 Halpert to Seary, 20 April 1965, Canada Council, Seary Papers, ELRC, MUN.
83 Sharpe and O'Dea in Macpherson, *Four Centuries and the City*.
84 Guigné, *Folksongs and Folk Revival*.
85 Overton, "Sparking a Cultural Revolution."
86 Halpert to Seary, 15 April 1966, Canada Council, Seary Papers, ELRC, MUN. Halpert encouraged Harris to write a book based on the riddles he remembered and the social context in which they were told. It culminated in Leslie Harris's *Growing Up with Verse*, an autobiography of his childhood that included poetry from oral tradition and literature.
87 Halpert and Widdowson, *Folktales of Newfoundland*, vol. 1, xxiv.

88 Halpert to Seary, 15 April 1966, Canada Council, Seary Papers, ELRC, MUN.

89 Report on field trip in dialect and folklore made to the Bonavista Bay, Notre Dame Bay, and Green Bay Areas by J.D.A. Widdowson, August 10–22 1965, Canada Council 1965–67, PO 26, President's Office, MUN.

90 Halpert to Seary, 15 April 1966, Canada Council, Seary Papers, ELRC, MUN.

91 Farley Mowat to Smallwood, "Some Unsolicited Suggestions on How to Start a Cultural Revolution in Newfoundland," 10 March 1966, 3.05.006, Smallwood Collection, ASC, MUN.

92 Mowat to Smallwood, "Some Unsolicited Suggestions."

93 Pocius, "The Mummers Song," 61.

94 Halpert to Don Yoder, 27 January 1967, Halpert Papers, Department of Folklore, MUN.

95 Halpert to Yoder, 27 January 1967, Halpert Papers, Department of Folklore, MUN.

96 Story and Halpert to Widdowson, 25 November 1969, 1969, *DNE* files, ELRC, MUN.

97 Halpert to Austin Fife, 12 October 1967, Halpert Papers, Folklore Department, MUN.

98 Halpert and Rosenberg, "Folklore Studies as Memorial University," 4.

99 Lovelace and Narváez, "Neil V. Rosenberg: Odyssey of a Folklorist," in Lovelace, Narváez, and Tye, *Bean Blossom to Bannerman*, 1–15.

100 Story to Kirwin "MUNFLA and its *Critical* Use," 1978, Canada Council file, Seary Papers, ELRC, MUN.

101 Story to Kirwin "MUNFLA and its *Critical* Use," 1978, Canada Council file, Seary Papers, ELRC, MUN.

102 Halpert, interview with Henderson-Carpenter, 25 March 1970, C3674, 78–57, MUNFLA.

103 Annual Report, Department of Folklore, 1969–70, 26 November 1970, Dean of Arts and Science, Reports – Departmental 1966–67 file, Box 2, President's Office, MUN.

104 Halpert and Story, *Christmas Mumming*, 3.

105 Halpert, "A Typology of Mumming," in Halpert and Story, *Christmas Mumming*, 61.

106 Melvin M. Firestone, "Mummers and Strangers," 73.

107 Firestone to Whitaker, 20 January 1961, Firestone, ISER, President's Office, MUN.

108 Firestone, "Mummers and Strangers," 73.

109 Firestone, "Mummers and Strangers," 73n10.

110 Melvin Firestone, interview with the author, 13 March 2012.
111 Louis J. Chiaramonte, "Mumming in 'Deep Harbour': Aspects of Social Organization in Mumming and Drinking," in *Christmas Mumming* by Halpert and Story, 82.
112 Szwed, "The Mask of Friendship."
113 James C. Faris, "Mumming in an Outport Fishing Settlement: A Description and Suggestions on the Cognitive Complex," in *Christmas Mumming* by Halpert and Story, 129.
114 J.D.A. Widdowson and Herbert Halpert, "The Disguises of Newfoundland Mummers," 147–64; G.M. Story, "Mummers in Newfoundland History: A Survey of the Printed Record," 167–85; Herbert Halpert and G.M. Story, "Newfoundland Mummers' Plays: Three Printed Texts," 187–207, in *Christmas Mumming* by Halpert and Story.
115 *Daily News*, 28 April 1970; Ray Guy, *Evening Telegram*, 25 April 1969, 5.06.004, George Story Papers, Coll. 243, ASC, MUN.
116 Cyril Poole to Les Harris, 3 December 1973, Harris Papers, ASC, MUN.
117 W. Edson Richmond, *Journal of American Folklore* 84 (April–June 1971): 255–256, 5.06.004, George Story Papers, ASC, MUN.
118 Pocius, "The Mummers Song," 59–60.
119 Story and Halpert to Widdowson, 25 November 1969, file 1969, *DNE* files, ELRC, MUN.
120 Story to Widdowson, 2 February 1970, file 1970, *DNE* files, ELRC, MUN.
121 Story to Widdowson, 16 May 1973, *DNE* files, ELRC, MUN.
122 Widdowson to Story, 17 July 1970, file 1970, *DNE* files, ELRC, MUN.
123 Widdowson to Story, 12 March 1970, file 1970, *DNE* files, ELRC, MUN.
124 Larry Youther to Story and Kirwin, 5 August 1971, file 1971, *DNE* files, ELRC, MUN.
125 Story to Youther, 28 July 1971, file 1971, *DNE* files, ELRC, MUN.
126 Harris, interview with Henderson-Carpenter, 25 March 1970, C3908, 78–57, MUNFLA.
127 Widdowson to F.A. Aldrich, 5 February 1973, file 1973, *DNE* files, ELRC, MUN.
128 Printed version of Story address upon being accepted as fellow of the Royal Society, 5.10.003, George Story Papers, ASC, MUN.
129 Klinck, *Literary History of Canada*.
130 George Story, "Notes from a Berry Patch," in his *People of the Landwash*, 105.
131 Story, "Notes from a Berry Patch," 107.
132 Phil Warren to Story, 19 July 1973; Bill Rowe to Story, 13 July 1973, 5.10.001, George Story Papers, ASC, MUN.
133 Stephen Taylor, 17 July 73, 5.10.001, George Story Papers, ASC, MUN.

134 F.G. Cassidy to Story, 25 July 1973, file 1973, *DNE* files, ELRC, MUN.
135 President's Report 1973–17, Folklore Department, Annual Report file, Box 12, President's Office, MUN.
136 Peter Narváez, interview with the author, 29 April 2011; Rosenberg, "Introduction," ix–xxi; Narváez, "The Protest Songs."
137 Meeting of archives committee of MUNFLA, 28 September 1974, file 1974, *DNE* files, ELRC, MUN.
138 Halpert to Carl-Herman Tillhagen, 30 August 1975, Halpert Papers, Department of Folklore, MUN.
139 Gerald Sider, interview with the author, 27 June 2011.
140 Gerald Sider, interview with the author, 27 June 2011.
141 Sider, "Christmas Mumming."
142 Bill [Kirwin] to Story, 21 February 1987, 5.06.009, George Story Papers, Coll. 243, ASC, MUN.
143 Gerald Sider, interview with the author, 27 June 2011; Pocius, "The Mummers Song," 60–1.
144 Sider, "The Ties That Bind."
145 For critiques of Sider, see the roundtable response to his book: Hiller, Narváez, and Vickers, "Newfoundland Past as Marxist Illustration."
146 Story to Andrew Fuller, the City University of New York, 28 March 1983, 2.02.018, George Story Papers, ASC, MUN.
147 Breslau, "Sociology of Science."
148 Brookes, *A Public Nuisance*, 10–11.
149 Brookes, *A Public Nuisance*, 17.
150 Pocius, "The Mummers Song," 63–4.
151 Pocius, "The Mummers Song," 63–4, 76.
152 Sider, "Christmas Mumming," 125.
153 McKay, *Quest of the Folk*; McKay and Bates, *In the Province of History*.
154 Michael Taft interview with the author, 28 March 2011; I. Sheldon Posen and Michael Taft, "The Newfoundland Popular Music Project," *Canadian Journal for Traditional Music* (1973).
155 Michael Taft, interview with the author, 28 March 2011.
156 Doucette, "Voices Not Our Own," 128.
157 Widdowson to Story, 27 October 1977, *DNE* files, ELRC, MUN.
158 Widdowson to Story, 27 September 1978, *DNE* files, ELRC, MUN.
159 Widdowson to Story, 4 January 1979, *DNE* files, ELRC, MUN.
160 Widdowson to Story, 5 January 1979, *DNE* files, ELRC, MUN.
161 Widdowson to Story, 5 January 1979, *DNE* files, ELRC, MUN.
162 Lovelace and Narváez, "Rosenberg," 16–17.
163 Dorson, *Folklore and Fakelore*.

164 Bendix, *In Search of Authenticity*, 153–8.
165 Halpert and Widdowson, *Folktales of Newfoundland*, vol. 1, liv.
166 Halpert and Widdowson, *Folktales of Newfoundland*, vol. 1, xxviii.
167 Halpert and Widdowson, *Folktales of Newfoundland*, vol. 1, lxxxviii.
168 Halpert and Widdowson, *Folktales of Newfoundland*, vol. 1, xxviii.
169 Halpert and Widdowson, *Folktales of Newfoundland*, vol. 1, lxxxix.
170 Halpert to Carl-Herman Tillhagen, 5 May 1975, Halpert Papers, Folklore Department, MUN.
171 Halpert to Carl Lindahl, 25 September 1996, Halpert Papers, Folklore Department, MUN.

Chapter Four

1 Les Harris, "Remarks ISER 25th Anniversary," Harris Papers, ASC, MUN.
2 Morgan to L. Bradbury, Department of Fisheries, 30 June 1961, Enclosure: "Institute of Social and Economic Research at the Memorial University of Newfoundland," Dept. of Fisheries file, ISER, President's Office, MUN.
3 Whitaker to Don Martindale, 31 January 1961, Philbrook file, ISER, President's Office, MUN.
4 Whitaker to Jack Goody, 1 October 1963, Faris file, ISER, President's Office, MUN.
5 Whitaker to Faris, 4 September 1963, ISER, President's Office, MUN.
6 Brought up in Blackpool, England, Mars left school at the age of 16 and worked at a series of temporary jobs before doing his national service in the RAF. Night school and then university, during which he wrote a thesis on the fairground at which he had worked, earned him a place at Cambridge. He studied anthropology and economics and took up the ISER fellowship to work on longshoremen. He used that research as the basis of a PhD at the London School of Economics. www.theasa.org/networks/apply/profiles. Accessed 16 June 2012.
7 Minutes of meeting of Governing Committee, 24 January 1962, 3.09.058, Smallwood Collection, ASC, MUN.
8 Harris, "Chairman's Report," 1. Emphasis is in the original.
9 Martindale to Whitaker, 11 March 1961, Philbrook, ISER, President's Office, MUN.
10 Martindale to Morgan, as cited in Melvin Baker, "The Establishment of Memorial's Institute," M.O. Morgan, "Remarks of the 30th Anniversary of ISER," in *Special Anniversary Edition*, ISER Research and Policy Papers no. 15 (1992), 39.
11 Halpert and Story, *Christmas Mumming*, 4.

376 Notes to pages 204–10

12 First meeting of Advisory Council, 10 February 1962, 3.09.058, Smallwood Collection, ASC, MUN.
13 Kuklick, "The British Tradition," 63.
14 Kuper, "Anthropology," 371.
15 Steinmetz, "A Child of the Empire."
16 Whitaker, "Core Values," 78.
17 Whitaker, "Core Values," 78.
18 Whitaker to Philbrook, 16 February 1961, Philbrook, ISER, President's Office, MUN.
19 Whitaker to Morgan, 11 May 1961, Philbrook, ISER, President's Office, MUN.
20 Philbrook to Whitaker, 20 November 1961, Philbrook, ISER, President's Office, MUN.
21 Philbrook to Whitaker, 19 April 1962, Philbrook, ISER, President's Office, MUN.
22 Whitaker to Firestone, 7 May 1963, Firestone, ISER, President's Office, MUN.
23 "Shemul Ben-Dor," 3.05.012, Smallwood Papers, ASC, MUN.
24 Whitaker to Ben-Dor, 28 February 1962, Ben-Dor, ISER, President's Office, MUN.
25 Ben-Dor to Whitaker, 23 October 1962, Ben-Dor, ISER, President's Office, MUN.
26 Chiaramonte to Whitaker, 22 January 1962, Chiaramonte, ISER, President's Office, MUN.
27 "Louis J Chiaramonte," 3.05.012, Smallwood Papers, ASC, MUN.
28 Whitaker to Chiaramonte, 28 February 1962, Chiaramonte, ISER, President's Offic, MUN.
29 Whitaker to Chiaramonte, 1 November 1962, Chiaramonte, ISER, President's Office, MUN.
30 Chiaramonte to Conrad Arensberg, Columbia University, 10 March 1963, Chiaramonte, ISER, President's Office, MUN.
31 Chiaramonte to Whitaker, 10 January 1963, Chiaramonte, ISER, President's Office, MUN.
32 Whitaker to Arensberg, 13 March 1963, Chiaramonte, ISER, President's Office, MUN.
33 Chiaramonte to Arensberg, 10 March 1963, Chiaramonte, ISER, President's Office, MUN.
34 Whitaker to Arensberg, 13 August 1963, Chiaramonte, ISER, President's Office, MUN.
35 Chiaramonte, *Craftsman-Client Contracts*, preface.

36 Whitaker to Goody, 8 February 1962, Mars, ISER, President's Office, MUN.
37 Gerald Mars, interview with the author, 9 October 2012.
38 "Gerald Mars," Mars, ISER, President's Office, MUN.
39 Whitaker to Goody, 21 March 1962, Mars, ISER, President's Office, MUN.
40 Gerald Mars, "An Anthropological Study," A1/9–10.
41 Whitaker to William Breen, 21 March 1962, Mars, ISER, President's Office, MUN.
42 Mars, "An Anthropological Study," A1/12–13.
43 Gerald Mars, interview with the author, 9 October 2012.
44 Mars, "An Anthropological Study,"A1/14–18.
45 Mars, "An Anthropological Study," A1/18–19.
46 Whitaker to Mars, 1 February 1964, Mars, ISER, President's Office, MUN.
47 Raymond Firth to Ian Whitaker, 4 March 1964, Mars, President's Office, MUN.
48 Born in 1938, Sharon earned a BA in Spanish and an MA in library science from the University of Washington, and during her second year in the province was employed for a while at Memorial's library. Later, she received an MA and a PhD in history at Arizona State University, having written on the history of women in Savage Cove. Obituary: Arizona State University, http://asura.asu.edu/obitsEF. Accessed 3 February 2013. See Firestone, "To Plant with Women."
49 Firestone to Whitaker, 10 October 1963, Firestone, ISER, President's Office, MUN.
50 Melvin Firestone, interview with the author, 13 March 2012.
51 Whitaker to Watson, 3 June 1964, Firestone, ISER, President's Office, MUN.
52 Whitaker to Watson, 3 June 1964, Firestone, ISER, President's Office, MUN.
53 Melvin Firestone, interview with the author, 13 March 2012.
54 Junek, *Isolated Communities*.
55 Firestone, *Brothers and Rivals*, 85.
56 Melvin Firestone, interview with the author, 13 March 2012.
57 "John F Szwed," 3.05.012, Smallwood Papers, ASC, MUN.
58 Szwed, *Private Cultures*, 11.
59 Tom Nemec, interview with the author, 15 April 2011.
60 James Faris, interview with the author, 9 March 2012.
61 Goody to Whitaker, 8 October 1963, Faris file, ISER, President's Office, MUN.
62 Faris to Whitaker, 27 August 1963, Faris file, ISER, President's Office, MUN.

63 Whittaker to Faris, 12 August 1963, Faris file, ISER, President's Office, MUN.
64 Faris to Whitaker, 13 February 1964, Faris file, ISER, President's Office, MUN.
65 James Faris, interview with the author, 9 March 2012; Faris to Alex Wheaton, 22 January 1964, asking for help finding a house in Fredericton, NL, Faris Papers, ASC; Faris to Whitaker, 13 February 1964, Faris file, ISER, President's Office, MUN.
66 Faris to Jack, Marion and family, 28 November 1965, Faris Papers, ASC, MUN.
67 Head, *Community Geographical Surveys*, 78.
68 Faris to Webb, email correspondence, 25 May 2012.
69 Faris to Webb, email correspondence, 25 May 2012.
70 Faris to Whitaker, 13 February 1964, Faris file, ISER, President's Office, MUN.
71 Faris to Allan Williams, 15 February 1964, Faris Papers, ASC, MUN.
72 Faris to Szwed, 2 February 1965, Faris Papers, ASC, MUN.
73 Faris to Szwed, 2 February 1965, Faris Papers, ASC, MUN.
74 Faris notes, 27 August 1967, 662, Faris Papers, ASC, MUN.
75 Faris to Whitaker, 27 August 1963, Faris file, ISER, President's Office, MUN.
76 Faris field notes, 10 April 1964, 206, Faris Papers, ASC, MUN.
77 Faris, interview with the author, 9 March 2012.
78 Faris to Webb, email correspondence, 17 March 2012.
79 Faris field notes, 15 December 1964, 980, Faris Papers, ASC, MUN.
80 Faris field notes, 26 March 1964, 132, Faris Papers, ASC, MUN.
81 Faris field notes, 15 May 1964, 377, Faris Papers, ASC, MUN.
82 Faris field notes, 9 June 1964, 458–9, Faris Papers, ASC, MUN.
83 Faris field notes, 9 June 1964, 458, Faris Papers, ASC, MUN.
84 Faris, interview, 9 March 2012.
85 Faris, interview, 9 March 2012.
86 Faris, interview, 9 March 2012.
87 Faris to Colin Story, 8 June 1964, Faris Papers, ASC, MUN.
88 Tom Nemec, "A Multi-Disciplinary Approach to the Reconstruction of the History and Culture of Rural Populations: A Newfoundland Example," paper presented to the second annual conference of the Canadian Aural/Oral History Association, St John's.
89 Faris, interview, 9 March 2012.
90 George Story to Colin Story, 30 June 1965, 3.16.124, Smallwood Collection, ASC, MUN.

91 Robert Paine to George Story, 8 July 1965, 2.01.15, George Story Papers, ASC, MUN.

92 Chiaramonte to Paine, 23 August 1965, Chiaramonte, ISER, President's Office, MUN.

93 Cohen, "The Anthropology of Proximate Cultures," 217.

94 Paine, "By Chance By Choice," 147.

95 Draft letter from Story to Paine, n.d., 2.01.15, George Story Papers, ASC, MUN.

96 Alan Macpherson, interview with the author, 15 November 2010.

97 Gerald Mars, interview with the author, 9 October 2012.

98 MacKay, "The Problem of Newfoundland," in MacKay, *Newfoundland*, 38.

99 Harris, "Chairman's Report," 1.

100 Harris, "Chairman's Report," 1.

101 The colloquium, titled The Comparative Sociology of Friendship, was held 6–8 March 1969. Participants from universities other than Memorial came from Columbia, Bergen, Harvard, North Carolina, Clairmont, Sorbonne, Bristol, British Columbia, Cornell, and Rutgers. See Robert Paine, "Colloquia," in his *Third Report* (1971), 37–8.

102 Melvin Firestone, interview with the author, 13 March 2012.

103 Faris, *Cat Harbour*, 1–4.

104 Faris, *Cat Harbour*, 22. Head and Matthews's work, which questioned the role at the supposed illegality of settlement and suggested other factors that were responsible for the settlement pattern, was unavailable to Faris at the time he was writing.

105 Faris to Harris, 28 November 1964, Faris Papers, ASC, MUN.

106 L. Harris to Faris, 16 December 1964; Rothney to Faris, 17 December 1964, Faris Papers, ASC, MUN.

107 Nemshi Crewe to Faris, 3 December 1964, Faris Papers, ASC, MUN.

108 Faris, *Cat Harbour*, 100.

109 Faris, *Cat Harbour*, 64.

110 *DNE*, 2nd ed., 128.

111 Kirwin to Paine, 4 January 1977, Kirwin Papers, ELRC, MUN. These definitions of *buck* and *scoff* are taken from *DNE*, 2nd ed., 70–1, 438–9.

112 Chiaramonte to Whitaker, 19 November 1962, Chiaramonte, ISER, President's Office, MUN.

113 Szwed to Whitaker, 22 October 1962, Szwed, ISER files, President's Office, MUN.

114 Melvin Firestone, interview with the author, 13 March 2012.

115 Faris to George and Aunt Ida, 5 December 1965, Faris Papers, ASC, MUN.

116　Faris to Jack, Marion, and family, 28 November 1965, Faris Papers, ASC, MUN.
117　Faris to M.O. Morgan, 15 November 1965, Faris file, ISER, President's Office, MUN.
118　Faris to Paine, 16 March 1966, Faris file, ISER, President's Office, MUN.
119　Nadia Robbins to Faris, 4 November 1972, Faris Papers, ASC, MUN.
120　"Life in a Rural Fishing Community: 'You Can Never Tell about Strangers,'" *Evening Telegram*, 24 February 1967, 14.
121　Faris to Paine, 15 June 1972, Faris Papers, ACS, MUN.
122　Widdowson to F.A. Aldrich, 5 February 1973, *DNE* files, ELRC, MUN.
123　Ray Guy, "Enough's, Enough," *Evening Telegram*, 1 February, 1968, 1.
124　Nadia [Robbins] to Faris, 11 December 1965, Faris Papers, ASC, MUN.
125　Faris to Jack, Marion, and kids, 19 October 1972, Faris Papers, ASC, MUN.
126　Faris to Hellen Hantler [Ellen Antler], 23 June 1972, Faris Papers, ASC, MUN.
127　Ross, *The Origins of American Social Science*, 254.
128　Wright, *A Fishery for Modern Times*, 3–4.
129　Philbrook, *Fisherman, Logger, Merchant, Miner*, 1.
130　Melvin Firestone, interview with the author, 13 March 2012.
131　Gerald Mars, interview with the author, 9 October 2012.
132　John Szwed, interview with the author, 16 March 2011.
133　Melvin Firestone, interview with the author, 13 March 2012.
134　Whitaker to James Watson, 18 October 1963, Firestone file, ISER, President's Office, MUN.
135　Cohen, "The Anthropology of Proximate Cultures," 214–15.
136　Whitaker, "Core Values," 78–9.
137　Whitaker to Faris, 4 September 1963, ISER, President's Office, MUN.
138　Chiaramonte to Arensberg, 10 March 1963, Chiaramonte, ISER, President's Office, MUN.
139　Chiaramonte to Arensberg, 10 March 1963, Chiaramonte, ISER, President's Office, MUN.
140　Chiaramonte to Paine, 23 August 1965, Chiaramonte, ISER, President's Office, MUN.

Chapter Five

1　Mannion, introduction, *The Peopling of Newfoundland*, 1.
2　O'Flaherty, "Looking Backwards," 150.

3 Peter Pope, personal communication, 18 September 2013; Pope, *The Many Landfalls of John Cabot*, 70–1.

4 Richard Whitbourne, *A Discourse and Discovery of Newfoundland* (London: Felix Kingston, 1612). Another example would be William Vaughan, *The Newlanders Cure* (London: N.O. for F. Constable, 1630).

5 Alexander, "Newfoundland's Traditional Economy," 17.

6 An exception would be William Gilbert Gosling, *Labrador: Its Discovery, Exploration and Development* (Musson, 1910).

7 W.E. Cormack, *Narrative of a Journey across the Island of Newfoundland* (St John's: 1873).

8 His name is generally rendered as "Joe Sylvester," although this was likely a reversal of his Christian and surnames since "Sylvester" is unknown as a surname among the Mi'kmaq. See Hewson, "Joe, Sylvester."

9 Howley, *Geography of Newfoundland*.

10 Howley, *The Beothucks or Red Indians*.

11 Gordon Handcock, interview with the author, 10 December 2013.

12 Perret, *La Géographie de Terre-Neuve*.

13 Bassler, *Vikings to U-boats*, 193–9. The quotation appears on page 200.

14 See, for example: J.B. Jutes, *Excursions in and about Newfoundland during the years 1839 and 1840* (London: John Murray, 1842); Richard Henry Bonnycastle, *Newfoundland in 1842* (London: Colburn, 1842).

15 Newfoundland settlers lived on the coast and knew little of the interior of the county, wrote Rogers, it was like a "husk without a kernel." Rogers, *Historical Geography*, 59.

16 Prowse, *Cartological Material*; Pope, *The Many Landfalls of John Cabot*.

17 *DNE*, 1st ed., 116.

18 Howley, *Geography*, viii.

19 Gordon Handcock, interview with the author, 10 December 2013.

20 Macpherson, "The Early Development of Geography."

21 Robic, "Geography."

22 Story, "The View from the Sea," 1–2.

23 Seary, "Regional Humanism," 14.

24 Unsigned Memo, "Toponymy of Newfoundland," 1955, *DNE* files, ELRC, MUN.

25 E.R. Seary, interview with Carole Henderson-Carpenter, 17 March 1970, C3911, 78–57, MUNFLA.

26 Les Harris, interview with Carole Henderson-Carpenter, 25 March 1970, C3908, 78–57, MUNFLA.

27 Harris, interview with Henderson-Carpenter, 25 March 1970, C3908, 78–57, MUNFLA.

28 Harris, interview with Henderson-Carpenter, 25 March 1970, C3908, 78–57, MUNFLA.
29 Gordon Handcock, interview with the author, 10 December 2013.
30 Story, "The View from the Sea," 5–7.
31 Seary, *Place Names of the Avalon Peninsula*.
32 Seary, with Sheila Lynch, *Family Names of the Island of Newfoundland*.
33 Macpherson, "The Early Development of Geography."
34 Macpherson, "The Early Development of Geography."
35 Summers, *Geography of Newfoundland*.
36 *Department of Geography Annual Report 1965–66*, Departmental Reports, Box 1, Dean of Arts and Science, President's Office, MUN.
37 Alvin Hamilton to W.T. Keough, 31 January 1963, 3.16.123, Smallwood Collection, ASC, MUN.
38 "ARDA's Proposed Role," 7.01.009, Edward Roberts Collection, ASC, MUN.
39 Federal-Provincial Rural Rehabilitation and Development Agreement: Background Notes and Comments Regarding the Proposed Agreement, October 8 1964, pp. 6–7, 7.01.007, Edward Robert Collection, ASC, MUN.
40 Untitled document, 4 March 1965, 7.01.009, Roberts Collection, ASC, MUN.
41 The geographer Grant Head believed that Jack Pickersgill had arranged for some of the money, which had been earmarked for agricultural development under the program, to be directed to research. It's possible that Pickersgill had a role in ensuring federal funds for research. He had been a senior civil servant in Ottawa and a Smallwood ally before Newfoundland had joined Canada, and the premier had helped him get elected as the member of Parliament for Bonavista-Twillingate. He served in that position from 1953 to 1967. Pickersgill was in the cabinets of both Prime Ministers Louis St Laurent and Lester Pearson and was well positioned to serve as Smallwood's conduit to influence and money in the federal government. On the other hand, the act did provide for social and economic research into rural areas, and I have not seen any corroborating evidence that Pickersgill intervened.
42 The federal government was aware that there were many small farmers in Canada who worked on marginal land and hoped to find a way of improving their income by better use of land and forming more economically viable units. See Hamilton to Smallwood, 30 March 1961, 3.01.003, Smallwood Collection, ASC, MUN.
43 Training Course for Newfoundland Government ARDA Fieldmen, 1 February to 30 April, 3.16.123, Smallwood Collection, ASC, MUN.

44 Training Scheme for ARDA Rural Development Officers, 16 November 1964 to 16 April 1965, 3.16.123, Smallwood Collection, ASC, MUN.

45 Smallwood, "For information," 13 May 1965, 3.16.123, Smallwood Collection, ASC, MUN.

46 Alan Williams, *Land Use Surveys*, 110.

47 C. Grant Head, interview with the author, 3 November 2011. Head, *Community Geographical Surveys*.

48 C. Grant Head, interview with the author, 3 November 2011.

49 The Canadian-born Andrew H. Clarke, after a BA at McMaster, had worked with Harold Innis at Toronto, which encouraged his interest in historical geography, and studied at Berkeley with Carl Sauer. Turning his attention back to PEI and Nova Scotia, during the period that Head worked with him, Clarke stressed the "transference of agricultural and pastoral patterns" across the Atlantic. Wynn, "Geographical Writing on the Canadian Past," 101, 108–9.

50 C. Grant Head, interview with the author, 3 November 2011. Head, "The Changing Geography of Newfoundland."

51 Head, *Eighteenth Century Newfoundland*, 20–1, 35, 66–7.

52 Head, *Eighteenth Century Newfoundland*, 94.

53 C. Grant Head, interview with the author, 3 November 2011.

54 Head, *Eighteenth Century Newfoundland*, 111–37.

55 Harris, "A Life between Geography and History."

56 John Mannion, interview with Carole Henderson-Carpenter, 23 March 1970, C3968, 78–57, MUNFLA.

57 Mannion, *Irish Settlements in Eastern Canada*.

58 Williams, *John Guy of Bristol*.

59 Williams, *John Guy of Bristol*, xii–xiv.

60 Department of Geography to Dean of Arts and Science, 15 December 1966, Dean of Arts and Science, Box 1, President's Office, MUN.

61 "Fisheries Research Centre Proposal," "North-West Atlantic Fisheries Research Project," Departments – Plans and Proposals, 1967–68, Box 1, Dean of Arts and Science, President's Office, MUN.

62 Alan Macpherson, interview with the author, 15 November 2010.

63 Michael Staveley, "Migration and Mobility in Newfoundland and Labrador: A Study in Population Geography," PhD thesis, University of Alberta, 1973.

64 Alan Macpherson, interview with the author, 15 November 2010.

65 Chesley Sanger, "Technological and Spacial Adaptation in the Newfoundland Seal Fishery During the Nineteenth Century," MA thesis, Memorial University 1973.

66 Gordon Handcock, interview with the author, 10 December 2013.

67 Handcock, *Soe longe as there comes noe women*, 9–11.

68 Sharpe and O'Dea, "Heritage Conservation in the City of St John's," 159–61.

69 Mannion, *The Peopling of Newfoundland*.

70 Graeme Wynn, "'As We Discover We Remember; Remembering, We Discover': Placing the MUN School of Historical Geography," unpublished lecture, 24 September 2010.

71 Mannion, *The Peopling of Newfoundland*, 12.

72 Wynn, "As We Discover We Remember."

73 Piternick, "The Historical Atlas of Canada."

74 Cole Harris to Gordon Handcock, 20 August 1987, Geography 1987, Geography Box, Dean of Arts, President's Office, MUN.

75 Not everyone was impressed. See Pierson, "A Diatribe."

76 Piternick, "The Historical Atlas of Canada."

77 Wynn, "As We Discover We Remember."

78 Wynn, "As We Discover We Remember."

79 Wynn, "Geographical Writing on the Canadian Past," 112.

80 C. Grant Head, interview with the author, 3 November 2011.

81 Pocius, *A Place to Belong*.

82 In 1975 Staveley chaired a sub-committee of the university's Advisory Committee on Newfoundland Studies. "Report of the sub-committee on a Proposed Programme of Newfoundland Studies," 27 February 1975, VPA Advisory Committee on Newfoundland Studies file, 1974 – 1976, Box C-6, President's Office, MUN.

83 Harris, "A Life between Geography and History," 437.

84 Wynn, "Geographical Writing on the Canadian Past," 107.

85 Frickel and Gross, "A General Theory," 219.

Chapter Six

1 Ian Whitaker, "Research Fellowships in Sociology and Anthropology," Firestone, ISER, President's Office, MUN.

2 Ralph Matthews, interview with the author, 31 August 2014.

3 Smallwood, "What Is Liberalism?"

4 Gwyn, *Smallwood*, 130–1.

5 Raymond W. Miller, "Preliminary Report on Extension," 30 January 1953, 8, Box 3, Extension Service Records, Archives and Special Collections (ASC), QEII Library, MUN.

6 Gwyn, *Smallwood*, 309.

7 Johnston, "Government and University," 228, 241–7.
8 S.J. Colman, "Memorial University of Newfoundland Extension Service," 27 July 1960, 10.03.002, Alain Frecker Papers, ASC, MUN.
9 Colman, "Memorial University," 27 July 1960, 10.03.002, Alain Frecker Papers, ASC, MUN.
10 Colman, "Memorial University," 27 July 1960, 10.03.002, Alain Frecker Papers, ASC, MUN.
11 S.J. Colman, "Memorial University of Newfoundland Extension Service," 3 May 1960. Copy sent to Joseph Smallwood by Colman, 9 May 1960, 3.09.035, Smallwood Papers. ASC, MUN.
12 Colman, "Memorial University of Newfoundland Extension Service," 3 May 1960, 3.09.035, Smallwood Papers, ASC, MUN.
13 "University's Extension Program Being Arranged," *Evening Telegram*, 4 August 1960, 4.
14 Biographic note, Julia Morgan Papers, Coll. 211, ASC, MUN.
15 "MUN Extension Man to Visit West Coast," *Evening Telegram*, 20 June 1961, 2.
16 S.J. Colman to Fred Earle, 10 January 1964, 2.01.027, Fred Earle Papers, ASC, MUN.
17 George Lee, interview with the author, 20 September 2010.
18 Latham, "Modernization," 724.
19 Shore, *The Science of Social Redemption*, 93.
20 Latham, "Modernization," 727.
21 Blake, *Canadians at Last*; Wright, *A Fishery for Modern Times*.
22 Riggins, "Memorial University's First Sociologist," 47–60.
23 Donald Willmott to William G. Skinner, October 1956, as quoted in Riggins, "Memorial University's First Sociologist," 61.
24 Willmott as quoted in Riggins, "Memorial University's First Sociologist," 69.
25 Neis, "The Uneasy Marriage," 322–3.
26 Overton, "With Their Rubber Boots On."
27 Alexander Brady, commentary in "Needs and Opportunities for Economic and Socio-Economic Research in Canada's Atlantic Provinces," Halifax, Atlantic Provinces Economic Council, 1958, 4.
28 Harris, "Chairman's Report" (1971), 2.
29 Baker, "The Establishment of Memorial's Institute of Social and Economic Research."
30 Gushue to Smallwood, 22 May 1961, 3.09.058, Smallwood Collection, ASC, MUN.
31 Morgan, *Research Report 1963–1965*, 1.
32 Morgan, *Research Report 1963–1965*, 2.

33 "Raymond Vernon Dies at 85," *Harvard University Gazette*, 23
    September 1999. Accessed 22 March 2013. http://news.harvard.edu/
    gazette/1999/09.23/vernon.html. "Raymond Vernon," *The Economist*.
    Accessed 22 March 2013. www.economist.com/node/238854.
34 Smallwood to Raymond Vernon, 26 September 1963, 3.16.123, Smallwood
    Collection, ASC, MUN.
35 Vernon to Smallwood, 26 May 1964, 3.16.123, Smallwood Collection,
    ASC, MUN.
36 Vernon to Smallwood, 26 May 1964, 3.16.123, Smallwood Collection,
    ASC, MUN.
37 Report on the Second Meeting of the Inter-Departmental Co-ordinating
    Committee Held in the Board Room of the Department of Public
    Works, 5 February 1965, 7.001.009, Edward Roberts Collection,
    ASC, MUN.
38 Smallwood to Maurice Sauvé, 29 May 1964, 3.16.123, Smallwood Collec-
    tion, ASC, MUN.
39 Sauvé to Smallwood, 11 June 1964, 3.16.123, Smallwood Collection,
    ASC, MUN.
40 Memorandum to Executive Council ED 60-'64; Subject: Application for
    Funds for ARDA Rural Development Action and Research Projects,
    3.16.123, Smallwood Collection, ASC, MUN.
41 Federal-Provincial Rural Rehabilitation and Development Agreement:
    Background Notes and Comments Regarding the Proposed Agreement,
    8 October 1964, p. 6–7, 7.01.007, Edward Robert Collection, ASC, MUN.
42 S.J. Colman to D.J. MacEachern, 4 May 1964, 2.01.027, Fred Earle Papers,
    ASC, MUN.
43 George Story to Colin Story, 30 June 1965, 3.16.124, Smallwood Collection,
    ASC, MUN.
44 Raymond Gushue to Angus MacLean, 21 June 1961, Department of
    Fisheries, ISER, President's Office, MUN.
45 Riggins, "Memorial University's First Sociologist," 72–3.
46 Morgan to L. Bradbury, Department of Fisheries, 30 June 1961, Enclosure:
    "Institute of Social and Economic Research at the Memorial University of
    Newfoundland," Department of Fisheries, ISER, President's Office, MUN.
47 Government of Newfoundland, *Report of the Royal Commission*, 38.
48 Whitaker, "Sociological Preconditions."
49 Whitaker, "Sociological Preconditions," 377.
50 Whitaker, "Sociological Preconditions," 377.
51 Overton, "With Their Rubber Boots On."
52 Newfoundland, *Royal Commission on the Economic State*, 1–2.

53 For a critique of the common discourse on "work ethic," see High, "Working for Uncle Sam."
54 Newfoundland, *Royal Commission on the Economic State*, 2.
55 Newfoundland, *Royal Commission on the Economic State*, 28.
56 Overton, "With Their Rubber Boots On."
57 James Faris, interview with the author, 9 March 2012.
58 Faris to Colin Story, 8 June 1964, Faris Papers, ASC, MUN.
59 Faris to Colin Story, 29 July 1964, Faris Papers, ASC, MUN.
60 Faris to Colin Story, 29 July 1964, Faris Papers, ASC, MUN.
61 Faris to Colin Story, 29 July 1964, Faris Papers, ASC, MUN.
62 Colin Story to Smallwood, nd, marginal note ER, 4 August 1964, 3.16.123, Smallwood Collection, ASC, MUN.
63 Edward Roberts, who had been Smallwood's executive assistant during this period, told me that Smallwood read only a fraction of the correspondence coming into his office. Roberts was in the habit of placing a check mark on the upper corner of the document if Smallwood read it, or if he read it to Smallwood. No check mark appears on this document. Edward Roberts, personal communication, 10 November 2012.
64 "ARDA Programming," 7.01.008, Edward Roberts Papers, ASC, MUN.
65 Alan Williams to Faris, 15 May 1964, Faris Papers, ASC, MUN.
66 Donald Snowden to Robert Paine, 12 April 1966, Noel Iverson, President's Office, MUN.
67 George Lee, interview with the author, 20 September 2010.
68 Snowden to Paine, 15 April 1966, Iverson, President's Office, MUN.
69 Ralph Matthews, interview with the author, 31 August 2014.
70 Iverson and Matthews to informants, 2 July 1966, Iverson, President's Office, MUN.
71 Ralph Matthews, interview with the author, 31 August 2014.
72 Matthews, "Ethical Issues in Policy Research," 208.
73 John Widdowson, interview with the author, 16 July 2012.
74 Matthews, "Ethical Issues in Policy Research," 207.
75 Iverson and Matthews, *Communities in Decline*. Iverson had taught sociology at Memorial and was working at the University of New Brunswick when he was contracted to conduct the study. Matthews was a Newfoundland native with an undergraduate degree from Memorial who was then a doctoral candidate at the University of Minnesota.
76 Matthews, "Ethical Issues in Policy Research," 210–11.
77 Ralph Matthews, interview with the author, 31 August 2014.
78 Edward Roberts to F.W. Rowe, 21 March 1967, 3.24.032, Smallwood Papers, ASC, MUN.

79 Roberts to Rowe, 21 March 1967, 3.24.032, Smallwood Papers, ASC, MUN.
80 R. Hart to Robert Paine, 2 May 1967, 3.24.032, Smallwood Papers, ASC, MUN.
81 Neis, "The Uneasy Marriage," 323.
82 Zenon Sametz to Paine, 27 February 1967, Department of Fisheries, ISER, President's Office, MUN.
83 DeWitt, *Public Policy and Community Protest*, 14.
84 DeWitt, *Public Policy*, 47.
85 DeWitt, *Public Policy*, 53.
86 DeWitt, *Public Policy*, 67.
87 DeWitt, *Public Policy*, 79.
88 Crocker, "Filmmaking and the Politics of Remoteness," 65.
89 Low, "Grierson and Challenge for Change," 17.
90 Newhook "The Godfathers of Fogo." The popular memory of Extension's role in Fogo, for example, was that it helped empower people to resist the government's plan to resettle their community though creating a cooperative. As Newhook has shown, there was no real effort to resettle the communities in Fogo Island. Furthermore, Extension often worked hand in glove with government in encouraging modernization, and the province provided significant financial support to the Fogo Fishermen's Co-operative. To present Fogo as an example of Extension helping people resist Smallwood's modernization agenda is to misrepresent a more complex story.
91 Paul McLeod, interview with the author, 3 September 2010.
92 George Lee, interview with the author, 20 September 2010.
93 Fred Earle to Cato Wadel, 27 September 1969, 2.01.155, Fred Earle Papers, ASC, MUN.
94 Earle to Cato Wadel, 29 February 1968, 2.01.155, Fred Earle Papers, ASC, MUN.
95 Skolnik, *Viewpoints on Communities in Crisis*; Robert Paine, "Anthropology, Archaeology, Sociology," in his *Third Report* (1971), 10–11.
96 Barth and Brox, "My Life as an Anthropologist."
97 Ottar Brox, "Resettlement in Newfoundland: Some Sociological Comments," in Skolnik, *Viewpoints*, 22.
98 DeWitt, *Public Policy and Community Protest*, vi.
99 Robert Paine, preface, in DeWitt, *Public Policy and Community Protest*, v.
100 Robert Paine, preface, in DeWitt, *Public Policy and Community Protest*, v.
101 Neis, "The Uneasy Marriage," 321–38.
102 Unnamed federal official cited in Wright, *A Fishery for Modern Times*, 149.

103 Matthews, "Ethical Issues in Policy Research," 208.
104 House, *Against the Tide*, 271n4.
105 Neis, "The Uneasy Marriage," 324–5.
106 Story and Alexander, *Report: Committee on Federal Licensing Policy*.
107 Copes, "The Fishermen's Vote in Newfoundland," 583.
108 Copes, "The Fishermen's Vote in Newfoundland," 583.
109 Copes, "Fisheries Research and the Pursuit of Controversy."
110 Parzival Copes to Story, 23 November 1976, 2.01.002, George Story Papers, ASC, MUN. *Evening Telegram*, 17 February 1976.
111 Story to Copes, 21 December 1976, 2.01.002, George Story Papers, ASC, MUN.
112 Copes to Story, 8 February 1977, 2.01.002, George Story Papers, ASC, MUN.
113 Copes, "Fisheries Research and the Pursuit of Controversy."
114 Al Pittman and Pat Byrne, "Ode to Parzival Copes," unpublished lyrics, circa 1972. I thank Pat Byrne for permission to reproduce the song.
115 Gieryn, *Cultural Boundaries of Science*.
116 Copes, "Fisheries Research and the Pursuit of Controversy."
117 George Lee interview, 20 September 2010.
118 Matthews, "Ethical Issues in Policy Research," 211.
119 Neis, "The Uneasy Marriage," 324.
120 Neis, "The Uneasy Marriage," 324.
121 Helm-Hayes and McLaughlin, "Public Sociology in Canada."
122 Matthews, *The Creation of Regional Dependency*.
123 Steinmetz, *The Devil's Handwriting*, 145.
124 Harris, "Chairman's Report" (1974), 1.
125 Harris, "Chairman's Report," 1.
126 Burawoy, "Disciplinary Mosaic," 878.
127 Ralph Matthews, interview with the author, 31 August 2014.
128 Barth and Brox, "My Life as an Anthropologist," 109.

Conclusion

1 Patrick O'Flaherty, "Guide to Family Names," *MUN Gazette* (18 November 1977), 3.
2 O'Flaherty, *The Rock Observed*, 142.
3 G.M. Story to Leslie Harris, 3 July 1968, "Centre Newfoundland Studies," President's Office, MUN.
4 Samuel Gilmore, "Schools of Activity and Innovation," 207.
5 Frickel and Gross, "A General Theory," 204–32.
6 Frickel and Gross, "A General Theory," 209–14.
7 Frickel and Gross, "A General Theory," 226.

8 Leslie Harris, interview with Carole Henderson-Carpenter, 25 March 1970, C3908, 78–57, MUNFLA.

9 Harris, interview with Henderson-Carpenter, 25 March 1970, C3908, 78–57, MUNFLA.

10 Harris, interview with Henderson-Carpenter, 25 March 1970, C3908, 78–57, MUNFLA.

11 Michael Taft, interview with the author, 28 March 2011.

12 Matthews, "Class of '32."

13 Sager, Fisher, and Pierson, "Introduction," in Alexander, *Atlantic Canada*, vii.

14 Webb, "Constructing Community and Consumers."

15 Michael Taft, interview with the author, 28 March 2011.

16 Story to Harris, 3 July 1968, "Centre Newfoundland Studies," President's Office, MUN.

17 Pang, *Empire and the Sun*, 124.

18 Story to Harris, 3 July 1968, "Centre Newfoundland Studies," President's Office, MUN.

19 Story to Harris, 3 July 1968, "Centre Newfoundland Studies," President's Office, MUN.

20 Halpert to Harris, 9 October 1968, Dean of Arts and Science, Academic Planning Committee file, 1968–9, Box 4, President's Office, MUN.

21 Minutes of Advisory Committee on Newfoundland Studies, 23 January 1974, Dean of Arts – VP's Committee on Newfoundland Studies file, Box 29, President's Office, MUN.

22 Minutes of Advisory Committee on Newfoundland Studies, 7 January 1975, VPA Advisory Committee on Newfoundland Studies file, 1974 – 1976, Box C-6, President's Office, MUN.

23 Helen Carew to Harris, 30 May 1975, VPA Advisory Committee on Newfoundland Studies file, 1974–1976, Box C-6, President's Office, MUN.

24 Farrell, *Collaborative Circles*.

25 McLaughlin, "How to Become a Forgotten Intellectual," 241.

26 Harris, interview with Henderson-Carpenter, 25 March 1970, C3908, 78–57, MUNFLA.

27 Whisnant, *All That Is Native and Fine*, 247.

28 Whisnant, *All That Is Native and Fine*, 261.

29 Kozlov, "Athens and Apocalypse," 393.

30 Bannister, "Whigs and Nationalists."

31 Whisnant, *All That Is Native and Fine*, 13.

32 Whisnant, *All That Is Native and Fine*, 14.
33 Robert Paine, "In Praise of the Locative," 60.
34 Gulliver, "Preserving the Best."
35 Charles Camic has emphasized the importance of attention to the local context in understanding the history of ideas. See Camic and Xie, "The Statistical Turn."
36 Story, interview with Westhues, 2 March 1983, 5.13.033, George Story Papers, ASC, MUN, 59–60.
37 Doug House observed that in the 1970s, in part as a reaction to the Resettlement Program, a grass roots movement worked to preserve rural Newfoundland through local economic development. See House, *Against the Tide*, 180.
38 Peckford, *The Past in the Present*, v.
39 Peckford, *The Past in the Present*, 61.
40 Story, interview with Westhues, 2 March 1983, 5.13.033, George Story Papers, ASC, MUN, 47–8.
41 Anderson, *Imagined Communities*.
42 Bender, *Intellect and Public Life*.
43 Paine, "In Praise of the Locative," 59.
44 Overton, "With Their Rubber Boots On."
45 Overton, "Towards a Critical Analysis of Neo-Nationalism in Newfoundland."
46 Overton, "A Newfoundland Culture?" 45–61.
47 Jackson, "The Marxist Mystification."
48 Jackson, "The Marxist Mystification," 267–8.
49 Jackson, "The Marxist Mystification," 268, 270.
50 Jackson, "Local Communities and the Culture-Vultures," 7.
51 Jackson, "Local Communities and the Culture-Vultures," 9.
52 MacLeod, *A Bridge Built Halfway*, 89.
53 Donald Willmott quoted in Riggins, "Memorial University's First Sociologist," 61.
54 Memorial University of Newfoundland Extension Service and National Film Board, *Fogo Project – Specialists and Memorial Discuss the Fogo Films*, 1969.
55 Pocius, *A Place to Belong*.
56 Farrell, *Collaborative Circles*, 2.
57 Shils, "The University, the City, and the World."
58 Breslau, "Sociology of Science," 467.
59 Head, *Community Geographical Surveys*, iv.

392   Notes to pages 348–50

60 Harris to P.J. Gardiner, 16 April 1975, VPA Advisory Committee on Newfoundland Studies file, 1974–1976, Box C-6, President's Office, MUN.
61 Paine, "In Praise of the Locative," 60.

Bibliography

Archival Collections

Archives and Special Collections, Queen Elizabeth II Library, Memorial University Libraries
Fred Earle Papers.
James Faris Papers.
Alain Frecker Papers.
Leslie Harris Papers.
M.O. Morgan Papers.
Robert Paine Papers.
Edward Roberts Papers.
J.R. Smallwood Papers.
George Story Papers.
English Language Research Center, Memorial University of Newfoundland
Dictionary of Newfoundland English files.
W.J. Kirwin files.
E.R. Seary Collection.
G.M. Story Correspondence.
President's Office Memorial University
Institute of Social and Economic Research files.
President's Office files.
Memorial University Folklore and Language Archive, Memorial University of Newfoundland
Carole Henderson-Carpenter Collection 78–57
Halpert, Herbert. C3673.
Halpert, Herbert. C3674.
Halpert, Herbert. C3967.

Harris, Les. C3908.
Kirwin, William. C3925.
Mannion, John. F4412.
Rosenberg, Neil. C3904.
Rosenberg, Neil. C3906.
Seary, E.R., and Agnes O'Dea. C3911.
Story, George. C3909.
E.R. Seary Collection.
Malcolm MacLeod: Oral History of Memorial College Project. 82–282, 84–221.
    Harris, Les. C7184.
    Pitt, David G. C5966.
Department of Folklore, Memorial University of Newfoundland
Herbert Halpert Papers.
Maritime History Archives, Memorial University of Newfoundland
Keith Matthews Collection.
University of Toronto Archives
Harold Adams Innis Papers.

Oral Interviews

Gillian Townsend Cell, interview with the author, 8 May 2010.
James Faris (University of Connecticut), interview with the author, 9 March 2012.
Melvin Firestone (Arizona State University), interview with the author, 13 March 2012.
Gordon Handcock (Memorial University), interview with the author, 10 December 2013.
C. Grant Head (Wilfred Laurier University), interview with the author, 3 November 2011.
George Lee (Memorial University), interview with Makaela Gulliver, 20 September 2010.
Gerald Mars (University of London), interview with the author, 9 October 2012.
Ralph Matthews (University of British Columbia), interview with the author, 31 August 2014.
Paul McLeod (Memorial University), interview with Makeala Gulliver, 3 September 2010.
Alan MacPherson (Memorial University), interview with the author, 15 November 2010.

Peter Narváez (Memorial University), interview with the author, 29 April 2011.
Tom Nemec (Memorial University), interview with the author, 15 April 2011.
S.J.R. Noel (University of Western Ontario), interview with the author, 29
    August 2011.
Shane O'Dea (Memorial University), interview with the author, 15 December
    2010.
Rosemary Ommer (Simon Frazer University), interview with the author,
    13 October 2010.
Neil V. Rosenberg (Memorial University), interview with the author, 4 March
    2011.
Gerald M. Sider (City University of New York), interview with the author,
    27 June 2011.
John Szwed (Yale University), interview with the author, 16 March 2011.
Michael Taft (Library of Congress), interview with the author, 28 March 2011.
John D.A. Widdowson (University of Sheffield), interview with the author,
    13 July 2011, and 16 July 2012.

Printed Sources

Alexander, David. *Atlantic Canada and Confederation: Essays in Canadian
    Political Economy*. Edited by Eric Sager, Louis Fischer, and Stuart O Pierson.
    Toronto: University of Toronto Press, 1983.
Alexander, David. "Newfoundland's Traditional Economy and Development
    to 1934." In *Newfoundland in the Nineteenth and Twentieth Centuries: Essays in
    Interpretation*, by Hiller and Neary. Toronto: University of Toronto Press, 1980.
Anderson, Benedict. *Imagined Communities: Reflection on the origin and spread of
    nationalism*. London: Verso, 2006.
Atlantic Provinces Economic Council. *Needs and Opportunities for Economic
    and Socio-Economic Research in Canada's Atlantic Provinces*. Halifax: Atlantic
    Provinces Economic Council, 1958.
Ayre, Agnes Marion (Miller). *Newfoundland Names*. St John's: n.p., 1936.
Bailey, Richard. "National and Regional Dictionaries of English." In *The
    Oxford History of Lexicography*, vol. 1, edited by A.P. Cowie, 279–301. Oxford:
    University of Oxford Press, 2009.
Baker, Melvin. "The Establishment of Memorial's Institute of Social and
    Economic Research in 1961." *Newfoundland Quarterly* 92, no. 3 (Winter 1999):
    21–5.
Baker, Melvin. "Memorial University's Role in the Establishment of a
    Provincial Archive for Newfoundland in 1960." *Newfoundland Studies* 9, no.
    1 (Spring 1993): 81–102.

Bannister, Jerry. "Whigs and Nationalists: The Legacy of Judge Prowse's History of Newfoundland." *Acadiensis* 32, no. 1 (Autumn 2002): 84–109.

Barth, Fredrik, and Ottar Brox. "My Life as an Anthropologist." *Ethnos: Journal of Anthropology* 61, no. 1–2 (1996): 103–20.

Bartlett, Kenneth R. *A Short History of the Italian Renaissance*. Toronto: University of Toronto Press, 2013.

Bassler, Gerhard P. *Vikings to U-boats: The German Experience in Newfoundland and Labrador*. Kingston and Montreal: McGill-Queen's University Press, 2006.

Béjoint, Henri. *The Lexicography of English: From Origins to Present*. Oxford: Oxford University Press, 2010.

Bender, Thomas. *Intellect and Public Life: Essays on the Social History of Academic Intellectuals in the United States*. Baltimore and London: Johns Hopkins University Press, 1993.

Bendix, Regina. *In Search of Authenticity: The Formation of Folklore Studies*. Madison: University of Wisconsin Press, 1997.

Bentley, Michael. *Modernizing England's Past: English Historiography in the Age of Modernism, 1870–1970*. Cambridge: Cambridge University Press, 2005.

Berger, Carl. *The Writing of Canadian History: Aspects of English-Canadian Writing since 1900*. 2nd ed. Toronto: University of Toronto Press, 1986.

Blake, Raymond B. *Canadians at Last: Canada Integrates Newfoundland as a Province*. Toronto: University of Toronto Press, 1994.

Brebner, John Bartlet. *North Atlantic Triangle: The interplay of Canada, the United States and Great Britain*. New York: Columbia University, 1945.

Breslau, Daniel. "Sociology of Science: The Real and the Imaginary in Economic Methodology." In Steinmetz, *The Politics of Method in the Human Sciences*, 451–69.

Brison, Jeffrey. *Rockefeller, Carnegie, and Canada: American Philanthropy and the Arts and Letters in Canada*. Kingston and Montreal: McGill-Queen's University Press, 2005.

Bruneau, William. "'Quiet Flow the Dons': Towards an International History of the Professoriate." In Stortz and Panayotidis, *Historical Identities*, 31–60.

Bronner, Simon J. *American Folklore Studies: An Intellectual History*. Lawrence: University Press of Kansas, 1986.

Brookes, Chris. *A Public Nuisance: A History of the Mummers Troupe*. St John's: ISER Books, 1988.

Burawoy, Michael. "Disciplinary Mosaic: The Case of Canadian Sociology." *Canadian Journal of Sociology* 34, no. 3 (2009): 869–86.

Burrow, John. *A History of Histories: Epics, Chronicles, Romances and Inquiries from Herodotus and Thucydides to the Twentieth Century*. London: Penguin Books, 2007.

Camic, Charles. "The Making of a Method: A Historical Reinterpretation of the Early Parsons." *American Sociological Review* 52, no. 4 (August 1987): 421–39.

Camic, Charles. "Three Departments in Search of a Discipline: Localism and Interdisciplinary Interaction in American Sociology, 1890–1940." *Social Research* 62, no. 4 (Winter 1995): 1003–33.

Camic, Charles, and Neil Gross. "The New Sociology of Ideas." In *The Blackwell Companion to Sociology*, edited by Judith R. Blau, 236–50. Malden: Blackwell Publishing, 2001.

Camic, Charles, and Yu Xie. "The Statistical Turn in American Social Science: Columbia University, 1890 to 1915." *American Sociological Review* 59, no. 5 (October 1994): 773–805.

Camic, Charles, Neil Gross, and Michèle Lamont. *Social Knowledge in the Making*. Chicago: University of Chicago Press, 2011.

Carpenter, Carole Henderson. *Many Voices: A Study of Folklore Activities in Canada and Their Role in Canadian Culture*. Ottawa: National Museums of Canada, 1979.

Cell, Gillian T. *English Enterprise in Newfoundland 1577–1660*. Toronto: University of Toronto Press, 1969.

Cell, Gillian T. *Newfoundland Discovered: English Attempts as Colonisation, 1610–1630*. London: Hakluyt Society, 1982.

Chiaramonte, Louis J. *Craftsman-Client Contracts: Interpersonal Relations in a Newfoundland Fishing Community*. St John's: ISER, 1970.

Clarke, Sandra. *Newfoundland and Labrador English*. Edinburgh: University of Edinburgh Press, 2010.

Cohen, Anthony. "The Anthropology of Proximate Cultures: The Newfoundland School and Scotland." *Scottish Journal of Sociology* 4, no. 2 (1980): 213–26.

Collins, Randall. "On the Acrimoniousness of Intellectual Disputes." *Common Knowledge* 8, no. 1: 47–70.

Colton, Glenn David. *Newfoundland Rhapsody: Frederick Emerson and the Musical Culture of the Island*. Kingston and Montreal: McGill-Queen's University Press, 2014.

Copes, Parzival. "Fisheries Research and the Pursuit of Controversy." Lecture presented in response to the award of the Ted and Nora Sterling Prize in Support of Controversy on 20 September 1994. Accessed 9 July 2015. https://www.sfu.ca/content/dam/sfu/sterlingprize/recipients/copes/Lecture-by-Parzival-Copes.pdf.

Copes, Parzival. "The Fishermen's Vote in Newfoundland." *Canadian Journal of Political Science* 3, no. 4 (December 1970): 579–604.

Crocker, Setphen. "Filmmaking and the Politics of Remoteness: The Genesis of the Fogo Process on Fogo Island, Newfoundland." *Shima: The International Journal of Research into Island Cultures* 2, no. 1 (2008).

Denning, Michael. *The Cultural Front: The Labouring of American Culture in the Twentieth Century*. New York: Verso, 1996.

Darnell, Regna. "North American Traditions in Anthropology: The Historiographic Baseline." In *A New History of Anthropology*, edited by Henrika Kuklick, 35–51. Malden, MA: Blackwell, 2008.

Desmond, Adrian. *Huxley*. London: Penguin, 1998.

Devereux, E.J. "Early Printing in Newfoundland." *Dalhousie Review* 43 (1960): 57–66.

Devine, P.K. [Patrick Kevin]. *Devine's Folk Lore of Newfoundland in Old Words, Phrases and Expressions, Their Origin and Meaning*. St John's: Robinson, 1937.

DeWitt, Robert L. *Public Policy and Community Protest: The Fogo Case*. St John's: ISER, 1969.

Dorson, Richard M. *Folklore and Fakelore: Essays toward a Discipline of Folk Studies*. Cambridge: Harvard University Press, 1976.

Dorson, Richard M. "Is Folklore a Discipline?" *Folklore* 84, no. 3 (Autumn 1973): 177–205.

Doucette, Laurel. "Voices Not Our Own." *Canadian Folklore Canadien* 15, no. 2 (1993): 119–38.

English, L.E.F. *Historic Newfoundland*. St John's: Department of Tourism, 1955.

Faris, James C. *Cat Harbour: A Newfoundland Fishing Settlement*. St John's: ISER, 1966. Revised edition 1972.

Farrell, Michael P. *Collaborative Circles: Friendship Dynamics and Creative Work*. Chicago: University of Chicago Press, 2001.

Fay, Charles Ryle. *Life and Labour in Newfoundland*. Cambridge: W. Heffer and Sons, 1956.

Firestone, Melvin M. *Brothers and Rivals: Patrilocality in Savage Cove*. St John's: ISER, 1967.

Firestone, Melvin M. "Mummers and Strangers in Northern Newfoundland." In Halpert and Story, *Christmas Mumming*.

Firestone, Melvin. "Sephardic Folk-Curing in Seattle." *The Journal of American Folklore* 75, no. 298: 301–10.

Firestone, Sharon A. "To Plant with Women: Women's Lives in Savage Cove, Newfoundland." PhD diss., Arizona State University, 2003.

Freed, Richard D. *Eloquent Dissent: The Writings of James Sledd*. Portsmouth, NH: Boynton/Cook Publishers, 1996.

Frickel, Scott, and Neil Gross. "A General Theory of Scientific/Intellectual Movements." *American Sociological Review* 70, no. 2 (April 2005): 204–32.

Gieryn, Thomas F. *Cultural Boundaries of Science: Credibility on the Line.* Chicago: University of Chicago Press, 1999.

Gilmore, Samuel. "Schools of Activity and Innovation." *The Sociological Quarterly* 29, no. 2 (Summer 1988): 203–19.

Gough, Barry M. "The Royal Navy and Empire." In *The Oxford History of the British Empire,* vol. 5, *Historiography,* edited by Robin Winks. Oxford: Clarendon Press, 1998.

Gosling, William Gilbert. *Labrador: Its Discovery, Exploration and Development.* London: A. Rivers, 1910.

Government of Newfoundland. *Report of the Royal Commission on the Economic State and Prospects of Newfoundland and Labrador.* St John's: Queen's Printer, 1967.

Graham, Gerald S. "Fisheries and Sea-Power." *Report of the Annual Meeting of the Canadian Historical Association* 20, no. 1 (1941): 24–31.

Great Britain. *Newfoundland Royal Commission 1933: Report.* London: HMSO, 1933.

Guigné, Anna Kearney. *Folksongs and Folk Revival: The Cultural Politics of Kenneth Peacock's Songs of the Newfoundland Outports.* St John's: ISER Books, 2008.

Gulliver, Mekaela. "Preserving the Best: Newfoundland's Cultural Movement." PhD diss., Memorial University, 2014.

Gunn, Gertrude. *The Political History of Newfoundland, 1832–64.* Toronto: University of Toronto Press, 1966.

Gwyn, Richard. *Smallwood: The Unlikely Revolutionary.* Toronto: McClelland and Stewart, 1968.

Gwyn, Sandra. "The Newfoundland Renaissance." *Saturday Night* 92, no. 2 (April 1976): 38–45.

Hall, Joan Houston. "Frederic Gomes Cassidy, October 10 1907–June 14 2000." *Dictionaries: Journal of the Dictionary Society of North America* 22 (2001): 1–30.

Halpert, Herbert. "American Regional Folklore." *The Journal of American Folklore* 60, no. 238 (October–December 1947): 355–66.

Halpert, Herbert. "Breadth versus Depth." *The Journal of American Folklore* 71, no. 280, (April–June 1958): 97–103.

Halpert, Herbert. "Coming into Folklore More than Fifty Years Ago." *The Journal of American Folklore* 105, no. 418 (Autumn 1992): 142–457.

Halpert, Herbert. "Coming into Folklore More than Fifty Years Ago." In *Folklore: An Emerging Discipline Selected Essays of Herbert Halpert,* edited by Martin Lovelace, Paul Smith, and J.D.A. Widdowson. St John's: Memorial University of Newfoundland, 2002.

Halpert, Herbert. "Folklore and Newfoundland: An Informal Introduction to the Materials and Methods of Folklore." In *Papers of the Bibliographic Society of Canada*, vol. 8, 10–22. 1969.

Halpert, Herbert. "Some Underdeveloped Areas in American Folklore." *The Journal of American Folklore* 70, no. 278 (October–December 1957): 229–305.

Halpert, Herbert, and G.M. Story. *Christmas Mumming in Newfoundland: Essays in Anthropology, Folklore and History*. 2nd ed. Toronto: University of Toronto Press, 1990. First published 1969.

Halpert, Herbert, and J.D.A. Widdowson. *Folktales of Newfoundland: The Resilience of the Oral Tradition*. Vols. 1 and 2. St John's: Breakwater Books, 1996.

Handcock, W. Gordon. *Soe longe as there comes noe women: Origins of English Settlement in Newfoundland*. St John's: Breakwater, 1989.

Harris, Cole. "A Life between Geography and History." *Canadian Historical Review* 93, no. 3 (September 2012): 436–62.

Harris, Leslie "Chairman's Report." In Paine, *The Institute of Social and Economic Research: Third Report*.

Harris, Leslie. "Chairman's Report." In Paine, *The Institute of Social and Economic Research: Fourth Report*.

Harris, Leslie. *Growing Up with Verse: A Child's Life in Gallows Harbour*. St John's: Harry Cuff Publications, 2002.

Harris, Leslie. *Newfoundland and Labrador: A Brief History*. Toronto: J.M. Dent and Sons, 1968.

Harrison, Julia, and Regna Darnell, eds. *Historicizing Canadian Anthropology*. Vancouver: UBC Press, 2006.

Hart, Anne. "Dr Agnes O'Dea, 1911–1993." *Newfoundland Studies* 8, no. 2 (Fall 1992): 179–81.

Head, C. Grant. "The Changing Geography of Newfoundland in the Eighteenth Century." PhD diss., University of Wisconsin, 1971.

Head, C. Grant. *Community geographical Surveys: The North-east Coast, the Southern Avalon, the Northern St. Barbe; a Study Under ARDA*. St John's: ISER, 1963.

Head, C. Grant. *Eighteenth Century Newfoundland: A Geographer's Perspective*. Toronto: McCelland and Stewart, 1973.

Head, C. Grant. "Settlement Migration in Central Bonavista Bay, Newfoundland." In *Canada's Changing Geography*, edited by R. Louis Gentilcore, 92–110. Scarborough: Prentice Hall, 1967.

Helm-Hayes, Rick, and Neil McLaughlin. "Public Sociology in Canada: Debates, Research, and Historical Context," *Canadian Journal of Sociology* 34, no. 3 (Summer 2009): 572–600.

Hewson, John. "Joe, Sylvester." In *Dictionary of Canadian Biography*, vol. 6. University of Toronto/Université Laval, 2003–. Accessed 30 June 2014. http://www.biographi.ca/en/bio/joe_sylvester_6E.html.

High, Steven. "Working for Uncle Sam: The 'Comings' and 'Goings' of Newfoundland Base Construction Labour, 1940–1945." *Acadiensis* 32, no. 2 (Spring 2003): 84–107.

High, Steven. "The 'Narcissism of Small Differences': The Invention of Canadian English, 1951–67." In *Creating Postwar Canada: Community, Diversity, and Dissent, 1945–75*, edited by Magda Fahrni and Robert Rutherdale, 89–110. Vancouver: UBC Press, 2008.

Hiller, J.K. "Is Atlantic Canadian History Possible." *Acadiensis* 30, no. 1 (Autumn 2000): 16–22.

Hiller, J.K. "The Foundation and Early Years of the Moravian Mission in Labrador, 1752–1805." MA thesis, Memorial University, 1967.

Hiller, J.K. "A History of Newfoundland, 1874–1901." PhD diss., Cambridge University, 1971.

Hiller, J.K, and M.F. Harrington, eds. *The Newfoundland National Convention, 1946–1948*, vol. 1, *Debates*. Montreal and Kingston: McGill-Queen's University Press, 1995.

Hiller, J.K., Peter Narváez, and Daniel Vickers. "Newfoundland Past as Marxist Illustration," *Newfoundland Studies* 3, no. 2 (Fall 1987): 265–76.

Hobsbawm, Eric, and Terence Ranger, eds. *The Invention of Tradition*. Cambridge: Cambridge University Press, 1983.

Hollett, Calvin. *Shouting, Embracing, and Dancing with Ecstasy: The Growth of Methodism in Newfoundland, 1774–1874*. Kingston and Montreal: McGill-Queen's University Press, 2010.

House, J.D. *Against the Tide: Battling for Economic Renewal in Newfoundland and Labrador*. Toronto: University of Toronto Press, 1999.

Howley, James P. *The Beothucks or Red Indians: The Aboriginal Inhabitants of Newfoundland*. Cambridge: Cambridge University Press, 1915.

Howley, James P. *Geography of Newfoundland: For the Use of Schools*. London: Edward Stanford, 1876.

Iggers, Georg G. *Historiography in the Twentieth Century: From Scientific Objectivity to the Post Modern Age*. Hanover, NH: Wesleyan University Press, 2005.

Iggers, Georg G., and Q. Edward Wang, with contributions from Supriya Mukherjee. *A Global History of Modern Historiography*. Harlow: Pearson Education Limited, 2008.

Iverson, Noel, and Ralph Matthews. *Communities in Decline: An Examination of Household Resettlement in Newfoundland*. St John's: ISER, 1968.

Jackson, F.L. "The Marxist Mystification of Newfoundland History."
    Newfoundland Studies 6, no. 2 (1990): 267–81.
Jackson, Lin. "Local Communities and the Culture-Vultures." *Newfoundland
    Quarterly* 81, no. 3 (Winter 1986): 7–10.
Johnston, K. Brian. "Government and University: The Transition of Memorial
    University of Newfoundland from a College to a University." PhD diss.,
    University of Toronto, 1990.
Junek, Oscar Waldemar. *Isolated Communities: A Study of a Labrador Fishing
    Village*. New York: American Book Company, 1937.
Kirwin, W.J. "Either for Any in Newfoundland." *Regional Language Studies*, no.
    1 (October 1968): 8–10.
Kirwin, W.J. "Standardization of Spelling in the Editing of the *Dictionary of
    Newfoundland English*." *Regional Language Studies*, no. 19 (September 2006):
    19–24.
Klinck, Carl Frederick. *Literary History of Canada: Canadian Literature in English*.
    Toronto: University of Toronto Press, 1965.
Korneski, Kurt. "Development and Diplomacy: The Lobster Controversy on
    Newfoundland's French Shore, 1890–1904." *International History Review* 36,
    no. 1 (2014): 45–69.
Kozlov, Denis. "Athens and Apocalypse: Writing History in Soviet Russia." In
    Schneider and Woolf, 393
Kuhn, Thomas. *The Structure of Scientific Revolutions*. London: Chicago
    University Press, 1962.
Kuklick, Henrika. "The British Tradition." In *A New History of Anthropology*,
    edited by Henrika Kuklick, 52–78. Malden, MA: Blackwell, 2008.
Kuper, Adam, "Anthropology." In *Cambridge Histories Online*, edited by
    Theodore M. Porter and Dorothy Ross. Cambridge University Press, 2003.
    Accessed 12 October 2011. doi:10.1017/CHOL9780521594424.020.
Lamont, Michèle. "How to Become a Dominant French Philosopher: The Case
    of Jacques Derrida." *American Journal of Sociology* 93, no. 3 (November 1987):
    584–622.
Latham, Michael E. "Modernization." Cambridge Histories Online, edited by
    Theodore M. Porter and Dorothy Ross. Cambridge University Press, 2003.
    Accessed 12 October 2011. doi:10.1017/CHOL9780521594424.020
Lorenz, Chris. "History and Theory." In Schneider and Woolf, 32–3.
Lovelace, Martin, Peter Narváez, and Diane Tye, eds. *Bean Blossom to
    Bannerman, Odyssey of a Folklorist: A Festschrift of Neil V Rosenberg*. St John's:
    Memorial University of Newfoundland, 2005.
Low, Colin. "Grierson and Challenge for Change (1984)." In *Challenge for
    Change: Activist Documentary at the National Film Board of Canada*, edited by

Thomas Waugh, Michael Brendan Baker, and Ezra Winton. Kingston and Montreal: McGill-Queen's University Press, 2010.

Low, Jacqueline, and Gary Bowden, eds. *The Chicago School Diaspora: Epistemology and Substance*. Kingston and Montreal: McGill-Queen's University Press, 2013.

Ludlow, Peter. "Searching for the Past, Writing for the Present: Charles Ryle Fay and Newfoundland's Contested Past." *Acadiensis* 39, no. 2 (Summer/Autumn 2010): 89–108.

MacKay, R.A., ed. *Newfoundland: Economic, Diplomatic and Strategic Studies*. Toronto: Oxford University Press, 1946.

MacLeod, Malcolm. *A Bridge Built Halfway: A History of Memorial University College, 1925–1950*. Kingston and Montreal: McGill-Queen's University Press, 1990.

MacLeod, Malcolm. "Crossroads Campus: Faculty Development at Memorial University of Newfoundland, 1950–1972." In Stortz and Panayotidis, *Historical Identities*, 131–57.

Macpherson, Alan. "The Early Development of Geography as a 'Subject of Instruction' and the Origins of the Department of Geography and Memorial University of Newfoundland, 1946–1963." Department of Geography, 2000. Accessed 27 July 2011. http://www.mun.ca/geog/about/Goodridge_Summers.pdf.

Madden, Frederick. "The Commonwealth, Commonwealth History and Oxford, 1905–1971." In *Oxford and the Idea of the Commonwealth: Essays Presented to Sir Edgar Williams*, edited by Frederick Madden and D.K. Fieldhouse. London: Croom Helm, 1982.

Mars, Gerald. "An Anthropological Study of Longshoremen and of Industrial Relations in the Port of St John's, Newfoundland, Canada." PhD diss., University of London, 1972.

Mars, Gerald. "Fieldwork in Newfoundland." Unpublished memoir. 7 October 2012.

Mannion, John J., ed. *The Peopling of Newfoundland: Essays in Historical Geography*. St John's: ISER Books, 1977.

Mannion, John J. *Irish Settlements in Eastern Canada: A Study of Cultural Transfer and Adaptation*. Toronto: University of Toronto Press, 1974.

Matthews, Keith. "Class of '32: St John's Reformers on the Eve of Representative Government." *Acadiensis* 6, no. 2 (Spring 1977): 80–94.

Matthews, Keith. "Historical Fence Building: A Critique of the Historiography of Newfoundland." *Newfoundland Studies* 17, no. 2: 155: 143–65.

Matthews, Keith. *Lectures on the History of Newfoundland 1500–1830*. St John's: Breakwater Books, 1988.

Matthews, Ralph. *The Creation of Regional Dependency.* Toronto: University of Toronto Press, 1983.

Matthews, Ralph. "Ethical Issues in Policy Research: The Investigation of Community Resettlement in Newfoundland." *Canadian Public Policy* 1, no. 2 (Spring 1975): 204–16.

McArthur, Tom, ed. *The Oxford Companion to the English Language.* New York: Oxford University Press, 1992.

McDonald, Ian D.H. *"To Each His Own": William Coaker and the Fishermen's Protective Union in Newfoundland Politics, 1908–1925.* Edited by J.K. Hiller. St John's: ISER, 1987.

McDonald, Ian D.H. "W.F. Coaker and the Fishermen's Protective Union in Newfoundland Politics 1908–1925." PhD thesis, University of London, 1971.

McKay, Ian. *Quest of the Folk: Antimodernism and Cultural Selection in Twentieth Century Nova Scotia.* Montreal and Kingston: McGill-Queen's University Press, 1994.

McKay, Ian, and Robin Bates. *In the Province of History: The Making of the Public Past in Twentieth-Century Nova Scotia.* Kingston and Montreal: McGill-Queen's University Press, 2010.

McLaughlin, Neil G. "Collaborative Circles and Their Discontents: Revisiting Conflict and Creativity in Frankfurt School Critical Theory." *Sociologica*, no. 2 (2008).

McLaughlin, Neil G. "How to Become a Forgotten Intellectual: Intellectual Movements and the Rise and Fall of Erich Fromm." *Sociological Forum* 13, no. 2 (June 1998): 215–46.

McLaughlin, Neil G. "Why Do Schools of Thought Fail? Neo-Freudianism as a Case Study in the Sociology of Knowledge." *Journal of the History of the Behavioral Sciences* 34, no. 2 (Spring 1998): 113–34.

McLintock, A.H. *The Establishment of Constitutional Government in Newfoundland, 1783–1832.* London: Longmans, Green and Co., 1941.

Megill, Allan. *Historical Knowledge, Historical Error: A Contemporary Guide to Practice.* Chicago: University of Chicago Press, 2007.

Mellin, Robert. *Newfoundland Modern: Architecture in the Smallwood Years, 1949–1972.* Montreal and Kingston: McGill-Queen's University Press, 2011.

Memorial University of Newfoundland Extension Service and National Film Board. *Fogo Project – The Specialists at Memorial Discuss the Fogo Films*, 1969. http://collections.mun.ca/cdm/ref/collection/extension/id/3847.

Morgan, M.O. *The Institute of Social and Economic Research Report 1963–1965.* St John's: Memorial University, 1965.

Narváez, Peter. "The Protest Songs of a Labor Union on Strike Against an American Corporation in a Newfoundland Company Town: A Folkloristic

Analysis with Special References to Oral Folk History." PhD thesis, Indiana University, 1986.

Neary, Peter, and Melvin Baker. "Allan Fraser's 'History of Newfoundland's Participation in World War II'." *Newfoundland Quarterly* 102, no. 4 (Spring 2010): 12–15 and 40–5.

Neary, Peter, and Melvin Baker. "Introduction to Allan Fraser 'History of the Participation of Newfoundland in World War Two.'" Unpublished manuscript. 2010.

Neis, Barbara. "The Uneasy Marriage of Academic and Policy Work: Reflections on the Newfoundland and Labrador Experience." In *Fragile Truths: Twenty-Five Years of Sociology and Anthropology in Canada*, edited by William K. Carroll, et al., 321–38. Ottawa: Carleton University Press, 1992.

Nemec, Tom. "A Multi-Disciplinary Approach to the Reconstruction of the History and Culture of Rural Populations: A Newfoundland Example." Paper presented at the second annual conference of the Canadian Aural/Oral History Association, St John's, 1975.

Newhook, Susan. "The Godfathers of Fogo: Donald Snowden, Fred Earle and the Roots of the Fogo Island Films, 1964–1967." *Newfoundland and Labrador Studies* 24, no. 2 (Fall 2009): 171–98.

Noel, S.J.R. "Government and Politics in Newfoundland, 1904–1934: Prelude to the Surrender of Dominion Status." D.Phil., Oxford, 1965.

Noel, S.J.R. *Politics in Newfoundland*. Toronto: University of Toronto Press, 1971.

Novick, Peter. *That Nobel Dream: The "Objectivity Question" and the American Historical Profession*. Cambridge: Cambridge University Press, 1988.

O'Dea, Agnes. *Bibliography of Newfoundland*. Edited by Anne Alexander. Vol. 1. Toronto: University of Toronto Press, 1986.

O'Flaherty, Patrick. *Leaving the Past Behind: Newfoundland History from 1934*. St John's: Long Beach Press, n.d., ca. 2011.

O'Flaherty, Patrick. "Looking Backwards: The Milieu of the Old Newfoundland Outports." In *The Blasty Bough*, edited by Clyde Rose, 145–8. St John's: Breakwater Books, 1976.

O'Flaherty, Patrick. *Lost Country: The Rise and Fall of Newfoundland, 1843–1933*. St John's: Long Beach Press, 2005.

O'Flaherty, Patrick. *Old Newfoundland: A History to 1843*. St John's: Long Beach Press, 1999.

O'Flaherty, Patrick. *The Rock Observed: Studies in the Literature of Newfoundland*. Toronto: University of Toronto Press, 1979.

Overton, James. "A Newfoundland Culture?" In *Making a World of Difference: Essays on Tourism, Culture and Development in Newfoundland*, 45–61. St John's: ISER, 1996.

Overton, James. "Sparking a Cultural Revolution: Joey Smallwood, Farley
    Mowat, Harold Horwood and Newfoundland's Cultural Renaissance."
    Newfoundland and Labrador Studies 16, no. 2 (Fall 2000): 166–204.
Overton, Jim. "With Their Rubber Boots On: Sociologists as Modernizers,
    Strip Miners, Necrographers, Romancers and Revivalists." *Sociology on the
    Rock*, no. 5. Accessed 8 July 2012. http://www.mun.ca/soc/newsletter/
    issue5/rock-5-overton.html.
Overton, James. "Towards a Critical Analysis of Neo-Nationalism in
    Newfoundland." In *Underdevelopment and Social Movements in Atlantic
    Canada*, edited by R. Brym and R. Sacouman, 219–49. Toronto: New
    Hogtown Press, 1979.
Paine, Robert. "By Chance By Choice: A Personal Memoir." *Ethnos*, 63, no. 1
    (July 2010): 133–54.
Paine, Robert, ed. *The Institute of Social and Economic Research: Third Report*. St
    John's: Memorial University of Newfoundland, 1971.
Paine, Robert, ed. *The Institute of Social and Economic Research: Fourth Report*. St
    John's: Memorial University of Newfoundland, 1974.
Paine, Robert. "In Praise of the Locative (With Revolving Doors)." In *The
    University as It Is/As It Could Be*, by James R. Black, 57–70. St John's:
    Memorial University, 1997.
Paine, Robert, and Lawrence Felt. "Reflections on ISER Books." *Papers of the
    Bibliographical Society of Canada* 48, no. 1 (Spring 2010): 169–74.
Pang, Alex Soojung-Kim. *Empire and the Sun: Victoria Solar Eclipse Expeditions*.
    Stanford: Stanford University Press, 2002.
Patterson, George. "Notes on the Dialect of the People of Newfoundland [pt.
    1]." *Journal of American Folk-lore* 8, no. 28 (1895): 27–40.
Peckford, A. Brian. *The Past in the Present: A Personal Perspective on
    Newfoundland's Future*. St John's: Harry Cuff, 1983.
Perlin, A.B. *The Story of Newfoundland: Comprising a New Outline of the Island's
    History from 1497 to 1959, a Brief Account of Some of the Social and Economic
    Life of the Province and of Its Resources, Natural History, Public Services and
    Culture, and a Description of Some of Its Principal Industries, Public Utilities, and
    Commercial Institutions*. St John's: n.p., 1959.
Perret, Robert. *La Géographie de Terre-Neuve*. Paris: 1913.
Philbrook, Tom. *Fisherman, Logger, Merchant, Miner: Social Change and
    Industrialization in Three Newfoundland Communities*. St John's: 1966.
Pierson, Stuart O. "David Alexander: A Reminiscence." In Alexander, *Atlantic
    Canada*, x–xviii.
Pierson, Stuart O. "A Diatribe." In *Hard-Headed and Big-Hearted: Writing
    Newfoundland*, edited by Stan Dragland, 50–78. St John's: Penneywell, 2006.

Piternick, Anne B. "The Historical Atlas of Canada: the Project Behind the Product." *Cartographica* 30, no. 4 (Winter 1993): 21–31.

Plumptre, A.F.W., A.M. Fraser, and Harold Innis. "Newfoundland, Economic and Political: The Amulree Report (1933) A Review." *Canadian Journal of Economics and Political Science* 3, no. 1 (February 1937): 58–83.

Pocius, Gerald L. *A Place to Belong: Community Order and Everyday Space in Calvert, Newfoundland.* Athens, Kingston and Montreal: University of Georgia Press and McGill-Queen's University Press, 1991.

Pocius, Gerald L. "The Mummers Song in Newfoundland: Intellectuals, Revivalists and Cultural Nativism." *Newfoundland Studies* 4, no. 1 (1988): 57–85.

Poole, Cyril. *Mose Morgan: A Life in Action.* St John's: Harry Cuff Publications, 1998.

Pope, Peter. *The Many Landfalls of John Cabot.* Toronto: University of Toronto Press, 1987.

Prowse, G.R.F. *Cartological Material.* Winnipeg: self published, 1936.

Reeves, John. *History of the Government of the Island of Newfoundland: With an Appendix; Containing the Acts of Parliament Made Respecting the Trade and Fishery.* London: Sewell, 1793.

Riggins, Stephen Harold. "Memorial University's First Sociologist: The Dilemmas of a Bureaucratic Intellectual." *Newfoundland and Labrador Studies* 29, no. 1 (Spring 2014): 47–83.

Robic, Marie-Claire. "Geography" and "The Modern Social Sciences." In *Cambridge Histories Online,* edited by Theodore M. Porter and Dorothy Ross. Cambridge University Press, 2003. Accessed 12 October 2011. doi:10.1017/CHOL9780521594424.020.

Rogers, J.D. *Historical Geography of the British Colonies. Vol. 5, part 4: Newfoundland.* Oxford: The Clarendon Press, 1911.

Rosenberg, Neil. "Introduction." In *Sonny's Dream: Essays on Newfoundland Folklore and Popular Culture,* by Peter Narváez, ix–xxi. St John's: Memorial University, 2012.

Ross, Dorothy. *The Origins of American Social Science.* New York: Cambridge University Press, 1991.

Rothney, G.O. *Newfoundland: From International Fishery to Canadian Province.* Ottawa: Canadian Historical Association, 1959.

Rothney, G.O. "The History of Newfoundland and Labrador 1754–1783." MA thesis, University of London, 1934.

Rudin, Ronald. *Making History in Twentieth-Century Quebec.* Toronto: University of Toronto Press, 1997.

Ryan, Shannon. *Fish Out of Water: The Newfoundland Saltfish Trade, 1814–1914.* St John's: Breakwater, 1986.

Ryan, Shannon. "The Newfoundland Cod Fishery in the Nineteenth Century."
    MA thesis, Memorial University, 1972.
Sager, Eric W. "Newfoundland's Historical Revival and the Legacy of David
    Alexander." *Acadiensis* 11, no. 1 (Autumn 1981): 104.
Said, Edward. *Orientalism*. New York: Vintage Books, 1979.
Schneider, Axel, and Daniel Woolf. *The Oxford History of Historical Writing:
    Historical Writing since 1945*. Vol. 5. New York: Oxford University Press,
    2011.
Schumaker, Lyn. "Women in the Field in the Twentieth Century: Revolution,
    Involution, Devolution." In *A New History of Anthropology*, edited by
    Henrika Kuklick, 277–92. Malden, MA: Blackwell, 2008.
Seary, E.R. "The Anatomy of Newfoundland Place Names." *Names* 6, no. 4
    (December 1958): 193–207.
Seary, E.R. *Place Names of the Avalon Peninsula of the Island of Newfoundland.*
    Toronto: University of Toronto Press, 1971.
Seary, E.R. "The Place of Linguistics in English Studies." *Journal of the
    Canadian Linguistics Association* 1, no. 2 (October 1955): 9–13.
Seary, E.R. "Proposals for Developments in Research and Tuition in the
    Department of English." *Regional Language Studies*, no. 21 (April 2009): 23–8.
Seary, Edgar Ronald. "Regional Humanism." *Newfoundland Quarterly* 65, no. 2
    (November 1966): 14–16.
Seary, E.R., with Sheila Lynch. *Family Names of the Island of Newfoundland*. St
    John's: Memorial University, 1976.
Seary, E.R., and G.M. Story. *Reading English: A Handbook for Students*. Toronto:
    Macmillan, 1959.
Seary, E.R., G.M. Story, and W.J. Kirwin. *The Avalon Peninsula of Newfoundland:
    An Ethno-linguistic Study*. Ottawa: National Museum of Canada, 1968.
Sharpe, Christopher, and Shane O'Dea. "Heritage Conservation in the City
    of St John's." In *Four Centuries and the City: Perspectives on the Historical
    Geography of St John's*, edited by Alan G. Macpherson, 156–221. St John's:
    Memorial University, 2005.
Shils, Edward. "The University, the City, and the World: Chicago and the
    University of Chicago." In *The University and the City: From Medieval
    Origins to the Present*, edited by Thomas Bender, 210–30. New York: Oxford
    University Press, 1988.
Shore, Marlene. *The Science of Social Redemption: McGill, the Chicago School, and
    the Origins of Social Research in Canada*. Toronto: University of Toronto Press,
    1987.
Sider, Gerald M. "Christmas Mumming and the New Year in Outport
    Newfoundland." *Past and Present* 71 (May 1976): 102–25.

Sider, Gerald M. *Culture and Class in Anthropology and History: A Newfoundland Illustration*. Cambridge: Cambridge University Press, 1986.

Sider, Gerald M. "The Ties That Bind: Culture and Agriculture, Property and Propriety in the Newfoundland Village Fishery." *Social History* 5, no. 1 (1980): 1–39.

Skolnik, Michael. *Viewpoints on Communities in Crisis*. St John's: ISER, 1968.

Sledd, James. "Bi-Dialectalism: The Linguistics of White Supremacy." In Freed, *Eloquent Dissent*.

Sledd, James. "Dollars and Dictionaries: The Limits of Commercial Lexicography." In *New Aspects of Lexicography: Literary Criticism, Intellectual History, and Social Change*, edited by Howard D. Wienbrot, 119–37. Carbondale and Edwardsville: Southern Illinois University Press, 1972.

Smallwood, J.R., ed. *The Book of Newfoundland*. St John's: Newfoundland Book Publishers, 1937.

Smallwood, Joseph R. "Memorial University of Newfoundland – 'A Live, Dynamic Centre of Learning [and] Culture,'" edited by Melvin Baker. *Newfoundland Quarterly* 93, no. 2, (Winter 2000): 3–5.

Smallwood, J.R. "What Is Liberalism? A Restatement of Its Aims, Objects and Ideals." Edited and introduced by Melvin Baker and James Overton, *Newfoundland Studies* 11, no. 1 (Spring 1995): 75–126.

Smith, Roger. *The Fontana History of the Human Sciences*. London: Fontana Press, 1997.

Steinmetz, George. "British Sociology in the Metropole and the Colonies, 1940s–1960s." In *The Palgrave Handbook of Sociology in Britain*, edited by John Holmwood and John Scott, 302–37. London: Palgrave Macmillan, 2014.

Steinmetz, George. "A Child of the Empire: British Sociology and Colonialism, 1940s–1960s." *Journal of the History of the Behavioral Sciences* 49, no. 4 (2013): 353–444. doi:10.1002/jhbs.21628.

Steinmetz, George. *The Devil's Handwriting: Precoloniality and the German Colonial State in Qingdao, Samoa, and Southwestern Africa*. Chicago: University of Chicago Press, 2007.

Steinmetz, George, ed. *The Politics of Method in the Human Sciences: Positivism and Its Epistemological Others*. Durham: Duke University Press, 2005.

Story, G.M. "A Critical History of Dialect Collecting in Newfoundland." *Regional Language Studies*, no. 6 (May 1975): 1–4.

Story, G.M. "Edgar Ronald Seary." In *A Festschrift of Edgar Ronald Seary: Essays in English Language and Literature Presented by Former Colleagues and Students*, edited by A.A. Macdonald, P.A. O'Flaherty, and G.M. Story, 1–5. St John's: Memorial University of Newfoundland, 1975.

Story, G.M. "A Newfoundland Dialect Dictionary: A Survey of the Problems." Paper read before the Humanities Association of Canada, 13 April 1956 (later published).

Story, G.M. *People of the Landwash: Essays on Newfoundland and Labrador*. Edited by Melvin Baker, Helen Peters, and Shannon Ryan. St John's: Harry Cuff Publications, 1997.

Story, G.M. "Research in the Language and Place-Names of Newfoundland. Paper read before the Canadian Linguistic Association, Ottawa, 13 June 1957.

Story, G.M. "The Role of the Dictionary in Canadian English." Paper presented at the In Search of the Standard in Canadian English conference, Kingston, ON, October 1985.

Story, G.M. "The View from the Sea: Newfoundland Place Naming." Plenary lecture presented at the 16th International Congress on Onomastic Sciences, Quebec City, August 1987.

Story, George, and David Alexander. *Report: Committee on Federal Licensing Policy and Its Implications for the Newfoundland Fisheries*. St John's: Memorial University, 1974.

Story, G.M., and W.J. Kirwin. "The Dictionary of Newfoundland English: Progress and Promise." *Regional Language Studies*, no. 5 (January 1974): 15–17.

Story, G.M., and W.J. Kirwin. "National Dictionaries and Regional Homework: A Dictionary of Canadianisms on Historical Principals." *Regional Language Studies*, no. 3 (January 1971): 19–22.

Story, G.M., and W.J. Kirwin. Transcript of interview by Robert Paine, November 1982, 5.09.015. George Story Papers, AMD, 4–5.

Story, G.M., W.J. Kirwin, and J.D.A. Widdowson. *Dictionary of Newfoundland English*. Toronto: University of Toronto Press, 1982.

Stortz, Paul, and E. Lisa Panayotidis. *Historical Identities: The Professoriate in Canada*. Toronto: University of Toronto Press, 2006.

Summers, William. *Geography of Newfoundland*. Toronto: Copp Clark, 1972.

Szwed, John F. "The Mask of Friendship: Mumming as Social Relations." In Halpert and Story, *Christmas Mumming*, 105–18.

Szwed, John. *Private Cultures and Public Imagery*. St John's: ISER, 1966.

Thompson, Frederic F. *The French Shore Problem in Newfoundland: An Imperial Study*. Toronto: University of Toronto Press, 1961.

Webb, Jeff A. "Constructing Community and Consumers: Joseph R Smallwood's *Barrelman* Radio Programme." *Journal of the Canadian Historical Association* 8 (1997): 165–86.

Webb, Jeff A. "The Newfoundland and Labrador Fieldwork of Harold Adams Innis." In *Harold Innis and the North: Appraisals and Contestation*, by William

J. Buxton, 167–185. Kingston and Montreal: McGill-Queen's University Press, 2013.

Webb, Jeff A. *The Voice of Newfoundland: A Social History of the Broadcasting Corporation of Newfoundland, 1939–1949.* Toronto: University of Toronto Press, 2008.

Whisnant, David E. *All That Is Native and Fine: The Politics of Culture in an American Region.* Chapel Hill: University of North Carolina Press, 1983.

Whitaker, Ian. "Core Values among Newfoundland Fishermen in the 1960s." *Anthropologica* 30, no. 1 (1988): 75–86.

Whitaker, Ian. "Sociological Preconditions and Concomitants of Rapid Socio-Economic Development in Newfoundland." In Government of Newfoundland, *Report of the Royal Commission,* 369–95.

Williams, Alan. *Land Use Surveys: Part One North East Coast.* St John's: ISER, 1963.

Williams, Alan. *John Guy of Bristol and Newfoundland.* Edited by Gordon Handcock and Chesley Sanger. St John's: Flanker Press, 2010.

Williams, Raymond. *Key Words.* London: Fontana Press, 1976.

Wright, Donald. *The Professionalization of History in English Canada.* Toronto: University of Toronto Press, 2005.

Wright, Miriam. *A Fishery for Modern Times: The State and the Industrialization of the Newfoundland Fishery, 1934–1968.* Don Mills, ON: Oxford University Press, 2001.

Wynn, Graeme. "Geographical Writing on the Canadian Past." In Michael P. Conzen, Thomas A. Rumney, and Graeme Wynn, eds. *A Scholar's Guide to Geographical Writing on the American and Canadian Past,* 91–124. Chicago: University of Chicago Press, 1993.

Index

Harris, Leslie (Les), 61, 96; agenda
for Newfoundland studies,
162, 321; background, 112–4;
informant, role as, 67, 169, 231;
interdisciplinary research, 349;
ISER, on role of, 199–200, 203,
230, 315; leadership, 3, 113–4,
116, 142, 323, 337–8; place names,
interest in, 154; public support
for Newfoundland studies, 180;
scholarship, 109, 113–4, 125;
university, view of, 3, 329
Head, C. Grant, 347, 382n41; economic
geographer, 259–60, 267; historical
geographer, 251, 260–3, 266, 275–7;
historical geography, on decline of,
273–4; historiography, critique of,
135–6, 138–9, 187, 327
heritage revival, 42, 168
Herrick, Clinton, 305
Herzog, George, 148
Hewson, John, 59, 167
High, Steven, 79–80
Hiller, James, 120, 131–2, 141, 331
Hilliard, Robert, 67
Historical Research Committee,
104–6, 114
Hollett, Calvin, 97, 109
Hollett, Robert, 76, 78
Horwood, Harold, 24, 45, 168
House, J.D., 307
Howley, James P., 23, 78, 84, 247–8, 250
Howley, Michael F., 27–8, 78, 80, 247, 253
Hufford, David, 183
Hunter, A.C., 29

informants: agenda, 223–4; earning
trust of, 208, 211–3, 218–21, 226–7;
resistance to being interviewed,
49–50, 180

Innis, Harold Adams, 90–1, 129, 261,
275
ISER (Institute of Social and
Economic Research), 13, 158, 327,
342; applied research, 279–80,
292, 299, 305–8, 311, 321, 323;
community studies of, 200–4, 206,
221, 230, 237–43, 286, 293, 295;
creation, 200, 288–9; geographic
research, 259, 269; graduate
student funding, 120–1, 131;
mumming, research on, 166–7,
176; oral culture research, support
for, 53; publications, 210, 227, 326;
research agenda, 230; research
fellows, 161, 239–41; resettlement,
study of, 302, 313; role, 199–201,
203, 227, 278, 292–3
Iverson, Noel, 203, 280, 299–302,
305–6, 315

Jackson, F.L., 339–41
Jeffery, C.E.A., 103–4
Jutes, J.G., 249

Karpeles, Maude, 146, 160
Kealey, Greg, 142
Kealey, Linda, 142
Keough, William, 281
Kirwin, William J.: career, 47–8,
78; collaborations, 27, 180;
commitment to Newfoundland
scholarship, 57, 77–8, 80–1, 321;
culture change, view of, 343;
dialect questionnaires, 160–1;
DNE, on role of, 72; editorial work,
74, 76; ethnolinguistic survey,
52; etymology, 58, 357n95; Faris,
James, view of, 232–3; lexical
research, 59–60, 323; linguistic

intellectual, 28, 84–6, 92–3, 103, 323, 334; public support for, 300, 333; rhetorical style of, 232–3
Snowden, Donald, 299, 303
sociology, 205
speech, 27, 75, 163, 180; efforts to correct, 50–2; social stigma of, 37, 44–6, 73–4, 158, 214; variations, 43–4
Staveley, Michael, 266, 269, 271
Story, Colin, 226, 291–2, 296–8
Story, George M.: agenda for Newfoundland studies, 38–9; applied research, 308; archival collection, 100, 120; brother Colin, and, 291–2; celebration of, 181; collaborations, 18, 27, 181, 322; collection of words, 39–41, 153; cultural change, view of, 348; cultural revival, encouragement of, 189–90, 333; death, 77; dialect questionnaires, 160; dialect variety, view of, 355n49; DNE, on the nature of, 42–3, 67–8, 70–2; DNE, role in, 73, 75, 78; education, 25–30, 31–2, 81; ethical concerns, 61, 180; ethnolinguistic survey, 47, 52; faculty recruitment, role in, 56, 119–20, 143, 228; Halpert, Herbert, relationship with, 158; heritage movement, 168, 268, 322; historical research group, 105; ISER, 229; Kirwin, William, and John Widdowson, collaboration with, 52–4, 58; language, awakening interest in, 30; language, encouragement of pride in, 51; leadership of Newfoundland studies, 9, 26, 83, 119, 320–2, 324, 347; lexicographers, consultations

with, 57; Memorial, hired at, 32–3; mumming, study of, 146, 166–7, 174, 177–8; MUNFLA, 173, 184, 192; nationalism, 71–2, 183, 334–6; Newfoundland culture, view of, 47, 343; Newfoundland language agenda 33, 39, 252; oral culture, view of, 181–2, 318; pejorative stereotypes, response to, 46–7; popular speech, view of, 43–6, 275; reflection on Newfoundland studies, 75–6, 161–2, 317, 330, 350; research centre, proposal for, 324–5; research chairs, promotion of, 179; public policy, debate over, 309–10; research interests, 76–7; Sider, view of, 186–8; social history, interest in, 143, 146; Widdowson, John, relationship with, 165–6
students as researchers, use of, 125, 154–7, 160–1, 179–80, 205
Summers, William, 256–7, 260, 265–6
Szwed, John, 158, 206; fieldwork, 215–6, 230, 234; mumming, research on, 176–7, 185

Taft, Michael, 184, 191–2, 322, 324
Tallman, Richard, 183
Taylor, Stephen, 114, 182, 193
Thompson, Frederic F., 118
Thompson, Stith, 151–2
Thornton, Patricia, 266, 269

University of London, 85, 96, 105, 109
University of Minnesota, 203

Vernon, Raymond, 289–90

Wadel, Cato, 229, 304–5, 307
Wareham, Wilfred, 183–4

Warren, Phillip, 182, 342
Westhuse, Kenneth, 334
Whisnant, David, 329, 332
Whitaker, Ian, 166, 227, 299; economic
development, research on, 259,
312, 314; ISER, role of, 278, 292–3,
308; modernization, view of, 293–5,
303; research, 205–6, 209, 241, 243,
274; research agenda, 200–1, 230;
research fellows, 201, 207–14, 224,
238–9, 240–1, 323–4
Whitbourne, Richard, 246
Whitely, William, 109, 130
Widdowson, John D.A.: career, 53, 59,
179; collaborations, 27, 58, 179–80;
commitment to Newfoundland
scholarship, 80–1, 321; dialect
questionnaire, 161; DNE,
contribution to, 56, 63–4; doctoral
research, 58–9; Earle, Fred, fieldwork
with, 164–7; ethical concerns, 61,
180, 198; fieldwork, 161, 163, 165,
167, 170, 181, 227, 233; folklore,
concern about the future of, 192–4;

Halpert, Herbert, collaboration with,
59, 162–4, 196–8; mumming, research
on, 177; MUNFLA, contribution
to, 184, 193; phonology, research
on, 161; Story, George, and William
Kirwin, collaboration with, 52–4, 81
Williams, Allan, 266–7; economic
development, research on, 258–60,
299, 314; historical research, 264–5,
275–7
Williams, Harold, 20
Willmott, Donald: career, 114,
292, 341; early life, 286, 314;
Historical Research Committee,
105; ISER, contribution to, 288;
Newfoundland government,
work for, 287–8, 312
Wise, T.F., 259
Wood, Harold, 260
Wright, Miriam, 237, 286
Wynn, Graeme, 269–73

Young, Murray, 105–6, 109, 114
Youther, Larry, 180, 339